Music Sociology

D1528588

Music Sociology

Examining the Role of Music in Social Life

Edited by

Sara Towe Horsfall,
Jan-Martijn Meij, and
Meghan D. Probstfield

Paradigm Publishers
Boulder | London

Copyright © 2013 Paradigm Publishers

Published in the United States by Paradigm Publishers, 5589 Arapahoe Avenue, Boulder, CO 80303 USA.

Paradigm Publishers is the trade name of Birkenkamp & Company, LLC, Dean Birkenkamp, President and Publisher.

Library of Congress Cataloging-in-Publication Data
Music sociology : examining the role of music in social life /
edited by Sara Towe Horsfall, Jan-Martijn Meij, and Meghan D. Probstfield.
    pages ; cm
Includes bibliographical references and index.
ISBN 978-1-61205-313-4 (paperback : alk. paper)
1. Music—Social aspects. 2. Music—Philosophy and aesthetics. I. Horsfall, Sara.
II. Meij, Jan-Martijn. III. Probstfield, Meghan D.
ML3916.M8783   2013
306.4'842—dc23
                                                                    2013008566

Printed and bound in the United States of America on acid-free paper that meets the standards of the American National Standard for Permanence of Paper for Printed Library Materials.

17 16 15 14 13   1 2 3 4 5

Contents

II. Experience of Music: Ritual and Authenticity

III. Experience of Music: Stratification and Identity

VI. Commodification of Music

Preface for the Instructor
How to Teach This Book

There are a variety of ways that this book can be taught. As you can see from the table of contents, it follows a logical order that would fit naturally in any sociology of music course. It starts with a history of the field and a description of what the sociology of music is, followed by three sections that deal in one way or another with how people experience music. The final section of the book examines the commodification and sale of music. As such, one can start reading the first chapter and proceed throughout the chapters in a logical order.

This book could also be used as a supplementary text in sociology courses not focused on the study of music. Many of the themes presented in the book are essential to sociology. For example, the notion of socialization, the importance of culture, the existence of inequality and stratification, the role of institutions, and the role of music as social change—as well as the idea that our world is a social construction—are all addressed in readings of this collection. Additionally, we are living in an increasingly globalized world, and several of the readings deal with this topic. Some of these readings confront the notion of authenticity of the audience and the musicians involved. What happens, for example, when due to globalization, the traditional and sometimes sacred music of a particular society becomes popular in other countries?

One of sociology's unique characteristics is the multi-theoretical framework of the discipline. Whether it is structural functionalism, conflict perspective, symbolic interactionism, feminist theory, or critical race theory, there are readings that approach music from that perspective. The readings illustrate the diversity within sociology.

Not only sociologists will find this a useful teaching aid. A musicologist interested in exploring the sociology behind music could adopt this book as one of the course materials. The editors of this volume made a conscious effort to include as many genres as possible in order to offer the richest experience of a variety of musical expressions. There are readings that explore each of the genres of spiritual music, jazz, heavy metal, rap, hardcore, ska, indie, straight-edge, and taqwacore. As such, this volume has a great potential for compare-and-contrast assignments. For example, are the rituals describing a mosh pit at a metal show similar to rituals in a different genre? Are the conflicts involved in being a child of a biracial parent unique to rap music? Do other countries or fans of a particular genre have specific requirements about authenticity as described in Chapter 8's study of Hispanic music? These and other questions could be turned into assignments for both sociology of music and musicology courses.

Adopting the approach of a sociological imagination as described by C. Wright Mills, a course on the sociology of music could explore the interconnections between biography, history, and sociology. Many of the readings in this volume are written with that goal in mind. One could use the book as a starting point to explore the connections to historical, social, economic, cultural, and political events. Music is a form of entertainment, information, education, inspiration, and as such it is a meaningful art to explore in the classroom.

Preface for the Student

An intellectually important question posed both implicitly and explicitly in this fine collection of essays is, I believe, the key to the development of a sociology of music. The question is, simply put, What is the sociological definition of music? What does a sociologist see, hear, feel, or think of when addressing—no, encountering—music? The best answer is that a sociologist should see, hear, feel, or think of music in ways that are unique—and creative—among scholars, musicians, critics, and fans.

Sociologists define things by conceptualizing them, that is, by seeing them as examples or illustrations of broader analytical categories. Most of the readings in this collection apply trustworthy and useful sociological concepts to music as a social phenomenon: social class, stratification, social identity, ritual, and authenticity. Will Roy and Tim Dowd's piece, "What Is Sociological about Music?" (Chapter 5) does this very well. A few others, however, entice the reader to embark on novel ways of *seeing* music. Howard Becker's "American Popular Song" (Chapter 3), for example, sees the popular song form in a unique way: as a social accomplishment among writers, musicians, singers, and audiences who are searching for music of which everyone can be part. My point is that the ultimate goal of music sociology is twofold. First, we should *see* something—a behavior, activity, value, aesthetic, or perception—that no one else sees in music. Second, we should appreciate music itself as a special pleasure. Close encounters with music should leave us in awe, and individuals—such as your professor and you!—who study music sociology are generally people who experience music just this way in their own everyday lives.

Let me give you an example of this from my own research. During the summer of 2012, I taught an online course in the sociology of popular music. The most popular song that summer—a song that you heard all the time on the radio and simply could not escape—was "Call Me Maybe" by Carly Rae Jepsen. Before her song became a number-one hit, Jepsen was perhaps best known as a Justin Bieber protégé from Canada. On December 11, 2011, Justin Bieber blogged, "Call me maybe by Carly Rae Jepsen is possibly the catchiest song I've ever heard lol." "Call Me Maybe" went viral. All sorts of people, from star celebrities like Jimmy Fallon and Katy Perry, and college baseball teams from Harvard and Texas State, to the USA Olympic swim team, posted their versions of CMM videos. Everyone seemed to refer to the song as "catchy."

I asked my class to analyze CMM phenomenologically, that is, in terms of describing their actual experiences of the song and under what circumstances a song like this becomes "catchy." This assignment applied to all students who had any exposure at all to the song, whether they liked the song or hated it. The students' responses were both marvelous and distinctively sociological. One female student indicated that she had heard the song numerous times on the radio but didn't realize how much she "knew" about the song until it came on the office radio and she and a coworker both simultaneously started singing along with the song. She was able to enjoy the song and *surrender* to it in the presence of another who did the same in the mailroom. On the other hand, a male student indicated that he hated the song but put up with it when his girlfriend was driving and played it over and over. He tolerated this foolishness because he controlled the radio when they were driving in his truck! Our finding was that the "catchiness" of a song is highly affected by the social contexts within which the song is played, defined and evaluated, and enjoyed (Kotarba et al. 2013).

Now, my class exercise was a very microscopic view of music experiences, but my argument should be clear. Music sociology works when it discovers historical, demographic, organizational, and other social aspects of music. But it also works when the sociologist can unpack— or deconstruct, as the postmodernists put it—aspects of music that are seen, heard, or felt by audience members but ordinarily taken for granted. "Catchy" is such a social feature. The readings in this collection discover and unpack a wide range of music experiences, styles, and related social phenomena. I am very pleased that the authors do not get caught up in irrelevant debates not clearly sociological, for example, the differences between popular and classical music. That is a distinction best left to musicologists and historians, especially since the distinction is increasingly fuzzy. (Is Tchaikovsky's *Nutcracker Suite* classical music when it is performed in over a hundred venues in the United States at Christmastime as a way for ballet and orchestra companies to raise funds to support their less popular "serious" programs, to an audience as likely to dress in jeans and sweaters as suits and dresses, and to an audience who purchased their tickets through the same Ticketron office where they purchased their Neil Young and Crazy Horse tickets, and to an audience who can purchase their Nutcracker coffee mugs at the gift shop on the way out?)

This book escorts us into musical worlds quite familiar (e.g., heavy metal, rap, and jambands) and some that may be new to the student. My advice to you is to enjoy both approaches. You may think you are an expert metalhead, but you may not be aware that, like jazz, metal is evolving into a "highbrow" art form, as Roscoe Scarborough demonstrates (Chapter 9). We have all experienced the ongoing debate regarding authenticity between white and black rap, but Matt Oware illustrates the world of multiracial rap music (Chapter 11). In contrast, readers—including me—are introduced to Muslim American punk rock and southern Italian tarantism, or "noise music," by Sarah Hosman and Lee Blackstone (Chapters 17 and 19, respectively). Above all, my best and last piece of advice is to find and listen to the music you are reading about. Become part of the music, share the music experience, and absorb all the pleasure of this wonderful array of music you can. After all—it is music!

Joseph A. Kotarba
Department of Sociology
Texas State University–San Marcos

Introduction

Why Sociology of Music?

More appropriately, why *not* sociology of music? Music is so much a part of us, affects our lives, and is endemic to our culture—almost any culture—why shouldn't we study it? To a musician and music appreciators, life without music is like life without color, or food without salt or spices. Something is missing if it is not there. Yet within sociology, music, like art and emotions, has not been addressed as a legitimate area of inquiry in the United States. In contrast, in Europe, where sociology is generally less quantitative, sociology of music is well established. Ironically, much of the popular music being studied there has its origins in the United States.

Part I: Journey into American Music

So, what is sociology of music, then? According to Will Roy and Tim Dowd (Chapter 5), it is both an object and an activity. As an object of culture, music is similar to cars, computers, art, fashion, cell phones, and any number of other artifacts that reflect our cultural values. An artifact has a creator—an individual or a group in whom the idea arose. Artifacts can also be bought and sold. As a commodity, music has been one of the largest US exports for more than a century. Today rap music is found worldwide, as is jazz and rock, and as were minstrels in the nineteenth century.

As an object, popular music changes over time, as society itself changes. The practice of copyrighting a song started in Stephen Foster's time. At the turn of the twentieth century, prior to recordings, it was the published sheet music of popular songs, rather than records or CDs, that was consumed by the public. When sound began to be recorded, the commercial focus changed from the song to the performer, and from sheet music to a recording (and to video). Today the music industry is well established and an object of study in itself—as is examined more thoroughly in Section VI. And many people make a very good living making and selling music.

Women sing the traditional Maori welcoming for visitors to the Rongopai Marae (Tribal Meeting House) just outside Gisborne, New Zealand.

So what is music as an activity? It includes the venue in which music is performed. Minstrels, for instance, America's first musical form, were a form of entertainment in rowdy drinking halls. This musical venue changed after the Civil War, when vaudeville, which was performed in theaters and cabarets, became common. Another popular venue was informal parlor singing—a favorite pastime at the turn of the century, when the sale of pianos and sheet music reached their peak. Then came the venues spawned by recordings. Almost as soon as records were invented, they became a favorite way to transport the musical experience from place to place. Today, much as Emile Durkheim (1995 [1912]) predicted in religion with his Cult of the Individual, iPods and earphones have made a group activity and social event into a personal experience. But popular music as an activity still persists at concerts and other venues.

What does music reveal? As discussed in "Music as Ritual" (Chapter 6) in Section II, for many African Americans music does more than express their life situation. It gives them a collective identity. From spirituals during slavery, to ragtime, jazz, rock (or rhythm and blues), and now rap, African Americans who participate in the music have a place where they belong. Music is not only an expression of their lives, it *is* their lives. Perhaps that strong sense of culture is what makes African American forms of music so dynamic and popular. Music also tells others about the culture from which the musicians came. As Alan Lomax (1968) observed, in sexually repressed societies, singers tend to use a tense, high-pitched voice; in societies where women's contribution to society is acknowledged, a relaxed, wide voice is more common.

And what about the music itself? What does it tell us? The varied world musics reveal some surprising similarities. As Paul Robeson (Chapter 1) notes, the pentatonic scale (black keys on the piano) is found in many cultures around the world. It was a scale commonly used in Africa, and as a result, most spirituals use the pentatonic scale—as does rock, jazz, and many (most?) musical forms that have their origins in African American culture. There is a simplicity in its use that makes the music accessible to all (although it must be said that Eastern music, which also uses the pentatonic scale, is not necessarily simple or accessible to Westerners). Similarly, the American popular song that developed during the vaudeville era has a form that is so commonly used, most people know it without realizing they know it. It is the basis for many musical performances, as well.

Part II: Experience of Music: Ritual and Authenticity

What is the experience of music? Are all musical experiences authentic? Does the music inspire individual feelings, or does the listener "borrow" feelings from someone else? Does the music express a real-life situation for the listener (or the artist)? Or does it tap into generic, preexisting emotions, and thereby exploit the listener?

Authenticity is a recurring theme not only in Section II but through-out the book. Philosophically, we might think of authenticity as the original piece of music composed in a particular style. Any music of that style that deviates from that first piece, then, is a little less authentic. But is that always the case? And is that the only way to think of it? When discussing authenticity, sociologists also talk about reification—making something that is not real, something that is just an idea, into a real commodity. Race, for instance, is the idea that there is a real difference between groups of people, even though most academics agree that it is really only a social construction—there is no biological trait that definitively separates one race from another. Individuals are at risk of reifying culture and meaning in music as a result of music migration or cultural assimilation, personal experience, and even knowledge.

There are more questions. How does the individual construct mean-ing in his or her listening experience? Most people experience music as a social event. Does ritual play a part in that experience? What role do rituals have in guiding people into authentic experiences of musical meaning? To separate and understand the authentic as distinct from the reified, we must consider the significance of time (e.g., temporal and historical), space (i.e., public or private, region of the world, and music venue), and the rituals that not only enable a person to have a more authentic understanding of a music form but also link him or her to important meaning and experiences from the past.

As you read through Section II, use your own experience as a guide to your thinking. What is your preferred style of music? How do you define it? Are there rituals that are important to the definition of that musical style? Are those rituals necessary to achieve an authentic understanding of this music? For example, can people who have not participated in the ritual (dress, concert activity, and so on) understand? Are there inauthentic versions of this music? What are the historical links to its current form?

Part III: Experience of Music: Stratification and Identity

A crucial question for sociologists is, How are the resources available to us divided up among the different demographic, socioeconomic, and cultural groups that exist in our society? No sociological investigation of music would be complete without addressing this key issue. Do minorities or women, for instance, have less access to performance or publishing opportunities? And, relatedly, how does the experience of music differ in the different social groups? Section III examines the significance of musical genres as they relate to African Americans, Hispanics, Native Americans, and Asian Americans. Russell Potter (Chapter 10) takes us on a journey through the music of one group, African Americans. He points out that in a postmodern world race is supposed to be insignificant, but in terms of music, that is not the case. His conclusion sheds light on the reality of race beyond postmodernism. While reading this chapter, think about the music that you listen to. Why do you listen to that music? Is it simply because it's pleasing to your ears, or is there a deeper cultural meaning behind it?

Going a step further, Matthew Oware (Chapter 11) uses symbolic interactionism to examine the musical identity of people who are multiracial. He presents us with an interesting question: How do rap artists who come from a multiracial background include their non–African American identity in their music? While we often discuss race using particular racial groups (e.g., whites, Latinos, African Americans) there are of course many people who have a much more complex and multidimensional racial and ethnic background. In this light, it is particularly noteworthy that various rap artists wrestle with the question, and it's interesting to observe their resolutions. The question we should ask ourselves while reading Oware's essay is, Why do certain multiracial rap artists identify not as biracial but as African American, or another particular racial group?

Potter and Oware examine meaning and the importance of a racial identity for both performer and audience. Daniel Sarabia (Chapter 12) shifts our attention to a diffusion of racist attitudes and behavior in music. Sometimes a particular minority genre is co-opted by another group. In the case he examines, ska music—which originated with skinheads and a working-class environment with borrowed symbols from West Indian immigrants—developed into a subcultural expression that included a racist faction. A key question once again is authenticity. Which is the "real" skinhead culture? Sarabia's study illustrates that there are similar discussions within other musical genres as well.

Roscoe Scarborough (Chapter 13) directs our attention back to the question of authenticity. He explains that while both jazz and heavy metal music started as niche genres, the image of jazz today is more easily associated with highbrow culture whereas heavy metal doesn't have that same image. As such, these images are constructed.

Part IV: Experience of Music: Subcultures and Musical Enclaves

Music, perhaps uniquely, has both material and nonmaterial cultural components. Socialization is the primary way that meaning is transferred from one generation to the next, and culture plays a vital role in that process. Music can be thought of as the embodiment of patterned ways of thinking, feeling, and behaving. And like other cultural values, much of it is learned through the socialization process, although not necessarily in the family. These patterns are learned through interaction with other people, and the notion of value consensus or shared values and norms is important. Just as there are many musical styles, there are also many subcultures where individuals—who belong to the dominant culture—simultaneously share a different set of values with other like-minded individuals. In other words, a subculture.

Section IV identifies and examines the characteristics of contemporary music enclaves that could also be defined as subcultures. Most of us are familiar with the subculture that surrounds jazz, but we may not have thought of it in religious terms. Neil Leonard (Chapter 14) compares innovative jazzmen to religious prophets in the devotion shown to them by their mentors and followers. Kerry Hendricks (Chapter 15) looks at hardcore, and the meaning it has to its listeners. Similarly, Pamela Hunt (Chapter 16) examines the ritual interaction among those in the jamband community. And finally, Sarah Hosman (Chapter 17) introduces us to Muslim American punk rock, or taqwacore.

As you read, ask yourself, What are the characteristics that distinguish the music I listen to? Is there a specific style of clothing that I and other fans wear that identifies us to each other? Are there common themes in the lyrics? Does the music generate recognizable emotional responses? How do I, and others, act when listening to the music in a public venue? Where did this music begin? What are the cultural influences? How has it been modified from its original source?

Part V: Music as Social Change and Commentary

How do people use music? Section I discussed changes in hymns—music that was and is used as an aid to devotional practice in churches. Most people instantly recognize this particular kind of music whenever it appears. At the other end of the spectrum, music is used as a social commentary. Artists let their listeners know what they think of leaders and social situations. This is exactly what Mark Mengerink (Chapter 18) found in heavy metal's use of Hitler images. While this dark part of history is used to shock unsuspecting listeners, it often contains a warning about the concentration of power in current economic and political systems. William Tsitsos (Chapter 20) also examines the use of music for political commentary. European "straight-edge" music is used to challenge what the group sees as capitalist oppression. American straight-edge, in contrast, is less political, primarily reflecting an individual morality stemming from the 1960s.

Lee Blackstone (Chapter 19) examines how music that was originally a form of solace for members of an alienated southern Italian region has been adopted as a sort of fashionable trend, despite its earlier stigmatized and rejected sound. This raises the question of how a culture determines that something is valuable or not valuable, and it happens in music as with other cultural artifacts.

Another common use of music is to inspire social change. Jeneve Brooks (Chapter 21) looks at folk music as a ritual component for those involved in social activism. Music has created unity among singers, inspired action, and informed others of the need for action. It is a seemingly painless way to garner public support—a catchy melody and easy-to-remember words. Another dramatic and touching story of music inspiring change occurred in Estonia in the 1980s. A successful nonviolent protest against the Soviets was organized primarily through song, as told in the film *The Singing Revolution*. Unfortunately, the reader will have to research the Estonia protest on his or her own, as it is not included in this volume.

Part VI: Commodification of Music

The sixth section of our book addresses the notion of commodification. You probably heard someone say that "band X is a sellout." What does that mean? What is the difference between a band performing in a small garage and performing in a giant stadium? This may seem like a relatively new question, but one answer dates back to the foundation of sociology as a discipline. One early social thinker, Karl Marx, used the concept of alienation to explain the difference. Here Simon Frith (Chapter 22) explains alienation in music as a situation where "something human is taken from us and returned in the form of commodity."

Think about how we express love in our society. Love is something deeply intimate and personal, yet we see it packaged all around us: expensive jewelry, songs, Valentine's Day gifts. Our deepest intimate emotional and personal relationships are transformed into things we can buy and sell. The same is true in music. Frith encourages us to look at the production methods behind the end product. Blaming individual musicians for selling out ignores the pressures of the record industry. Even "independent" music labels have become part of the music industry, with their own particular role to play. Technological innovations have made it easier to copy and replicate music. While the current focus is on illegal file-sharing through the Internet (as is discussed in Chapter 26), this has been a recurring debate throughout the history of popular music. It was of great concern when cassette tapes became popular. When CDs replaced cassettes, the concern shifted to the ability to "burn" your own music onto a compact disc.

Once again, someone claims a band or musician is a sellout. For the record industry to make money, it limits itself to signing only those artists that fit a particular mold. Usually what it boils down to is that a band or musician signed with a major label; typically, the bands that aren't perceived as sellouts sign with independent labels. Jennifer Lena (Chapter 23) focuses on the notion of authenticity of rap and country artists. She explains that this is often a created identity. While reading her piece, ask yourself how it is that you decided your favorite musicians were authentic? What is it about them or their music that makes them authentic? Also think back to the readings on stratification in Section III (another dimension of authenticity)—is there an element of advantage or disadvantage that the musicians enjoy or suffer?

Jeffrey Nathanial Parker (Chapter 24) shifts our attention back to the musical acts themselves. He illustrates that sometimes individual musicians speak out about developments in the larger music industry. In the cases he observed, the musicians took a stand on a particular issue. However, a band is sometimes confronted with a tough decision. Does it have to be affiliated with a giant organization that charges a lot of money for tickets in order to be able to perform throughout the country? And how do band members feel about fans recording their live shows? Or, does the band want to take the risk of offering its music directly to the fans through the Internet and asking fans to make a donation?

What This Book Is Not

There are some things that are not addressed in this book. The editors strongly argue that the subject is so vast, and the different genres and subcultures so varied, it would be impossible for one person to cover them adequately. The chapter authors are obviously invested in their particular genres. As such, the reader has a unique opportunity to observe these subcultures from the inside and to develop an appreciation for music that may have heretofore been unappealing. Harriet Martineau (1989 [1838]), one of the first female sociologists, warned that anyone doing field studies needs to be aware of observing through the lens of their own prejudices. In a similar vein, Joseph Kotarba (2009) coined the term *ethnographic tourist*, which also captures the idea of being open to new experiences.

Many sociologists have written about music over the past century or so, such as Theodor Adorno, Tia DeNora, Alfred Schutz, and Howard S. Becker. Their writings were not included in this volume because we wanted to focus on contemporary music, but, as it turns out, most of these theorists do, in fact, inform the analyses that appear here. So they are included indirectly, if not directly. Most of the significant works are cited in the bibliography.

Although we have called this *music sociology,* it is more correctly sociology of *popular* music. Classical music has not been included—not because it is not worthy, and certainly not because we don't like classical music (we are all serious classical music lovers). A book on sociology of music *should* include it. A sociologist's view of music may be different from the way classical musicians view it, however. The latter tend to look down on popular music as of lesser quality. Certainly the lesser is the greater when it comes to consumption of music around the world. Donald Clark (2001 [1994]) claims that classical musicians created names for other categories of music to distinguish themselves as something of higher quality and more deserving of a place in academia.

There is a whole area of music that is not covered—the social functions of music. Peter Martin (1995) argues that Western music has been separated from its social functions as it became an autonomous sphere of social activity. But that is not exactly true. We still have music that is instantly recognized as functional: "The Star-Spangled Banner," the "Wedding March," lullabies, children's songs, Muzak, advertising jingles, theme music for TV programs, practice pieces and scales, beginner music, and so on. Again, another volume.

Part I
Journey into American Music

Mayteana Morales of The Pimps of Joytime, a band from Brooklyn, NY. Their style, which blends afrobeats, latin rhythms, and rock and roll, represents the international mixing of music in popular culture. Photo by Meghan Probstfield at the New Orleans Music Fest, 2012.

1

A Universal Body of Folk Music—
A Technical Argument
Paul Robeson

Renowned African American singer (1898–1976) Paul Robeson explains
the importance of the pentatonic scale, which is found in native traditions
around the world, to African American music, including jazz and rock.
Despite its seeming universality, few classical composers have used the
pentatonic scale, and it rarely is a part of Western classical music training.

During the recent years of my enforced professional immobilization
[during the 1950s McCarthy era], I have found enormous satisfaction
in exploring the origins and interrelations of various folk musics, and
have come to some interesting and challenging ideas—supported by
many world renowned musicologists—which further confirm and explain my own and Lawrence Brown's interest in and attraction to the
world body of folk music.

Continued study and research into the origins of the folk music of
various people in many parts of the world revealed that there is a world
body—a universal body—of folk music based upon a pentatonic (five
tone) scale. Interested as I am in the universality of mankind—in the
fundamental relationship of all peoples to one another—this idea of
a universal body of music intrigued me, and I pursued it along many
fascinating paths.

My people, the Negro people of America, have been reared on the
pentatonic scale and pentatonic melodies, in Africa and in America. No
wonder Lawrence Brown introduced me to the music of Mussorgsky

Originally published as Appendix C in Here I Stand *(New York: Othello Associates, 1958), pp. 123–125. Reprinted with permission.*

(of the Russian "Five"); to the music of Dvorak and Janacek; to ancient Hebraic chants; to the old melodies of Scotland and Ireland; to the Flamenco and de Falls of Spain; to the music of all of Eastern Europe; Armenia, Bulgaria, Romania, Hungary, and Poland, especially to the songs of Kodaly and Bartok; the music of contemporary Soviet composers; to the music of ancient Africa; to S. Coleridge Taylor; to the music of Ethiopia; the melodies of Brazil and to the music of the North and South American Indian peoples. And I have found my way to the music of China, of Central Asia, Mongolia, of Indonesia, Vietnam and of India.

And always, with my "pentatonic ears," my interest in the fundamental five-tone scale grew. J. Rosamond Johnson's comments on African and Afro-American music are extremely interesting in this connection. In his book *Rolling Along in Song* (Viking Press, N.Y. 1937) he writes:

> The Negro hesitated, pondered for a while, and then with fond affection hung his banjo on the wall and found the inspiration for a new style of rhythm simply by pounding on the black keys of the piano. His native instinct had led him into the pentatonic scale. Staying on the black keys, he found easily the five-tone formula so distinctively characteristic of African music.

Very interesting and illuminating in this connection are Marion Bauer's comments on the pentatonic in her book *Twentieth Century Music* (G.P. Putnam's Sons, New York and London, 1947):

> The pentatonic, which may be found by playing the black keys on the piano, was doubtless a universal scale, not belonging to any one nation or race, but marking a stage in the evolution of man's consciousness. The Chinese and Japanese have clung to it throughout the centuries; it is familiar to us through many characteristic Scotch and Irish folk songs; traces of the pentatonic are to be found in the music of the American Indians and Eskimos, as well as in that of the Africans.

It is very interesting to me to note that in recent years many Western composers have turned to their old pentatonic modal folk music, finding new inspiration in this wealth and basing many of their new compositions upon it, just as Bach based much of his music on the ancient modal folk Chorales. These composers have found richness in pentatonic modal melodies because, as Joseph Yasser conclusively demonstrates, there is also a pentatonic harmony which has long existed and been developed in China, Africa, Indonesia, etc., and in Europe up to 1500. That is to say, there is a pentatonic system of music which preceded and co-exists with the better known diatonic or seven-tone system—the one in general use in the classic music of Europe after

1700. However, this pentatonic system has always continued in folk music. My dear friend and colleague Lawrence Brown has also drawn upon this richness, and has made many beautiful arrangements of our own folk music. And as Kodaly and Bartok point out and conclusively demonstrate, their harmony is drawn from the inner logic of the pentatonic modal melodies.

In *Musical Form* (Harvard University Press, 1951), Hugo Leichtentritt says of Bartok:

> Among modern composers, Bela Bartok has, more than anybody else, exploited unusual scales and strange harmonic effects derived from them. . . . In the "Allegro barbaro" for piano he uses a scale composed of C major and F sharp minor-major plus the same scale a fifth higher—G major and C sharp minor-major. . . . Here is seen a nine- or sometimes even a ten-tone scale.

Bartok himself gives a real clue in his Microcosmos (Vol. 2), written for children, entitled, "Two Major Pentachords," precisely C and F sharp. So the scale could be looked at as two contrasting pentatonics, providing a kind of natural folk-song bitonality. This gives Bartok's work a very advanced and modern harmonic feeling.

If children, who learn their model and pentatonic melodies at an early age, could be taught to look at the piano as comprised of two pentatonic scales, or two folk songs (with two auxiliary tones common to each scale), it might shorten the time of instruction and ease the work load for them. Each pentatonic is in itself a folk tune. Since this musical language is as much a part of children as their spoken tongue, they might be taught to experiment with these two pentatonics and with their interrelationships, especially the tri-tone relationship.

It may well be that today, after many fascinating and rewarding digressions, we are flowing back into the mainstream of world music— which includes the music of Asia, Africa, Europe, and the Americas— with a future potential of immense musical wealth, all giving to and taking from each other through this wonderful world bank of music.

2

Five Important Moments in America's Musical History— The Rest of the Story
Sara Towe Horsfall

Cultural moments often change what music means to a society. Our past includes these five important moments: (1) the eighteenth-century development of hymns as church music; (2) the wild popularity of nineteenth-century blackface minstrels (including Stephen Foster songs); (3) the gentrification of music entertainment on vaudeville, which set the stage for our modern music industry; (4) the continued popularity of the *Little Red Songbook* and folksingers such as Pete Seeger; and (5) Alan Lomax's extensive nonprofessional recordings, which give us a glimpse of music among the rural African Americans and others around the country in the early twentieth century.

The good thing about the past is that we can see things better retrospectively. The bad thing is that important things are often forgotten. In terms of music, both are true. There are several outstanding musical events in America's popular music past that are today unknown, or unappreciated. Understanding these gems leads to greater appreciation of our multifaceted and unique cultural heritage. Five such events are examined here: hymns, minstrels, vaudeville, the "little red songbook" or protest music, and folk music. As musical forms they may be familiar, but their role in the development of our musical culture may not be fully appreciated.

1. Hymns: Dr. Isaac Watts and the Controversial New Church Music

Most people don't think of hymns when they think of popular music, yet when hymns first appeared, they were very popular. Our knowledge of many popular hymns is limited. We know that "A Mighty Fortress Is Our God" was written by Martin Luther, and that "John Brown's Body"—the pre–Civil War protest song—borrowed a melody from the "Battle Hymn of the Republic." We probably hummed the Gaelic hymn "Morning Has Broken" along with Cat Stevens. Everyone sings Christmas hymns, and most know that "Silent Night" was composed in haste (for guitar) because the organ wasn't working. But we rarely think about the origin of this instantly recognizable genre.

Three hundred years ago, church music in this country consisted of "lining out," or psalmody. The latter form of singing began just after the Protestant Reformation—the congregation repeats a line or verse from the Bible sung a capella by a lead singer, who may have changed and embellished a melody. The slow, familiar melodies were further slowed by congregational hesitations. Psalmody was approved as a temporary measure by the British Parliament in 1644 in order to encourage the poor and illiterate to participate in the worship service. It came to the United States with the Puritans, who didn't have songbooks (Leonard, n.d.; Ruggles 1997).

By the late seventeenth century, psalmody had many critics—including teenager Isaac Watts. Challenged by his father to write something better, Watts embarked upon a prolific career of hymn writing. He composed a song a week and published his first volume of hymns in 1706, when he was thirty-two years old. Over the years he wrote some 750 hymns—some with borrowed melodies, others with borrowed words, but many with his own words and melodies. Each hymn had the block form four-part harmonies now recognizable as hymns. Among his better-known hymns are "Joy to the World" (to a tune by Handel) and "O God Our Help in Ages Past" (Ruggles 1997; J. M. K., n.d.).

Hymns were a new and controversial form of church music not only because congregants were reluctant to change, but because as liturgy they contained non-Biblical poetry. Watts used common phrases that were easily understood. His hymnals became the second most sought after book by churches around the country (Best 2006). Watts is today known as the father of English hymnody.

Watts's hymns were particularly popular among the African American slaves who had recently converted to Christianity. The pentatonic scale[1] used in many of the songs reminded them of

African songs (Robeson 1958). Today, however, the singing style known among African Americans as "Dr. Watts" style is more like the lining out (call and response) than the hymns that Watts composed (Wallace 2006).

Gospel hymnody further popularized religious music in the United States. The gospel hymns of the 1800s were musically and harmonically simple (although often rhythmically complex—reflecting African American influence) and had a simple text with little or no theological overtones. They were sung at camp meetings and were an important part of the Second Great Awakening (Smith Creek Music 2001). A system of shape note music was developed for part singing in large groups.

> One of the artifacts of the camp meeting was the Pocket Hymn Book. . . . The songbooks were generally 4×6 inches, making them easy to carry. On each page was a hymn without music, since the melodies were based on popular standards that everyone already knew. In other instances the tunes were simplistic and catchy, consequently easy to learn. . . . The prime function of the revival song was emotional response. The songs were based on the appeal of singing ecstasy, that is, total physical and emotional involvement. (Denisoff 1972:50, 52)

Sacred Harp music, the most famous songbook in that style, was compiled in 1844. After the Civil War, churches printed their own hymnals with words but no written music (Clark 2001 [1994]). In later years, secular movements such as the Socialists, Wobblies, and Communist Party used a similar method of developing emotional appeal by singing familiar songs.

2. Minstrels and Stephen Collins Foster

The racist caricature of the slave music from plantation jubilees was *the* music of the mid-1800s, both in this country and in Europe—just as rock 'n' roll was a century or so later. Minstrels gave America its first unique musical form. It was exciting music, even though it lacked the African American syncopation (white musicians didn't quite get it) (Cockrell, n.d.). It began in the 1830s, when performer T. D. "Daddy" Rice jumped up on stage between acts and did a lively, animated dance to the song "Jump Jim Crow."[2] This imitation of slave humor and music developed into a whole show of songs and jokes by at least five performers, who sat in a semi-circle. An adapted African American instrument, the banjo, accompanied the singing. Bones and Tambo, with their expected roles, sat on each end. In later years the shows ended with a cake walk. Some of the larger troupes, such as the Sweeny Minstrels or

the Christy Minstrels, had up to a hundred performers, mostly whites who "blacked up." But talented African American performers also became known (they also "blacked up"); the highest paid "minstrel man" of all time, James Bland, was African American.

We still sing minstrels, although we don't think of them as such: "Jingle Bells," "Oh! Suzanna," "Clementine," "Turkey in the Straw," "Dixie," "Pop Goes the Weasel," and "The Yellow Rose of Texas."[3] One of the most famous minstrel composers was Stephen C. Foster, who had his first big hit when he was only twenty-one: "Oh! Suzanna." It became so well known that people thought it was a folk song. Foster developed sympathies for African Americans and so dropped the caricature of slaves in favor of dignity and humanity, as seen in "Old Folks at Home," "Old Black Joe," and "Nelly Was a Lady," a song about a loving African American husband and wife. Foster was the first to negotiate payment for the rights to his songs—thus beginning the modern music industry. But that came too late for his most popular songs. He didn't perform his songs and was not well-known. Toward the end of his life he sold the rights to his songs for very little, and he died as an alcoholic with thirty-eight cents in his pocket.

> Altogether he made $15,091.08 in royalties during his lifetime and almost nothing in performing rights. . . . The total known royalties on his songs amounted to $19,290. Today, it would be worth millions. (Center for American Music 2010)

Minstrels died out after the Civil War[4]—eventually replaced by vaudeville. Despite most minstrels' racist overtones, northerners became more aware of the situation of slaves through these songs. Minstrels probably fueled antislavery feelings among the sympathetic. On the other hand, they created the caricature of the African American as an entertainer. It has taken more than a century for African Americans to outgrow that popular image.

3. Vaudeville—American Entertainment

Vaudeville replaced minstrels, medicine shows, Wild West shows, and circuses after the Civil War. Unlike the rowdy minstrel shows, vaudeville appealed to the ladies. In the larger theaters, signs were posted to teach theater etiquette:

> Gentlemen will kindly avoid stamping of feet and pounding canes on the floor. . . . All applause is best shown by clapping of hands. Please don't talk during acts, as it annoys those about you and prevents a perfect hearing of the entertainment. (Trachtenberg 1982)

By 1890 vaudeville programs included a physical act (escape artist, high divers, strong man, balancing act), a silent act, a singing act, a comedy routine, a novelty act, a rising star, an animal act, and a headliner (big star). Many twentieth-century entertainers started in vaudeville: Jack Benny, Bing Crosby, Abbott and Costello, George Burns, Gracie Allen, Judy Garland, Charlie Chaplin, and Will Rogers. In big cities there were continuous performances twelve hours a day, but those who hit the "big time" performed only twice a day in the best theaters.

At the other end of the spectrum were "small-time" performers who toured around the country. A vaudeville troupe was on the road forty weeks a year or more. By 1900 there were some 2,000 theaters in Canada and the United States. If a town had no theater, troupes would use barns, churches, or bars. Vaudeville theaters themselves are important to our cultural past. They were grand palaces, luxuriously fitted out with wrought-iron decoration, stained glass, gargoyles, arches, marble pillars, elegant lighting, upholstered seats, private boxes, velvet curtains, large mirrors, and paintings. Although the theaters varied, all were ornate and outstanding.

You may have unknowingly admired a vaudeville theater; as a child, I remember wondering why movie theaters had balconies and velvet curtains. I didn't realize that many of the 2,000 venues so popular at the turn of the century later became movie houses. In Bozeman, Montana, I became fascinated by an ornate, covered walkway that crossed a street high above the traffic from a hotel to a building across the street. The building, I was told, was a theater. It wasn't until I learned about vaudeville that I realized the walkway was for performers and patrons to avoid the freezing Montana winter weather.

In historic Tombstone, Arizona, the vaudeville craze also left its mark. The Birdcage Theater,[5] a combination theater, saloon, and bordello, opened on Christmas Day 1881. Artifacts on display include photos of vaudeville performers who came to Tombstone when it was one of the largest towns west of the Mississippi.

With vaudeville, public consumption of music changed. There was a boom in piano sales, with some 25,000 pianos sold during the vaudeville era. Sheet music became popular with sales reaching a peak at the end of the nineteenth century. By 1880 Chicago, Cincinnati, Baltimore, and Philadelphia were squeezed out by New York's Tin Pan Alley[6] as the dominant sheet music publishing center. Vaudeville performers were initially used to encourage sales of sheet music. Later, publishers paid artists to have their picture on the cover of sheet music. This led to a focus on the performer.

The vaudeville era also gave birth to the American Song—the characteristically happy, peaceful, warm, and nostalgic music of the 1890s: "Good Ole Summertime," "Give My Regards to Broadway," "Shine on Harvest Moon," "Down by the Old Mill Stream," "Let Me Call You Sweetheart" (see Chapter 3).

By the end of World War I, popular recordings began to replace sheet music as the major form of popular music consumption. Similarly, radio and movies replaced vaudeville. In 1932, the New York Palace was the last vaudeville theater to close its doors.

4. The Little Red Songbook *and the Song "Strange Fruit"*

Music was essential to the Wobblies (Industrial Workers of the World, or IWW), the revolutionary socialist movement founded in 1905. "Almost every Wobbly hall had a piano," one member recalled (Moore, n.d.). Music was used to recruit and inspire. Migrant workers and unskilled laborers could get the message in a song quicker than verbally or in writing (Herrmann 1998). Irreverent, zany rhymes were sung to well-known melodies. For example, the words "solidarity forever" are sung in place of "glory, glory hallelujah" in the "Battle Hymn of the Republic." "The Preacher and the Slave" used the melody from the hymn "Sweet Bye and Bye": "You will live, bye and bye; In that glorious land above the sky; Work and pray, live on hay; You'll get pie in the sky when you die."

"The Big Question" is sung to the tune of "America":

> *My Job now is no more*
> *The boss has slam'd the door;*
> *What shall I do?*
> *Seems like my end is near,*
> *My guts feel awful queer—*
> *Where do we go from here?*
> *This is up to you.*
>
> *No, I've not lost a leg,*
> *Why must I starve and beg?*
> *What Shall I do?*

Where can the answer lurk?
Why am I out of work,
Gazing on all this murk?
This is up to you.

First published in Spokane, Washington, in 1909, the *Little Red Songbook* sold 10,000 copies within a month. Within four years, it had print runs of 50,000. The songs maintained their popularity throughout the twentieth century. The songbook has been published more than thirty times—the most recent printing in 2010 (Herrmann 1998; Seeger 1972). Roy (2010:73) calls it "one of the most famous and widely distributed sources of radical songs in American history."

The songs' popularity owes much to the goals of the Wobblies, who wanted to get everyone to join one big union and then go on strike "to decide who was going to run the world." A songbook was given out with the union card. The motto on the cover—"To Fan the Flames of Discontent"—conveyed its purpose. "The songs were roared out by Wobblies at meetings, on picket lines, in jails . . . on freight trains through South Dakota" (Seeger 1972:74). This breaking into "the universal language of song" at an IWW strike meeting was unforgettable; according to Helen Keller, it created a "curious lift" and a "strange sudden fire of mingled nationalities" (Herrmann 1998:173).

Because this music was used to create a particular attitude or inspire a particular action, Denisoff (1972:58) calls it *propaganda music* rather than protest music. It appeals to emotions to get support, to promote cohesion, and to reinforce particular values and solutions. Woody Guthrie is the singer that most symbolizes the propaganda song. "Woody took his tunes mostly from different kinds of American folk songs and ballads. . . . He felt that the old four line stanza, which told a story and slowly unfolded a moral, was as good as any he could use" (Seeger 1972:50).

The Communist Party also used music in the 1930s and 1940s, but its leaders wanted to influence American culture as well as inspire activism (Roy 2010:89). Their first attempt was relatively unsuccessful—the 1934 release of a *New Workers Song Book* of "proletarian" music created by the Workers Music League. Then, through the efforts of Pete Seeger, son of league member Charles Seeger, they embraced folk music as "the people's music." The People's Songs, Inc. was formed in 1946 with the hope of creating a "singing labor movement" with music for picket lines, publicity, and meetings (Dunaway in Roy 2010:122). The PSI *Bulletin* was edited by Pete Seeger, who later started *Sing Out!* in order to revive folk and labor songs. According to Seeger, many later song collectors did not really understand the meaning of the words (Seeger 1972:76–81).

By 1949, when the funds ran out for the People's Songs, many of the musicians left the labor union. But the *Sing Out!* magazine continued.

For a few years it barely stayed alive. . . . [It] now has a worldwide circulation of 15,000. Magazines like it started up in England and on the Continent, in Australia, NZ and Japan and several North American cities. The basic idea is sound: to combine songs and criticism. (Seeger 1972:21)

Denisoff identifies four distinct periods of the propaganda song: (1) 1905–1915—the Wobblies and their *Little Red Songbook*; (2) just before World War II—publication of the Communist Party's *Red Song Book*; (3) just after World War II—publication of the People's Songs Inc. and the *People's Song Book I* and *II* (1948); and (4) the late 1950s and early 1960s—folk song revival era, when the SNCC published its *We Shall Overcome Songbook* (1964) (Denisoff 1972:77).

"Strange Fruit"

A powerful propaganda song about lynchings, "Strange Fruit" is one of the ten "songs that actually changed the world" (Margolick 2001:8). It was written by a communist Jewish school teacher, Abel Meeropol, but was co-opted by African American singer Billie Holiday. People sometimes walked out or became hysterical when she sang it. It was well known by black and white intellectuals alike, although it was never heard on the radio—too risky. For some African Americans it was almost "sacred," but it played a role in Holiday's demise (Margolick 2001:75).

> *Southern trees bear a strange fruit*
> *Blood on the leaves and blood at the root,*
> *Black body swinging in the Southern breeze,*
> *Strange fruit hanging from the poplar trees.*
>
> *Pastoral scene of the gallant South*
> *The bulging eyes and the twisted mouth,*
> *Scent of magnolia, sweet and fresh*
> *And the sudden smell of burning flesh!*
>
> *Here is a fruit for the crows to pluck*
> *For the rain to gather, for the wind to suck,*
> *For the sun to rot, for a tree to drop*
> *Here is a strange and bitter crop.*

5. Alan Lomax, Folk Music, and Cantometrics

Alan Lomax and his father, John Avery Lomax, traveled the rural South and then the world looking for and recording indigenous music. Much of their work is now in the Library of Congress (Archive of American

Folk Song). Among the singers first recorded by the Lomaxes in the 1930s and 1940s are Leadbelly, Woody Guthrie, Muddy Waters, Pete Seeger, and Burl Ives. Recording equipment was bulky and heavy, and it was Alan's job to "tote the 500-pound recording machine on loan from the Library of Congress" (S. Kennedy, n.d.). The Lomaxes also carried automobile batteries to use when there was no electricity. With this simple equipment they recorded more than 3,000 songs.

Following his father's death, Alan Lomax continued recording and performing on his own. During the McCarthy era he sought refuge in England because of his extreme politics. Back in this country he participated in the civil rights movement, organized musical events, and generally "ruffled feathers" in his attempt to preserve and disseminate indigenous music (Cohen 2002). It was not uncommon for musicians who gathered in his New York apartment to spend an entire weekend making music (S. Kennedy, n.d.).

Cantometrics

Lomax's system of analyzing world musical styles is largely unknown today, primarily because neither he nor his father traveled in academic circles. *Cantometrics* ("song measurements") was developed in the 1960s, when Lomax and a colleague coded some 700 songs from 233 different cultures. Indigenous music is largely regular: words are repeated, and rhythm, melody, tempo, volume, and singing styles are all regular. This regularity indicates a cooperative effort of music making that adheres to accepted rules. Norms develop as to the number of performers, their arrangement, and their interactions. Other norms develop for solo performances, and for the audience. This "tacit agreement" among all present "to abide by the musical formulas of their culture and of the particular song" is what allows music to be produced and enjoyed (Lomax 1968:14, 15).[7] A single culture, however, is likely to have a limited number of musical performance norms.

After analyzing more than 3,000 songs from all over the world, Lomax found some relationships between social structure and music.[8] An aggressive, masculine culture, for instance, was likely to have music that is forceful and aggressive, and the interaction between musicians would be similar to the social interactions in their society. Societies that favor solo singers with a complex style that deters others from joining in are likely to have a highly centralized political authority. In contrast, a communal culture, as found among the American Indians, is more likely to have group singing. In Lomax's estimation, technicians, office workers, and scientists are likely to prefer an explanatory singing voice.

According to Lomax's investigation of cantometrics, six factors determine a society's musical style: (1) the type of economic production,

(2) the political activity, (3) the amount of stratification, (4) sexual restrictions, (5) the amount of male dominance, and (6) social cohesiveness. Complex societies will likely have music that is wordy, precisely articulated, and sung in mid-volume with a normal accent. Complex societies will also have music with multiple parts and rhythms, a variety of music instruments, use of embellishment, and free rhythms.

Simple societies, in comparison, will have songs that are repetitive and nonexplicit, with simple rhythms. A cohesive group performance of such music allows everyone to join in easily. Group rather than solo performances are found throughout Africa, where societies are likely to have a simple political structure. Their performances are also polyphonic and polyrhythmic.

Lomax believed that interlocking and counterpoint tended to decrease as the complexity of a society increased. He thought of counterpoint as a feminine invention, because he observed that polyphony and complementarity tend to increase when feminine involvement in the society increases. Choral cohesiveness also increases when feminine contribution to subsistence increases. When men occupy positions of leadership and specialized competence and are more assertive, women tend to sing in interlocked choral groups, where leadership and individual voices are submerged in the collective vocalization.

Most interestingly, Lomax observed that people sang in "wide voices" where women are secure, productive, and free to relate fully to men; conflict between the sexes does not result in inner tension. This voice is found in most societies of Africa and Oceania, and in the villages of Old Europe. But in societies where sex is repressed, singers will "express themselves over assertively in rasp, or appeal for sympathy in nasality, or express sexual tensions by vocal narrowing" (Lomax 1968:200).

Lomax concluded that there were five different unique musical traditions in the world. The first area is North Africa and Eurasia from the Mediterranean to East Asia. The second is the North American Indian, also found in South America. The third is Australia, Polynesia, and New Guinea. The fourth is a "remarkable contrapuntal style" of African hunters that was "reproduced" in America. And fifth is European, which actually has three distinctive traditions: Old Europe, Eastern Mediterranean, and Western Europe (Lomax 1968:79).

A study of fifty-six world cultural areas with forty songs for each area roughly confirmed this typology. The researchers ranked song similarity line by line. Making use of computer analysis, they identified six large regions: (1) North America; (2) South America (bounded at the Isthmus of Tehuantepec); (3) the Pacific, excluding Australia; (4) Africa, except Ethiopia and Muslim Sudan, but including Madagascar and Afro-America; (5) Europe—except Lapps, but including

Anglo-America, French Canada, and Ibero America; and (6) Old High Culture—Afro-Eurasian region from North Africa to East Asia and Malaysia.

CODA: A Note about Folk Music

Although considered a separate genre today, the term *folk music* is a bit of a misnomer. The usual definition of folk music is a song important to a people's cultural tradition with no known composer. Many of the songs that Alan Lomax and his father recorded fit that definition. Early African American songs also fit this definition: "Oh When the Saints," "Swing Low," "Let My People Go," "Drinkin' Gourd," and others. But these are also known as spirituals.

Many songs regarded as folk music are not anonymous compositions. "Greensleeves," for instance, first appeared in a book called *A Handful of Pleasant Delights,* by Clement Robinson in 1584 (Nelson-Burns, n.d.). Neither was it important to a cultural tradition. It was simply a popular song. Because of its age and familiarity we have come to regard it as a folk song. There are other songs now called folk songs that were written, sung, printed, and passed around during the sixteenth, seventeenth, and eighteenth centuries. Many of these are broadside ballads—songs that were sold and performed on the streets to discuss the day's events or tell tales of heroes (Bodleian Library, University of Oxford).

Some songs become folk songs only because the composer isn't well known—as with Stephen Foster. And to complicate things, there are modern songs written in the 1960s folk style—lyrical melodies with meaningful words sung to the accompaniment of a guitar or other stringed instrument. These too are called folk music. Researchers and musicians agree that the term is not the best one. Nelson-Burns explains on her very extensive website that folk music "is not a completely accurate term for the music I post here. Many of the tunes do have known authors. . . . 'Traditional and Popular Music' . . . would probably be a better name." She continues to use the term, however, because that is how people know the music. Similarly, Pete Seeger explains,

> The term "folk music" was invented by 19th century scholars to describe the music of the peasantry, age-old and anonymous. Nowadays it covers such a multitude of sins as to be almost meaningless. To me it means homemade-type music played mainly by ear, arising out of older traditions but with a meaning for today. I use it only for lack of a better word. Similarly I have had to accept the label "folksinger," although a "professional singer of amateur music" would be more accurate in my own case. (Seeger 1972:5)

Roy's comments are even more pointed. He notes that the Folk Song Society of London (founded in 1898) did not preserve music performed by "the folk." Rather, melodies, harmonies, and lyrics were freely used and adapted by others, including classical composers. In this country, the American Folk Lore Society (founded in 1888) was not interested in African American music.

> Few societies other than modern Western ones make a distinction between the culture of the educated elite and the culture of "the folk." The social roots of the distinction between folk and high culture lie in a nationalist and often aristocratic project to define a people while registering a genteel critique of industrial, urban society. (Roy 2010:54)

In the end, Nelson-Burns is probably right that people are too used to the term to be able to change it easily. However, academically it should be used with caution.

Notes

1. Pentatonic scale is a five-note scale common in Africa and the Far East. An easy way to play it on the piano is to play only the black keys. Most spirituals are in pentatonic scale.

2. In the wording of the time, Jim Crow referred to a plantation slave, whereas Zip Coon was a city dandy.

3. Published in 1858, "The Yellow Rose of Texas" was a love song by an African American longing for his girlfriend. During the Civil War it was a campfire song (Clark 2001 [1994]).

4. The banjo and minstrel style of singing is now found in bluegrass music, although few acknowledge its minstrel heritage.

5. According to its current owners, the Birdcage Theater had continuous performances for only a few years before it closed its doors because of the decline in Tombstone's population. It sat empty for close to 100 years before being opened again to the public.

6. Many sheet music publishers were located in New York on 28th street between Fifth and Broadway. Before air conditioning, pianos could be heard on all sides through the open windows, hence the name Tin Pan Alley.

7. Lomax and his colleague identified eight ways that musical cultures differ: (1) the social organization of the vocal group; (2) the social organization of the orchestra; (3) the cohesiveness of the vocal group and the orchestra; (4) the explicitness of the text; (5) the rhythm of the vocal group and orchestra; (6) the melodic complexity; (7) the degree and kind of embellishments used; and (8) the vocal stance. They also noted that the individual performer had certain freedoms: use of ornamentation (although only a small number of patterns are used in any one culture), adaptation of their voice, and use of melodies and phrases. Specifically, Rpa (parlando rubato), embellishment, glissando,

melisma, tremolo, glottal shake, melodic form, phrase length, and number of phrases are left up to the individual.

8. "Our working rule at that time was to stop coding in a culture when we ceased to find notable differences between the songs. In some cases, of course, we had only one or two songs from a culture. At the end of the period, we sorted the profiles by eye and drew master model profiles for the main regional types as they emerged from this purely visual kind of statistics. Although the sample has quadrupled in size and has twice been reorganized in its cultural spread since that first summer, the main characteristics of the regional types discovered then have not been drastically affected" (Lomax 1968:21).

3

American Popular Song
Howard S. Becker[1]

Our common, popular song form developed at the end of the vaudeville
era. These distinctly American songs came from the collective contributions
of song writers, musicians, singers, and audiences. They have simple
melodies in a limited voice range, suitable for untrained musicians.

The United States produced, over a period of perhaps seventy to eighty
years, and most importantly in the first half of the twentieth century,
an enormous body of popular music. James Maher estimates (in
Wilder 1972, p. xxxviii) that about 300,000 songs were copyrighted
from 1900 to 1950. Before that period, American popular song was
an amalgam of derivations from European parlor music and some
native ballad traditions, including those of the large black population recently released from slavery. It was meant to be performed
in the parlors of middle-class people, who owned and knew how to
play pianos, flutes, and violins, and is best represented in the work
of Stephen Foster.

I confess immediately to a deep cultural chauvinism. I think it un-
questionable that American popular song of what is sometimes called
"The Golden Age" is a striking cultural achievement that one does
not find elsewhere in the world. It has now been superceded by the
somewhat different genres of rock, rap, and their relatives, on the one
hand, and by the further branching of its musical theater based genre
into the simpler sounds of Andrew Lloyd Weber . . . and the more
sophisticated and chromatic ones of Stephen Sondheim on the other.

Originally published in Tom Bevers, ed., Artists—Dealers—Consumers: On the
Social World of Art *(Hilversum: Verloren, 1994), pp. 9–18. Condensed from the
original. Reprinted with permission.*

So I'm talking about a tradition that was once widespread, popular, and culturally dominant, which has now become esoteric, of concern mainly to antiquarians and aficionados.

The development of this characteristic American song style coincided with the growth of institutions in which that music, now moved out of the parlors of private homes, could be performed for the public: the vaudeville houses, musical theaters, taverns, and night clubs that became increasingly common after the turn of the century. Later, it was a creature of the recording industry, and then radio and the movies. I haven't studied all these matters, and can only guess at how they work. My guesses are based on looking at some of the voluminous literature but, to be truthful, as much on my own experiences growing up in the heyday of this music and performing it for many years as a pianist in dance bands, night clubs, and the like (thus doing my part to prolong the tradition).

The Sound: Alec Wilder

The songs that make up this achievement have a characteristic sound and ambience. They are immediately distinguishable from the popular musics of other countries, although American popular song eventually came to dominate, or at least influence strongly, that of most other countries which shared the same western musical tradition. . . .

In a prodigious act of scholarship, Alec Wilder examined over 17,000 American popular songs to produce his book, *American Popular Music 1900–1950*, a definitive analysis of that distinctive sound and form. Wilder, however, operated in a peculiar and idiosyncratic way, never enunciating, in the over 500 pages of his book, an explicit aesthetic. He proceeded entirely by what I sometimes think is the ultimate critical act: pointing, pointing to specific instances of songs, and specific places in songs, which he thought epitomized the characteristic aspects and virtues of the form. So you have to read between the lines of his book to find the generalizations which, though hidden and implicit, are nevertheless there. . . .

The characteristic features of the musical form Wilder analyzed can be simply listed. There were many variations, some of which I will mention, but the archetypal form was thirty-two bars long, divided into four sections: an eight-bar statement of a theme (A), a repetition of that theme (A'), a second theme (B), often referred to as "the bridge," and a final repetition of the first theme (A").[2] Common variations were ABAB and ABAC (in which C would consist of a slight variation of B). The major exception to this was the blues. Blues seldom had a real melody, though some ("St. Louis Blues" is a well-known example) did. Rather than a melody, its characteristic feature was an invariant twelve-bar succession of chords, again with certain common variations.

The thirty-two bar form could almost be called traditional, except that, as Hobsbawm and others have taught us about so many other traditions, it had a relatively recent origin. Wilder notes that "There were few instances of it in any type of popular music until the late teens. And it didn't become the principal form until 1925–1926" (p. 56).

The melodies of these songs were so constructed that they could be sung by a person with no more than an average vocal range, seldom reaching beyond a tenth, and usually not even that much. Nor did they involve unfamiliar, uncommon, or "difficult" skips or intervals between successive notes, since they consisted mostly of scalewise movements or broken arpeggios (the notes of a simple chord played in turn). The melodies were harmonized with chords native to the scale or ones that were reached through the circle of fifths, thus retaining the diatonic flavor. They did not ordinarily contain unexpected harmonies or dissonant melodic notes. . . .

It will be obvious from this description that these songs could be sung, as they were meant to be, by people who were musically untrained. No knowledge or ability beyond what someone might have acquired in school or from singing traditional songs was really necessary. Perhaps more to the point, the songs could be understood and "appreciated" by people with a similar lack of specialized training and skill. Hearing such a song was something like filling in the blanks in a printed form: you did not have to guess at the form but could quickly see which of the common ones you already knew it was. The melodies were familiar in their intervals and formats, proceeding by the familiar steps and skips contained in scales and triads. The harmonies were likewise familiar. Together, at a higher level of organization, they produced familiar patterns that could be interpreted in traditional ways as sad or happy, romantic, and so on. Composers of "mood music" for Hollywood films eventually codified these effects in libraries of readymade music for standard situations. (The similarity of all this to the creation and recognition of standard visual patterns will be apparent to readers of William Ivins and Ernst Gombrich.)

This music acquired its characteristically "American" sound when composers began to incorporate into what they wrote the sounds being created by the musicians who were developing jazz, particularly syncopation, and "blue" and other altered notes in melodies and harmonies. Musicians had also adapted their playing to the requirements of the situations they were playing in, particularly by accepting the steady, unvarying tempos required by dancers, thus avoiding the characteristically "European" sound created by the extensive use of rubato and the fermata. These changes, and others, made a distinctively "American" sound.

Most Americans had learned to recognize this set of components and the typical ways of organizing them, and to respond to them in predictable ways, in their sleep so to speak. In their sleep? Almost literally in their sleep. When I played professionally in bars and taverns which stayed open until late at night, it sometimes happened that I fell asleep, and continued playing without getting lost. Which is only an extreme example of the deep level at which people acquired this knowledge. It was what some people in the field of performance studies now call "embodied" knowledge, a phenomenon studied in sociology only in David Sudnow's unique book *Ways of the Hand* (Sudnow 1978). That book, for those who have not read it, describes how, when Sudnow learned to play jazz as an adult (who had, it should be added, become an ethnomethodologist!), his hand learned things that, it could be said, his mind did not know; the knowledge was in his body.

Since this knowledge was so widespread, it could be taken for granted. It became a resource composers and performers could use, knowing that the resulting songs would be playable or singable by anyone who could play or sing at all, and understandable, musically and emotionally and unthinkingly, by anyone who heard it.

Many variants of these musical forms occurred, some extremely simple. . . . If a few composers create some new forms and styles, that in no way guarantees that a successful, widely accepted popular music with great cultural penetration will develop. For these songs to be written and played, to be heard and responded to . . . a network of organizations, institutions, and customary practices had to . . . maintain the music and carry it to the world. What was that network? Traditions do not exist without people to keep them alive, especially so in a performed art like music. . . .

Briefly, the tradition continued because one group of people—song writers—continued to write songs in these genres; because another group—musicians and singers—learned them and kept them alive by continually performing them; because commercial institutions existed— sheet music stores, record stores—to distribute them; because other commercial institutions—dance halls, night clubs, theaters, vaudeville houses—provided the places where audiences might hear the music in ways that gave it added cachet and meaning; and because the people who heard them continued to be able to "hear" them and to invest them with emotional meaning. It was never in any way "necessary" or given that such organizations and activities would arise and persist. But had those organizations not developed as they did, American popular song would not have been what it became. One might say that the music consisted, in a real sense, of the sounds *and* all that organization, conceived as a unity, somewhat as Bruno Latour (1987, pp. 103–44) conceives networks of machines, people, and social organizations as unities. The development of each of the phenomena I have mentioned is a sociological study in itself, in the growth and maintenance of institutionalized ways of doing things.

Wilder, Aesthetics, and the Music Business

Sociologists are frequently criticized for refusing to make aesthetic judgments. Alec Wilder's book is filled with judgments about which songs are good and what is good about them, most of which I share. Although he never states any explicit or systematically argued for criteria of what is musically good, it is easy to discern the outlines of one in his meticulously phrased analyses and judgments of particular songs and even musical phrases.

What Wilder is most concerned with is that a song be *interesting*: that in the construction of the melody and in the arrangement of the harmonies that underlie that melody the composer has made interesting choices between available alternatives, choices which show wit and elegance and sophistication. He concerns himself with the most minute aspects of a song: where notes are repeated and with what effect, what kinds of melodic skips are employed and where, what melodic and harmonic patterns are established against which a witty variation can be heard, which of the harmonizations of a song that might be employed are used.

. . . Listeners to music (or readers of poetry) develop expectations as they proceed through a work. Given what they have so far seen or heard they expect, on the basis of the conventional patterns they are familiar with, that certain words or notes or harmonies will probably follow. When the work does not satisfy these expectations, listeners experience tension and discomfort, resolved when the expectations are finally satisfied. The most satisfying works (the "best") are those which reveal that listeners had mistakenly relied on the wrong models in generating their expectations, works in which the final notes or words turn out to be completely appropriate once the appropriate model is recognized. A musical culture of the kind I have described having come into existence, performers and audiences alike had plenty of models to use as the basis of their guesses as they listened to any song. . . .

Do listeners go through all this consciously when they listen to a popular song? No. They know that a song sounds fresh or interesting, but they do not know, or cannot put into words, the means the composer used to produce that result.

Songwriters

Behind the deluge of songs Wilder analyzed, of course, were the composers, the songwriters (to use the less dignified term most of them would have recognized) who created these popular songs. It cannot be overemphasized that this was an industry, which ground out a continual supply of what would be called today, in the argot of Hollywood and television, "product." Songs came out of the publishing houses, who originally made their profits by selling sheet music to people who would take it home and play it, and later made them by collecting royalties for the performance (especially the recorded performance) of songs they had published.

Most of these songs, like most of the production of any large-scale cultural industry, were forgettable. So much like hundreds of other songs, so banal in their melodic contrivances and harmonies, so trivial and derivative in their lyrics (the endless rhyming, in English, of "June" and "moon" became the object of many jokes). They were written to be recorded, played on the radio, sold in record stores, perhaps to become "hits" which would sell thousands, maybe millions, of copies and make the publishers (and perhaps the authors, if they were not cheated of their due, as they often were) a fortune. These songs seldom had the wit, freshness, elegance, sophistication, or any of the other qualities Wilder makes much of, and which musicians and singers treasured so that the songs became classics, and entered what became a standard repertoire.

Some few had these qualities. They came, disproportionately, from a few writers, who mostly wrote their songs not for the sheet music factories of what was called Tin Pan Alley, but for the musical stage and the films. These are the composers to whom Wilder devotes the bulk of his book (but not all of it, to which I will return): Jerome Kern, George Gershwin, Irving Berlin, Cole Porter, Harold Arlen, Richard Rodgers.

Writing scores for musical comedies gave composers room for innovation, though in a very limited range. . . . The audiences who attended those shows were more sophisticated and capable of taking innovation in stride (though it was still a common criterion of judgment that you be able to whistle the tunes as you left the theater . . . and the songs were supposed to carry some dramatic weight and move the narrative along (when there was one). Something like that was true of film music as well. . . .

The people who worked in this genre thus produced the characteristic product of a relatively closed and stable cultural organization: vast numbers of songs whose quality varied enormously within quite narrow limits. Within the conventions of the form, composers could and did make works of great skill, art, and beauty, recognized as such by knowledgeable members of the world of popular song.

Musicians

Wilder's aesthetic is very much that of the world of the popular musician, the kind of musician I was in my youth. Such musicians, the people who played in bars and clubs, who played for dances and parties, routinely "knew" hundreds of such songs and could play thousands. When I say that they "knew" these songs, I don't mean that they had memorized each one note for note, but rather that they could play all these songs once you gave them a bare minimum of information. In the best case, they might know both the melody and the harmonies that had been set to it. But they might, with only a general idea of which of the several available harmonic models the song fit, and relying on the melody to provide sufficient clues to the harmony or vice versa, then be able to perform it adequately. So a player might identify a song his fellow players did not know as "I Got Rhythm" with a "Honeysuckle [Rose]" bridge and others would be able to play along. If even one player knew the melody, or if someone in the audience could just hum it for them, the others could pick it up as they played.

To these musicians, certain of the thousands of songs they "knew" in this way seemed especially good, in just the ways Wilder suggested. These songs have, as musicians liked to say, "interesting changes," that is, harmonies they found it interesting to improvise on and melodies which provoke interesting variations in the improvisations built on them. They are, in that sense, interesting and "fun" to play.

Because musicians liked these songs, they played them often, whenever they could choose what they would play, which was often enough. As the musicians made their choices of particular songs to play, based on their own preferences, on what they found "interesting," they constructed a shared standard of judgment which then made those songs even more likely to be chosen again, since "everyone" would be more likely to know them. This is a specific version of what social scientists speak of as "culture."

The application of these shared standards, put into practice in countless specific situations, weeded out the endless succession of similar songs produced by songwriters, most of them ephemeral and not worth anyone bothering to memorize because they would not be asked for in the future. This left a smaller repertoire known to everyone. Because they were played a lot, those songs become the basis of a repertoire, the "standard" songs which every competent player in the genre ought to know and, in fact, did know. Although no two players would know exactly the same "standards," most players and singers knew enough of them to make it easy for groups to perform an evening's worth of music even if they had never met before, let alone rehearsed. (Bruce McLeod (1993) has described this phenomenon in detail for the case of the "club date musicians" of the Greater New York area.)

When musicians who had not rehearsed, who perhaps did not even know each other, met to play in situations where they could assume, almost always correctly, that the other players there would know the same songs they did, it was sufficient to say "Sunny Side of the Street" and indicate a tempo for the group to then play a competent collective version of that song. They did not even have to indicate the key, because everyone "knew" that the "standard" key was C; if it was not to be played in C, perhaps to accommodate a singer's range, someone would add "in F."

This repertoire is an important foundational element of jazz playing. Most jazz performances are performances of a song chosen from among these standard tunes. Even if the melody is never played, even if a different melody is substituted over the distinctive harmonies, a competent player will recognize the song whose harmonies and format underlie what is being played, and will say, "Yeah, that's really 'Cherokee' (or 'Exactly Like You' or 'All the Things You Are')." Thus, the song made famous by Dizzy Gillespie and Charlie Parker as "Ornithology" was, in this sense, "really" "How High the Moon." In short, the existence of the standard repertoire is what made most jazz possible. Even when jazz players composed songs not based on an already existing popular song, they usually used the same thirty-two bar format and variations of well-known harmonic patterns.

It was not just the small jazz groups, whose work was mainly improvised, who carried this tradition. Big bands, of the kind that began to develop after the end of World War I, reached their peak in the Thirties and Forties and, unfortunately, began to die out in the Fifties. Made up of anywhere from twelve to twenty musicians, playing from written arrangements—led by household names like Benny Goodman, Tommy Dorsey, and Count Basie—they supported the large numbers of musicians from among whom the more talented improvisers could emerge and in which they could get their training. While much of what they played consisted of ephemera, the 300,000 songs from which Wilder made his selections, they always played some of the standards as well, keeping them alive for the members of the national audience and making them part of everyone's experience.

Singers

Singers deserve special mention as carriers of the tradition. For most laypeople the songs were indissolubly connected to the lyrics that accompanied them (which was the case for musicians as well, most of the time). People learned the words from the singers who recorded them and sang them in films and on the radio and, later, television. Popular singers came and went—Perry Como, Bobby Darin, Dinah Shore.

Some singers—Frank Sinatra, Tony Bennett, Nat "King" Cole, and Ella Fitzgerald and Mel Torme are major examples—became, in their own way, "standards." They outlived the vagaries of the entertainment markets and sang, as jazz players played, the standards of the repertoire. Still others—Mabel Mercer, Bobby Short, Michael Feinstein—specialized in a more esoteric repertoire, the lesser known or almost unknown works of the masters Wilder writes about, and of others who were not well known at all beyond the inner circles of the music business—like Wilder himself, whose works fill albums by such champions of the esoteric as Marian MacPartland, and Jackie Cain and Roy Kral. Though they are not so widely known, a more specialized audience supported them and their work.

These singers carried the tradition, as can be seen in the albums and CDs recorded by them—Ella Fitzgerald's "songbooks" of works by Gershwin, Rodgers and Hart, Johnny Mercer, and others, and Sinatra's albums of classics. They kept the songs alive by continually performing them, thus training succeeding generations of listeners to prize them. The recordings of Short, Feinstein, and others kept even the more esoteric branches of the tradition alive.

Audiences

The repertoire of standards, brought to the public by the singers and the big bands, was also what most lay people knew. Growing up surrounded by this music, several generations of Americans heard it on the radio, in films, on the records they brought home, at the dances and clubs they went to. The songs were immediately accessible because of the simple, recognizable structures I have already discussed. They became the language in which courtship was conducted, in which one learned to "feel" what one was supposed to feel in romantic situations, and in other emotional situations as well. Thus, all those Americans, and many people around the world, learned to associate the winter holidays with Irving Berlin's "White Christmas" and Easter (in America, a day for promenading in new finery) with his "Easter Parade." We fell in love to "Moonlight in Vermont," celebrated our sweethearts with "My Funny Valentine," and suffered heartbreak with "Don't Get Around Much Any More."

Coda

I had trouble thinking how to end this talk. I was tempted to call on the show business tradition on which I have relied for my knowledge, and "play myself off" with a chorus of "Fine and Dandy." But that is hardly suitable for a serious occasion, so I will, instead, close with the suggestion that this kind of integrated look at the institutions of an art and the various kinds of actors who made those institutions viable is transportable across the lines of time, place, and genre, and suggest that comparative studies by sociologists make a special point of taking into account, in a serious way, the fine details of the works themselves, arising as they do out of the continued interactions of all those people and groups.

Notes

1. Author Note: When this paper was first presented, at a conference in Rotterdam, I gave it from the piano, accompanied by a drummer and bass player, illustrating the points by playing relevant music.

2. Editor's Note: An example of the AA'BA form is "Rudolph the Red-Nosed Reindeer."

A = *Rudolph the Red-Nosed Reindeer, had a very shiny nose,*
   And if you ever saw it you would even say it glows.

A' = *All of the other reindeer used to laugh and call him names.*
   They never let poor Rudolph join in any reindeer games.

B = *Then one foggy Christmas eve, Santa came to say,*
   "Rudolph with your nose so bright, won't you drive my sleigh tonight."

A = *Then all the reindeer loved him, as they shouted out with glee,*
   "Rudolph the Red-Nosed Reindeer, you'll go down in history."

4

The Industrialization
of Popular Music—Part I
Simon Frith

The author examines how the production of music has changed over the years, and how this has changed our understanding of what music is and who the musicians are. New technologies include records, radio, tape, and CDs. With each change, major industries developed strategies to sell their music. As music production changes, so does our understanding of what music is, and who the musicians are.

When I was a child I lived in dread of having to sing in public. This was a common forfeit in party games, but I'd do anything else humiliating in preference. Singing was too personal, too exposed an activity.

Singing still seems to me the rawest form of personal expression (which is why I love soul music) and music making, more generally, still seems the most spontaneously human activity. Without thinking much about it, people sing in the bath and on the playground, beat out rhythms on the dance floor, and whistle while they work. It is because of our experience of the immediacy of music making that its industrial production has always been somehow suspect. In fact, of course, people today work with piped-in music and skip to the beat of a ghetto blaster; they're more likely to listen to the radio than to sing in the bath. Most of the music we hear now, in public or private, has been mechanically produced and is tied into a complex system of money making. And we take these "artificial" sounds for granted. A couple

Originally published in James Lull, ed., Popular Music and Communication, *2nd ed. (Thousand Oaks, CA: Sage, 1992), pp. 49–74. Condensed from the original. Reprinted with permission.*

of years ago I went to see Al Green in concert in the Royal Albert Hall in London. At one point he left the stage (and his microphone) and walked through the audience, still singing. As he passed me I realized that this was the first time, in thirty years as a pop fan, that I'd ever heard a star's "natural" voice!

The contrast between music as expression and music as commodity defines twentieth-century pop experience and means that however much we may use and enjoy its products, we retain a sense that the music industry is a bad thing—bad for music, bad for us. Read any pop history and you'll find in outline the same sorry tale. However the story starts, and whatever the authors' politics, the industrialization of music means a shift from active musical production to passive pop consumption, the decline of folk or community or subcultural traditions, and a general musical deskilling—the only instruments people like me can play today are their disc players and tape decks. The rise of the multinational leisure corporation means, inevitably, efficient manipulation of a new, global pop taste that reaches into every first, second, and Third World household like Coca-Cola (and with the same irrelevance to real needs).

What such arguments assume (and they're part of the common sense of every rock fan) is that there is some essential human activity, music making, which has been colonized by commerce. Pop is a classic case of what Marx called alienation: something human is taken from us and returned in the form of a commodity. Songs and singers are fetishized, made magical, and we can only reclaim them through possession, via a cash transaction in the marketplace. In the language of rock criticism, what's at issue here is the *truth* of music—truth to the people who created it, truth to our experience. What's bad about the music industry is the layer of deceit and hype and exploitation it places between us and our creation.

The flaw in this argument is the suggestion that music is the starting point of the industrial process—the raw material over which everyone fights—when it is, in fact, the final product. The "industrialization of music" can't be understood as something that happens *to* music but describes a process in which music itself is made—a process, that is, that fuses (and confuses) capital, technical, and musical arguments. Twentieth-century popular music means the twentieth-century popular record; not the record of something (a song? a singer? a performance?) that exists independently of the music industry, but a form of communication that determines what songs, singers, and performances are and can be.

We've come to the end of the record era now (and so, perhaps, to the end of pop music as we know it) and I'll return to the future later. What I want to stress here is that from a historical perspective rock and roll was not a revolutionary form or moment, but an evolutionary one, the climax of (or possibly a footnote to) a story that begins with Edison's phonograph. To explain the music industry we have, then to adopt a much wider time perspective than rock scholars usually allow. The pop business itself—the nature of its sales activities—is in a constant state of "crisis." Business analysts should, by contrast, keep cool. To be examining always the entrails of the "latest thing" is to mistake the trees for the forest, and, as I hope to show, there is more to be learned from the continuities in pop history than from the constantly publicized changes. "New things" are rarely as novel as suggested. In 1892, for example, "song slides" became a promotional craze for sheet music publishers. Pictures telling the story were, for years, a necessary sales aid for a new song sheet—they survived the coming of radio and talkies and had a measurable effect on the types of songs marketed and sold (Witmark and Goldberg 1939). Video promotion doesn't just go back to 1930s jazz shorts!

To analyze the music industry through its history means focusing on three issues.

The Effects of Technological Change

The origins of recording and the recording industry lie in the nineteenth century, but the emergence of the gramophone record as the predominant musical commodity took place after the 1914–1918 war. The history of the record industry is an aspect of the general history of the electrical goods industry, and has to be related to the development of radio, the cinema, and television. The new media had a profound effect on the social and economic organization of entertainment so that, for example, the rise of record companies meant the decline of the music publishing and piano-making empires, shifting roles for concert hall owners and live-music promoters.

The Economics of Pop

The early history of the record industry is marked by cycles of boom (1920s), slump (1930s), and boom (1940s). Record company practices reflected first the competition for new technologies and then the even more intense competition for a shrinking market. By the 1950s the record business was clearly divided into the "major" companies and the "independents." Rock analysts have always taken the oligopolistic control of the industry for granted, without paying much attention to how the majors reached their position. What were the business practices that enabled them to survive the slump? What is their role in boom times?

A New Musical Culture

The development of a large-scale record industry marked a profound transformation in musical experience, a decline in amateur music making, the rise of a new sort of musical consumption and use. Records and radio made possible both new national (and international, American based) musical tastes and new social divisions between "classical" and "pop" audiences. The 1920s and 1930s marked the appearance of new music professionals—pop singers, session musicians, record company A & R people, record producers, disc jockeys, studio engineers, record critics, and so on. These were the personnel who both resisted and absorbed the "threat" of rock and roll in the 1950s and rock in the 1960s.

The Making of a Record Industry

The origins of the record industry are worth describing in some detail because of the light they cast on recent developments. The story really begins with the North American Phonograph Company which, in 1888, got licenses to market both Edison's phonograph and the Graphophone, a version of the phonograph developed by employees of the Bell Telephone Company. When Edison had predicted, ten years earlier, how his invention would "benefit mankind," he had cited the reproduction of music as one of its capacities, but this was not the sales pitch of the North American Phonograph Company. They sought to rent machines (as telephones were rented) via regional franchises to offices—the phonograph was offered as a dictating device.

The resulting marketing campaign was a flop. The only regional company to have any success was the Columbia Phonograph Co. (Washington had more offices than anywhere else!). The company soon found that the phonograph was more successful as a coin-operated "entertainment" machine, a novelty attraction (like the early cinema) at fairs and medicine shows and on the vaudeville circuit. And for this purpose, "entertaining" cylinders were needed. Columbia took the lead in providing a choice of "Sentimental," "Topical," "Comic," "Irish," and "Negro" songs.

Meanwhile, Emile Berliner, who in 1887–1888 was developing the gramophone, a means of reproducing sounds using discs, not cylinders, was equally concerned in making recordings—he needed to demonstrate the superiority of his machine over Edison's. . . . Berliner, unlike Edison, regarded the gramophone as primarily a machine for home entertainment and the mass production of music discs such that "prominent singers, speakers or performers may derive an income from royalties on the sale of their phonautograms" (Gelatt 1977, p.13), and in 1897

Gaisberg opened the first commercial recording studio. For the next five years there was an intense legal struggle between disc and cylinder. . . .

At a certain moment in the development of a new electronic medium, though, the logic changes. If people begin buying records, any will do (train noises, the first compact disc releases, whatever one's tastes), just to have *something* to play. Then, as ownership of the new equipment becomes widespread, records are bought for their own sake, and people begin to buy new improved players in order to listen to specific sounds. Records cease to be a novelty. In the record industry this switch began in the 1920s, the real boom time for companies making both phonographs and phonograph records. . . .

It follows that these companies' musical decisions, their policies on who and what to record, were entirely dependent on the judgments and tastes of the "live" music entrepreneur (just as the "new" form, pop video, has been dependent so far on the skills and tastes of existing short film—that is, advertisement—makers). Companies competed to issue material by the same successful stage and concert hall performers, to offer versions of the latest stage show hit or dance floor craze, a practice that continued into the 1950s and rock and roll with the "cover version." Few companies were interested in promoting new numbers or new stars, and there was a widely held assumption in the industry that while pop records were a useful novelty in the initial publicizing of phonographs, in the long run the industry's returns would depend on people wanting to build up permanent libraries of "serious" music. . . .

There is an irony here that has a continuing resonance: while each new technological change in mass music making is seen to be a further threat to "authentic" popular music, classical music is seen to benefit from such changes, which from hi-fidelity recordings to compact discs have, indeed, been pioneered by record companies' classical divisions. The record industry has always sold itself by what it could do for "serious" music. . . .

For anyone writing the history of the record industry in 1932, there would have been very little doubt that the phonograph was a novelty machine that had come and gone, just like the uneventful passing of the piano roll. Sales of records had dropped from 104 million in 1927 to 6 million; the number of phonograph machines manufactured had fallen from 987,000 to 40,000.

The 1930s slump was marked not just by an overall decline in leisure spending but also by a major reorganization of people's leisure habits. The spread of radio and arrival of talking pictures meant that a declining share of a declining income went toward records (just as in the late 1970s and early 1980s, when there was, after the rise in gas prices, less money overall to spend on new leisure time products like video recorders and computer games). I won't go into the details of the slump here, but simply note its consequences. First, it caused the collapse of all small recording companies and reestablished the record business as an oligopoly, a form of production dominated by a small number of "major" companies. This wasn't just a matter of rationalization in the recording business itself—failing companies going bankrupt or being taken over—but also involved the surviving companies covering the crisis in record sales by putting together more wide-ranging music interests. . . .

As radios replaced record players in people's homes the primary source of music profit shifted from record sales to performing rights and royalties, and the basic technological achievement of this period, the development of electrical recording by Western Electric, marked a fusion of interests among the radio, cinema, and record industries. Western Electric could claim a royalty on all electrical recordings and was the principal manufacturer of theater talkie installations. Film studios such as Warner's had to start thinking about the costs (and profits) of publishers' performing rights, and began the Hollywood entry into the music business by taking over the Tin Pan Alley publisher, Witmark, in 1928.

The following year RCA (with money advanced by GE and Westinghouse) took over the Victor Talking Machine Company and, with General Motors, formed GM Radio Corporation, to exploit the possibilities of car radio. The subsequent making (and unmaking) of the United States' electrical-entertainment corporations is too complicated to go into here, but in the resulting oligopoly, competition for sales got more intense and, quickly, changed its terms. The initial response to falling sales was a price war—records were sold for less and less and the assumption was that people would go for the cheapest record on the market, but this eventually came up against the "irrationality" of tastes—people's musical choices aren't just a matter of price. New sales tactics had to be developed and, for the first time, record companies, led by Decca, ran aggressive advertising campaigns in newspapers and on billboards. . . .

Decca was the first company to realize that an investment in advertisement and promotion was more than justified by the consequent increase in sales. The peculiarity of record making is that once the break-even point is past, the accumulation of profit is stunningly quick. The costs of reproduction are a small proportion of the costs of producing the original master disc or tape. It follows that huge sales of one title are much more profitable than even cost-covering sales of lots of titles and that the costs of ensuring huge sales are necessary costs. . . .

In the 1930s the recording star system was dependent on a tie-in with film and radio (hence the arrival of Bing Crosby—again, Decca was the first company to realize how valuable he was). But in the 1980s, again in a time of recession, we saw very similar strategies being followed—an emphasis on a few superstars at the expense of the mass of groups just getting by, those stars in turn being marketed via films and film soundtracks and, more especially, with video promotion on MTV. Industry statistics suggest that the average of 4,000–5,000 new albums per year in the 1970s had become less than 2,000 per year in the 1980s.[1]

Aggressive selling and a star system in the 1930s meant a new recording strategy. Companies became less concerned to exploit existing big names, more interested in building stars from scratch, as recording stars; they became less concerned to service an existing public taste than to create new tastes, to manipulate demand. . . . But radio mattered most of all, and by the end of the 1930s it was the most important musical medium. It gave record companies a means of promoting their stars, and record companies provided radio stations with their cheapest form of programming. Media that had seemed totally incompatible—radio killed the record star—ended up inseparable.

The 1930s marked, in short, a shift in cultural and material musical power—from Tin Pan Alley to broadcasting networks and Hollywood studios, from the publisher/showman/song system to a record/radio/film star system—and the judgment of what was a good song or performance shifted accordingly—from suitability for a live audience to suitability for a radio show or a jukebox. It was in the 1930s that the "popularity" of music came to be measured (and thus defined) by record sales figures and radio plays. Popular music came to describe a fixed performance, a recording with the right qualities of intimacy or personality, emotional intensity or ease. . . . The record industry became a mass medium in the 1930s on the back of two assumptions: first, that the pop audience was essentially malleable; second, that pop music (and musicians) were, in cultural terms, vacuous. These assumptions were challenged after World War II by the rise of rock and roll.

Note

1. Thanks to Reebee Garofalo for these figures.

5

What Is Sociological about Music?
William G. Roy and Timothy J. Dowd

The sociology of music has become a vibrant field of study in recent
decades. While its proponents are well aware of this field's contributions
and relevance, we focus here on demonstrating its merit to the broader
sociological community. We do so by addressing the following questions:
What is music, sociologically speaking? How do individuals and groups
use music? How is the collective production of music made possible? How
does music relate to broader social distinctions, especially class, race,
and gender? Answering these questions reveals that music provides an
important and engaging purchase on topics that are of great concern to
sociologists of all stripes—topics that range from the microfoundations of
interaction to the macrolevel dynamics of inequality.

. . . Like many specializations in sociology, scholars have often gravitated toward the sociology of music because of a personal interest.
Not surprisingly, they have also found a ready audience in other music
lovers. As evidenced by the seminal works of Max Weber, W. E. B.
Du Bois, Alfred Schutz, Howard Becker, Richard Peterson, Pierre
Bourdieu, and Tia DeNora, sociology has long offered an important
vantage from which to understand music, the people who do it, and
its effect on people. . . .

[The] broader relevance of music sociology is our focus here . . .
demonstrating how the sociological salience of music can be framed
in terms of the following questions: (a) What is music, sociologically
speaking? (b) How do individuals and groups use music? (c) How is
the collective production of music made possible? (d) How does music

Originally published in Annual Review of Sociology 36 (2010):183–203. Con-
densed from the original. Reprinted with permission.

relate to broader social distinctions, especially class, race, and gender? By addressing these questions, we show that the sociology of music is relevant for such varied subfields as stratification, social movements, organizational sociology, and symbolic interactionism. . . .

A. What Is Good Music, Sociologically Speaking?

Music is not a singular phenomenon and, hence, is not captured by one definition. . . . Following musicologist Phillip Bohlman (1999), we bring . . . construction to the fore by discussing how music can be conceptualized as both object and activity. . . .

1) Music as Object

Music is often treated as an object—a thing that has a moment of creation, a stability of characteristics across time and place, and potential for use and effects. As such, music can be abstracted from its time and place and put into new contexts, such as when Bach's B minor Mass is performed in a secular, rather than a religious, setting more than 250 years after its creation. . . .

Music as an institutionalized system of tonality means, fundamentally, that certain notes are regularly utilized and repeated frequently enough that they can be treated as things: the sonic building blocks for songs, symphonies, and other compositions. One fundamental aspect of tonality is the division of pitch into distinct tones (i.e., notes). . . . Although this system[1] is neither the only nor the most scientific way for dividing pitch into notes (Duffins 2007; see Becker 1982, pp. 32–33), this musical object is taken for granted, especially in the West, and it shapes the very manner in which individuals hear music (see Cross 1997).

The achievement of music as an object goes far beyond its codification in notation and the rationalized system of tonality. In many places, music is embodied in objects of exchange (commodities). This buying and selling of music has occurred for centuries, with the range of commodities growing more expansive. An early precursor involved the buying and selling of [musical] labor, with the state, Church, and aristocracy serving as patrons that secured the services of musicians and composers (Abbott and Hrycak 1990, DeNora 1991, Scherer 2001).[2] Outright commodification of musical objects took root in the (late) 1700s with the expansion of commercial music publishing and the rise of copyright laws that fixed sets of notes as distinct entities. The objectification of notes and words into a product helped composers move from patronage into the freelance marketplace (Lenneberg 2003, Scherer 2001). . . . Commodification expanded further in the late 1800s and early 1900s, when the application of technologies freed music from the fleeting nature of performance and the static nature of the printed page. . . . The commodification of music is now commonplace and a fact of life in most societies, which Adorno (2002 [1938]) and others lament. What exactly is owned—the notes on the page, the performance, the technological reproduction—is a matter of conflict, whose adjudication has far-reaching consequences for the social dynamics of music (see Leyshon et al. 2005, Sanjek and Sanjek 1991). . . .

2) Music as Activity

Scholars critical of the treatment of music as an object have frequently asserted that music is more fruitfully understood as a process—an activity. Rather than treating it as an object with fixed qualities, we can treat music as something always becoming that never achieves full object status, something unbounded and open, something that is a verb (musicking) rather than a noun. . . .

In the realm of jazz, which is known for improvisation that can render a song differently every time, the development of improvisational skills is an ongoing process, as well. In order to improvise, jazz musicians develop such cognitive skills as understanding the relationship between chords and individual notes and identification with the character and role of their particular instrument. They acquire such corporal skills as knowing how to use their body in the delivery of this instantaneous music. They learn interactional skills and etiquette for collective performance that involves the spontaneous musical passages of soloists, turn-taking among soloists, and accompaniment that ably responds to the expected and unexpected directions that improvisation takes. Their mastery of improvisation, in turn, is shaped by a larger context containing familial support, mentorship, social connections among musicians, and the changing landscape of performance opportunities (Berliner 1994, Dempsey 2008, Gibson 2006, MacLeod 1993, Sudnow 1978). What appears to be ephemeral—the improvisation that is commodified at jazz venues and on recordings—is actually embedded in extended activity that connects both the musical and the nonmusical. . . .

B. *How Do Individuals and Groups Use Music?*

. . . Many scholars . . . focus on how music is embedded in social life (e.g., social relations). Hence, DeNora (2000) speaks of "a range of strategies through which music is mobilized as a resource for producing the scenes, routines, assumptions and occasions that constitute 'social life'" (p. xi). That is, people use music to give meaning to themselves and their world. . . .

1) Embeddedness of Musical Meaning

The embeddedness of music complicates the construction of meaning, as meaning is not solely located in either a musical object or activity. Drawing inspiration from DeNora (1986), we address two broad approaches to this complication: those who emphasize the musical object (what we label here as textualists) and those who emphasize the activity (contextualists).

The textual approach often treats music as analogous to language. The most straightforward example comes from numerous studies focusing on song lyrics. Sociologists and others probe meaning by interpreting one set of words (lyrics) into another set describing it. For instance, in an ambitious analysis of more than 400 songs found on best-selling hip-hop albums, Kubrin (2005, p. 366) ultimately interprets their lyrics as "[helping] construct an interpretive environment where violence is appropriate and acceptable." Acknowledging that rappers could have different lyrical intentions and listeners could have divergent interpretations of these lyrics, Kubrin nevertheless roots the meaning in violence while connecting it to inner-city streets that he notes are familiar to hip-hop artists and audiences (but see Rodriquez 2006, p. 664). . . .

The contextual approach differs markedly. Contextualists particularly focus on listeners, who, in the textual approach, are often ignored, imagined, or simply the academics themselves. . . . The most explicit argument is by Small (1998, p. 13):

> The act of musicking establishes in the place where it is happening a set of relationships, and it is in those relationships that the meaning of the act lies. They are to be found not only between those organized sounds . . . but also between the people who are taking part, in whatever capacity, in the performance.

. . . The contextual approach maintains that the meaning is never purely in the music because there is never "a" meaning. . . . According to contextualists, whether rap music foments violence or conciliation depends less on its lyrics and sounds than on what people do with it. . . .

2) Music and Meaningful Construction of Identity

Music and its meanings inform people, quite profoundly, about who they are. From aging punk rock fans (Bennett 2006) and passionate opera connoisseurs (Benzecry 2009) to youthful dance club devotees (Thornton 1996) and bluegrass music enthusiasts (Gardner 2004), music both signals and helps constitute the identity of individuals and collectivities.

DeNora (2000) is the leading sociologist addressing musical meaning and individual identity. Through interviews and observation, she finds that individuals construct an identity (a "me") by using music to mark and document important aspects of their lives—including memorable events and evolving relationships—and to guide how they negotiate such activities as shopping, aerobics, and lovemaking. . . .

Music is a "technology of the self" (DeNora 2000). It is something in which to lose oneself apart from others. Classical music aficionados can seek transcendence while listening to albums in the confines of their home (Hennion 2001), and iPod users can create sonic solitude while surrounded by strangers in a bustling city (Bull 2007). Music is also something by which to find oneself amid others, which is of particular interest to sociologists. . . .

Groups likewise use music as a tool for building identity—an "us" (Roy 2002). The relationship between a group and music flows two ways: music is identified by people inside (and outside) the group as belonging to it, and membership in the group is marked partly by embracing this music. . . . Musicking "recreates, reestablishes, or alters the significance of singing and also of the persons, times, places, and audiences involved. It expresses the status, sex, and feelings of performers, and brings these to the attention of the entire community" (Seeger 2004, p. 65). Music does not simply reflect this group but plays a performative role in defining it. The two-way relationship can also occur in a deliberate and sudden fashion, as when groups come to see particular music as signifying both their us-ness and their plight. African American slaves used spirituals with religious lyrics to define themselves and covertly critique deplorable conditions (Douglass 1993 [1845]; see also Du Bois 1997 [1903]). In the early 1900s, some 400,000 textile workers walked off the job after encountering local music that taught them of their solidarity and offered prescriptions for action (Roscigno and Danaher 2004). Serbian students of the late 1990s drew upon rock music to mobilize against Miloševic, simultaneously constructing "a collective identity and a discourse of opposition that demarcated them not only from the regime but from other oppositional forces" (Steinberg 2004, p. 22).

Music can be a "technology of the collective" because people gravitate toward those who share similar tastes (Bourdieu 1984, Roy 2002). This is particularly important in contemporary societies, as individuals can potentially be members of many (disparate) groups (see DiMaggio 1991). . . .

C. How Is the Collective Production of Music Made Possible?

Musical creation is deeply social. Even when one person is apparently responsible for music (e.g., recording original songs in a bedroom studio), her efforts are most likely intra-individual (Becker 1982). This occurs when that person uses the long-established system of tonality (Weber 1958), relies upon technologies devised by others (Jeppesen and Frederiksen 2006), or engages conventions shared by many (Hesmondhalgh 1998). Particularly intriguing are frequent instances in which musical production is explicitly collective—where individuals and organizations with their own respective interests come together for delivery of music (Regev 1998).

Several approaches take this aggregation as something to explain, including the art world's approach (Becker 1982), the production-of-culture approach (Peterson and Anand 2004), field theory (Prior 2008), and neo-institutional theory (Johnson et al. 2006). They all point to widely shared cognition that enables this collective production to work: (often times) taken-for-granted ways of viewing the world (institutions) that bring together individuals and organizations into a (somewhat) coherent field. . . .

1) Genre as Collective Enactment

A distinctive feature of modern Western music is the way that genre simultaneously categorizes cultural objects and people. Some definitions of genre emphasize the content of cultural objects more than the people engaging such objects, as when Rosenblum (1975, p. 424) defines genre (i.e., style) as "particular mannerisms or conventions that are frequently associated together." Other definitions bring people a bit more into the mix, as when Walser (1993, p. 29) summarizes, "Genres . . . come to function as horizons of expectations for readers (or listeners) and as models of composition for authors (or musicians)." Still other definitions emphasize more fully that genres are socially relevant in different ways for different actors and that people, as well as the music itself, can be categorized by genres. . . .

Businesses collectively enact genres too, but in a less dynamic fashion than musicians. Rather than focus on all available genres, large music firms have historically mined relatively few, taking a mainstream approach that emphasizes well-known conventions and established musicians rather than the cutting-edge developments of unheralded musicians. . . .

Collective enactment of genre highlights issues of classification that have informed sociology since the days of Durkheim (Lamont and Molnár 2002). For many, classification is a cognitive map imposed upon reality, as though reality is there before its classification. . . .

2) Hierarchy and Classical Music

Differentiation of music can also entail hierarchy. The hallmark of subcultures is their members' insistence on the superiority of their favored genre (punk rock rules!) and the attendant hierarchy of people based on their associations with that genre (Bennett 2004). More remarkable is when disparate individuals from many groups acknowledge the merit of a particular genre(s). To illustrate such a widely held hierarchy, we turn to a broad ranking that has centuries-old roots and has been upheld internationally: the touting of classical music as superior to popular music.

The ranking of classical music over popular music requires that those categories have relevance. Yet the former category has not always existed (Weber 1984, 2006). European patrons and audiences long favored contemporary music—often devised for one-time performance at social events—rather than the repeated performance of complete works from the past (i.e., classics). . . .

Hierarchy took root on both sides of the Atlantic with the proliferation of performance organizations that offered only classics, cordoning them off from popular music of the day (Allmendinger and Hackman 1996, Benzecry 2006, Levine 1988, Santoro 2010). . . .

Developments in the broader field of musical production further solidified this hierarchy but, recently, have contributed to its erosion. In Europe and North America, recording companies and broadcasters of the early 1900s gave prominent attention to classical music, using albums and shows to educate listeners on the merits of this music. By the mid-1900s, these for-profit corporations began marketing classical music as a specialty product, if at all (Dowd 2003, Katz 1998, Maisonneuve 2001). From the mid-1900s, educators and critics in multiple nations instructed many on the importance and worth of classical music, showing surprising agreement on its exemplars (e.g., Beethoven). In recent years, educators and critics have given increasing attention to the worth of popular music, raising its stature relative to classical music (Bevers 2005, Dowd et al. 2002, Janssen et al. 2008, van Venrooij and Schmutz 2010). Meanwhile, in the United States, nonprofits may have grown less effective at insulating classical music from popular music, as declining audiences and dwindling donations have made ticket sales a central concern (DiMaggio 2006). Despite these recent developments, this institutionalized hierarchy remains surprisingly robust. This simple ranking enabled, and was enabled by, a transnational field of musical production. . . .

D. How Does Music Relate to Broader Social Distinctions?

If musical differentiation and hierarchy aligned smoothly with the stratification of society, sociology of music would have little to say about broader social distinctions such as race, class, and gender. However, various aspects of music sometimes invert stratification, turning it on its head. Although white listeners have sometimes devalued music by

African Americans because of racial associations (Frith 1996, Lopes 2002), they sometimes imbue black with a positive value (e.g., authentic) and white with a negative value (e.g., inauthentic) (Cantwell 1997, Grazian 2003). As one ethnographer observes about hip-hop, "Whites who pick up on African American styles and music do not necessarily want to be black; they seek to acquire the characteristics of blackness associated with being cool" (Rodriquez 2006, p. 649). Music consequently plays a complex role: It upholds stratification when people use it to reinforce social distinctions but undermines it when used to reach across distinctions (Roy 2002, 2004). As such, music enters into social relations and helps to constitute fundamental distinctions on a micro- and macrolevel.

1) Musical Bounding of Distinctions

Bounding is one mechanism that shapes a society's system of alignment between conceptual distinctions (e.g., how music is classified into genres) and social distinctions (e.g., race, class). It thus links consequential distinctions, as when (de)valued musical genres are aligned with (de)valued groups of people (Lamont and Molnár 2002, Roy 2001, Zerubavel 1991). . . .

Commercial producers and distributors probably have the greatest impact on how the general public forms associations between musical genres and social distinctions (e.g., race). The racialization of music has been at the core of commercial music in America since its origins. The first genre of American commercial popular music arguably was the minstrel, which was based on white men's appropriation of black culture. Throughout much of the 1800s, minstrelsy was not only the place where most non-Southerners learned about African Americans, but it substantially informed immigrants about what it meant to be a white American (Lott 1993). Minstrelsy even supplied the name for the oppressive apparatus of legal segregation that framed race relations for much of the twentieth century: Jim Crow. In the late 1800s, when publication of sheet music became the most profitable part of the music business, visual images added new power to racial stereotypes. Music publications were adorned with cover pages displaying Sambo caricatures—African American cartoons with exaggerated lips, bulging eyes, flat noses, mocking top hats, and gigantic bow ties—which all congealed into an icon of derision (Lhamon 1998, Lott 1993, Roy 2010).

The sharp racialization carried over into the era of recorded music. In the 1920s, record companies targeted racial groups in their marketing. Although some executives were surprised that people other than white middle-class urbanites would buy records, most record companies created special labels and catalogs for "race records" and "hillbilly music," before eventually adopting the names rhythm and blues and country and western (Dowd 2003; Peterson 1997; Roy 2002, 2004). Concurrently, large recording firms prominently featured jazz orchestras of white musicians while hoping to avoid the stigma that purportedly flowed from the hot jazz of black musicians—as when they relied on pseudonyms to hide the identity of well-known black musicians such as Louis Armstrong (Phillips and Kim 2009, Phillips and Owens 2004).

. . . Compared with men, women musicians have historically faced a narrow range of instruments and responsibilities (Bayton 1998, Clawson 1999, DeNora 2002), unstable employment (Coulangeon et al. 2005), limited commercial success (Dowd et al. 2005), and disgruntlement from fellow instrumentalists when their presence in symphony orchestras moves from token numbers to a sizable minority (Allmendinger and Hackman 1995). The alignment between genre and gender has often worked against women in popular and classical music.

Listeners of various types are involved in bounding. A notable strand of British scholarship, for instance, details the symbolic fit between the values and lifestyles of a particular subculture—its subjective experience—and the music it uses to express or reinforce its focal concerns (Bennett 2004). Hence, punks' general rejection of respectability is reflected in their strident music that subverts mainstream musical aesthetics, just as piercing their faces with safety pins subverts the meaning of mundane objects (Hebdige 2004 [1979]). Although members of subcultures may intentionally use music to construct their position in the social order, Bourdieu (1984) argues that members of classes do so with little forethought. The economic situation of each class shapes its members' disposition toward music in a particular fashion, with this disposition seeming natural. Given the limited finances and free time of the French working class, they favor pleasurable music that requires little training to appreciate. The French upper class, possessing considerable resources and leisure time, tends toward the cerebral rather than the entertaining, such as the classical music that requires much training and cultivation to appreciate. The privileged standing of the upper class means that its disposition is widely seen as legitimate, as when familiarity with classical music serves as cultural capital that facilitates opportunity and success in a variety of domains. . . .

2) Musical Bridging of Distinctions

Bridging is another mechanism that shapes the alignment of conceptual and social distinctions (Roy 2002, 2004). It blurs the linkage between distinctions, as when a musical genre once limited to a particular social group is embraced by other groups (Lamont and Molnár 2002, Roy 2001, Zerubavel 1991). . . .

Although businesses played a substantial role in early racialization of American music, some later moved away from a strict segregation of black and white music(ians). Since the early 1900s, a single organization, ASCAP (American Society of Composers, Authors, and Publishers) worked on behalf of composers and publishers to secure payment whenever venues or broadcasters used their compositions; however, its leaders resisted dealing in race and hillbilly music, leaving these genres and their composers (e.g., Jelly Roll Morton) without economic representation. Chafing from fees charged by ASCAP, broadcasters established their own organization in 1939, BMI (Broadcast Music, Inc.). It aggressively represented genres that ASCAP had ignored and provided the economic foundation for the burgeoning of those genres from the 1940s onward (Dowd 2003, Ryan 1985). These genres further benefited when record companies of the mid-1900s moved away from the stringent categorization of an earlier era. Folkways Records purposefully mixed African American and rural white performers on key albums without identifying their race for listeners. Large recording firms did not go as far, but they did complement their focus on pop music by investing heavily in country music and R&B. Moreover, these firms soon realized the value of crossover success. . . . Although not completely eliminating racialization in American music (Negus 1999), such bridging has made it less blatant and provided opportunities for once marginalized genres to reach new audiences.

The discourse of well-placed individuals likewise can bridge across distinctions. Even in that despicable era, the relationship of slaves to music was complex (Roy 2010). Owners used the music of slaves to regulate the pace of labor and to entertain at white social events, but they often heard as noise the spirituals that slaves enacted on their own in richly symbolic and, at times, defiant ways. To great effect, abolitionists, folklorists, and academics convinced some whites that this noise is actually important music. Frederick Douglass and others argued compellingly that spirituals dramatized the humanity of African Americans, revealed their relationship to the almighty, and portrayed them as full, if not equal, human beings (Cruz 1999). In subsequent eras, critics and academics have (successfully) made the case to whites that other genres associated with African American musicians—particularly jazz and hip-hop—are neither noise nor immoral but emergent art forms that merit careful consideration (Binder 1993, Lopes 2002; see Lena and Peterson 2008). . . . The alignment between genre and race is growing more fluid in much discourse.

Recent scholarship suggests that listeners, particularly high-status individuals, are engaged in considerable bridging, aligning a varied range of music to their own daily experiences (see Peterson 2005). This bridging is not new, however. Despite early commercial classification and segregation of race and hillbilly music, many black and white musicians of the time, even in the South, knew each other, learned from each other, and sang each other's songs (Roscigno and Danaher 2004; Roy 2002, 2010). Musicians, academics, and others created the genre of folk music in opposition to those commercial classifications and as part of a project to trace various national musics to the primordial past. . . .

Because the groups that are bounded and bridged by music are rarely socially equal, music plays an important role in sustaining and reconfiguring stratification. Not surprisingly, the relationship of music to inequality has been the focus of some of the theoretically richest and most widely discussed work in the sociology of music. This work should be of interest, then, to students of stratification because it reveals the role of what may seem innocuous—musical tastes and preferences—in helping to create and mark such socially consequential distinctions as race, gender, and class.

Conclusion

The sociology of music illuminates how sociologists examine various dimensions of social life more generally. From the microsociological concerns of how precognitive interaction shapes the way we relate to each other to the macrosociological concerns of how social distinctions are constituted and reinforced, the sociology of music offers important lessons. Although we can do little more than baldly make a claim, we would argue that the most profound lessons for nonmusic sociology are found in the distinctive qualities of music.

While music's nonunique qualities are studied by other specializations in sociology (e.g., its organizational and interactional aspects), probing its unique qualities highlights the taken-for-granted qualities of nonmusical interaction. For example, Bourdieu (1984) explains how it is music's abstract, content-less quality that makes it appropriate for cultural capital. This insight has transformed the study of stratification to include the ineffable as well as the countable. Similarly, it was the attribution of music to slaves that abolitionists used to assert their humanity. Although the Christian content of spirituals might have boosted the sympathy that white audiences felt for the enslaved, it was the act of making music that mitigated the image of savagery. Cruz (1999) has described how the use of music to humanize American slaves presaged a new kind of relationship between dominant and subordinate groups that he calls "ethnosympathy": a simultaneous embracing of and distancing from a group seen as culturally different. Thus, the study of stratification and ethnic relations has benefited from the sociology of music, not when music is treated like another form of signification or a vehicle for lyrical expression, but when it is treated as a special kind of activity that people do. Indeed, by answering the four questions listed at the outset of the paper, we hope to have shown the import of music for all kinds of sociologists.

We as a discipline are just beginning to develop the conceptual and methodological tools to capture fully the social dynamics of music, but as we make further progress, it will benefit the discipline and the store of human knowledge as a whole.

Notes

1. Editor's Note: Reference is to the Western twelve-tone scale, which is further organized into major, minor, and modal scales. This organization of tones, which fostered the typical Western harmonies, is uniquely Western in its development. See original for more explanation of this and other items.

2. Editor's Note: In early Europe, musicians at court, in the church, and elsewhere were paid by patrons.

Part II
Experience of Music: Ritual and Authenticity

Sara Towe Horsfall playing classical guitar, 2009.

6

Music as Ritual
A Hotline to the Collective Conscious
Sara Towe Horsfall

Randall Collins's theory of Interaction Ritual Chains is used to analyze the emotional energy and connection to the collective that comes with music rituals. African American spirituals exemplify the importance of music to the collective and to the individual. They connected slaves to each other and allowed them to reconstitute a cultural identity using Christian imagery as a common language. Musical venues such as the "ring shout" reaffirmed their value as individuals.

The Study of Music in American Society

During the past century, there have been many studies on the role of music in American society, but little or no continuity. In Europe, music is an established area of sociological inquiry, with culture and music as commodities being the primary foci. Here I argue that music is more intimate to our daily lives. It can be commercial, and it can reflect our cultural values, but it does more. It is part of a social ritual that creates our social world and connects us to the collective. Early sociologist Emile Durkheim identified the collective consciousness as a sort of group mind—an experience of being "in sync" with others in your group, such as happens with fans at a football game.

Experiencing music gives us a feeling of this group mind. Through their interaction with music, people can actually create a collective experience. Kassabian (1999) and others believe that music is a lived experience, and that people with the same lived experiences become connected to each other. People live the music together in a ritual that becomes an end in itself. Music listeners are not only receiving a culture, they are creating a common group identity. Music does such a good job of connecting otherwise isolated individuals to the social that I have come to call it a "hotline" to the collective consciousness.

In his book *Interaction Ritual Chains*, Randall Collins uses Durkheim's analysis of the Aborigines to support his idea of ritual. In a ritual, people meet together, focus on something, and act together. Rituals create "a sort of electricity," which Durkheim called "collective effervescence." Collins calls it emotional energy (Collins 2004:35). A successful ritual makes us think that others have the same views and the same feelings that we do, and it gives us energy.

Individuals are attracted to the most intense ritual charge they can get. Failed rituals don't give us a buzz—they are emotionally flat, boring, or depressing, and they drain our energy. Successful rituals, in comparison, are exhilarating, and create energy. At peak times in the ritual, people touch each other—high fives, hugs, a reassuring hand on the shoulder. This individual emotional expression feeds back into the collective, creating a cycle of increasing energy. By expressing the emotion that we feel in a group setting, the collective energy becomes even greater (Collins 2004).

The emotional energy given to the individual during a ritual is carried to the next social encounter. In addition to energy, we take symbolic objects that were also charged with energy from the ritual. These are Durkheim's totems. Finally, we take the memory of solidarity of the ritual group with us. This is Durkheim's collective consciousness. Long after the ritual is over, we relive the experience when we look at the object, or when we meet someone from the ritual group. Two old acquaintances meeting together after a gap of several years are often heard to say, "Do you remember that time when we . . . ?" They are reliving their experiences and reviving the emotional energy of an earlier time. Because it is emotional energy we seek, when the ritual charge wanes, we hold assemblies to revive the feeling once again. It is emotional energy and unity, not utilitarian self-interest, that holds society together (Collins 2004).

This theory is clearly seen in popular concerts. Concert attenders get charged up by the music. They buy paraphernalia and T-shirts to remind them of the experience. Every time they wear the T-shirt, or see someone else wearing the band T-shirt, they relive the experience together. They play their CDs and regenerate the experience—for themselves and for those who didn't go to the concert. They relive other rituals of other performances—even if they didn't experience them in person. They relive the rituals they never actually experienced with other people who also never experienced them. They carry all those ritual experiences with them, all those songs—hundreds of songs. The songs and the rituals go with them all day long. Listeners are constantly connecting to the collective. They are constantly receiving a buzz, constantly creating more energy, even if they are by themselves.

Early African American Music

African Roots

To understand African American music we have to first look briefly at the African musical heritage. African culture has often been regarded as primitive, which is a misnomer born of ignorance of its history. Early historians created an artificial division of the African continent into north and south and then overlooked an important culture in the middle that spanned both areas (Hilliard 1998). Also, many of the sophisticated African cultures had oral traditions rather than preserving their heritage in writing. More important, African culture was impacted by the slave trade, which had a devastating effect on existing institutions and created an atmosphere of distrust that further eroded societal structures. The loss of an estimated 60–100 million people to the slave trade over several hundred years confused the social norms. Physically, entire cities were abandoned or in disrepair (Hall 2005, Rublowsky 1971). By all accounts, much of the continent's early greatness remains unknown.

Similarly, African music is often regarded as primitive. It has no musical notation and is produced on simple, humble instruments. But a closer examination reveals a complexity and inherent subtlety that can only indicate sophisticated musical traditions. A complete discussion is beyond the scope here, but some characteristics are worth noting. Most African music is intended for group participation. The syncopated rhythms inspire movement and dance. The call-and-response forms allow everyone to participate. The hypnotic and cyclical phrases provide the leaders with a means of adjusting and manipulating the group mood. Repetition gives participants the time they need to find their own unique voice, and to improvise. The tradition of dense textures and buzzy tones lets participants create rhythm using whatever is at hand (Turino 2001).

In Africa, the drum is king, and music is a part of every facet of life. It is there at birth, at important community celebrations, and at death. There is music for every occasion—both trivial and familial. There is music to accompany everyday life activities such as child-minding, tilling the soil, going to war, and hunting (Martin 1995:15). In this traditional setting, music cannot be separated out as an artifact—or a commodity. Music binds people together; it is a part of every person's emotional and spiritual expression and experience of society (Nzewi 2006).

Spirituals—A Ritual of Survival

African Americans, coming from African cultures with strong oral traditions, took advantage of every opportunity to create music—which was for them a recreation of their own culture. Deprived of dignity, separated from loved ones, isolated in a foreign country, and unable to communicate verbally—including with other slaves because of their different languages—it is not surprising that music became central to their lives. Singing was allowed, and the songs they sang were transformed to express their inner feelings, struggles, and longings. When no song existed that could do the job adequately, new songs were created as a salve to treat the bitterness of their lives. Through music, a communal spirit was forged, going beyond language to make use of the common cultural skills they all brought with them from Africa. The music and the venues were familiar to them, and the songs had meanings that were not always obvious to others in their new environment (Genovese 1974).

To be sure, African American music is not the same as African music. A European harmonic structure was incorporated. But the characteristic elements that identify African music remained: syncopation, call and response, cyclical phrases, improvisation, dense and buzzy textures, and, above all, group participation.

The Ring Shout

One of the most important venues for the slaves was the "ring shout." This was a tradition that developed sometime after 1667, when a Virginia law stated that slaves could be Christians. Prior to that, little thought was given to religious education for the slaves. After the law was passed, many slave owners felt obliged to provide exposure to Christianity. Initially, this meant attending church services by standing or sitting in the back or in the gallery (Boyer 1999).

Including African Americans in congregations of the Southern plantation churches coincided with the introduction of hymns as a more contemporary form of worship music in the English-speaking world. These hymns were composed and collected by various concerned religious ministers who wanted to instill the worship service with more spiritual vitality. A popular book published in 1707, *Hymns and Spiritual Songs*, by an English minister was soon adopted by many Protestant churches in the United States (NetHymnal 2010). Many of these new hymns used the pentatonic scale. This was particularly true of the "Dr. Watts songs," as they became known, which were favorites of the slaves. Reminiscent of pentatonic African melodies, they were easily learned and remembered.

The "ecstatic delight" that the slaves took in singing these songs is likely to have led to a separate meeting place for them. In the eighteenth and nineteenth centuries, itinerate white or black ministers taught African Americans in separate buildings designated for such purpose. Although the first ring shouts may have occurred in slave quarter cabins, in the woods, in the simply constructed "praise houses," or out in the open around a fire (Harding 2005), they came to be synonymous with a regular service when the benches or pews were pushed back to make room for the congregation to move around in the middle of the room.

Someone would begin singing, and soon the whole group was singing and shuffling in a counterclockwise direction around the room. They were careful not to cross their feet—which would make the movement dancing (forbidden). Nevertheless, the ring shout was reminiscent of African dances. "Through the diaspora, enslaved people used their homes, wooded and isolated places, and structures they built with the express purpose of sheltering their gatherings, to meet, to dance, to sing and to thus call spirit into their midst" (Harding 2005). Ring shouts often continued for hours as the participants got caught up in an ecstasy. The following description appears in *Slave Songs of the United States,* published in 1867:

> But the benches are pushed back to the wall when the formal meeting is over, and old and young, men and women . . . all stand up in the middle of the floor, and when the "sperichil" is struck up, begin first walking and by and by shuffling round, one after the other, in a ring. The foot is hardly taken from the floor, and the progression is mainly due to a jerking, hitching motion, which agitates the entire shouter, and soon brings out streams of perspiration. Sometimes they dance silently, sometimes as they shuffle they sing the chorus of the spiritual, and sometimes the song itself is also sung by the dancers. But more frequently a band, composed of some of the best singers and of tired shouters, stand at the side of the room to "base" the others, singing the body of the song and clapping their hands together or on the knees. Song and dance are alike extremely energetic, and often, when the shout lasts into the middle of the night, the monotonous thud of the feet prevents sleep within half a mile of the praise-house. (Allen, Ware, and Garrison 1995:xiii–xiv)

Some people objected to the ring shout, but black leaders were likely to counter that without a ring, a sinner could not be converted (Southern 1997:130). A description of *Negro Spirituals* by Thomas Wentworth Higginson, published in the *Atlantic Monthly* in 1867, gives further insight into the meaning of group singing. One song would be personalized, and continue for up to a half an hour, until everyone present was mentioned by name in one of the verses. This very effective group technique shows support and reaffirmation of the value of each participant. Sometimes the songs were known, but sometimes they were made up on the spot, with others joining in on the chorus as if they knew the song.

It is easy to conclude that each occasion of the ring shout provided the participants with cultural elements uniquely fitted to the circumstances. It was not just music, but the reconstitution of a culture left behind. As such, it was a means of survival.

> Now let me tell you what happens. You start singing a song, and when you're singing it first, according to the slaves, you're just singing the words. But after awhile, it's almost like therapy. It begins to take the frown out of the face. The shoulders begin to come back to their natural position. What's happening is, you're going through a cleansing process. You're coming back to where you wanted to be. Things are not quite as bad as you think they are. And the more you sing it, huh, the more you find relief, the more you believe that there is a way out of this.
>
> Remember that the slaves endured days of hard work, mistreatment, little food, little clothing, little rest. And they had to get up the next day to work hard, get little food, little clothing, a little rest . . . so they had to have something which would inspire them, which would keep them getting up from day to day. And that's what these spirituals did for the slaves. I'll tell you, had we had psychiatrists during that time, and sent the slaves to them, I don't know whether they could have done the effective job that these spirituals did for them. (Boyer 1999–2000)

Psychiatrists *couldn't* have done as well, because they could not have created the collective effervescence, the emotional energy that comes from a group ritual. They couldn't have connected the individual slaves to a larger cultural group that restored meaning and value to their lives. They couldn't have given them the energy that was created in the group singing—the "buzz" from a successful ritual.

> The spirituals are a transforming and transformational music. A principal aim of the song, when sung in ceremonial context, has been to invoke the presence of spirit. Like Hepworth, other 19th and early 20th century observers remarked at palpable changes in the energy of the meetings and churches where spirituals were being sung. . . . A central objective of collective worship is to create the space for the sacred to enter and engage with the people present. The spirit is not simply to be considered and acknowledged, but to be felt, experienced and relished. The combination of chanted or sung prayer, ritual music and dance is intended to transform the space and the individuals present so that they are open to another quality of experience. So too, the spirituals, especially when accompanied by rhythmic movement and the ring shout, were designed to manifestly change the nature of the space. (Harding 2005)

Christian Imagery

The Christian stories appealed to the slaves—stories of Daniel in the lion's den, or Jonah in the whale, and other heroic examples of faith. The Israelites as slaves in Egypt had special meaning: It was a story that resonated with their own. Songs about the suffering of the Israelites expressed their own suffering, and the hopes of the Israelites expressed their own hopes. Listening to sermons about God's justice, they no doubt understood nuances of meaning in the Christian message that the white congregation did not (Du Bois 1969, Watermulder et al. n.d.).

Christian imagery became a new language that went beyond the words. A belief in human justice was reaffirmed with the song "Didn't My Lord Deliver Daniel? . . . Why Not Every Man?" Death and hope for a better world were sung about in "Swing Low, Sweet Chariot" and "I Got Shoes" ("you got shoes, all God's children got shoes. When I get to heaven gonna put on my shoes I'm gonna walk all over God's heaven, heaven, heaven.") By other accounts, "chariot" or "gospel train" might refer to the Underground Railroad and its various stations. One such station was Ripley, a town by the Ohio River where the fugitives had to wait for help to cross the river. "Home" in this case meant freedom (NegroSpirituals 2010). Yet other vivid images include the Big Dipper and the North Star. "Follow the Drinking Gourd" gives specific directions to the runaway. Similarly, "Wade in the Water" tells runaways there were sniffing dogs nearby, and they should travel in the river so as not to get caught.

As clever verbal manipulators, this group was adept at using Christian images and symbols to express other things. Many innocent-sounding songs had secret, coded meanings. It is unlikely that any one song had only one meaning, or was sung in the same way each time. Verses were created and added as needed. The drum was left out of their music—it was forbidden by the slave owners everywhere except in New Orleans. Clapping, stomping, and beating on the floor with sticks substituted for the drum and kept the rhythm. The melodies used to express their longing and sadness were poetically called "Sorrow Songs" by W. E. B. Du Bois. Though the content of these songs was different, there is some evidence that the melodies may not have been that dissimilar to traditional African songs. Studies of spirituals reveal that more than 20 percent have melodies that are identical or closely related to West African songs (Rublowsky 1971).

Spirituals Made Public

The early African Americans became connected to a collective, a newly constituted collective, through their music. It was a new tradition, combining the important traditional forms brought from Africa with new imagery and meaning that they found in America. And it incorporated Western harmonic structure. After working hard all week, new energy from the ring shout recharged them. New identities were forged in the collective experience. Music was a way to support others in the community; it provided a venue to reaffirm a belief in justice and the conviction that the institution of slavery was wrong, and that one day they would be free. It gave some of the slaves the determination needed to escape to a better life. And the songs gave them directions along the way.

Today, these same songs provide us with a historical record of the experiences of slavery. In a sense, the experience became an artifact. The first collection of spirituals was *Slave Songs of the United States,* published by Lucy McKim Garrison in 1867 (Rublowsky 1971).

About the same time, a group of African American students from Fisk University in Nashville, Tennessee, started performing spirituals under the direction of their music teacher, George L. White. They sang songs that had been set aside since Emancipation, presented authentically to white audiences. With "grit and grime and . . . passion" the Fisk Jubilee Singers gave many people their first glimpse of this musical tradition. They toured the country, and Europe, singing wherever they could, and managed to raise a considerable amount of money for the university.

At the turn of the twentieth century, an accomplished African American musician, Henry Thacker Burleigh, was responsible for writing down the version of the common spirituals that many people know today. Early in his life, Burleigh was a student of Antonin Dvorak, who incorporated "American" melodies in his subsequent symphonies. Dvorak is quoted as saying, "In the Negro melodies of America I discover all that is needed for a great and noble school of music. They are pathetic, tender, passionate, melancholy, solemn, religious, bold, merry, gay, or what you will" (Southern 1997:167).

Other Venues

A discussion of early African American music would not be complete without a discussion of other venues for music making, and the music that came from these venues. Jubilees and corn shucking were plantation traditions that provided occasions for the creation of unique African American music. But in truth, the music produced in these venues was a different kind of music. It was not the music that created a collective identity, so much as an artifact that reflected the thinking and skill of the artists of the occasion.

Jubilee celebrations on holidays were a time when everyone—black and white—participated in the festivities. A program of music, dance, and comedy was developed, sometimes starting in the "big house" and later moving outside for a slave show. There were infectious rhythms, dance, and song. The performances of these occasions were the ones musicians and actors imitated in the minstrel shows (Rublowsky 1971).

Another occasion for music, dance, and wit was corn shucking. It was tedious work, done at night—all night, perhaps for a dollar prize, but also for a bit of whiskey and certainly with songs and dancing. Workers from several nearby plantations would gather.

> They were gala affairs. The jug passed freely, although drunkenness was discouraged; the work went on amidst singing and dancing; friends and acquaintances congregated from several plantations and farms; the house slaves joined the field slaves in common labor; and the work was followed by an all-night dinner and ball at which inhibitions, especially those of class and race, were lowered as far as anyone dared. . . . The combination of festive spirit and joint effort appears to have engaged the attention of the slaves more than anything else. (Genovese 1974:316)

The slaveholders joined in the work and demanded that the slaves sing—which they did. Songs were made up on the spot.

> [The songs were] bristling with sharp wit, both malicious and gentle . . . they turned their wit and incredible talent for improvisation into social criticism. . . . Blacks—any blacks—were not supposed to sass whites. By the device of a little flattery and by taking advantage of the looseness of the occasion, they asserted their personalities and made their judgments. (Genovese 1974:317)

"Field hollers" and work songs are two other less celebratory venues for early African American music. Field hollers were the personal expressions of slaves who worked in isolation on small farms. They were a strong, strident lament of the hardship and sorrow of the black man. In contrast, work songs were communal endeavors where the pace of work was set, slow and steady, by the valued lead singer. It gave comfort to those who were tired and overworked (Landeck 1969, Genovese 1974).

Music Rituals after Emancipation

After the Civil War, music continued to play a central role in the lives of African Americans. Tracing the development of new musical forms or genres is like relating the social history of African Americans. Each genre arose at a time when large numbers of the community faced, and dealt with, significant social situations. Space does not permit more than a hint of this most fascinating correlation. Suffice it to say that ragtime, blues, jazz, rhythm and blues, and rap all continue to be an expression of the community.

7

Moving Past Violence and Vulgarity
Structural Ritualization and Constructed Meaning in the Heavy Metal Subculture

Jan-Martijn Meij, Meghan D. Probstfield, Joseph M. Simpson, and J. David Knottnerus

Fans of heavy metal music have often been portrayed as mindless zombies who are only interested in getting drunk, getting high, or causing mayhem. It is not uncommon for people to believe that these individuals identify with the "darker" side of life, such as satanism, addiction, depression, anger, and alienation. Though some individuals embody these characteristics, scholars tend to overlook the more positive attributes represented by this diverse community with a shared cultural taste for music. In this selection, the authors use a descriptive study to explore the diversity within the heavy metal subculture. An online questionnaire was created to learn more about the meaning fans use to describe this music, and Knottnerus's structural ritualization theory helped explain the way this meaning was structured and modified by heavy metal fans, in particular, through one of the more conspicuous collective events: the concert venue.

Historically, heavy metal music has generally been met with skepticism, disdain, or even disregard by the typical music lover, Parent Music Resource Center (PMRC) member, or anyone who does not enjoy loud, obnoxious, screaming music about death, anger, suppressed rage, sadness, and satanism (Gross 1990, Binder 1993). For the non–metal music fan, there is not much logic to banging your head to loud music, throwing fists in the air, and body slamming as a form of dance or as a period of relaxation following a long workday. The notion that fans actually enjoy this music and attend live concerts because it is fun seems to be lost on others as they attempt more psychoanalytic understanding. This makes it easier for these individuals to label or perceive of heavy metal music as extremely aggressive and representative of antiestablishment, antireligious, potentially satanic, and unconventional values that have immoral implications (Gross 1990, Binder 1993). Images of these fans include an angry "white trash" teenager who primarily wears black and concert T-shirts; a trouble maker; and a misfit of low intelligence with suicidal ideation and some mental issues, who engages in fighting, drug and alcohol abuse, or other destructive behavior. Individuals that continue to enjoy this music in their late twenties, thirties, forties, and beyond are seen as immature, unintelligent, peculiar adults, who also have mental issues and trouble leaving their younger years behind. In other words, many non–metal music fans consider this genre to be part of a youth culture phenomenon (Gross 1990), especially as it pertains to the louder, faster, and angrier styles of metal—such as death metal and black metal—with indecipherable lyrics.

Is the common metal fan really that limited in personal characteristics? Are the lyrics without substance? Is it accurate to assume that fans of metal music cannot separate lyrical meaning from reality in matters of death, murder, and violence? The answer is a resounding no. In fact, it would not be prudent social science to support a causal relationship between music and the more negative behavior that often becomes the focus of attention among the public (Epstein and Pratto 1990; Epstein, Pratto, and Skipper 1990; Wright 2000; Anderson, Carnagey, and Eubanks 2003).

Meaning among Heavy Metal Fans

To understand the diverse meanings attributed by individuals to the music and their affiliated behavior, a series of both open-ended and closed-ended questions were used. The topical matter included everything from identity and community, to music knowledge and behavior. The Internet questionnaire generated a sample of respondents from various regions in Europe, Canada, and the United States and provided a greater understanding about the role of beliefs, emotions, and special collective ritual events that promote group solidarity.

Being a Heavy Metal Fan

When explaining what being a metal fan means, many respondents simply stated, "listening to heavy metal music." This was often stated with a sense of humor or hint of sarcasm, a common characteristic for the typical heavy metal fan. Several respondents articulated a sense of empowerment or group identity beyond the typical stereotypes:

Of course it means I listen to metal, but it can go further than that. It seems that most metal fans don't give a shit about what other people do/say to you, rather that someone who listens to lets say any pop girl and cares about every single thing someone would say to them. Because when I listened to poppy music, I was really insecure about myself. Now that I listen to metal. It kinda opened new doors for me and I could care less what people think about me.

I do consider myself a metal fan, but not in the traditional sense. When I say "traditional" I mean the stereotypical "caveman," long-haired, beer-swilling, leather and spikes, et al. description; I'm in fact quite the opposite. Being a metal fan, to me, is, well, being a fan of metal. If one can enjoy the music and get into it, then one is a metal fan, regardless of sex, ethnicity, appearance, etc.

Being a metal fan means that you do not applaud someone when they say they listen to "heavy metal" then follow with a list of bands consisting of AC/DC, Godsmack, Disturbed, Saliva, Drowning Pool, etc.

Other characteristics listed by respondents to define being a metal fan included terms such as "unique," "open-minded," "tolerant," "expressive," "creative," "intelligent," "independent," "free thinker," "rebellious," and "does not conform." It is interesting that all of the responses included positive answers and not a single respondent indicated anything related to being aggressive or violent. However, within the metal community, there is often a noticeable use of vulgarity in lyrical content, on album cover artwork, and during interaction at live shows (Halnon 2006). Sometimes band members will refer to their fans as "motherfuckers," "maggots," and "fuckers," and they often include profanity in prompting the crowd, for example, "We're going to have a fucking awesome show tonight, alright?!" The use of vulgarity should not be misconstrued as any sign of disrespect to the fans; rather, it should be interpreted as another way to emphasize a value regarding the freedom of expression. In other words, in many circumstances it is a statement about the notable absurdities of everyday life. For some, the use of profanity is another way to more strongly emphasize an emotive state.

A Metal Community and Other Sources of Meaning

To learn more about the individual meaning applied to being a fan of heavy metal, we also explored other potential sources of meaning. In this line of questioning, respondents were asked about a metal community in or around their residential areas, band preferences, whether changes in these preferences occurred over time, and what bands were considered to be the origins of heavy metal music.

The existence of a metal community was thought to be significant because having other fans of the music in the immediate area would serve as an important resource for participation and group cohesion in the broader culture of metal. Approximately 12 percent of the respondents indicated that there were barriers to participation and full expression of a preference for this style of music. These barriers included small residential areas with even fewer fans of the music, and the stigma that is typically placed on those with preferences for metal music. However, since the same negative connotations are also applied to the metal culture milieu, they primarily functioned to reinforce the individual's identity, shared values, or commitment to the broader metal culture.

An ongoing debate within the metal community involves discussion about the first metal band or the music's origin. Respondents listed forty-five different bands, and unsurprisingly, Black Sabbath topped the list in frequency, followed by Judas Priest, Led Zeppelin, Iron Maiden, Metallica, and Deep Purple. Perhaps a more interesting fact was that several respondents indicated no real knowledge or interest on the matter and claimed to be only repeating what other people said. Others mentioned they did not listen to these bands and that metal consists of multiple genres each with their own origins. Generally, respondents did not seem too concerned about the genealogy of heavy metal or the most significant bands and preferred just describing what constitutes metal music. While the majority of respondents simply mentioned one or more bands in their answer, others actually provided an explanation. Some of these phrases and words used to articulate this understanding were "first to use distortion power chords," "heavy sound," "speed," "brought harder tone," "reference to Satan," "includes dark themes & lyrics," and "first use of devil's note." However, respondents had more critical insights and antidotes for what constituted real heavy metal music.

Authenticity: Real versus Fake Metal

It is clear that real heavy metal is in the eye of the beholder. In fact, the most popular responses were that real metal is a "feeling" that cannot really be described and that it is a "personal decision" and "subjective." Perhaps the most telling answer to the question of false metal was that rather than describing what makes a band fake, respondents simply listed specific bands. There appears to be a generational factor involved in the varied responses to authentic heavy metal. For example, during the 1990s people grew up with nu-metal, which is a fusion of rap and heavy metal (e.g., Korn, Limp Bizkit, Slipknot), and today these bands are sometimes considered too light, not heavy enough, or in the case of Slipknot too much of a gimmick. One could argue for a similar occurrence in the 1980s with the rise of hair bands and glam metal (e.g., Poison, Motley Crüe, Cinderella); though they were popular, many fans in the 1990s did not define this as metal. The following response from one metal fan illustrates this point:

> "Real metal" is just a term used by ignorant fans of extreme metal who feel that open-minded people should not be exposed to those more "extreme" bands. To give an example in mainstream terms, Cannibal Corpse is "real metal" as opposed to a band like Slipknot.

Other respondents provided more detailed answers, and it seems that to some, "false metal" refers to whatever mainstream media calls metal or whatever is considered popular. For example, bands that replicate a popular culture trend are considered less authentic than original bands:

> "Real" metal really should be a personal decision. But in my opinion, real metal cannot conform. It will never be radio friendly or MTV friendly. Looks, i.e. hair, clothing, etc. has nothing to do with it. What constitutes real metal to me is the subject material, the style and form of the melodies and guitar playing, musical style of percussion and vocals. If a band is singing about how much they miss their "baby girl," the guitar parts are catchy and follow typical chord progressions, the entire drum part can be recreated in my kitchen with 2 pots and pans, and my little sister can sing along karaoke style, it's not metal.

Other respondents used a variety of descriptors and references to instrumental styles to describe authentic heavy metal: heavy, technical, integrity, brutal, subject matter, not catchy, good riffs, melodic, sound angry, no conformity, cannot be a corporate sellout, influenced by other metal bands, leads to head banging, thoughtful, intelligent, creative, style and form of melodies and guitar, intensity of vocals, no melodic singing, style of percussion, double bass, no typical chord progression. Generally, they described authentic metal as being original, not something based on corporate-sponsored gimmicks or individual ego. The music should matter the most. Probably the most salient characteristic in defining real heavy metal is that regardless of any individual's definition or band preferences, each respondent was aware of the bands and styles under consideration. In other words, a single respondent might define a group like Hatebreed as metal and Poison as nonmetal, but she or he still recognized both bands as part of the discussion. This suggested a cultural recognition of heavy metal as a genre even though individual meaning for authentic metal varied.

Meaning for the Darker Side of Heavy Metal

The "dark side" of heavy metal referred to criticisms that have been historically attributed to this music, such as church burnings, satanism, aggression, and suicide. Generally, respondents dismissed most of the satanic themes and proposed church burnings as being silly, a gimmick, a marketing ploy, or an act:

> Again, who cares. Life's too short to be involved in any sort of idiotic shit like that. People take themselves and their hobbies far too seriously.

Others pointed to the fact that metal music is direct and often covers issues related to personal and societal problems, things that are not always popular to discuss:

> I'd say it's just a more realistic approach to life. In much of modern music the focus seems to be on the good things in life, but not everything is good. No matter how much modern society might want to blind us from the evil in the world, these things exist, and metal is willing to accept that. It is entirely foolish to blame metal for these things, however, as they would still be occurring without the presence of metal. Metal simply brings their existence to the forefront, it's just that people are not willing to see things the way they truly are, and instead of trying to change things, they would rather demonize the messenger.

Still others focused their attention on the artistic expression of heavy metal and the fact that much of the negative connotations stem from stereotyping and overgeneralizing based on the extreme actions of a very small group of people:

> There is a dark side in all cultures. Suicide and aggression feature in all areas of society and are not just limited to metal fans. Not all satanists are metal, and not all metalheads are satanists. It is a minority of people who believe in this and should not be reflected on the whole. As for the church burnings, these were a localized series of events performed by a small group of individuals who have been dealt with in accordance to the law. Because metal is a minority, and "promotes" violence and evil, this was seen as how all metalheads act, which is not a fair judgment. There are extremities such as this in all walks of life.

It seems that when addressing the issue of satanic metal most respondents equated it to publicity stunts or artful expression that was effective in generating emotion. For the typical heavy metal fan, emotion seems to be a very significant part of his or her experience with the music, especially with a music that is about passion and the freedom to express what one is feeling. The icons of heavy metal—including symbols of death, war, Satan, and sadness—were generally viewed as artful ways to discuss real-world social, political, historical, and psychological issues.

Meaning for the Positive Side of Heavy Metal

According to the fans of this music, heavy metal provides identity, acceptance, emotional release, and a sense of community, or a place for some self-proclaimed misfits to call home. There were a significant number of references to emotional release. The music appears to serve as an outlet for aggression, frustration, anger, depression, and the like. Many respondents even indicated that the music makes them feel happy, noting that even though the music is loud and often includes someone screaming, it makes him or her feel better and come out of a negative mood:

> Sometimes the expression of anger, pain, and disdain through music can alleviate the feelings that the listener may suffer. It can offer a point of reflection that is impossible with the sickening pop that plagues the radio and mass culture.

> Sometimes it's just nice to know that there ARE other people out in the world who feel the same way you do, whether it be pissed off at political situations, aspects of life, death, whatever.

Others point out the potential educational value of the music that encourages either the exploration of historical and literary events or critically thinking about the world we live in:

> Due to many bands' lyrical themes, I have been inspired to read Norse mythology, Moby-Dick, and many other things I never would have considered otherwise. Many bands have intelligent lyrics that are thought-provoking and meaningful, but they are not as widely recognized as the gore and Satan lyrics.

Overall, it seems that metal fans tend to emphasize the music and what it has to offer by means of creativity, complexity, diversity, intellect, uniqueness, personal therapy, and direct confrontation with social life. Additionally, there appeared to be an interactive effect between the multilayered domains of interaction that structure the heavy metal subculture and ritualized symbolic practices (RSPs) that generate, modify, and perpetuate meaning among the fans of this subculture. The authors applied structural ritualization theory to one of the more conspicuous and salient characteristics of being a heavy metal fan, that is, attendance at heavy metal concerts, to articulate this understanding.

The Concert Venue—
the Application of Sociological Theory

Structural ritualization theory (SRT) is a contemporary theory that integrates structural dimensions with the construction of symbolic meaning through ritual practices. The theory postulates that rituals or RSPs are action repertories that are grounded in cognitive schemas.[1] The original formulation of the theory focused on organizations where the dominance or importance—rank—of RSPs that individuals engage in are influenced by four factors: salience, homologousness, repetitiveness, and resources (Knottnerus 1997, see also 2010). These principles put forth in SRT can be applied to many different situations where people engage in ritualized behaviors (see, for example, Guan and Knottnerus 1999; Knottnerus and LoConto 2003; Mitra and Knottnerus 2004; Wu and Knottnerus 2005; Ulsperger and Knottnerus 2006, 2010).

More recent work in SRT has discussed how the *emotional intensity* of people in special collective ritual events (e.g., musical concerts, political rallies, festivals, religious events) are influenced by four factors: *shared focus of attention, rates of interaction, interdependence of actors,* and *resources* (Knottnerus 2010).[2] It is argued that as the emotional intensity of actors increases in such events the greater will be their commitment to and integration into the group. A brief look at a typical heavy metal concert demonstrates these characteristics.

First, heavy metal shows require many *material resources*. Before the show, trucks drive to the back of the venue and roadies begin to unload and rig the stage. Fans have traveled from near and far spending hard-earned cash on tickets for the anticipated show. In and outside of the venue there are booths where fans can buy merchandise such as CDs, DVDs, T-shirts, posters, beer mugs, and shot glasses. At the metal show, the stage becomes the *shared focus of attention* for the crowd, drawing people toward the security railing that separates the stage from the crowd. As the band comes on stage, the screaming fans become *interdependent actors* within the performance, reacting to the gestures and calls of the band and the hierarchy of the crowd.

As the band plays, the tempo and rhythm of the music set the *interactional pace* of the mosh pit, putting demands on the hardcore fans to give it their all in bursts of timed aggression. Sometimes these timed bursts of aggression are direct responses to the request of the band whereas other times they seemingly appear out of nowhere, thus making the energy and pace of interaction bi-directional. Additionally, fans will "throw their horns," or maloik, a hand gesture used to show appreciation for the music and used as a response to whatever question the band may have for the crowd. The *human resources* amassed in a metal crowd change the dynamics of the show. The energy of the band and the proportion of headbangers versus uninterested "hangers-on" dramatically impact the intensity and meaning of a show. When a metal show is in full verve the *emotional intensity* generated by this event involves a powerful release of tension and excitement. When all of these factors are present to a high degree, these widely shared, emotionally charged ritualized practices, which are grounded in strongly held beliefs (or symbolic meanings), reinforce a *commitment to the community* of metal maniacs who are both participating in the event and scattered all over the globe.

Positive emotions generated in this quite conspicuous and unique domain of interaction, the concert venue, increase people's commitment to the beliefs and meanings associated with this music. This is the result of the aforementioned factors, such as repetitious patterns of behavior and interaction occurring in the concert event, for example, mosh pitting, crowd surfing, headbanging, showing the horns hand gesture, yelling, and singing along with the band. These interactive action repertoires are schema driven, which enable many individuals to participate through the ritual in the production of meaning. Though these rituals vary in intensity and style by the respective heavy metal genre, the individuals within the subculture regardless of their location or national language understand them because they are familiar forms of interaction.

These behaviors appear extreme, but they promote positive emotional states that connect participants to the ritual event and create positive associations with other participants. The positive emotional states created by the repetition of rituals generate shared experiences, shared commitments, shared norms, and group cohesion (see also Willis 1977; Lawler and Yoon 1993, 1996, 1998; Rose 1994; Lawler, Thye, and Yoon 2000; Lawler 2001). It is significant that metal music, much like metal fans, is quite diverse. The rituals, however, signify a cultural recognition of heavy metal (Weinstein 1991, 2000), and they point to the same bonding process that occurs for non–metal music fans that construct meaning by ritualistic behavior in their preferred musical venues.

Our respondents indicated that meaning arises through the process of structured interaction that takes place at heavy metal shows; the everyday life or communities of respective fans due to societal responses to the music and them when their musical preference is discovered; and the digital interactive spaces that let fans know there are other people around the world who understand and share values for this music. Metal bands and music may vary by individual preferences; however, it is the collective action at events such as the concert venue that provides the necessary ritualized symbolic practices that unite people and reproduces meaning that gets passed on from one person to the next and from one generation to the next.

Notes

1. Ritualized symbolic practices are action repertoires that are schema driven. These action repertoires are standardized or habitual social behaviors. Schemas are defined as cognitive structures or maps for behavior. This perspective does not focus specifically on cognitive processes operating in individual actors, as cognitive psychology would do. In other words, meaning results from both individual cognitive schemas and social structure simultaneously. The focus, then, is on domains of interaction or bounded social arenas based on social context, time, and place. There may be one or many domains of interaction that significantly influence the development of RSPs. Domains of interaction refer to the settings in which ritualized behaviors occur. The rank or strength of an RSP is determined by the four following factors: *salience* = degree to which an RSP is perceived to be central to an act, action sequence, or bundle of interrelated acts (p. 262); *repetitiveness* = relative frequency with which an RSP is performed (p. 262); *homologousness* = degree of perceived similarity among different RSPs; *resources* = human and nonhuman materials needed to engage in RSPs that are available to actors (p. 264). Further details of the original theory are available in the book *Ritual as a Missing Link: Sociology and Structural Ritualization Theory and Research* (Knottnerus 2011.)

2. To more clearly understand the role of emotional intensity in collective ritual events, see Knottnerus (2010), "Collective Events, Rituals, and Emotions." The strength of the *emotional intensity* of actors engaged in a special ritual collective event is determined by the following four factors: *shared focus of attention* = the degree to which actors participating in a ritual event are focused on a particular aspect of that event; *interdependence of actors* = the degree of contribution to the ritual performance and the level of complexity involved (i.e., a contribution can be stratified or equal and simple or complex); *interactional pace* = the rate of interaction (i.e., frequency with which people interact) and the degree to which participants engage in rhythmic motion (i.e., unified action or movement within a group); and *resources* = both the human and nonhuman items needed to engage in the ritual event such as knowledge or the physical setting in which the ritual occurrence is located. *Emotional intensity* = emotional state of participants that is generated by participation in a ritual event, which affects commitment to and integration within the group.

Authenticity in Latino Music

Scenes of Place

Kathryn M. Nowotny, Jennifer L. Fackler, Gianncarlo Muschi, Carol Vargas, Lindsey Wilson, and Joseph A. Kotarba

Traditional Latino music scenes are vibrant features of their respective communities. We use four interactionist concepts—the scene, idioculture, place, and authenticity—to examine musical experience as a symbolically meaningful social activity. Our basic research question is, How do members of the various Latino communities in Houston, Texas, use music to make sense of their selves and everyday life in a large metropolitan city? Further, we argue that members of traditional Latino music scenes use the narrative of authenticity primarily to validate their participation as a scene member. Authenticity is especially problematic in Latino music scenes that invoke potentially conflicting criteria of quality—particularly scenes that are populated by Anglos as well as Latinos. Through the use of ethnography we examine the established music scenes of conjunto, mariachi, salsa, and Latin jazz.

Music is an especially salient feature of Latino culture, informing migration, citizenship, spirituality, and other aspects of the contemporary Latino experience (Natella 2008). In this chapter, we examine conjunto, mariachi, salsa, and Latin jazz. We refer here to these varieties as established music scenes, that is, as having been part of the existing landscape of Latino music for many decades. Established scenes are characterized by more tightly written scripts. These scripts include

Originally published in N. K. Denzin, ed., Studies in Symbolic Interaction 35 (2010):29–50. *Condensed from the original. Reprinted with permission.*

fairly specific definitions of authenticity in music. The perception of authenticity in music scenes is an important dimension for all participants, including both the artists and audience members. Authenticity can be conceptualized as something strategically invoked as a marker of status or method of social control. Authenticity is not so much a state of being as it is the objectification of a process of representation, that is, it refers to a set of qualities that people in a particular time and place have come to agree represent an ideal or exemplar (Vannini and Williams 2009, p. 3).

Our approach in designing the present study has been to survey, or map, the various Latino music scenes with a methodological temperament best thought of as discovery.[1] Over the course of this study, we came to appreciate the value of four interactionist concepts in helping us understand the social dimensions of Latino music scenes. First, the concept of scene directs our attention to the comprehensive, everyday cultural world within which Latino music provides meaning for self, identity, and nationality (Irwin 1977). Second, the concept of idioculture directs our attention to the ways all interactive groups develop and maintain a local culture. This system of knowledge, values, and customs provides communicative resources to help members engage in various interactional activities (Fine 1979). Third, the concept of place directs our attention to how Latino music as an idioculture creates a sense of place in each of these established Latino music scenes (Cohen 1995; Gruenewald 2003). Lastly, the fourth concept is authenticity. In this chapter, we use these interactionist concepts to explore established Latino music scenes and to examine the musical experience as a symbolically meaningful social activity.

Conjunto

The roots of conjunto music are firmly embedded in the traditional culture and values of northern Mexico and Texas (Guerra 2001; Valdez and Halley 1996). Emerging in the early 1900s, the lyrics, instrumentation, and melody artfully recreate the traditional Mexican folk music of ranchera of that time period (Guerra 2001). The notions of family and traditional cultural values play a key role in the continued popularity of conjunto music, specifically in the Houston scene. Valdez and Halley (1996) contend that conjunto is a durable and significant cultural expression among working-class and poor Mexican Americans. It has also served as a cultural vehicle for reproducing gender roles in more traditional forms than are typical of the majority society (p. 149).

Conjunto, which literally means "a musical group," utilizes the unique sound of the accordion accompanied by a German polka-style beat, traditional instrumentation, and arrangements. Like *conjunto*, *tejano* music is flourishing in the Houston area. Though similar in style and content (both feature the accordion), *tejano* music blends Texas and American country music, western music, and rock 'n' roll with the traditional *conjunto* sound. Often referred to as *norteño* (of the North), *tejano* music is best described as the music of Texas Mexicans.

The Music and the Artists

The diatonic accordion is perhaps the most definitive characteristic of conjunto music. The sound of a traditional conjunto ensemble, for example, is designed to showcase the accordionist. Not until after World War II did lyrics play a role in conjunto (Peña 1985). Incorporating the singing tradition of the guitarreros into their music, pioneer accordionists began to add song lyrics with duet harmonies to their instrumental dance music. The issues of lyrical content and interpretation are controversial in Houston's conjunto and tejano scenes. Because traditional conjuntos (which were performed for dance) do not have lyrics or vocal melodies, purists prefer an instrumental ensemble. The musicians who play this pure form of *conjunto* create a joyously nostalgic mood that audiences relish.

When lyrics are incorporated into *conjunto* music, romanticized depictions of lost or unrequited love are the most popular themes. In describing *conjunto* songs, one respondent said, "I like the fact that live *conjunto* music is not just a show but a form of expression. The songs are associated with real life experiences such as heartbreak, prison time, or working at the job, and this is sincere and more genuine when it is heard live." While romanticized stories are not unique to this scene, the seemingly unbending devotion to singing about these topics is unique to the *conjunto* scene. The lyrics express emotions that respondents feel cannot be expressed accurately outside of the Spanish language. Many *conjunto* and *tejano* artists are sensitive to the unique demands of their multilingual audience, and they sometimes utilize a combination of Spanish and English lyrics, trying to stay true to the original conception of the song.

The Audience

The audience for conjunto music consists of predominantly second- or third-generation Mexican Americans. A common theme among fans of this scene is a strong sense of nostalgia and historical appreciation of the music and its traditional characteristics. When Albert listens to live *conjunto* he says, "I feel like I am at home. I feel like I have something in common with other people and a sense of camaraderie fills my heart." Because the music is often enjoyed at family gatherings and traditional celebrations, there is an inherently conservative connection between *conjunto* and the past. One audience member noted, "This is my grandparents' music and I want my grandchildren to love it too."

Traditional *conjunto*s were initially written and performed for family gatherings. Groups were (and still are) often comprised of relatives who performed together at birthdays, holidays, and quinceañeras (birthday parties for fifteen-year-old females). Modern *conjunto* is still very much a family experience. Traditional songs and dances are passed on from generation to generation. One respondent felt it was particularly important to expose his young son to the scene, stating, "I want to teach him to be aware of our culture. And now at this stage in my life, I find myself having to tell him of what this unique area had, how it evolved and what it became, because we had to create our own identity through our music." He also spoke at length concerning regional identity, and how he wanted his son to understand the unique situation that early Tejanos faced, particularly the ambiguous nature of identifying as a Tejano people that were "accepted neither by the Mexicanos on the other side of the border nor by the Anglos on this side."

Mariachi

The urban mariachi tradition emerged in the post-revolutionary period of the 1920s as a symbol of Mexican identity (Jaquez 2002). The charro suit in which mariachis perform symbolizes manhood, nationhood, and power and is an important national symbol for Mexico (Vanderwood 1981). In Houston, the mariachi scene can be found in two distinct locations: in public at Mexican restaurants and at private family events. Many people see mariachi bands performing al talon, for a fee per song, at Mexican restaurants. Many mariachi ensembles begin performing at restaurants in order to practice their skills and to advertise their musical talents. The restaurants are a means to get their mariachi ensemble name out to the public so that they will be hired for family events.

The Music and the Artists

The instruments that mariachis use have changed over the years. Traditionally, the instruments included a harp, one or two violins, the vihuela, guitars, and a guitarron (Sheehy 1999). The trumpet was introduced into the mariachi orchestra in the 1930s. Today, all but the harp are still visible in a mariachi ensemble. The vihuela is a unique instrument that looks like a small guitar with a deep-bodied V-shaped back and five strings. It produces a crisp, high-pitched sound that fades away quickly. The vihuela and the guitar help support the melody by providing chords and rhythmic strums. The guitarron is the heart of the contemporary mariachi band. The guitarron resembles a larger version of the vihuela. It is a very large and deep-bodied six-string instrument that has a much deeper sound. This deeper sound allows the bass part to carry its own rhythms underneath the other rhythms.

Typical mariachi songs focus on the topics of love, *machismo*, betrayal, death, politics, and animals. While traditionally mariachi ensembles played songs like "La Bamba" that contained a mixture of folk traditions and were associated with different regions of Mexico (Gonzales 1991), mariachi ensembles now play other types of songs such as salsa, *cumbia*, mambo, *ranchera*, polka, *balada*, *huapango*, and other popular music. The *grito* is an important part of the music as well and involves audience participation. *Gritos* are small shouts that are usually heard during the instrumental solo of a song.

The Audience

Audience members can best be characterized as participants in the live performance. Although there are some audience members who participate as spectators simply by watching the live performance, many audience members actively participate by singing or dancing in close proximity to the mariachi band. It is not uncommon for the vocalist to give the microphone to audience members so that they can sing along. Jorge, a thirty-eight-year-old male from Mexico, commented, "I like that they put on a show while they are singing. They not only play their instruments but also dance and perform for the audience. They even allow the audience to become part of their show." When the mariachis play a melancholy song, the dancers join together and sway from side to side at a slow tempo.

When the mariachis play upbeat music, dancers will dance around a sombrero or engage in a *zapateado*, kicking the floor with their shoes. One scene participant, Isabel, commented on the dancing, "This [dancing] allows me to express my love towards the traditions and culture of my heritage." As Isabel hints, the Latinos who enjoy mariachi express a connection or bond with the music. The music allows them to connect with their Mexican heritage or culture and to reflect back to time spent in Mexico. Jorge offered a similar statement: "I like listening to mariachi music because it reminds me of my roots. I'm in a country that is not mine. It [the music] helps me forget that I am in United States." For Jorge, listening to mariachi music reminds him of Mexico. It brings back memories of the time when he was young, before he left his wife, children, and friends to find work in the United States. "I love this music because it is a part of me," Jorge stated. "In a way, it involves you with the music and with your past [culturally]."

Salsa

Salsa combines both African and Caribbean rhythms and almost always involves both singing and dancing. Salsa emerged in the US, particularly New York, during the 1960s, a decade of great social changes. By the 1980s, salsa was entrenched as a transnational musical genre (Waxer 2002). According to Julio Flores, a Latin jazz and salsa DJ, salsa really picked up in Houston in the late 1970s. There was a single salsa club on the southwest side, and people congregated there to dance and listen to Latin music. People of varying ethnicities, including Caribbeans, Colombians, Dominicans, Puerto Ricans, Cubans, and Venezuelans, all participated in the early scene. By the 1980s, salsa really exploded in Houston.

Today, there are two main types of salsa venues in Houston: the traditional salsa club and the Latin restaurant. Salsa clubs are designed around the dance floor and tend to be upscale with select clientele and a strictly enforced dress code. These venues are recognized as important places to dance salsa since they draw the most acclaimed salsa performers (e.g., Willie Colon, El Gran Combo de Puerto Rico, and Oscar de Leon). In the restaurants that feature salsa the bands play on small dance floors, allowing for interaction between the audience and the performers. While individuals do listen to and dance salsa at restaurants, the primary service is dining. A unique feature of this scene is the establishment of salsa dance schools, some of which are located within salsa clubs and some of which are freestanding dance studios. The first salsa schools opened in Houston in the early 1990s. These schools are important because they promote the musical genre to a broader sector of the public, reaching beyond just Latinos. This is largely because dancing is an important feature of salsa music. The dance schools significantly contributed to the popularization of salsa among a variety of ethnic groups.

The Music and the Artists

In the 1960s and 1970s, salsa musicians typically played a kind of "Son Montuno" (Cuban popular music) with lyrics that talked about the "hard life" and urban stories common to people living in big cities like New York and Los Angeles. Stories of legendary characters like "Pedro Navaja" and "Juanito Alimana," both Latin gangsters, were made into songs and popularized by salsa. In the 1980s, however, the salsa market fell. Other Latin genres became popular instead. In an effort to save the genre and keep their audiences, salsa musicians began to play "Salsa Sensual." Salsa Sensual constituted a new style of playing and singing salsa. The lyrics did not talk about social and urban situations, but instead focused on love and often described sexual encounters between couples and stories about lovers.

Salsa is played by an orchestra, or band, and traditionally composed of a minimum of eight musicians. Salsa orchestras use piano, congas, trumpets, *tres cubano*, trombones, timbal, bass, and violin. The instruments that create the salsa sounds have not been modified until recently. For instance, as technology has advanced, new instruments like the electric guitar, drums, and keyboards have been added to many salsa bands. Additionally, the use of computers has allowed for smaller bands. For example, a band of just five musicians can play salsa music with prerecorded tracks substituting for some of the instruments. Antonio Garza, the cofounder and director of the popular Orchestra Salerum, discusses his band's music and the issue of authenticity:

> While the band plays merengue, bachata, and cumbia, all the musicians are salseros at heart. Musicianship is the key, and having the best musicians in Houston wanting to play in your band always helps. We all want to sound authentic and not steer too far away from what the actual recording sounds like. In other words, we are not trying to play the Salerum version of the song.

The Audience

Latin Americans and Afro-Caribbeans constitute the majority of the salsa scene audience in Houston, particularly at restaurants featuring salsa. However, there are an increasing number of Anglos and Asians in the scene, many who attend the salsa schools. For example, the Sky Bar offers salsa lessons prior to the band's performance and coincidently has the most ethnically diverse audience. Sam, a forty-year-old male from Japan, goes out every Thursday to dance and have fun with his classmates from salsa school. Even though Sam does not understand the lyrics, he learned to feel the music through dance, explaining, "That's the [best] way to dance salsa. The essence of dancing salsa is in you, in what you feel and interpret that sounds in dance steps." For these non-Latino participants, the focus of the salsa music is the emotionality of the dance. Carol, a twenty-five-year-old Anglo college student, is also a salsa school student. She loves salsa because the dance is more rhythmical than other musical genres, and she admits that people who dance salsa look "elegant and sensual."

Thus, for the non-Latino audience members who attend salsa schools, salsa is heavily tied to dance and most participate in the scene because they enjoy dancing and experiencing the music through dance. The audience at restaurants featuring salsa is more often than not composed of Latinos, and frequently includes a variety of Latin ethnicities. This audience tends to be older couples or families. Sandro, a forty-five-year-old Colombian male, frequents Las Haciendas because it is a "nice and quiet place to have fun with [his] family." For Sandro, salsa also reminds him of his home country. He explained, "Everybody in the neighborhood listened to this kind of music at home, in the public institutions, buses, and even in the streets." Sandro further commented on this idea of being reminded of home, noting that the song "En Barranquilla Me Quedo" reminded him of his home city, and the many things he left in Colombia. He said, "When I listen to songs about my country, I get goose bumps and innumerable memories come to my mind." For Sandro, like other salsa school participants, the scene allows him to have fun and to experience salsa music through dance. However, it also inspires memories and reminds him of his home country.

Latin Jazz

Latin jazz is an instrumental idiom that combines Afro-Cuban music with bebop, a type of American jazz in the 1940s that features complex harmonies, melodies, and rhythmic patterns (Pinckney 1989). This genre includes a variety of Afro-Caribbean, Latin American, North American, and traditional Puerto Rican structures in both vocal and instrumental music.

In fact, "the Latin jazz idiom is spawning the same kind of stylistic diversification that has characterized the field of jazz as a whole" (Pinckney 1989, p. 259). This evolution of jazz, with a distinctive Latin flair, is especially prominent in the Latin jazz scene in Houston. The heart of the scene is Sambuca, an upscale jazz café located downtown.

The Music and the Artists

The Zenteno band plays at Sambuca every Thursday and is headed by singer Norma Zenteno, who took over from her father. Since many of Norma's songs are written for her audience at Sambuca, words relating to dancing and movement are often used to inspire audience members to dance. Norma's voice is what makes her Latin jazz different than other artists because she has a sultry voice and frequently sings very romantic lyrics. Norma's daughter, a regular audience member, noted, "My mother's music makes you feel like you want to dance, and whenever I bring a date here, the music makes you feel so romantic." Norma describes the sound of the Zenteno band as Latin, explaining that "the music has a certain Latin twist to it, it sounds very tropical and upbeat, and it has that Latin rhythm that makes you want to dance." One audience member confirmed Norma's description, explaining, "The Latin music all seems very authentic due to the interaction between the drums, percussion, bass and horn sections. It is so refreshing to see all these live instruments in concert on a local stage."

The Audience

The genre of Latin jazz music draws a diverse crowd in terms of age, gender, race, and ethnicity. However, this diversity does not extend to class. Since Sambuca is located in an affluent area of the city, the audience is typically composed of prosperous individuals who are often considered "uptown." Although the music in this scene is distinctly Latin, the majority of the audience members are not. Illustrating exactly this point, one audience member explained, "Norma's music is so great that it attracts all different types of people, all races, and age groups."

The crowd at Sambuca Jazz Café on Thursday evenings is generally made up of "regulars," people who attend the performances of the Zenteno Band almost every week. This group of regulars, however, can be broken into two groups: (1) those who come to Sambuca and participate in the scene because of their loyalty to the Zentenos, and (2) those who come simply to engage in social interaction and generate social capital (Coleman 1988). One audience member told us, "I used to come here to listen to Norma's father, Roberto, and now I continue to come, even after he died a few years ago. He used to play some good music, and he's given that to his children." Thus, many audience members attend because of their long history of involvement. Another group of fans attends not simply because of loyalty to the Zentenos or a love of Latin jazz, but because of a desire for interaction with similar, affluent, socially mobile people as means of acquiring social capital (Coleman 1988). One audience member explained this trend, saying, "I come here because I know the band members, I know Norma, and I know all the staff here." Another audience member explained, "I come here because I work across the street, I know everybody here. Most of these people are regulars and I come to talk to them after work on Thursdays." Thus, the goal of scene participation is simply social interaction with familiar and similar individuals.

Discussion and Conclusion

The traditional Latino music scenes we have observed and described are vibrant features of their respective communities. Conjunto and mariachi are very much like other forms of family-oriented ethnic music (see Kotarba 1998). The purpose of these forms of music is not to create new cultural worlds, but rather to preserve the ongoing cultural world. Additionally, both conjunto and mariachi are family oriented in two ways: (1) the music groups themselves are frequently composed of family members, and (2) the music is utilized at celebrations that typically involve the family like weddings, birthdays, and quinceañeras. This makes it a family-oriented feature of their perceived authenticity. Interestingly, neither scene is anchored to specific geo-social locations, as Irwin (1977) might expect. In other words, individuals do not typically go to a specific place to hear the music, rather the music is brought to a specific place (like a wedding, birthday party, or quinceañeras) for the purpose of celebration.

Latinos who listen to *conjunto* and mariachi feel a strong sense of connection with the music itself. The music acts as an aesthetic technology or "cultural vehicle" taking scene participants back to another time and place (DeNora 2000). By listening to the same music as their ancestors, fans of *conjunto* are able to share in a tradition that predates even the state of Texas. Therefore, the resultant sense of place is matched by a sense of time. As well, fans note that mariachi music allows them to connect with their Mexican heritage or culture and to reflect back to a different time and geographical place. In a sense, the place created by mariachi is wherever the family is: at home, at a marketplace, at a party, or at a friend's house. Also, much like *conjunto*, mariachis are embedded in the family traditions of Mexican Americans. The conservative nature of this music is a consequence of this connection to family tradition.

Salsa and Latin jazz are similar insofar as their Latino fans increasingly view them as inauthentic due to the invasion of non-Latino participants. Their authenticity is problematic because they are newer musical styles (having emerged in the mid-twentieth century), which have not maintained their traditional format and musical style, but instead have incorporated new styles and sounds, and they are frequented by non-Latinos who view scene participation as a means of acquiring social capital. These two musical genres do, however, maintain distinctly Irwinian (1977) scenes that include both the cultural phenomenon (artists, audience, music) and actual ecological locations like clubs, bars, and restaurants. For instance, it is clear in the Houston salsa scene that salsa has been adopted by people of many different ethnicities. Latin Americans used to feel like they had ownership of salsa (Urquia 2004), but the establishment of salsa schools in Houston has made it easier for non-Latinos to gain entrance to the scene. However, being Latino affords authority when participating in the salsa scene. Despite the changes to the music and dance and despite the ever-increasing number of non-Latino participants, Latino audience members continue to feel a deep sense of connection to the music and—like *conjunto*, *tejano*, and mariachi—it reminds them of another place: their home country. On the other hand, Latin jazz in Houston creates a sense of place that is "the place to be." When talking to audience members about the scene, interaction with others is mentioned far more often than the music, making the scene, as a meeting space, in some ways more significant than the music itself.

What seems to unite all four scenes is their conformity to tightly written scripts, as Irwin (1977) predicted about established scenes. One of the most crucial scripts in each of these scenes involves dancing. Participants in each music scene noted the importance of movement and dance to scene participation; in fact, not dancing in these scenes would be a violation of the tightly written scripts of the scene and would clearly mark one as an outsider. However, it is important to note that the style of dance varies. In the two scenes perceived most authentic, dancing is informal and spontaneous. However, in the two less authentic scenes, the dancing is more formalized. In the case of salsa, for instance, the dance is so formalized that schools have even emerged to teach people the dance steps.

In conclusion, this research highlights yet another important feature of the concept of authenticity in music sociology. Musicians, composers, critics, and others who create and manage music have a variety of aesthetic criteria to invoke in attributing meaning to music. They all view music in terms of its relative and variable beauty. Authenticity, on the other hand, may be the one distinctively sociological criterion to apply. Authenticity allows us to observe the ways various people position themselves around music in terms of its relative and variable truth. The former approach focuses on pleasure, whereas the latter sociological approach focuses moralistically on the correctness of the performance. Future sociological work on authenticity should further investigate the role that the social actor plays in relation to the importance and perceived authenticity of the music performance.

Note

1. See Kotarba, Fackler, and Nowotny (2009) for a discussion of the study methods.

9

The Jazz Solo as Ritual

Conforming to the Conventions of Innovation

Roscoe C. Scarborough

Drawing upon ethnographic observations at live jazz performances, the author argues that a successful solo is not an expression of unfettered creativity. If a solo is pure—if it is genuinely innovative—it will come across to any audience as noise. Conversely, a ritualistic solo draws upon the conventions of a particular art world. It involves strict adherence to prescribed roles by the soloist, other musicians, and the audience. When enacted correctly, the soloist, supporting musicians, and patrons experience an emotional charge that heightens group solidarity and reifies existing conventions of the jazz scene.

The colloquial understanding of soloing in jazz music is that the jazz solo is an expression of individuality and creativity that is channeled from one's mind, body, or soul. Musicians think of themselves as artists who possess an innate "gift" that facilitates innovation, which sets them apart from all other people (Becker 1973 [1963]:85). Drawing on ethnographic data from jazz performances, I argue that this perspective may accurately represent the belief system of musicians, but such a perspective entails a sociologically naïve conception of innovation. Music is a social enterprise. It is only communicable when all musicians and audiences share common artistic conventions and follow ritualistic scripts that define the types of musical expression that are acceptable and objectionable.

As enacted in live music performances, a *ritualistic solo* employs existing artistic conventions as a basis for on-the-spot "improvisations" by a performer. Conversely, a solo that is not in dialogue with genre or scene conventions—a *pure solo*—is received as noise by other musicians and audiences. A *pure solo* can only be enacted in complete independence from an existing "art world" (Becker 2008 [1982]). In other words, a *pure solo* can only occur if a musician develops his or her skills in complete absence of mentors, teachers, other players, audiences, and exposure to music. Though idealized as an outlet for expression of a musician's creativity and individuality, the jazz solo is fundamentally ritualistic in character. When enacted successfully, the soloist, other musicians, and audience patrons experience an emotional charge that builds solidarity and reifies existing conventions of the jazz scene.

Ritual in Music

Emile Durkheim's (1995 [1912]) pioneering work on primitive religion shows how participating in rituals binds a group together. According to Durkheim, objects in the world are divided into two categories: sacred and profane. Certain objects become sacred because they symbolize a group's identity. Ritualized action in collective ceremonies involving these sacred objects is an emotional experience that results in "collective effervescence" among participants. This experience builds solidarity, reaffirms group identity, and reasserts morality among practitioners.

Rituals are not only found in religion; they are integral to everyday interactions (Goffman 1967). Participation in recurrent rituals, such as greetings and goodbyes, condolences and congratulations, along with all the other little ceremonies of daily life, binds people together and provides structure for our lives in a complex social world. Specifically, rituals in everyday life engender high levels of mutual focus and emotional entrainment that result in a self-reinforcing feedback process of compelling emotional experience among those involved (Collins 2004). Thus, participants are continually drawn back to ritual experiences because they experience high "emotional energy" (Collins 2004) in these interactions. Just like in religious rituals, participating in everyday rituals binds people together, defines insiders and outsiders, and confirms conceptions of right and wrong.

Music is one area of social life where rituals occur. Musicians in the same "art world" adhere to conventions (i.e., production standards, common equipment, and shared culture) as they go about their artistic business. Participation in this ritualized action brings participants together and perpetuates norms of the scene.

These insights apply to the jazz solo as well. Soloing is the subject of in-depth analysis from a musicological perspective (e.g., Berliner 1994, Sudnow 1978). In particular, Berliner (1994) demonstrates how musicians acquire individual vocabularies and social competence through training, listening, and performing with others. Though sociological treatments of the solo generally occur in passing as part of a comprehensive ethnography of specific musical art worlds (e.g., Bennett 1980, Faulkner 1971, MacLeod 1993, Grazian 2003), some research focuses on the interaction among performers. This research demonstrates that an individual's improvisational process can only be understood by accounting for the social and cultural affiliations of players (Monson 1996), the contextual parameters of a musical performance, including harmony, rhythm, tempo, and style (Dempsey 2008), and the interaction among musicians (Hodson 2007, Sawyer 2003). Thus, to truly "solo" is to *not* play with the band (Chandler 2003). All of this suggests a conceptual difference between a solo as an unmediated expression of individual innovation—a *pure solo*—and a solo that draws upon existing artistic conventions—a *ritualistic solo*.

Research Design

The ethnographic data for this project are drawn from ninety hours of observation at jazz performances.[1] Utilizing my knowledge of music theory and lifelong patronage of live music performances, I observe musicians' solos as rituals. I attend to how the soloist, other musicians, and audience patrons all play roles in successfully enacting the ritual of the jazz solo. Inductively drawing upon two representative ethnographic accounts of solos from fieldwork in the jazz scene, I demonstrate why successful jazz solos involve the ritualistic enactment of genre conventions and not pure innovation.

Soloing in Jazz: Ritualistic and Pure Solos

As jazz soloists' performances are rooted in conventions of the jazz art world, unrestricted creativity is an ideal that is never quite realized. Musicians can only aspire to enact a pure solo. In the jazz art world, adherence to scripts associated with enacting the sacred ritualistic solo generates a heightened emotional state among musicians and aficionados. The charge of emotional energy motivates musicians and patrons to seek the ritualistic experience of the solo over and over again, which results in heightened solidarity among participants and a reification of scene conventions.

The Ritualistic Solo

On a November evening in 2009, world-renowned trumpeter John D'Angelo leads his quintet in a celebration of the "Golden Anniversary of Jazz" in a beautifully refurbished historical theater. About 400 attendees, ranging from senior citizens in formal evening garb to a smattering of young cultured bohemians, come to see five suit-clad middle-aged musicians perform renditions of canonical compositions by Dave Brubeck, Ornette Coleman, John Coltrane, Miles Davis, Paul Desmond, Bill Evans, and Charles Mingus.

Late in the final set of the evening, the band performs an upbeat version of "Moanin'" by Charles Mingus that incorporates considerable solo work by each musician. The trumpet player takes the first solo of the song. He performs a technically complex solo that closely adheres to the melody of the song, which does not earn significant applause from the audience. Similarly, the bassist and piano player faultlessly deliver solos that are quiet and conventional, but their efforts lack spirit and fail to facilitate any significant response from the crowd. Next, the drummer performs an unorthodox solo with a tribal-sounding beat that employs very loud rhythmic work on the floor tom and bass drum that he accents with wild gesticulations, an animated dance behind the drum kit, and an exaggerated ear-to-ear grin. Though musically unconventional, the intensity of this boisterous solo elicits a wall of applause from the audience that includes much whistling and cheering. Even more important, it raises the emotional energy of musicians and patrons.

After returning to the melody of "Moanin'," the band employs a gimmick to involve the audience in the solo. Everyone stops playing except the drummer, who keeps rhythm with footwork on the high-hat and bass drum. Exploiting the churchy, swinging, bluesy aspects of "Moanin'," the piano player, drummer, trumpet player, and bass player all begin to clap along with the drummer's rhythm, which primes the audience for the baritone sax solo.

Taking advantage of the high level of emotional energy among the captivated audience, the sax player walks up to the front of the stage and takes an extended, lively, fast-paced solo. Musically, he offers a high-pitched, technically complex solo interspersed with periodic guttural low note "barks." He matches this electrifying musical routine with a dynamic presentation of his physicality. At the apex of the stage in his shimmering blue pinstriped suit, he enacts an elaborate routine of knee bends and gyrations that includes repeated precarious backward bodily lunges paired with an expression of physical strain offset by deep bows delivered with a furrowed brow exhibiting thoughtful artistic contemplation. Throughout the ninety-second solo, he commands the full attention of the audience. At its conclusion, many audience patrons physically launch out of their seats to offer a mid-song celebratory ovation. The sax player reciprocates his gratitude with nods of acknowledgment and by repeatedly mouthing "thank you."

After this solo, the trumpet player and the sax player carry the melody of the song to its conclusion. Not only is this solo the climax of the song, but it is also the climax of the entire performance. The emotional charge left by the solo does not quickly dissipate. As the song ends, many members of the audience again jump to their feet and applaud while others shout accolades praising the performance. The musicians appear humbly appreciative as they offer nods and waves of acknowledgment to the cheering audience. They continue these gestures of acknowledgment until they are able to conclude the evening with a comparatively mellow rendition of "Freddie Freeloader" by Miles Davis.

Analysis

Because the solo is the primary medium through which jazz musicians display "innovation," it comes to symbolize the jazz culture itself. Without the solo, jazz is mundane; it would be everyday music. Thus, the solo is sacred. Due to its profound importance for members of the jazz art world, each participant in the ritual of the solo must enact his or her role in a ritualized manner. If enacted correctly, the jazz solo generates solidarity among all who participate and reifies the conventions of the jazz scene by affirming the appropriate content of a jazz solo.

Role of the Soloist

The soloist is the focal point of the ritualistic solo. However, the ritual of the solo involves much more than playing a series of notes for a specified amount of time. The soloist must enact an appropriate physicality and engage in expressive facial work suited to the performance. If the soloist neglects any component of the ritual then he or she will fail to generate a high emotional energy situation for all who are involved.

Colloquially, a solo is defined by its musical content. While technical proficiency, creativity, and artistry are all important components of a solo, it is essential that the musical elements of a solo, such as how notes are chosen and delivered, draw upon ritualized scripts. In the example I present here, the sax solo utilizes the song's chord progression as a basis for improvising a sequence of notes that form his solo. Further, his "barking" gimmick is not his own original innovation; it is but one possible device that is drawn from a toolkit of conventional variations that one can employ during a hard bop jazz solo. Musically, his solo is a success because it is familiar but not insipid, and it adheres to existing conventions of the scene.

How one chooses to solo depends upon the characteristics of the context, audience, and other musicians. Different contexts, such as a jazz concert hall, a nightclub, or a corporate luncheon, all call for a different role on the part of the soloist. At a formal jazz concert commemorating bebop jazz, the sax player's loud, fast, and high-energy solo is contextually appropriate.

Enacting a befitting musical performance is one of several components of a successful *ritualistic solo*. Nonmusical elements of the *ritualistic solo* performance, such as presenting an appropriate physicality, enacting expressive facial work, and acknowledging applause, are of central importance to the ritual of the jazz solo. In this case, the sax player's pinstriped suit is an appropriate selection for the formal atmosphere of this concert hall performance. Similarly, his vibrant routine of bounces, head bobs, facial expressions, and gesticulations is appropriate for the event and rightfully commands the audience's attention. Whether feigned or not, his expressive facial work, displaying his oscillation from the brink of physical exhaustion to thoughtful contemplation, demonstrates that he has given himself up to the "religious" experience of the jazz solo. Upon receiving thunderous applause mid-song, the saxophonist repeatedly mouths "thank you" to the audience as he waves in acknowledgment of their generous applause. This show of humility and gratitude for the audience's participation in the ritual is also important as it increases solidarity among all participants. When this type of acknowledgment follows a well-executed musical offering delivered with appropriate facial work and an appropriate physicality, the soloist has completed his or her part in the ritual of the jazz solo.

Supporting Musicians

Band members work together as a "performance team" (Goffman 1959) to ensure that the ritual of the solo is successful. In the "Moanin'" example, the other musicians support the sax player's solo work in a multitude of ways. First, the drummer provides a backbeat to accentuate the solo. Further, all of the musicians on the stage clap along with the drummer's beat, which directs everyone's attention to the soloist, emphasizes the consequence of the solo, and involves the audience in the ritual.

Supporting musicians also prompt inattentive or novice audiences to the beginning and end of a solo. These musicians mark the start of the solo by stepping to the side of the stage or offering an attentive gaze toward the soloist. Similarly, they mark the end of a solo by applauding or by beginning to play their own instrument at the solo's conclusion. If the audience remains disinterested, band members even cajole audiences to participate in the ritual. These actions attempt to construct a "pure performance frame" (Goffman 1974:251) in which the audience gives itself up to the ritualistic experience of the solo.

Audience Patrons

Though collective effervescence can occur among musicians without an audience, the attentive participation of an audience can exponentially increase the emotional energy of all those involved. If audience patrons attend a live jazz music performance, then it is likely that they seek to achieve a higher state of being and a temporary loss of self through participation in the ritual of the jazz solo. The audience's engagement and active participation in the ritual facilitates a high level of emotional energy and is a central ingredient for generating the quasi-religious atmosphere of the jazz solo.

The audience for the "Golden Anniversary of Jazz" concert is almost ideal for generating an emotionally charged situation. Most patrons who are willing to pay money to experience such a concert are undoubtedly familiar with canonical jazz selections and hold the competence to adequately participate in the jazz solo ritual. In the case of the "Moanin'" sax solo, the musicians' decision to encourage the audience to clap along with the expressive, loud, gimmicky, and technically proficient solo spawns a situation in which the musicians and audience both reciprocally feed off of each other's heightened emotional energy. This involvement engages and excites all participants, allowing them to be captivated and invigorated by the musical performance.

Though not the case in this example, seasoned audience patrons sometimes shoulder the burden of creating or maintaining a high level of emotional energy by offering conciliatory applause when the soloist does not adequately fulfill his or her role in the ritual. This often occurs when guest, amateur, or somehow deficient players do not solo in a manner that adheres to the standards or conventions of the jazz scene.

Only when all parties correctly enact their roles in the *ritualistic solo* do participants experience the charge from heightened levels of emotional energy. The successful ritual results in reification of existing scene conventions. Additionally, every participant leaves the experience feeling like he or she has experienced something special. This makes participants feel as if they are a part of a select jazz community, which reinforces their desire to experience the ritual again.

The Pure Solo

Six days after the "Golden Anniversary of Jazz" performance, a slightly different lineup of musicians performing as the John D'Angelo Quintet plays their weekly gig at Harry's—a local bar that attracts an eclectic gathering of jazz aficionado bohemians, post-fraternity social drinkers, and beer-swilling proletarians who congregate in the haze of a red neon sign and cigarette smoke to experience live local music. On this occasion, a typical Thursday-night crowd of jazz aficionados is displaced by a mass of people pursuing other late-night bar antics.

With the leader absent, the band's lineup includes sax, bass, drums, and two guitars. The band's regular guitar player, a forty-something-year-old black male wearing loose khakis, a long-sleeved black dress shirt, and glasses and with tight dreadlocks drawn back into a hair tie, is positioned in the rear of the stage. He is joined by a guest performer—a younger, white, balding male of similar age who dons a striped dress shirt with jeans and is positioned at the front of the stage.

During an extended jazz fusion selection, the sax player steps off the stage to have a drink at the bar while the drummer and bass player provide quiet rhythm support for the two guitar players to exchange dueling solos. The substitute player in the foreground performs fast-paced, technically elaborate solos with a rock flavor that include extensive work on the whammy bar, which he garnishes with a bouncing kinesthetic routine and expressive facial work that earns some applause from an unengaged crowd.

The regular guitarist, who is tucked behind the drummer, adopts a very different approach to his solo work. Musically, he shuns the hegemonic progressive, fusion-influenced, post-bop guitar style of John Scofield and opts for a minimalist approach that involves more silence and space than anything else. Juxtaposed against the elaborate solo work of the other guitarist and supported by the rhythm section, he offers a spattering of high notes picked quietly in rapid succession every few bars of the solo. This sparse musical performance is delivered in a stoic manner with no expressive facial work, minus a constant attentiveness to his finger position on the neck of the guitar. This brand of solo is repeated again and again throughout the solo duel. It does not pique the interest of audience patrons, who respond with comparatively meager applause.

As the solo exchange comes to an end, the sax player returns to the stage and the band returns to the melody one more time before concluding the song. By song's end, there is little energy in the crowd, and patrons clap politely as the band members discuss the next selection among themselves.

Analysis

A pure solo is a theoretical construct that represents absolute innovation. This is an ideal that many musicians strive to achieve but no musician is capable of realizing, as on-the-spot composition draws upon existing conventions of the genre or music scene that are learned through exposure to music through training, listening, and performing with others. True pure solos that do not adhere to these conventions lack the ritual dynamics that produce solidarity among participants and perpetuate the conventions of the jazz scene.

In the preceding example, the regular guitarist attempts to enact a *pure solo* that reflects his avant-garde artistic vision. Musically, his performance does not draw from the toolkit of common hard bop or jazz fusion solo techniques. Alternatively, he adopts a minimalist approach in an attempt to eschew existing jazz guitar conventions. Without adherence to conventions, audience patrons do not know how to evaluate his performance. It comes across as noise. Just as someone could not understand a foreign language they have never spoken, the bop audience cannot interpret and understand the guitarist's solo. This disconnect prevents their engagement in the listening process and inhibits a rise in the emotional energy level among patrons and performers.

Paralleling his anemic musical performance, the guitarist's presentation of his physicality is also lacking. His stoic demeanor, lack of any emotive facial work, rigid delivery, and position in the rear of the stage do not fulfill audience expectations for the role of the jazz soloist. Though some may construe an elaborate "performance" as charlatanism, his phlegmatic corporeal performance detracts from the level of emotional energy that he could generate with his physicality.

The blame for the failed ritual cannot be attributed solely to the soloist. The audience was unengaged and the supporting musicians did not beguile the audience into engaging with the atypical solo performance. In other words, no party intervened to save the ritual from failure.

In his effort to produce a *pure solo*, the guitarist's solo fails as a ritual. Although his performance is not vapid, other musicians and patrons cannot comprehend his solo through the logic of existing bop conventions. The solo lacks the ritualistic qualities that heighten the emotional energy of those who are present. Over time, solos of this sort lead to a lack of engagement by audiences, a weaker community, the eventual breakdown of musical conventions, and the possible dissolution or fragmentation of the jazz art world.

Discussion

In sum, a pure solo represents the unattainable ideal of unfettered artistic creativity among jazz musicians. Due to the conventions of existing art worlds, a pure solo characterized by genuine innovation is bound to fail as a ritual. Conversely, a ritualistic solo that draws upon existing genre conventions leaves all participants with an emotional charge that produces solidarity and results in the reification of the genre's conventions.

"Integrated professional" musicians—those who have the technical abilities, social skills, and conceptual apparatus necessary to fully participate in the jazz art world (Becker 2008 [1982]:228–233)—are most likely to uphold conventions and successfully enact a *ritualistic solo*. However, this does not mean that the jazz solo cannot evolve over time. Rituals are not mechanical and fixed; change and modification can occur (Knottnerus 2011).

Innovation comes from three sources: (1) mavericks, those who are marginalized by participants in an art world because their work strays too far from the accepted norms; (2) folk artists, everyday people who produce art in the course of their day-to-day lives; and (3) naïve artists, those who lack any training or connections to an existing art world (Becker 2008 [1982]:226–271). Naïve artists are most likely to enact an innovation that is genuinely pure because they are relatively uncorrupted by the conventions of existing art worlds. But much like folk artists, their contributions are largely ignored and labeled as illegitimate art. Conversely, mavericks have attenuated connections with networks of artists whom they can potentially influence, but their idiosyncratic peculiarities and radical innovations generally result in exile and hostile reception from other art world personnel. As a result, their products are unappreciated, or worse, unintelligible (Becker 2008 [1982]:63–66). New conventions can emerge from their art if audiences take time to learn and understand these innovations. However, these conventions only become accepted if they are continually enacted and constantly reinforced over time.

In general, most musicians operate under the false belief that their solos are genuinely innovative when, in fact, those that are highly lauded are *ritualistic solos* that draw upon existing conventions of the scene. Because audiences and other musicians understand the language of a *ritualistic solo*, they are engaged and seek to experience the jazz solo again in the future. All parties get a charge of emotional energy from participating in solos of this sort, which results in solidarity among participants and the reification of the scene's conventions.

The jazz solo, just like all rituals, keeps groups together and serves an organizing function in social life. It is clear that rituals perform a central role in maintaining the content of culture by reifying existing conventions and bracketing innovation. To be sure, the concept has not been fully exploited to explain social phenomena (Knottnerus 2011). Other arenas of social life can be analyzed through the lens of ritual (see Roy and Dowd 2010), which can facilitate a deeper understanding of how culture is produced and how it can change over time.

Note

1. All names of people and institutions, including some of their identifying details, have been changed to preserve their confidentiality.

Part III
Experience of Music: Stratification and Identity

Samba group playing on the train for money, Rio de Janero, Brazil, 2007.
Photo by Sara Towe Horsfall.

10

Race
Russell A. Potter

"Race" records were marketed to black audiences on the assumption whites would not want to listen to them. Alan Freed's famous 1952 Moondog Coronation Ball changed all that, and "rock 'n' roll" was born. The author discusses this and other racial aspects of the music industry.

In the history of popular music, perhaps no concept has been as vexed as that of race. From the "race" records of the 1920s to the political reception of rap music in the 1980s, race has been both calling card and wild card, draw and repulsion, essence and pose. No history of popular music or study of its contemporary formations can afford to neglect the issue of race, yet "race" as such has been continually elided, both within the music industry's discourse on its own modes of production and consumption, and by many of music's self-appointed critics. For even as popular music embodies and evokes a mosaic of racial identities and histories, its relationship with identity has never been as deterministic as those who see race as an essence have tried to construe it. "Black" music has always drawn "white" audiences, and indeed often drawn from "white" musical traditions.

Thus, there is no absolute test of authenticity to which either musicians or critics can turn—yet this has never prevented people from trying. Whether in the Afrocentric jazz genealogies of Amiri Baraka or Andrew Ross's postmodern celebrations of cultural indeterminacy, the question of the cultural authenticity of music has survived numerous attempts to reduce it to either bluntly racial fundamentalism or an ironic politics of pastiche. The reasons for this are caught up in the specific

Originally published in B. Horner and T. Swiss, eds. Key Terms in Popular Music and Culture *(Malden, MA: Blackwell, 1999), pp. 71–83. Condensed from the original. Reprinted with permission.*

histories of the music business, the cultural politics of consumption, and the shifting technologies by which audiences have been interpellated. In the process of entering into the subjectivities of musical space, each listener must construct his or her own eclectic map of these histories, and it is with my own first map, and the questions it raises, that I begin.

Digging in the Crates

In 1977, when I was seventeen, one of my friends told me that the best blues guitarist he had ever heard was someone named Blink Blake. He suggested that I pick up some of his records. Running off a strangely syncopated rolling bass line, he grimaced and remarked, "It's kinda like that, but better." I tried to copy the riff, but I couldn't quite get the timing right. Not long afterwards, I set out to the local record stores in search of this apparently unheralded guitar genius. No one, it soon appeared, had ever heard of him, at least not at the chain record stores, or even at the funkier independent record shops where Jethro Tull and Jeff Beck shared the shelves with bongs, pipes, and black-light posters. I finally found a store that said it had some of his recordings, a store on the other side of town, one of the first big music mega-stores. I went there—it took two bus rides lasting over an hour—and in one corner of its warehouse-like spaces I found a whole rack full of music by performers I'd never heard of before. Who was Georgia Tom? Victoria Spivey? Big Maybelle? Ron House? Their recordings, for the most part, consisted of reissues of scratchy old 78 r.p.m. records, compiled by equally obscure labels with names like Biograph, Yazoo, and Document. The covers of these albums featured grainy old black-and-white publicity photographs, sepia-toned images of young black men and women in dark suits, laced up leather shoes, and felt hats with downturned brims. There often seemed to be only one known photograph of any given artist, since the same photo would be used on every album. Some of them, like Bo Carter (author of the irresistible "Banana in Your Fruit Basket"), were eternally grainy and out of focus—their only surviving photograph must have been a small one, taken maybe in an early version of those take-your-own-picture photo booths. Almost all of these recordings had been made in the 1920s, 1930s, and 1940s, and the eerie surface noise of the originals ran over each of the albums like a Brillo Pad over Teflon, etching away the smooth musical surfaces and sticking their riffs to my mind. I picked up a couple of Blind Blake discs and was soon sitting at home with the eerie strains of songs such as "Black Dog Blues," "Dry Bone Shuffle," "Hard Pushin' Papa," and "Too Tight Blues #2" emanating from my Realistic speakers.

Reading over the closely printed liner notes, written evidently by a small group of aficionados and cognoscenti who actually possessed these old discs, I learned of something known as "race records," which seemed to me at the time to represent some ancient chapter in musical history when records and their audiences had a race. After all, this was the 1970s; my friends and I listened to a complicated mix of artists that didn't appear to line up along segregated racial lines. Music by the artists we listened to most—Joni Mitchell, Stevie Wonder, Jethro Tull, Aretha Franklin—seemed to appeal to everyone, and while race was certainly seen as an ingredient in their styles and personalities, it didn't produce anything approaching a one-to-one correspondence with audience. No doubt this had something to do with radio at that time, since you could still hear all these artists and more—everyone from Eric Clapton to Isaac Hayes, from the Pointer Sisters to Jackson Browne—on a single radio station, even in the course of a random half-hour listen. But it also had to do with a sense that my friends and I shared a sense that the promise of increasing racial equality and social justice was in some sense being fulfilled by the intensely inter-twined musical cross-influences that shaped our ears and excited our minds. There was a train a'comin, and whether it was sung on its way by Curtis Mayfield or Rod Stewart, we were ready to climb aboard. "Race" records, like segregated schools and the Negro Leagues, seemed a strange reminder of a worldview we thought had surely passed, or was soon to pass away.

Race and the Marketing of Popular Music

Alan Freed the waves just like Lincoln freed the slaves.
  —Chuck D of Public Enemy

It was not that long ago when things were quite otherwise. The history of the relationship between the recording industry and race is a long one and convoluted one, and not susceptible to a brief summary. Nonetheless, its pivotal points are hardly secrets. It is the stuff of legend that when, on August 10, 1920, Mamie Smith and her Jazz Hounds recorded "Crazy Blues," her record company did not anticipate substantial sales. After all, it was reasoned, how many black folks could afford to own Victrolas? When the record went on to become the industry's first million seller, that logic was refuted, but its fundamental assumptions went unquestioned. The recording companies did not consider the possibility that white folks were buying blues recordings (though they certainly were); they simply figured that black listeners were more numerous than they had imagined. All the major labels of the day—RCA, Paramount, Columbia—set up separate "race" labels with different names and catalog numbers. They then sought out publications, such as the *Cleveland Call,* the *Pullman Porters' Review,* and the *Chicago Defender,* where they could reach and target black consumers. When, a few years later, a similar market was discovered for the music of the Southeast and West, the record companies took the same route, establishing separate "Hillbilly" and "Mexican" labels, and advertising these titles in places where their presumptive audiences would see them.

And so it remained for the next thirty years and more. Even as white artists became immensely successful with their versions of "swing" and "jazz" music, the major labels kept separate catalogs and series numbers, a musical apartheid that reflected and amplified the historic divisions in theater and vaudeville. It was undeniable that black musical forms had given birth to the biggest sales boom in the history of commercial recordings, but this perception was safely sealed behind a wall of heavy black bakelite and wrapped in a brown paper sleeve festooned with images that evoked a world divided by stereotypes. How did the intended consumers react to record labels featuring darktown strutters in a panoply of latter-day minstrelsy, or straw-hatted hillbillies sipping moonshine from jugs? The record companies neither knew nor cared; it was the fiction of the audience that counted, and the music business still functioned with a largely top-down marketing attitude. The fantasy of the consumer took the place of actual market research, and there was little reason for anyone to question the assumptions that had so far brought in such substantial profits.

This system did not come to a crisis until the 1950s. In the postwar boom years, many things were changing. A bumper crop of young kids both black and white were craving something new and had little vested interest in the sounds of their parents' generation. . . . New neighborhoods and new industries, along with the GI Bill, were raising standards of living and creating a dynamic, rapidly growing audience of increasingly affluent listeners. More mobile in both class and regional terms, this generation was ready to cross over boundaries and tune its dial to wherever the musical action was found to be. The growing black middle class could tune to superstations of its own, such as Memphis's WDIA, where Martha Jean the Queen and Rufus Thomas ruled the waves. Yet, at the same time, ostensibly "white" radio began to flirt with DJs who, though white, consciously sought to talk "black." Radio (and later television) was a mass marketing tool that no one quite understood, and its potential for crossing over neighborhood lines was immense. One such DJ who discovered (belatedly) that he had tripped over a live wire was Cleveland's Alan Freed.

Freed, a DJ at Cleveland's WJW, played rhythm and blues (R&B) records for a largely black listening public. Unlike Memphis's WDIA, WJW did not, however, specifically target black listeners or advertisers, and only programmed R&B in the late night hours. This tacit acknowledgment of both black and white listenership was increasingly common as the 1950s rolled along, but in 1952 few people realized that such part-time fare was drawing a substantial audience, quite possibly more substantial than the regular daytime programming. Freed himself, known by his on-air moniker of Moondog, had little idea of the size of his audience, and when in March 1952 he decided to organize an R&B concert at the Cleveland Arena, his main concern was that he might not sell enough tickets to make back the cost of renting the hall. This was the infamous "Moondog Coronation Ball," advertised on its handbills as "The Most Terrible Ball of Them All." When the first fans began showing up around 8 p.m. on March 21, Freed was relieved that most of the tickets had sold in advance. The crowd was mostly black (though some music historians have promulgated the fiction that it was almost all white), and most of them had heard about the concert on Freed's radio show (aside from the handbills, the radio plugs were the show's only advertising). An hour later, as several hundred fans without tickets began to gather around the entrance, Freed realized there was going to be trouble. In Cleveland, a segregated city whose black population had grown substantially in the wake of the "Great Migration," a crowd of black folks made the all-white police on the scene nervous. Was this going to be some kind of riot? Around 9:30, when the crowd (now grown to more than six thousand) pushed in four of the arena's doors and walked right past the startled ticket-takers, the police called for reinforcements. After a tense period when the arena was filled far beyond its capacity (and with only the first song of the first act having been performed), the police shut down the concert and ordered everyone out, a process which took several more hours.

This is the show often hailed as the "first rock 'n' roll concert," usually because Freed was the one to introduce the term "rock 'n' roll" to describe the up-tempo R&B discs he played. Yet in many ways it was just another R&B concert, with the distinction that it was not advertised on a "black" radio station and did not appear at a "black" venue. In later years, Freed would be accused by some Afrocentric music critics of being instrumental in stealing black music and repackaging it for white consumers, but in 1952 Freed's audience was still mostly black, and he did nothing to consciously attract white listeners. In later years, Freed certainly tried to cash in on the huge crossover craze for rock 'n' roll, but he was far from alone. By then, the record companies themselves (belatedly, as usual) realized that R&B recordings were no longer being sold only (or even primarily) to black consumers, and having tried a variety of tactics to siphon off the profits made by the small labels that released most R&B records, began to sign R&B artists themselves, or acquire exclusive distribution deals. The industry magazine *Billboard* reflected this change, at first altering the chart listing of "Race Recordings" to "Rhythm and Blues," and finally (in 1963) eliminating the R&B chart altogether on the theory that R&B was then fully a part of pop.

Yet, two years later, the R&B charts were back, part of a trend that has continued to this day of listing individual charts for each genre and category of music. It turned out that the labels that were releasing R&B wanted to have a separate chart so that their sales figures could be sorted out from the burgeoning music marketplace, which was just then undergoing a "British Invasion" that denied most R&B recordings their top chart status. The double irony—that this supposed "British Invasion" was led by bands who imitated and followed in the footsteps of Little Richard, Bo Diddley, and Muddy Waters—was not lost on these originators of R&B, though most Americans today, with characteristic cultural amnesia, think of "rock" as a music without a race. Yet "R&B" is still an industry category, with "Urban Contemporary" as its sister label for radio station formatting, and most major record companies still divide their marketing and A&R departments along these lines.

Postmodernity in the Marketplace

But now it's the late 1990s. The new national Zeitgeist declares that because race as a category is now supposed to have been largely transcended, we don't need to acknowledge race as a meaningful question—in fact, to do so somehow marks us as cynical old leftists who can't get with the new post-racial reality. Yet, strangely enough, this is also the era when even more intensely racialized musical categories—"urban contemporary," "R&B," or "Latino"—dominate radio and music stores, and audience targeting and "formatting" guarantee that the listeners to one kind of music, however much they may overlap in reality, will be perceived and marketed as distinct groups. . . .

Within music criticism, a similar tension over race and genre has long been manifest. In the early criticism of jazz, the bulk of published critics were white men who venerated the sound of New Orleans in much the same way they lauded Michelangelo's David or Mozart's Requiem, as a cultural artifact in need of curatorial attention and meticulous cataloging. As Amiri Baraka (1967: 18) noted, this kind of care was in fact a kind of assassination, a reduction of a living tradition to "that junk pile of admirable objects and data that the West knows as culture." . . . In the years since the bop revolution, jazz finally won the critical and institutional recognition it long sought, but at a price very much like the one Baraka feared—it has become a cultural object, an institutional subject, but only in isolated cases the living breathing improvisational practice it once was.

The blues, a close second to jazz in terms of recording history, endured much different critical reception. The first "critics" of the blues were not aestheticians but folklorists, who were far more interested in classifying narrative tropes and variants than in looking at cultural politics. These early folklorists worked with the assumption that the blues was a characteristic—perhaps quintessential—folk art. Thus, they treated its performers as necessarily naïve and untutored practitioners of an oral tradition. This need to see musicians as untutored was so deeply rooted that when Big Bill Broonzy recorded an album for Mose Asch's Folkways label in the 1950s, the liner notes were written to suggest that Broonzy had scarcely left the plantation where his forefathers sharecropped. No mention was made of his twenty years' recording experience as an urban Chicago bluesman. . . .

Rock, the stepchild of the blues and R&B, received the most belated attention from critics who liked to think of themselves as "serious." Its critical beacons, from Lester Bangs to Greil Marcus, have tended to be eclectic and impressionistic in their approaches, as most of them cut their teeth writing for small independent rock magazines. . . . [Nelson] George's *The Death of Rhythm and Blue*s is quite possibly the most direct and cogent account of the cultural politics of race and music, as well as of the music industry's unsuccessful attempts to render such issues predictable.

Along with *Village Voice* page-mate Greg Tate, George was also one of the first critics to take a serious look at hip-hop culture. Hip-hop, more than previous musical forms, had a very specific cultural origin: the South Bronx. One could, in fact, make a map of its spread from Bronx to Queensbridge to Brooklyn and beyond (Tricia Rose offers one such map in her 1994 book *Black Noise*). Thus it was New York writers who first took notice, just as it was small New York–based record labels that first recorded it. Black-owned enterprises such as Enjoy, Winley, and Sugar Hill released the earliest hip-hop recordings in the late 1970s. Yet, as documented by Nelson George, once hip-hop became viable enough for the major recording companies to sit up and take notice, its path was frustratingly similar to that paved for R&B: appropriation, commodification, and an end to innovation. Small labels were absorbed, artists were dropped after their sophomore efforts had disappointing sales, artists were signed but left to rot on the shelf when the marketing breezes blew another way, and trends were relentlessly reproduced until they died. . . .

Redrawing the Map

My own route into hip-hop was a circuitous one which caused me to question many of my earlier figurations of the musical universe. In the wake of the self-immolation of punk in the 1980s, rock seemed eviscerated and all too-predictable. At the same time, R&B still bore the scars of its own disco inferno, and there was a sense that popular music in general no longer had the kind of raw, rebellious energy that had once, to quote Dylan Thomas, through the green fuse driven the flower. It was at this time that I remember my first dim inclinations towards musical nostalgia, the sense that what had come before was better than what was or what was likely to emerge in the near future. I spent hours listening to old protest songs by Bob Dylan and Phil Ochs, which seemed somehow far more urgent and pertinent than the blasé, ironic meanderings of Culture Club or OMD. MTV was on the air and commercial-free, but most of the videos were so predictably aimless that they were scarcely more stimulating than a test signal. Such occasional flourishes of music activism as there were sounded disappointingly smug and treacly to my ears. "USA for Africa"? "We Are the World, We Are the Children"? "No Nukes"?

In the midst of these musical doldrums, hip-hop was gradually emerging from the streets of New York as one of the brashest and most rebellious sounds of the century. Grandmaster Flash and the Furious Five released "The Message" in 1983, and the year after, Run-DMC broke out with their riff on "Walk This Way," but I never heard either song until years later. Why? Was it because the new generation of AOR (album oriented rock) superstations rarely played hip-hop, and mainline R&B stations shunned it as well? Was it because college kids were still noodling around with their own post-punk experiments and never looked at the wall to see what time it was? Was it because I was still assuming that revolutionary music could only be played on a guitar? What had really happened, I belatedly realized, was that the ostensibly egalitarian and eclectic notions of race fostered in the music environment of the 1970s had never really run that deep. At best, they were tenuous alliances: at worst, a kind of willed illusion, a dreamy Zeitgeist that temporarily papered over deep and persistent cultural and economic rifts. In seeming to move beyond race by imagining music as a transcendent force, my generation of suburban white boys had in fact abandoned the possibility of cultural crosstalk. In this we were aided and abetted by a music industry which studiously avoided risks, didn't put much stock in hip-hop and other emerging musical forms until well into the 1980s, and plugged into the popularity of hip-hop only after it felt it could market such dangerous music in a safety-sealed package.

The first time I actually stopped and listened to hip-hop, it was a strange and uncanny experience, something like the emergence of Chauncey Gardener from his late employer's mansion in the book and film *Being There*. Chauncey, a middle-aged gardener who has remained indoors for decades while the neighborhood outside slowly turned into a ghetto, attempts to deflect the threats of some local street kids by pointing his television remote at them and pushing the button. In a similar way, I found myself both enthralled and repelled when a friend sat me down and played the first few tracks of Straight Outta Compton. This was strong stuff, stronger than anything I'd imagined, and it cut across all my deep-seated liberal mores. "Fuck the Police," now that sounded fine, by Easy-E's and Ice Cube's luridly violent threats, many of which seemed aimed directly at the listener, overflowed the vessel of rebellion. Unlike leftist anthems such as Phil Och's "Cops of the World," this music did not allow its listeners the comfort of feeling good about themselves. These cops weren't in Cambodia or Santo Domingo. They were parked around the corner carrying badges and guns paid for by taxpayers like you and me. Police sirens, gunshots, and screeching tires were aurally imported into the mix, creating a tense environment within which white listeners were both vulnerable and culpable. There was no room for righteous empathy, at least not before confronting a few of the skeletons in the white liberal closet.

My early encounter with N.W.A. was only a very timid beginning, and it was only after many hours of listening that I could really hear it in the context of hip-hop as a whole. To endorse hip-hop was not necessarily to endorse N.W.A., any more than listening to rock meant that you had to become an apologist for Alice Cooper, but it took me a long time to be able to separate the issues. The subjective experience of any musical form or genre is such that no listener can take in the whole before understanding the formal codes of difference—which perhaps is part of the reason why hip-hop's long absence from radio made it so difficult for baby-boomer ears to grasp. It was not until a younger generation came of age that hip-hop gained a significant following among white teenagers. Unfortunately, this also meant that white listeners, who were generally more affluent, exercised a disproportionate influence over what the industry perceived as marketplace trends. So it was that, as the more militant black nationalism of late 1980s and early 1990s rappers began to fade, a new school of West Coast "gangsta" rappers took their place. One irony in all this is that the popularity of gangsta rappers among white listeners has sustained a large part of their sales (though that certainly does not much support the conspiracy theories of black anti-rap crusaders like C. Delores Tucker, who claims that rap records are a plot foisted on black communities by white-owned record companies). Another irony is that, as Chuck D has noted, the music industry only "let this shit succeed" when they were ready. The arrival of hip-hop on the stage at the Grammy Awards has in many ways been its death.

The most significant legacy of the past few years may ultimately be that the problematics of race must be acknowledged, and that we need to be suspicious of hazy constructions of musical utopia (especially when they take place on televised award shows). Even beyond that, we must be no less suspicious of the old pieties of liberal championing of black art forms. In fact, the traditional bifurcation between black and white can no longer be said to constitute the question of race, not in a United States where the Latino population will shortly outnumber

African Americans, and the number of Asian Americans has steadily increased. This is still more evident in popular music, where the recombinant influences of multiple generic and cultural threads have long since made it impossible to draw clear-cut ethnic or racial genealogies. Hip-hop backbeats have supported vocalists as far flung as Bruce Springsteen and Sinead O'Connor, and digital samples have crossed over still more unexpected territory. Hip-hop producers have recently sampled everyone from Sting to Joni Mitchell to Stephen Stills, and multimedia transcriptionists such as Beck have created aural textures so dense that, like James Joyce, they might well keep scholars busy for three hundred years and more.

In the end, we are back to the problematic articulated so many years ago by Walter Benjamin in his essay "The work of art in the age of mechanical reproduction." When audiences and artists can meet without meeting, sample without accompanying, and mix without mixing, the old sense of a music's cultural "aura" is one that cannot be maintained. The issue of race, and issues of identity politics in general, will certainly not, however, disappear as a result. For what brings us into contact with music is an affective politics, a subjective sense that the music speaks somehow to us, personally. Postmodern theorists have long asserted that the subjectivity is fragmented, but upon those fragments all kinds of animated ruins have been, and will continue to be, shored. T. S. Eliot (whose image this is) was in one sense a prescient literary "sampler," and it is possible to see in hip-hop, rave, and other aural recycling aesthetics something both before and beyond postmodernism. These art forms may mark the (re)emergence of what Paul Gilroy (1993) regards as "oppositional modernisms," of movements which have avowedly not thrown out the baby of art with the bathwater of romantic notions of originality and irreproducibility. (Eliot's "The Waste Land" (1992), particularly in its original draft ("He Do the Police in Different Voices"), is filled with dense intertextual collages, allusions, and borrowings, which Eliot felt strongly enough about to annotate with his own footnotes.) Put in other terms, the fact that identity is "complex and contradictory" does not mean the affective ties and social bonds secured by music (or any other art form) are false.

Complex subjectivity demands complex art, and the contradictions of one may well find their expression (if not necessarily their resolution) in the other. If, as Jean Baudrillard has claimed, the recombinant simulations of late twentieth century technology and culture have blurred or even reversed our notions of the "copy" and the "original," perhaps art in fact gains in power, as we need no longer apologize for the idea of art as collage, and can learn to be comfortable with the impure mixtures which mark both our social and aesthetic experiences. Popular music may indeed provide the quintessential insurance of this process, even as—and for the same reasons—it remains the most elusive matter for theoretical analysis. There can be no erasure of race, but that is not because it lies under everything like a seamless stone foundation, but because its conflicted histories are still the quarry and the quagmire in which all stones are born, heaved up, and lost.

11

(Re)Presentin' the Tragic Mulatto
An Analysis of Multiracial Identity in Rap Music
Matthew Oware

Cornell and Hartmann's constructionist approach is used to examine how rap artists with one black parent and another of a different race or ancestry discuss their racial identities in rap music. Four artists, whose lyrics reflect the situation faced by persons with multiracial identities, are examined: Chino XL, Drake, Afro DZ ak, and Michael Franti. Their resolutions vary. After expressing some confusion, Chino XL ultimately asserts a black identity, as does Drake. However, Afro DZ ak and Michael Franti adamantly claim a biracial or multiracial identity.

Extant research on racial identity formation among multiracial individuals with one black parent focuses on the determinants of a multiracial versus monoracial identification (Harris and Sim 2002) and the negotiation of racial identification with peers, family, or friends (Rockquemore and Brunsma 2002, Khanna and Johnson 2010, Khanna 2010). In addition, a fair amount of research examines whether multiracial identification harms or promotes the psychological well-being of these individuals (see Binning et al. 2009 and Cheng and Lively 2009 for contrasting findings). This chapter analyzes these debates within the popular genre of rap, focusing on rap artists who have one black parent and who discuss their racial identity in their music. Specifically, this research employs an extension of symbolic interactionism—the constructionist approach (Cornell and Hartmann 2006, Berger and Luckmann 1966), which states that racial identity is negotiated between the individual, his or her local environment, and the larger society—as a theoretical framework for analyzing how rap artists with multiple racial and ethnic ancestries express and explicate their identities. What follows is a brief discussion of the most current scholarship addressing multiracial identity. Next, I define the constructionist approach and apply it to the selected songs of artists Chino XL, Drake, Afro DZ ak, and Michael Franti. I conclude with the argument that, through their music, these rappers represent and embody the varying discourses and research related to multiracial and biracial identity.

The most current research on biracial and multiracial individuals posits that racial identity formation is contextual, contingent, and situational (Korgen 1998; Rockquemore and Brunsma 2002; Rockquemore, Brunsma, and Delgado 2009). Root (1992) argues that multiracial individuals have the right to change their identification whenever and wherever they want without criticism from other individuals. This process applies to individuals with one black parent as well (Khanna and Johnson 2010, Khanna 2010). Khanna and Johnson (2010) found that many of their black-white respondents situationally passed as black because they wanted to fit in with their black peers, or they perceived some advantage for doing so; for example, possibly benefiting from college affirmative action policies. Yet, these respondents did not actively claim a black identity without some validation or agreement from peers. When black-white biracials revealed their white ancestries to white peers they were still racially identified as black (Khanna 2010). Black peers responded similarly, stating that black-white biracials were "really black." These friends ostensibly adhered to the one-drop rule—the notion that if a person possessed any black ancestry then he or she identified as black (Davis 1991). Hence, identity formation for multiracial persons encompasses personal or internal views, as well as external or outsiders' views—reflective of the symbolic interactionist approach.

Constructionist Approach

Most of the research on the racial identity of multiracial individuals employs a symbolic interactionist framework (Cooley 1902, Mead 1934, Blumer 1969, Rockquemore and Brunsma 2002). According to this approach, "racial identity is described as a process in which identity is negotiated between the individual and larger society" (Khanna 2010:97). I use the constructionist approach as defined by Cornell and Hartmann (2006), which incorporates the above elements of symbolic interactionism but also adds two other components. Their theory argues racial identity formation should be understood as the intersection of asserted and assigned identities and thick and thin ties. Asserted identities are essentially individual claims about the self, who individuals say they are: for example, someone explicitly stating "I am black" or "I am white." Assigned identities are how outsiders view other individuals: for instance, peers, family members, friends, and so forth stating "you are black" or "you are multiracial." As symbolic interactionism states, identity formation entails negotiation between these two orientations. The constructionist approach includes the additional dimensions of thick and thin ties. Thick ties are defined as those racial or ethnic connections that primarily organize our social lives. An obvious example would be an immigrant residing in an ethnic neighborhood; for example, a Chinese immigrant's social life is daily influenced by living in a "Chinatown"—there are strong ties between this local community and the Chinese individual. Conversely, a thin tie is one that plays a nominal to insignificant role in social lives. Although race and ethnicity are social constructs, they nevertheless organize and influence the social lives of individuals, whether monoracial or multiracial (Omi and Winant 1994, Bonilla-Silva 1997). Thick and thin ties intersect with asserted and assigned identities. Therefore, according to Cornell and Hartmann (2006), there can be potential alignments and tensions between asserted and assigned identities, and thick plus thin ties. Multiracial individuals maneuver and navigate their identities with outsiders (family, friends, peers, strangers, etc.), members of their communities, and the "generalized other"—conventional, taken-for-granted interpretations and understandings of racial or ethnic identification that are embedded in a society (Cooley 1902, Mead 1934, Blumer 1969).

Despite the sudden increased analysis of multiracial identification over the past decade, a dearth of research exists on how multiracial identity is presented, expressed, and interpreted in popular media.[1] Even though the popular genre of rap music routinely explores racial politics (Rose 1994, Perry 2004, Oware 2009), little research focuses on racial identity, especially from mixed-race individuals. This work examines how a selected group of rappers reflects and embodies the racial dynamics of the aforementioned literature. Because black male artists predominate rap music, examining how black mixed-race male rappers represent themselves in this milieu provides insight on racial identity construction.

Methods

The criterion for selecting the rap artists consisted solely of examining artists who explicitly stated or revealed that they possess some black ancestry, specifically one black parent, and another different racial or ethnic background. I limit my sample to these specific characteristics because I want to focus on how partially black-mixed race individuals discuss negotiating their identities. I chose these individuals based on being introduced to their music, performing a Google search for black-mixed multiracial rappers, and being an avid listener of this genre in general. Thus, this research is not a systematic random selection of artists, nor do I make the claim that it is an exhaustive list of multiracial artists. My own research may not have unearthed every multiracial rapper.

The rap artists selected symbolize the larger conversations taking place around biracially black individuals. Essentially, each rapper is treated as a case study in racial identity construction. I performed an extensive examination of each artist's compilation of albums and found that besides the songs highlighted here, these individuals rarely discussed their racial identity in their music; they may reference it in passing (for example, stating that they are "black" or "biracial" in other songs) but there are not multiple songs devoted to identity construction. With this being said, the claims I make should not be understood as generalizable to all multiracial rappers. Below, I examine the similar identity selections of Chino XL and Drake (ultimately, black), and the parallel identity selections of Afro DZ ak and Michael Franti (that is, multiracial).[2]

Analysis

Chino XL and Drake

Chino XL, whose background includes black and Latino ancestry, emerged from the "underground" and gained nominal attention with the release of *Here to Save You All* in 1996. The song "What Am I" on this album reveals the hardships, from his perspective, of being an individual of multiple ancestries living in predominately white and black neighborhoods at different times. He first recounts his experiences growing up in the predominately white neighborhood of Middlesex, New Jersey:

> *About six, on my BMX, doin' tricks*
> *Back to Middlesex with a couple of poor white trashy brats*
> *Everything was coochie crunch till it was time for lunch*
> *They said to wait in the back, they said that Pops ain't like black...*
> *They want to see you jiggaboo with your/face painted*
> *They want to see you a failure so I never/became it*

Chino's problems began when he received invitations to his white adolescent friends' homes. He details the disparaging remarks received from the white adult parents. In this apparent testimonial, he uses the term *jiggaboo,* which was a derogatory phrase used to demean and belittle blacks during slavery and de jure segregation, as a description for black comportment around whites. He believes that whites in this community wanted him to behave as caricatured blacks during slavery, using exaggerated physical gestures such as their hands flailing about in an uncontrolled manner, speaking unintelligible gibberish. These behaviors purportedly represented black incompetence (Woodard 1955). Chino drives this point home in the next line when he states that whites wanted to see him (and all blacks) as a failure. He responds by asserting that he would never become that. Yet, he must balance this proclamation with how whites viewed him—assignment according to the constructionist approach.

Chino continues discussing his prejudicial and discriminatory treatment by whites, writing,

> *[They] Called me names, I was different, I was gifted, they made me ashamed*
> *Found out that I'm a different shade when I'm in the second grade*
> *Abe Lincoln's play, they want me to portray a slave*

Not only are members of this community discriminatory toward him, but he also receives similar reactions from his teachers at his local elementary school—implored to portray a slave in a play about Abraham Lincoln. Chino's lyrics ostensibly reveal that he was encouraged to feel embarrassed and self-conscious about his identity as a child among whites in his neighborhood and at his school. In the white community his mixed-race heritage was neither recognized nor acknowledged. He comes to view himself through the eyes of these individuals, similarly to Khanna's (2010) multiracial black respondents.

In his narrative, as a response to the racism that he receives in Middlesex, Chino's family moves to a predominately black area in Newark, New Jersey. Yet, as he rhymes, this engenders a "culture shock" because they moved into blighted, down-trodden, and poverty-stricken housing units: "Broadly called projects, black eyes, regrets/Torn lives, I've never seen so many people depressed." Albeit in dire poverty and seemingly hopeless, Chino finds that, ironically, even these individuals direct prejudice and discrimination toward him. When discussing the mistreatment by black people, Chino says,

> *My mental gets molested, physical takes violent threats*
> *Stress, walkin home from school's like a terrorist test*
> *I learned blacks could be racist too. . . .*
> *Even my teachers called me half-breeds and all of that*

Black youth physically and verbally assaulted Chino. As he profoundly states, blacks can indeed be just as racist as whites. He suffers what he believes to be terrorism by the local African American children. Similarly to authorities in Middlesex, he also receives a negative reaction from the teachers in Newark. Specifically, they refer to him as a "half-breed," a derogatory term that historically referred to a half-white and half-black person (Christian 2000). Thus, Chino was assigned a nonblack identity by blacks and not considered part of this community.

Chino concludes, "White people didn't accept me/. . . Black people didn't accept me/. . . Puerto Ricans didn't accept me/. . . Diggin' researchin' my identity it gots me goin cuckoo." In his most explicit statement to this point, Chino articulates not being accepted by whites, blacks, or Puerto Ricans. Indeed, this is the marginal man conundrum—lack of acceptance, acknowledgment, or recognition by any one particular race (Reuter 1969, Stonequist 1937). Not fitting in anywhere leaves him "cuckoo" when attempting to self-identify. Chino apparently personifies an unadjusted person both marginalized and confused about his identity (Cheng and Lively 2009, Reuter 1969, Stonequist 1937). Clearly, "race" and racial thinking permeate and are deeply embedded in the lives of people in these white and black communities, similarly to Khanna's (2010) respondents.

Drake, who possesses both black and Jewish ancestry (his mother is Jewish), is a platinum-selling artist who details similar reactions from whites in his song "S.T.R.E.S.S." released from his 2009 mixtape entitled *Room for Improvement*:

> *Picture when I was in school*
> *Me being the closest thing to black, and guess what, rap music [was what]*
> *   I was into*
> *Rest of the kids were sheltered*
> *I never liked to fight*
> *But when someone called me a "nigger" I'd punch them I couldn't help it*

Similarly to Chino XL, Drake attended a predominately white school when he was younger. He was called a racial epithet most often targeted toward blacks and responds violently to the verbal assault. As in Chino's case, whites are assigning a black identity to Drake via the use of this racial slur.

When of dating age Drake rhymes, "And your daddy want it very right/I make you happy, plus I'm Jewish, he don't approve, I think he want you to marry white." Here he reveals the anti-Semitism leveled against him by the white father of his girlfriend. Interestingly, he, and apparently the father, makes a distinction between being Jewish and being white. Jewishness as he (and the white father) defines it is non-white, not religiously connotated. Historically, some scholars argue that Jews were racialized; they became "white," undertaking a process of assimilation to the white Anglo-Saxon culture, along with other white immigrant groups (see Brodkin 1998). For Drake, his black and Jewish ancestries are "othered." Although Drake does not divulge and detail his experiences as much as Chino XL (these are the only lines where he refers to racial matters on all of his albums), race seems to have played a role in his life during this period.

Black identification
Both Chino XL and Drake ostensibly resolve the verbal and psychological assaults they receive by ultimately identifying as black. Chino states,

> *Don't call me red-boned, or light and bright and damn [near] white*
> *I ain't no zebra, ain't half of [an] original either*
> *Don't call me mulatto I['ll] stab you with a broken bottle*
> *Callin' your brother oreo get off it yo, now Tom consider*
> *He could be like Chino XL, a yellow ass nigga*

In these lines Chino specifically dis-identifies with a mixed-race identification, as expressed through the pejoratives "mulatto" and "zebra" (half white and half black). Rather, he asserts a black identity, as seen through the embrace of the term "yellow ass nigga." When mentioning the hue "yellow" Chino references the wide skin tone spectrum within the African American community, specifically dark to light shades of color. Attempting to align "light-ness" with "blackness," he samples the words of another song in his music:

> *I'm the yellow nigga right?*
> *I'm tired of that, I am not passing, I am black!*
> *I was born black, I live black*
> *And I will die, proud to be called black!*

Thus, albeit "yellow" he seems to claim a "black" identity. Moreover, although oftentimes deployed as a demeaning word, many blacks have attempted to reclaim and redefine "nigga" as a term of endearment; the debate continues as to whether this has been achieved (Kennedy 2003). In reference to the discrimination he receives from the white father of a girlfriend, Drake responds, "Black is Black honey, even if he's very light/ And so I never been for dinner at they places." Instead of identifying as biracial or multiracial, Drake (like Chino) adheres to the one-drop rule, implicitly stating that no matter the skin tone—even if lighted-skinned as a result of racially or ethnically different parents—black *is* black. Though both acknowledge their different racial and ethnic backgrounds and face prejudice and discrimination from blacks and whites in their respective communities, they each claim a black identity, paralleling the choices made by other black mixed-race individuals (Davis 1991, Khanna 2010). However, this is not the case with other multiracial rap artists.

Afro DZ ak and Michael Franti

Afro DZ ak, an "underground rapper," has black and undetermined ancestry. He proclaims in his song "Multiversity" that

> *Most cats limit themselves to one single category*
> *But when it comes to me*
> *that don't even tell half a story . . .*

> *Cuz I'm Multiracial, Multitalented*
> *Multilingual, finding the perfect balances . . .*

> *We become xenophobes*
> *equate different with trouble*
> *But me, I'm proud to speak French*
> *proud to be Congolese.*

Afro DZ ak seems critical of those who narrowly define themselves, whether along racial, linguistic, or other lines. He identifies as multiracial (as well as multilingual), specifically stating that he is proud to speak French and be Congolese, refuting that idea that difference of any type is problematic. He asserts a broad-based and all-encompassing identity with multiple cultural backgrounds, rejecting the idea of the one-drop rule. This "all inclusive" perspective is seemingly held by other mixed race rappers.

In the song "Socio-Genetic Experiment," Michael Franti, then lead member of the 1990s alternative group the Disposable Heroes of Hiphoprisy (and now part of the eponymous Michael Franti and Spearhead), writes about his experiences being "African [and] Native American [and] Irish and German." Initially projecting himself as a marginal man he writes, "sometimes I feel like a socio-genetic experiment/ a petri-dish community's token of infection." Similarly to Chino and Drake, he was "called . . . nigger on the walk home from school," identified as black through the deployment of the n word from whites. After he "cried until I found out what it meant," he remarks that he reacted with his "fists" and that he was a "hitman with no friends." Yet, he continues, "but who the hell am I cursing those whose skin/is half my DNA." Ostensibly, Franti contends that his genetic makeup (here a proxy for race) includes white genes; therefore, he questions his anger toward them.

Despite the forms of prejudice and discrimination he articulates, Franti does not choose to identify himself with only one race or ethnicity:

but I am not solely race, nor environment, nor destiny
I am the human scientific process
over and over and over again

but that is in fact my identity
uncluttered by the maskings of consumer addiction
ethno-centricity

Franti ostensibly views himself as part of the human evolutionary process, in this case individuals of different backgrounds intermingling and mating with one another over time. Furthermore, he rebuffs "ethnocentricity," refusing to espouse the cultural superiority of one racial or ethnic group over another. He ends his rhyme by asserting that he feels like a socio-genetic experiment and is "proud" of it, a declaration of multiracial identity and rejection of a narrowly defined monoracial identity.

Conclusion

The artists highlighted illustrate the constructionist approach. Through their interactions with peers, friends, teachers, and neighbors in their communities, as well as integrating or refuting conventional understandings of race, they project and articulate particular claims about their identities. In each instance, artists seemed to make classifications based on how they saw themselves, how others viewed them, and the manifestations (and resolutions) of racial tensions in their communities. Several dimensions and components of the constructionist approach were at work—assigned and asserted identities intersecting with thick ties. Yet, substantively, final racial selections elucidate how race and racial identity may be understood in broader society.

Chino XL and Drake ostensibly choose to align and classify their identities as black, maintaining the one-drop rule: any black ancestor makes a person black. Ultimately, these two rap artists promote essentialist perceptions of race and ethnicity, which leaves them potentially trapped in a "choose-one-race" racial paradigm. Their decisions reinscribe the conventional, hegemonic construction that an individual must represent one, and only one, racial classification because races are seen as distinct groups who are biologically and genetically determined. Indeed, this notion itself can result in the marginal man complex within mixed-race individuals, as explicated in previous literature (Cheng and Lively 2009, Reuter 1969, Stonequist 1937)—creating a disconnect between the selected racial group (by not being fully accepted) as well as the nonselected racial group. For example, Khanna and Johnson (2010) and Khanna (2010) find that black-white biracials who identify as black around monoracial blacks chose not to disclose their white ancestry for fear of stigmatization.

Afro DZ ak and Michael Franti apparently select a multiracial identity, freeing themselves of the potential problems that Chino XL and Drake face. Clearly, they critique those of multiple ancestries being forced to select one specific racial identification. This viewpoint aligns with academic scholars and various social movements addressing mixed-race identification who state that this population should not face limitations by individuals or government agencies in reference to how they classify themselves (Root 1992, Robbin 2000). Furthermore, some scholars argue that because members of this population selectively identify how they want when they want, there is not confusion or psychological distress on their parts (Rockquemore and Brunsma 2002). Indeed, Afro DZ ak and Michael Franti demonstrate this point. Concurring with these two, Leverette (2009:444), a biracial instructor, argues that revealing her identity as multiracial, not solely black, to her students "foster[s] new ground on which we can stand for a common cause as diverse individuals within heterogeneous communities." Thus, this orientation presents an alternative to that articulated by Chino XL and Drake. Yet, both these perspectives embody the larger discourse surrounding racial dynamics in the United States, especially for multiracial individuals.

Speaking to a larger conversation on race, some pundits and commentators posit that the United States has become (or will soon be) a post-racial/colorblind society because of the presidential election of Barack Obama. Yet, the influence of the one-drop rule still exists—our first mixed-race president checked the "black, African American, and Negro" box on the census, not white or other racial categories. He states that he, in part, identifies himself by how others see him. Hence, how "others" view "us," whether unconventional or rigid, impacts how we understand ourselves and, more important, our livelihoods, as illustrated by both symbolic interactionism and the constructionist approach. Yet, multiple researchers have found that blacks experience lower-quality education in comparison to other racial groups, and higher levels of concentrated poverty, joblessness, and prejudice and discrimination in comparison to other racial groups. Arguably, whether one is viewed as a black-white admixture, or some other black multiracial combination, the treatment they experience whether on the job or applying for a loan may be more in line with monoracial black experiences than their other nonblack racial or ethnic identities (see Chino XL and Drake). Nevertheless, it is important to recognize that racial identity is not static and rigidly defined. Race is a social construct; however, it has real consequences in a society where people are *still* judged along racial lines. Some multiracial rappers seem to express this point.

Discography

Chino XL. 1996. "What Am I." *Here to Save You All*. American Recordings.
Drake. 2009. "S.T.R.E.S.S." *Room for Improvement*. Mixtape.
Afro DZ ak. 2008. "Multiversity." *Elevation*. Gnawledge Records.
Disposable Heroes of Hiphoprisy. 1992. "Socio-genetic Experiment." *Hypocrisy Is the Greatest Luxury*. Pgd/4th & Broadway Records.

Notes

1. Hollywood movies such as *Imitation of Life* (1934) and *Jungle Fever* (1991) depict and characterize mixed-race identity as tragic or confused. Furthermore, Kraszewski (2010) finds that mixed-race young adults are presented on the popular MTV show *The Real World* as bewildered and in need of help from monoracial white cast members.

2. Lyrics were obtained from the website the *Original Hip Hop (Rap) Lyrics Archive*.

12

Skinhead Identity Contested
Ska Music, Racism, and Youth Culture
Daniel Sarabia

Far from uniform, the skinhead subculture is a splintered, heterogeneous, and consequently contentious cultural terrain. Factional divisions give rise to various claims to skinhead identity, including anti- and nonracist skinheads. Ideational expressions of skinhead identity in the musical genre of ska are analyzed. Informal interviews corroborate important cultural markers that delineate the factions.

Turf wars over authenticity and culture characterize the competing factions present in myriad subcultures. Despite mainstream public perception of a single, uniform group, skinheads are far more heterogeneous than many understand. When the term skinhead enters into public discourse it's often to single out a racist and xenophobic element to advance, through violence, a white separatist agenda. This characterization is largely accepted by the majority and speaks to the frustration expressed by some subcultural members. Media reports, along with coverage in the academic literature, fuel this perception and account for a distorted view. Violence within the subculture does make for sensationalist news, but when you begin to unpeel the homogeneous presentation you find a varied group that also includes nonracist and antiracist factions.

The splintered skinhead subculture has its origins in the working-class and immigrant neighborhoods of 1960s England (Marshall 1991). During this period, British youth culture drew from the music, language, and style of West Indian immigrants. The early influence of this immigration can be observed in the development of English "mod" culture, a precursor to the skinheads. Although the mods benefited from the cultural exchange with West Indian immigrants, they sought to distance themselves from the shared working-class existence. Escapism characterized a mod culture that through appearance and style wanted to shed its working-class roots. By the late 1960s, the mod subculture began to fracture, with "fashion mods" remaining faithful to the bourgeois aspirations of the group and "hard mods" reconnecting with their working-class backgrounds (Hebdige 2004 [1979]). Beyond a consideration of class, music also came to distinguish the two groups. Hard mods continued to follow the West Indian music imported by Jamaican immigrants, in particular ska, rocksteady, and reggae. The fashion mods gravitated toward the newly emerging acid rock and fashion-conscious hippie cultures of 1960s England (the Austin Powers films come to mind). While working-class elements found their way into hard mod culture, true to their subcultural history they maintained a distance from their working-class backgrounds.

Skinheads first surfaced in the England of 1967 and embraced elements of the hard mod style. Most important to the identity of the subculture, they celebrated their working-class backgrounds (Hebdige 2004 [1979], Marshall 1991, Zellner 1995). Additionally, the "caricature of the model worker" surfaced in the style and dress adopted by skinheads (Hebdige 2004 [1979]:55). The material elements of the culture became an important identifier that included the musical genre of choice for the group, Jamaican ska, which also went by the name of "bluebeat" or "skinhead reggae." Like their hard mod counterparts, early skinheads were a fixture in English reggae clubs and helped propel the popularity of the musical genre in the late 1960s.

To date, the contact with Jamaica's ska and "rude boy" subculture is observable in skinhead style, language, and dress. The terms *rude boy* and *rudy* not only describe supporters of ska music but historically have been used to refer to the marginalized Jamaican youth of the 1950s (Stolzoff 2000). Rude boy subculture, including its music, was exported to Britain and found its way into working-class neighborhoods. Early skinhead reggae recognized this history, and cultural borrowing, as references to rude boy culture were made in song and style. Jamaican artists who identified with rude boys recognized in their English audiences the frustration and alienation of youth (Stolzoff 2000). They also understood that music is important to youth culture and its expression. By the late 1960s, Jamaican artists began to acknowledge skinhead subculture in music. Emulating popular ska musicians, skinhead material culture adopted the neat and clean-cut look that characterizes the visual style of rude boys (Brake 1985). Image and appearance became important markers of skinhead identity and did have their origins in the cultural aesthetic advanced by both rude boys and hard mods.

The history of skinheads is intertwined with West Indian immigrants, and it's the roots of this relationship that become important to consider when the moniker "traditional" is introduced. Traditional skinheads emerged in Britain in the late 1960s and in the United States in the early 1980s. To identify as a traditional skinhead means to adopt the style, dress, music, and values of the original skinheads. These are self-described "purists" who distance themselves from the various permutations of skinhead culture and in particular a racist element. The essential material elements of skinhead culture can still be found today, and that includes contemporary music bands such as Scofflaws and Let's Go Bowling and journeymen Jamaican bands such as the Skatalites who continue to play traditional ska.

A racist skinhead faction first emerged in the Britain of the 1970s with the rise of the National Front Party. During a period of unemployment and economic instability, the party's message resonated with disenfranchised youth. The politics of racism soon found their way into music, and whereas the original skinheads continued to support Jamaican ska music, the racist element gravitated toward rock, punk, and Oi music. The genre of "white power" rock soon emerged to articulate the politics of nationalist groups. Bands such as Skrewdriver, whose lead singer was an organizer for the National Front Party, became torchbearers for the white nationalism advocated by racist groups. Speaking to the heterogeneity of the group, this period also saw the rise of other factions that included Oi, anarchist, and socialist skinheads.

When in the early 1980s skinhead culture, both traditional and racist, was exported to the United States, the media took note. However, the mainstream fascination with the subculture was with its racist faction. In spite of the sensationalism linked to white supremacist skinheads, traditional skinheads continued to have a presence in the United States, and in the past twenty-five years "antiracist" skinhead groups have surfaced. Unlike some traditional skinhead groups who prioritize style and music over an ideological agenda, antiracist skinheads actively seek to challenge and confront the ideology of white power skinheads. A militant stance toward combating racism within the subculture has been taken by groups such as Skinheads Against Racial Prejudice (SHARP). SHARP skinheads first emerged in New York City in 1987 and now have organized chapters throughout the United States and Canada (Wood 1999b). The group advocates violence as a means for "weeding out" the racist element within the subculture. As rationale, they argue that racism is inherently inconsistent with the values espoused and celebrated by the original skinheads. Zero tolerance for white power ideology has become mantra and is advocated not only by SHARP but by other antiracist factions, such as the United Front and Anti-Racist Action (Sarabia and Shriver 2004).

Without being dismissive of the importance of covering the presence of racism within the subculture, this chapter reveals the multiplicity and heterogeneity that aptly describes skinhead culture. The multiple factions don't all subscribe to one overarching perspective on race or racism. Traditional skinheads embrace original skinhead ideals and emphasize class consciousness and racial unity, but there also are racist groups who advocate racial violence, discord, and hate. In noting the shared material culture, it can be difficult for the layperson to distinguish between various skinhead factions if simply guided by appearance. Ideological differences do exist, and upon careful examination of cultural elements, material distinctions are also observed.

When surveying past studies, one finds that research on skinheads has largely led to investigations of racist factions with an emphasis on deviance within the subculture (Hamm 1993, Ridgeway 1990, Suall and Halpern 1993). Noting the interest in deviance in subcultural studies, it's not a shock that political disenfranchisement, inequality, and dissatisfaction would be treated as contributing factors to subcultural membership (Cohen 1955). More recently, studies have argued that far from existing at the margins of culture, subcultures may adopt values publicly known and shared by the mainstream (Young and Craig 1997). Whereas the mainstream may fall short of acting on values such as equality, subcultures may surface to lend criticism and put into practice ideals celebrated by the society. Taking a different approach, of particular interest in this chapter is the construction and maintenance of identity among traditional skinheads. Within the collective behavior and in particular new social movements literature, this has received much attention. *Collective identity* can be understood as a "shared definition of a group that derives from members' common interests, experiences, and solidarity constructed through interaction in social movement communities and as shaped by factors such as political opportunities, availability of resources, and organizational strength" (Taylor and Whittier 1995:172).

Three dimensions of collective identity are emphasized by Taylor and Whittier (1992) as important to group solidarity: boundaries, consciousness, and negotiation. Delineating between one's group and another is a critical component of collective identity when subcultural fissures are present. Developing a "sense of oneness" allows for the maintenance of group identity in the midst of competing group definitions (Chasteen and Shriver 1998:3). Participation in subcultural venues, whether physical or virtual, can facilitate group consciousness where opportunities exist for interaction. The exchanges that occur between group members in various settings allow for the negotiation of meaning. The third dimension, negotiation, is also important to collective identity as it reinforces established meanings that serve as a counterweight to negative definitions imposed by outsiders.

Studies have also examined the use of narratives and discursive practices that facilitate meaning construction and community solidarity (Steward, Shriver, and Chasteen 2002; Cutting 2000). Narratives not only provide nonmembers with a glimpse into a social world but allow members to produce new meaning and definitions. Likewise, "discursive communities" in virtual or physical environments form to assist the construction of identity and the diffusion of collective consciousness (Steward, Shriver, and Chasteen 2002; Swidler 1986). The Internet, music, and subcultural venues are integral parts of the communication networks that members draw on to maintain identity (Jenkins and Eckert 1986, Knoke 1990).

In a social environment where competing definitions abound, how do traditional skinheads secure identity and safeguard their presence within the subculture? Not only does this group combat factional divisions within the subculture, but mainstream perceptions cast public doubt on their claims to authenticity. When media contributes to the popular understanding of the group as racist, it leads to evaluations by members that the culture is threatened and continues to be hijacked. Beyond verbal barbs, this frustration has in the past led to violence between factions (Roddy 2002, Schreck 2004, Wernowsky 2006).

In one such incident, two former friends, split by ideology, found themselves in the hospital from injuries linked to a violent confrontation between antiracist and racist skinheads (Wernowsky 2006). For outsiders reacting to this account, the story of skinheads at each others' throats may further substantiate the perception of violence within the subculture. The layperson may not be shocked by reading the news story. However, at the center motivating the conflict is the ideological differences that exist between factions. According to Wernowsky (2006:1), "a closer examination of the dueling schisms reveals deeply rooted differences—most centering on race among so-called traditional skinheads, nonracist skinheads and those who advocate white power." Beyond a material lifestyle, in many instances, youth link a subcultural identity with values and beliefs (Brake 1985). Aspects of nonmaterial culture are often expressed by skinheads and pointed to by members to delineate groups.

Of the salient aspects of culture, observable within the skinhead community is where music and ideology intersect. In regard to the former, long before skinheads were associated with racism, black Jamaican artists were spotlighting and celebrating their skinhead audiences in song. Skinhead reggae bands such as the Ethiopians, Symarip, and Toots and the Maytals were all acknowledging skinhead culture. An example of this history can be linked to the music of Mr. Symarip, who to this day continues to give a nod to the skinheads in traditional ska music such as in the album title song "Skinheads Dem a Come" (2006) and much earlier in "Skinhead Moonstomp" (1969). The awareness of audiences compelled bands like Symarip to celebrate consumers of their music in song. According to one traditional skinhead, "the [Black skinhead reggae] performers recognize who we are and expect us at their shows. It's not unusual that they acknowledge our presence." To the admiration for black musicians, one skinhead shared, "I was at a Skatalites show once and [skinheads] were chanting Roland Alphonso's name [the tenor sax player]. Everyone there was excited to see him and the rest of the band" (cited in Sarabia and Shriver 2004).

From the perspective of traditional skinheads, the embracement of Jamaican artists is central to the subculture and its identity. Racial unity has been a hallmark of original skinhead culture from its inception. Subcultural members often point to the observable relationship between skinheads and Jamaican musicians. Noting this historically, Hebdige (1979:53) points out that white British youth developed an "emotional affinity with black people" that "was transposed into style." The skinhead audience that attended Britain's reggae clubs in the 1960s respected black musicians. By adopting the slang, music, and style of West Indian immigrants, white British youth were able to create a bridge between themselves and blacks. Early in the development of skinhead culture, black musicians were celebrated and played a significant role. In recognizing this history, traditional skinheads find it inconsistent that racism would be linked to the subculture.

Historically, racial inclusiveness is observed and surfaces in song. For those outside the group who characterize skinheads as racist, it's a surprise to come to find white youth following black artists. Furthermore, it's difficult to explain the presence of nonwhites in the culture. In fact, early in its inception, black skinheads were a fixture, and people of color continue to be involved. While conducting fieldwork, this researcher came to observe Asian, Hispanic, white, and black skinheads at group clubs. The message of solidarity and racial unity is also presented by contemporary ska bands. Ska-P, for example, expresses this sentiment in their song "Mestizaje" (2001):

> African . . . Asian . . . Indian . . . Muslim
> White European, Australian Aborigine,
> Five continents in the same heart
> Multiracial, multicultural, multiracial, multicultural . . .
> From the Philippines to Central America from the North Pole to
>   Madagascar
> This world doesn't belong to anyone it's for everyone . . .
> Long live the mixture, let's live together in community . . .
> Neither your residence, nor creed . . . nor your color,
> nor any difference makes you superior
> You stupid racist cheat of a human being

Skinhead collective identity from its early history has emphasized a message of racial unity. According to a traditional skinhead of Hispanic descent, "I've been involved with the scene since I was twelve;

I'm now 35. I have black, white, Asian, and Mexican friends who are also involved, they are all skins. . . . People from the outside think it strange, but they just don't know."

Multiracial ska bands such as the Specials, Mobtown, and the Rudimentals (the latter a band from South Africa) carried and continue to diffuse a message of cross-racial solidarity and the value of a multicultural world. The celebration of diversity is carried in ska music and emphasized by subcultural members. One traditional skinhead points out, "It's important to draw on our strengths and understand the similarities between us as human beings. . . . Integration makes more sense to me than an agenda that would separate people." Racial tolerance figures prominently in traditional skinhead culture and is expressed publicly in song and dress. To the former, a subcultural member referenced a traditional ska record by Desmond Dekker and the Aces, "Unity" (1967):

> This is the time that we all should live as one, brothers.
> This is the time that we all should live as one, sisters.
> So come along brothers,
> And come along sisters.
> U.N.I.T.Y.
> This unity.
> So come along brothers and sisters
> We must live as one . . .

Though Desmond Dekker's intention may not have been to write a song to be used as a moral guidepost for skinheads, the interpretation of cultural artifacts by subcultural members is significant. Ultimately, it's to further substantiate their own understandings of skinhead ideals and to distance themselves from racists that traditional skinheads turn to ska music. In spite of mainstream perceptions, nonracist and antiracist skinheads find support for their own definitions of skinhead identity through material culture and group interactions. Relational communities, where individuals share interests and worldviews, function to provide opportunities for individuals to negotiate and make clear meanings.

Of fissures that exist within the subculture, racism figures prominently in the division present within factions. However, in addition to race, politics and class orientation also surface. For many within the skinhead culture, you can't be a skinhead and be apolitical. As one subcultural member noted, "You literally wear your ideals when you are a skinhead." Fashion in the culture is tied to meaning and symbolism (Marshall 1991). Strategic decisions about dress are made to establish boundaries in the subculture, but they also distinguish members from the mainstream. Analysts note, youth cultures draw on fashion to express identity and to highlight ideals and history as understood by the group (Brake 1985, Sarabia and Shriver 2004). There's also the celebration of the aesthetic in music by artists such as Laurel Aitken and Prince Buster that encourages adherence to skinhead style. Specific material objects surface in skinhead dress that are meant to resemble the utilitarian clothing of the working man. Although stylized, the nod to work through dress expresses the "lumpen identity" linked to the beginnings of the culture in Britain's working-class and immigrant neighborhoods (Hebdige 2004 [1979]:55).

According to Widdicombe and Wooffitt (1995), group adoption coupled by social context lends significance to material objects. One such cultural marker, Dr. Martens work boots, was first introduced in Britain during the early 1960s. Consistent with skinheads' cultural interest in things working class, the boots became popular with government workers, police officers, and men working in factories. Soon, along with Fred Perry polos and other cultural objects, skinheads adopted the boots and made them their own. Dressing becomes important to doing identity, and in the social world of subcultures it's essential to the expression of meaning. One traditional skinhead remarks, "It's not just fashion, but the boots, my laces, and patches all mean something to me." An idealized working-class appearance is tied to the ideational aspect of skinhead identity, values of hard work and dedication. One skinhead adds, "We don't like women-beaters. We're not thugs full of disrespect for everything. We work for a living" (cited in Jones 1994). As interpreted by members, traditional skinhead identity is tied to ideals established by early skinheads that advocated racial unity and class consciousness. The former is emphasized in Laurel Aitken's "Skinhead Invasion" (1970):

> *This is our sensation, all over the nation!*
> *Read all about it! read all about it!*
> *Skinhead invasion . . .*
> *Is not black, is not white, is what is right*
> *Everything will be all right if we just unite . . .*

Symbols not only demarcate boundaries between groups but express meaning. More specifically, language is also employed to communicate the positions and attitudes of group members (Widdicombe and Wooffitt 1995). Verbal communication through song and slang further delineates boundaries and serves to create community. Group membership is strengthened when individuals recognize cultural cues, artifacts, and slang familiar to members. Regarding the latter, one such term that surfaces repeatedly to distinguish between skinhead factions is "boneheads." In attempts to create distance between themselves and racists, traditional skinheads use the derogatory term *bonehead* to identify those with a white-power agenda. Considering the history of the subculture, traditional skinheads are repulsed by the presence of racism. From their perspective, it's inconsistent with the embrace of West Indian culture by white working-class youth. As one traditional skinhead observes, "Neo-nazis . . . have adopted the skinhead look in an attempt to hijack the movement" (cited in Sarabia and Shriver 2004:284). The negative perceptions of the subculture don't escape traditional skinheads. It's in attempts to reclaim subcultural turf that some think it necessary to engage in efforts that would educate both the racist and layperson (Jones 1994, Smarsh 2001).

Through various means, traditional skinheads have sought to combat claims that link their culture with racism. Some have felt compelled to join antiracist organizations such as SHARP and Anti-Racist Action. The goals of these organizations are to create awareness of skinhead history and serve to counter the activities of racist elements. According to a member of Anti-Racist Action, "SHARPs exist . . . because the skinhead image predates the White Power skinheads and they want it back" (Wernowsky 2006:1). It's the feeling that their culture has been co-opted by racists that encourages proactive efforts to weed out the undesirable element—which has sometimes included violence (see Sarabia and Shriver 2004, Wernowsky 2006).

For all the generality that the term *skinhead* evokes, there is a multiplicity of definitions present in a splintered subculture that grapples with authenticity and competing meanings. Given the diversity, cultural ammunition is used by traditional skinheads to lay claims to their place in the culture. The interpretation of skinhead history and ideals becomes important to efforts to thwart negative stereotypes. Though for some traditional skinheads style and music take center stage—and not debates over class and race—they're aware of the political backdrop that underlies skinhead culture. In addition to traditional means of disseminating culture, traditional skinheads are a presence on Internet blogs, chat rooms, wikis, and websites. It's through traditional and alternative mediums that they seek to present a response to the racist label attached to the culture and bolster their claims to authenticity.

13

Lowbrow Entertainment to Highbrow Art Form
The Case of Jazz and Heavy Metal
Roscoe C. Scarborough

Drawing upon a comparative content analysis of news articles, editorials, and performance reviews concerning the jazz and heavy metal music genres in the *New York Times,* the author offers insight into how cultural products transition from lowbrow entertainment to highbrow art. The chapter shows how cultural entrepreneurs generate aesthetic mobility by framing a genre as legitimate culture and by authenticating its cultural products as highbrow art. Comparing the cases of jazz and heavy metal, the author argues that heavy metal has the potential for mobility to the status of highbrow art as it has fewer social hurdles to overcome than jazz a half century earlier.

In the early twenty-first century, jazz is consecrated as legitimate culture and authentic highbrow art while heavy metal remains disparaged as disreputable lowbrow entertainment. However, jazz was once understood to be illegitimate culture (e.g., *New York Times* 1935b), associated with disreputable musicians (e.g., *New York Times* 1935c), rioting (e.g., *New York Times* 1955), and delinquent behavior (e.g., *New York Times* 1935a). This is comparable to how heavy metal is still popularly received. Heavy metal is understood to be illegitimate culture (e.g., Riding 1985) that has associations with violence (e.g., Berlinkski 2005, Rockwell 1975), "death and madness" (Strauss 1995b), satanism (e.g., Palmer 1980c, Pareles 1985d), and misogynist gender values (e.g., Soyka 1985).

Bracketing concerns of form and content, I offer a distinctly sociological explanation that privileges how the actions of "cultural entrepreneurs" (DiMaggio 1982:35) result in the "aesthetic mobility" (Peterson 1994:179) of jazz and the immobility of heavy metal. Operating under the assumption that the perspectives espoused in the *New York Times* (*NYT*) are a proxy for the views of highly educated, influential, and culturally attuned Americans ("*New York Times:* Media Kit" 2011), I conduct a content analysis of eighty *NYT* news articles, editorials, and performance reviews on jazz and heavy metal. Drawing upon a systematic sample of jazz texts from 1935 to 2005 and heavy metal texts from 1975 to 2005, I analyze the actions of cultural entrepreneurs in an effort to identify social factors that lead to the aesthetic mobility of music genres.

Cultural entrepreneurs (including musicians, critics, producers, event managers, other gatekeepers, and even *NYT* writers) facilitate aesthetic mobility by framing a genre as legitimate culture and authenticating it as highbrow art. They frame music genres as legitimate culture by (1) idealizing a genre's disreputable past and (2) appropriating a suitable lineage to a genre's "roots" or to the European classical music tradition. Further, they authenticate genres as highbrow art by swaying critics and consumers that as cultural products they (1) appeal to an artistic aesthetic, (2) should be evaluated by the genre's own conventions, and (3) are attributable to specific composers.

Jazz and Heavy Metal: Analogous Genesis and Development

Beyond the objective characteristics of a genre, such as complex musical structures and the necessity for virtuosic, technically proficient players in jazz (Gioia 1997, Lopes 2002) and heavy metal (Walser 1993, Weinstein 2000), both genres have comparable developmental trajectories (Lena and Peterson 2008). Historically, both jazz and heavy metal were initially created and performed by marginalized groups and were not intended for commercial consumption (DeVeaux 1997, Gioia 1997, Walser 1993, Weinstein 2000). Both genres evolved into music scenes that are publicly reviled but then eventually transitioned into widely successful industrial stages (DeVeaux 1997, Early 1998, Lopes 2002, Waksman 2009, Walser 1993, Weinstein 2000). At present, those invested in each genre seek to preserve their genre's musical heritages (Early 1998, Gioia 1988, Lopes 2002, Walser 1993, Weinstein 2000). Despite the similarities in their development, jazz is consecrated as highbrow art and heavy metal is disparaged as lowbrow entertainment.

Framing a Genre's History

Before a cultural product can be authenticated as highbrow art, cultural entrepreneurs must properly frame it as legitimate culture among cultural and economic elites by (1) idealizing or disassociating the genre from a deviant past and (2) appropriating a legitimate developmental lineage for the genre. The efforts of jazz cultural entrepreneurs from the 1930s through the 1970s and heavy metal cultural entrepreneurs from the 1970s until the present to legitimate their genres have many similarities, but supporters of jazz have made greater headway in their efforts.

Overcoming the Conundrum of a Deviant Past

At various points in history, both jazz and heavy metal have been vilified as lowbrow entertainment that is steeped in negative connotations due to associations with immoral people and deviant activities. To establish their genre as legitimate culture, jazz and heavy metal cultural entrepreneurs have attempted to idealize or limit pejorative associations with deviant musicians and audiences. Compared to their jazz peers, heavy metal cultural entrepreneurs have had less success at cleaning up the reputation of their genre.

Until the 1970s, cultural entrepreneurs continued to battle "old myths" associated with jazz musicians, such as, "The jazz player can't read music. He comes to rehearsals late or drunk or high on narcotics. He cannot or will not do commercial jingles" (Goodman 1975). This documents jazz cultural entrepreneurs' now triumphant struggle to reframe pejorative conceptions enduring from a deviant past. Similarly, heavy metal cultural entrepreneurs' attempts to limit associations with a deviant past are captured in *NYT* texts with titles like "Being Smart about Music That Isn't" (Strauss 1995a), "A Kind of Boutique Metal Offers a Refined Approach to Headbanging" (Powers 2000), "Ozzy Osbourne, Without the Birds and Bats" (Pareles 2000), and "Heavy Metal Gets an M.F.A.: How Did Headbangers Become the Headiest Genre in Popular Music?" (Caramanica 2005). To offer an example, Caramanica (2005) writes, "Metal in general has long been unjustly maligned as solely the province of knuckle-dragging meatheads. . . . That said, there's never been a group of musicians like there is now, who are helping to advance the form." Reviews of this sort attempt to limit disreputable status of heavy metal, but heavy metal cultural entrepreneurs have made relatively little progress compared to those invested in cleaning up the reputation of jazz.

Establishing a Legitimate Pedigree

For a genre to be accepted by elites as highbrow art, it must not only lack a sordid past but also possess a legitimate social and cultural pedigree. Cultural entrepreneurs establish this through (1) association with or appropriation of the Western classical music tradition or (2) by framing the genre as having legitimate "roots" through an idealization

of a subcultural past. In jazz, cultural entrepreneurs have been successful at establishing ties to the classical music tradition while legitimizing
an understanding of jazz as a native, unique African American cultural
form. Conversely, heavy metal cultural entrepreneurs have been less
successful at establishing either of these associations.

In efforts to legitimate the genre, jazz cultural entrepreneurs parasiti-
cally draw upon the high status of classical music through performances
in classical music venues and with classical musicians (e.g., *New York
Times* 1945, Piazza 1995, Wright 1995). This can be characterized as
"[a] bold and transfiguring appropriation of a tract of the European
tradition" (Piazza 1995). Some even claim that the compositional rigor
of jazz makes it indistinguishable from contemporary classical music
(e.g., Rockwell 1985).

Cultural entrepreneurs also emphasize cultural and historical roots
of jazz in African American culture through efforts such as getting the
National Register of Historical Places to acknowledge the cultural
value of significant African American jazz landmarks (e.g., *New York
Times* 1985), through efforts to reinforce jazz communities (e.g., Ratliff
2005), and by raising awareness about the importance of jazz history
(e.g., Pareles 1985b). Jazz musicians also do their part to celebrate,
historicize, and canonize the genre by enacting live performances that
implicitly and explicitly offer historical lessons and highlight jazz as a
cultural form grounded in African American culture (e.g., Wilson 1965,
1975a; Pareles 1985a, 1985c). When combined with positive associations with highbrow classical music, these ties to African American
culture provide a lineage that legitimates the genre.

In the heavy metal world, cultural entrepreneurs vie for cultural
legitimacy by establishing associations with the classical music tradition, cultural "roots" in white working-class culture, and musical
"roots" in the African American blues musical tradition. Heavy metal
cultural entrepreneurs highlight comparable levels of virtuosity that
are required in both the classical and heavy metal genres (e.g., Pareles
1990). In addition, some bands are construed as using heavy metal "as
a jumping-off point for a range of experimental styles . . . [including]
modern classical music" (Caramanica 2005). However, there has been
little success at establishing this association with classical music outside
of select heavy metal scenes. Cultural entrepreneurs have had much
greater success at establishing cultural origins in the white working-
class culture of Birmingham, England (e.g., Palmer 1980b; Sanneh
2005; Strauss 1995c, 2000) and some success at emphasizing musical
foundations in the African American blues tradition, including Willie
Dixon, Muddy Waters, and Robert Johnson. For example, bands are
construed as having legitimate cultural roots if they can be historically
tied to "the cusp of the 1960s and 70s, the era of Cream and early Led
Zeppelin and Black Sabbath, when blues-rock was turning into heavy

metal" (Pareles 1990). As a whole, heavy metal cultural entrepreneurs have had less success than their jazz peers at establishing associations that offer a legitimate social and cultural pedigree for the genre.

Authenticating Highbrow Art

Beyond framing a genre as legitimate culture, cultural entrepreneurs can further facilitate aesthetic mobility by attempting to authenticate it as highbrow art among cultural and economic elites. To accomplish this task, cultural entrepreneurs must sway critics and consumers to accept that a genre's cultural products (1) appeal to an artistic aesthetic, (2) should be evaluated by the genre's own conventions, and (3) are attributable to specific composers.

Appealing to an Artistic Aesthetic

For a cultural product to experience aesthetic mobility to the status of highbrow art, it must be construed by cultural entrepreneurs as appealing to an artistic aesthetic. For jazz, an artistic rhetoric emerges in the *New York Times* during the 1950s but becomes the hegemonic manner for understanding the genre by the 1990s. Conversely, an artistic rhetoric is increasingly employed as a framework for understanding heavy metal, but this has not come to dominate how the genre is understood.

NYT texts from the first half of the twentieth century detail the characteristics of jazz performances based on entertainment qualities rather than musical form. As early as the 1950s, calls to recognize the artistic merits of jazz begin to appear in the newspaper—for example, jazz pianist Mary Lou Williams's claims that "jazz is the only true art in the world" (Wilson 1975b). By the 1980s, jazz is hegemonically understood as serious art. For example, a performance review outlining Chick Corea's trio employs an artistic rhetoric to describe the performances of individual musicians:

> Mr. Vitous often treats the acoustic stand-up bass as a self-contained orchestra. His signature style is a florid, frequently witty bowing of the instrument to produce overlapping conversational voices. Mr. Haynes's drumming supplies much more than a backbeat. In carefully blocked ensemble arrangements, it splices and redefines the spirit of a tune with an impressive split-second precision. (Holden 1985)

The language used in this review departs from earlier texts that focus on the entertainment qualities of a performance; instead, it assesses players' improvisational skill and ability to "say something" (Monson 1996). Though its entertainment purposes are not denied, jazz is now hegemonically assessed as serious art.

In the heavy metal world, art and heavy metal music have historically been understood to be mutually exclusive. A 1975 (Edwards) performance review of Led Zeppelin supports this position: "While there is plenty of heavy-metal rock in evidence, Led Zeppelin can now offer up a 'Stairway to Heaven.' The group's identity seems split exactly in half." In the 1970s, the art in Led Zeppelin's music is understood to be independent of the heavy metal elements of its music. This attitude persists, but cultural entrepreneurs have made some headway toward instituting an artistic rhetoric as the basis for interpreting heavy metal. For example, Powers (2000) reviews a Queens of the Stone Age performance:

> Mr. Homme's playing remained the focus on Saturday. He displayed the most unlikely quality: tastefulness. Spare solos only sometimes erupted into the climaxes one expects from a metal god. Mostly Mr. Homme toyed with choppy riffing or sinuous cadences, encouraging an introspective mood. His self-control, complemented by the resolute accuracy of the bassist, Nick Oliveri, and the drummer, Gene Troutmann, allowed for the crucial and uncommon element of sonic distance. This is not to say the music avoided the impact needed to stimulate headbanging.

While this review does not eschew the entertainment value of the show, it explicitly engages with the performance as serious art. Further, explicit lyrics, overt satanism, violence, and male-centered hypersexuality are increasingly interpreted as art, on par with "Picasso's *Guernica*, William Burroughs's *Naked Lunch*, [and] Alfred Ayler's 'Bells'" (Pareles 1985d). Art and heavy metal are no longer construed as antithetical. However, an artistic rhetoric has not yet supplanted the entertainment rhetoric as the dominant interpretive frame through which the genre is assessed.

Appropriating Internal Conventions of Evaluation

A second method used by cultural entrepreneurs to authenticate a genre as highbrow art is to establish a genre's own artistic "conventions" (Becker 2008 [1982]) as the legitimate criteria for evaluating its cultural products. Both jazz and heavy metal cultural entrepreneurs have made significant progress toward this end.

In *NYT* texts, calls for jazz music to be assessed using these internal conventions appear as early as the 1950s. In a 1955 editorial reflection upon the newspaper's treatment of jazz, Garner states,

> the point is that all the effective descriptions, pro and con, and even the more serious attempts, miss the point. Almost nobody gets down to jazz form! Maybe Duke Ellington beat us to it in 1932 when he wrapped it up in a song: "It don't mean a thing if you ain't got that swing."

This editorial argues the point that jazz should be assessed by its own conventions. This type of assessment does not become hegemonic until the 1980s. For example, a 1995 review of a live performance by aging first-generation beboppers Johnny Griffin and Milt Jackson privileges internal conventions in its assessment of the show:

> Mr. Griffin has always been a quick player, and an eccentric one, and he opened the show by playing "Just One of Those Things" at a nearly stupefyingly fast tempo. Yet his solo was coherent, with swoops and blues cries and runs that melted the notes into one another. With the next tune, his own "You've Never Been There," every note seemed to take on its own color. He swallowed some notes, hinted at others or bent them this way and that. His phrasing was wildly creative, with each idea taking on a new relationship to the steady pulse of the music, slowing down, rushing nervously or landing percussively on the bouncing syncopations between downbeats. (Watrous 1995)

By focusing on Griffin's improvisational ability, this evaluation privileges the internal conventions of jazz. At present, the conventions for the judgment of jazz are firmly institutionalized as the only legitimate standards for evaluating the genre. One critic (Pareles 1995) even argues that the conventions of jazz have become so reified that "there have been no significant innovations since Coltrane."

Historically, heavy metal has not been assessed on its own terms (e.g., Dove 1975). It is often critiqued by the conventions of rock music and characterized as "the loudest, crudest, most basic brand of rock" (Palmer 1980a). Beginning in the 1990s, cultural entrepreneurs begin to assess performances using the conventions of the heavy metal world. For example, a performance review of the band Slayer highlights how heavy metal has come to be assessed by its own standards:

> On Friday, Paul Bostaph, the band's new drummer, hammered out fast, mechanical tempos, his feet constantly kicking at two bass drums. Mr. Araya and the guitarists Kerry King and Jeff Hanneman constructed precise, synchronized riffs out of minor chords, occasionally breaking the pattern with a screeching solo or, during the long introduction to "Seasons in the Abyss," evocative horror-movie-style music. Unlike most other heavy-metal bands and hard-core bands, Slayer didn't provide a release for its audience but an anesthetic. (Strauss 1995b)

In this review, like most contemporary assessments, it is clear that the internal conventions of heavy metal have become established as the proper method for assessing and critiquing the genre.

Attribution of Compositional Credit

Highbrow art is attributable to a unique artist or composer. Attribution of compositional credit differentiates these products from profane, everyday cultural objects and takes strides toward creating an aura of originality and highbrow authenticity. It is yet another step taken by cultural entrepreneurs in their efforts to authenticate each genre's cultural products as highbrow art.

Departing from a history of being understood as anonymous entertainment, cultural entrepreneurs in both genres make strides toward attributing compositions and performances to specific individuals. Through the 1950s, jazz music is an anonymous entertainment spectacle that is not commonly attributed to a specific composer. By the 1980s, it becomes ubiquitous to acknowledge a specific individual as the composer of a piece of music. In the heavy metal world, the attribution of compositional credit for specific musical selections is uncommon in the early years of the genre but becomes commonplace by the 1990s. However, the composer remains somewhat anonymous in the heavy metal genre because selections are more often attributed to an entire band as opposed to an individual composer. Thus, the attribution of compositional credit in heavy metal does not provide a comparable boost of artistic authenticity as it does in the jazz genre.

Highbrow Art Worlds

Once a genre is framed as legitimate culture and its cultural products are authenticated as highbrow art in the minds of cultural and economic elites, the cultural entrepreneurs' task of facilitating aesthetic mobility is complete. Though jazz and heavy metal cultural entrepreneurs both attempt this process, jazz's cultural entrepreneurs have made much more progress toward legitimizing the culture of jazz and authenticating it as a highbrow art among elites than their heavy metal counterparts. Recognition and support from elites allow a highbrow jazz art world to exist, while heavy metal remains disparaged as lowbrow entertainment. Nevertheless, a heavy metal art world exists. Its participants simply operate without recognition or support from cultural and economic elites.

A Highbrow Jazz Art World

Cultural entrepreneurs have successfully framed jazz as legitimate culture and authenticated its cultural products as highbrow art. To place this transition in historical context, a 1975 (Goodman) article discusses jazz as receiving $550,000 in funding out of $16 million for the National Endowment of the Arts. In the piece, jazz trumpeter Jimmy Owens states, "It's our only indigenous music and such a small sum is disgraceful. But at least I can argue for more. That is more than a foot in the door" (Goodman 1975). Over time, jazz gained credibility. Cultural entrepreneurs successfully established a past-oriented, neo-classicist movement that marginalizes contemporary jazz (see Gioia 1988). In 1987, Congress officially authenticated jazz as "a true music of the people" that is "an indigenous American music and art form, bring[ing] to this country and the world a uniquely American musi-cal synthesis and culture through the African American experience" ("House Congressional Resolution 57" in Berliner 1994:759).

By the 1990s, Wynton Marsalis—a "magnetic jazz and classical trumpeter" (Wright 1995) and jazz's leading cultural entrepreneur (Nicholson 2005)—successfully emphasized jazz's roots in black history while upholding associations with highbrow classical music. With the support of cultural and economic elites, Marsalis was placed in charge of the Lincoln Center for Jazz in New York City in 2004 ("Jazz at Lincoln Center" 2011). As the world's first multimillion-dollar performing arts institution designed specifically for jazz performance, education, and broadcast ("Jazz at Lincoln Center" 2011), jazz now has an institutional base on par with a major opera company or a symphony orchestra, which is a testament to the genre's institutionalization as a highbrow art.

A Highbrow Heavy Metal Art World?

Heavy metal cultural entrepreneurs have made some progress toward authenticating the genre's cultural products as art, but they have had less success at destigmatizing the social and cultural history of the genre and establishing a legitimate pedigree. Heavy metal is not ac-cepted as legitimate culture by elites, which inhibits its authentication as highbrow art in the early twenty-first century.

Heavy metal remains culturally illegitimate lowbrow entertainment that is overwhelmingly performed in night clubs, arenas, amphitheaters, and stadiums, though it has been performed in several prestigious, elite venues. For example, Ozzy Osbourne and Tony Iommi performed "Paranoid" at Buckingham Palace for the royal family in 2002, and other heavy metal groups, such as Metallica, have recorded and per-formed in symphony halls (Christe 2004:352–362). To be sure, this is a sign of the increasing legitimacy of heavy metal in the minds of elites. Sir Ozzy Osbourne, anyone?

Just because cultural entrepreneurs have not successfully authenti-cated heavy metal as highbrow art among elites does not mean there is a dearth of serious artistry in the genre. Many heavy metal musicians are currently practicing the genre as a serious art (Caramanica 2005).

A heavy metal art world already exists today, but its network of artistic producers and fans operates with relative independence from any art world that is endorsed by elites.

If the historical case study of jazz offers a basis of comparison, heavy metal's current status is not permanent. Heavy metal has fewer social hurdles inhibiting its consecration as a highbrow art than jazz did in the 1930s. Despite being overwhelmingly practiced by working-class African Americans, jazz experienced aesthetic mobility beginning in the 1950s. This demonstrates that associations with working-class origins, a stigmatized race, or a deviant subculture does not provide insurmountable impediments to attaining highbrow status. If cultural entrepreneurs are able to establish a legitimate pedigree for the genre, heavy metal may yet be authenticated as serious highbrow art among cultural and economic elites. To be sure, heavy metal is not perpetually bound to the depths of the lowbrow. It has the potential to someday become institutionalized as highbrow art.

Authenticity in Art Worlds

In this chapter, I discuss a system of stratification oriented to the cultural and artistic conventions of institutionalized, hegemonic, upper-middle class culture. This is only one possible ranking system. For example, most practitioners of "death metal" and Baroque classical music probably do not view the same musical compositions as the pinnacle of artistic accomplishment. Various subcultures and scenes have their own systems of hierarchical assessment, which are often at odds with the predominant stratification system oriented to the standards of cultural and economic elites.

These competing systems of stratification offer different grounds for authenticity, which brings the constructed nature of authenticity in art into full relief. It can be based on originality, credibility, or purity. Highbrow artistic authenticity is associated with cultural and economic elites' acknowledgment of a cultural product as "serious" art. Alternatively, cultural products can be understood to be authentic when they are created in an unmediated environment independent of the culture industry or institutionalized art worlds. Clearly, authenticity is contested, and its criteria depend upon one's vantage point in the social world. Though authenticity offers legitimacy and social value, it is not an objective-free appraisal. It is a social construct with moral undertones that is always performed, staged, fabricated, crafted, or otherwise imagined by invested cultural entrepreneurs with particular goals operating in a complex social world (see Fine 2003, Grazian 2003, Peterson 1997).

In the world of music, highbrow authenticity and subcultural or scene-specific authenticity are fundamentally at odds with one another.

From the vantage point of elites who represent already institutional-ized art worlds, jazz is interpreted as legitimate culture and authentic highbrow art worthy of scholarly recognition and preservation in the major conservatories of classical music (Gennari 2006, Nicholson 2005). Meanwhile, heavy metal holds the infamy of being the most disliked music genre (Bryson 1996). It is characterized as simple, anti-intellectual music focusing on hatred, violence, rebellion, and substance abuse that is made by those who are slack-jawed, unsophisticated, and lack all originality (Weinstein 2000:1–2). From the perspective of elites, heavy metal is not viewed as legitimate culture or authentic highbrow art—it is simple lowbrow entertainment. Conversely, authenticity for heavy metal musicians, fans, and cultural entrepreneurs does not require endorsement from this elite-oriented stratification system. In fact, they often embrace their exclusion as "proud pariahs" (Weinstein 2000).

This struggle for authenticity provides an avenue for fruitful future research. Attention must be paid to how other social actors, such as musicians, audiences, academics, actors in prestige-granting institu-tions, critics, and music industry workers, are involved in the social construction and attribution of different types of authenticity, legiti-mation, valorization, and institutionalization. A critical examination of these social actors' actions takes a substantial step toward the "demystification of authenticity" (Grazian 2010) in the sociology of music and in the sociology of culture.

Part IV
Experience of Music: Subcultures and Musical Enclaves

Music is one of our biggest exports. This young couple in Argentina said they listen to Goth music and found it meaningful enough to emulate the American style. Photo by Sara Towe Horsfall (2007).

14

Sect and Prophets
Neil Leonard

The author argues that the devotion found among early jazz musicians for their mentors is similar to the devotion found in religious sects. He likens the innovative jazzmen who inspired these jazz sects to religious prophets.

It became almost a cult after a while, and the ones who felt themselves musically strong enough would enter it.

—Drummer Kenny Clarke, on the early bop movement

Sect

Jazz has had a turbulent history, perhaps as turbulent as that of any art form in the chaotic climate of the twentieth century. Detested by some Americans, ignored by more, exploited by predatory businessmen, tied to the growing pains and uncertainties of the mass media, and subjected to the whims of fickle audiences in search of endless novelty, the music has changed extraordinarily quickly. Yet, for all the confusion accompanying its rapid development, some general tendencies are evident. One is that broad jazz movements tend to take on sectarian qualities, in terms of the Troeltschean[1] metaphor.

In Troeltsch's typology the "sect-type" springs up in tension with the church. Whereas the "church-type" is exclusive, accommodating, and hierarchical, the sect is exclusive, relatively uncompromising, lay oriented, and minimally structured—a small group of true believers sharing faith and fellowship. And, whereas in the church status and role are ascribed, in the sect they rest more on merit, connected to an

---

Originally published in Neil Leonard, "Prophets" in Jazz: Myth and Religion *(New York: Oxford University Press, 1987), pp. 19–45. Condensed from the original. Reprinted with permission.*

awareness of transcendent truth inaccessible to outsiders and fostering an elitist identity. Seeking self-sufficiency and inner perfection, sectarians may welcome, even recruit, converts but do not try to penetrate other groups, toward which their attitudes range from indifference to hostility.

There have been three jazz movements loosely fitting this pattern. The first developed slowly and unself-consciously out of the music of ragtimers like Scott Joplin, New Orleans pioneers such as Buddy Bolden, and then, in the Twenties, blues singers including Bessie Smith and instrumentalists dominated by Louis Armstrong. By the end of the Twenties their styles, variations, and various syntheses (all lumped together here as "early jazz") began to be regarded as more than just catchy folk or popular music. Uninformed sympathizers had earlier sought to "refine" jazz for polite society and the concert hall; now knowledge adherents began to take it seriously as an art form in and of itself. In the early Thirties a growing cadre of critics, record collectors, and others excitedly spread the word, pointing out what was real jazz, defending it against attacks from the orthodoxy, and explaining it in ways palatable to an expanding following mostly drawn to the smooth dilutions of swing, which was rapidly becoming *the* popular music of the day. Before Pearl Harbor the maturing early sect, having survived, even flourished despite orthodox onslaughts, evolved its own hardening tradition with mystique, rituals, myths, and saints (original and latter-day)—all serving to guide and legitimize accepted beliefs and practices. But as World War II got under way all was not well among the faithful. Young musicians, feeling too constrained, departed from the fold to create a disturbing new music called bop; and fundamentalists, troubled by this aberration and the commercial impurities of swing, launched the evangelical "Dixieland Revival," which returned to untainted, original jazz.

This, then, was the situation as the second sect-like movement crystallized in the Forties around bop, which conflicted less with the church-like orthodoxy than with entrenched early-jazz forces. Whereas the early sect had gradually outgrown its folk roots, the bop movement developed more rapidly. Inspired by Charlie Parker, Dizzy Gillespie, and others who rebelled against the clichés, settled character, and restrictive rituals of early jazz and swing, bop was an electrifying new style with pyrotechnical virtuosity, harsh melodies, dissonant harmonies, and breathtaking tempos which held a powerful message for hip, streetwise youngsters. After a period of gestation in Harlem, it migrated downtown to West Fifty-second Street, where its circle of devotees, now including whites, widened into a full-fledged sect during and after World War II. In the process it generated its own rituals, mythology, and critical machinery which helped define its values and defend them from a thunderous attack from early-jazz loyalists.

The intersectarian battle over bop did not spill over into the nonmusical world as much as the church-sect controversy over early jazz had in the Twenties, but within its limits it was equally intense and raised similar issues. Conservatives complained that bop was shrill, anarchic, impure, and contagious—dangerous to music and morality alike. Elder prophet Louis Armstrong called it "jujitsu music" and ruinous to jazz. And trumpeter Max Kaminsky reported, "it had such an upsetting effect on my nervous system that it actually made me feel nauseous." The boppers seemed like incompetent upstarts reaching for sensational effects, not only through outlandish music but through bizarre speech, dress, humor, and also through drugs. Upholders of early jazz and the orthodoxy tried to expunge the new pollution, telling the world of its evils and doing what they could to keep it from the public ear. In 1946 radio station KMPC in Los Angeles, following the precedent of forerunners in the Twenties, banned bop on the grounds that "it makes degenerates out of our young listeners." And *Time* magazine called it "hot jazz overheated, with overdone lyrics, full of bawdiness, references to narcotics, and double talk."

As the Fifties wore on the dispute predictably quieted down. Having lost some of its original zeal, the bop movement settled into a tradition of its own and split into two factions: "cool," which watered the music with conventional elements; and "funky," or "regressive," hard bop, which sought a return to the sounds or spirit of the Forties. But despite the ardor of the regressives, the lines between early jazz and bop, once sharp, now blurred. Increasingly musicians synthesized the two styles, both were played on the same stage at concerts and festivals, and formerly partisan publications treated both sympathetically. Bop, in effect, had now joined early jazz in the increasingly respectable jazz world.

But as it did so a new "scourge" appeared. By 1960 the "new thing" or "free jazz" emerged in the work of restless youngsters moved little by formulas of bop. The new prophets, including Ornette Coleman, Cecil Taylor, and eventually (and most notably) John Coltrane, sought to liberate jazz from limitations—melodic, rhythmic, and especially harmonic—of the older styles. The departures of the "free-jazz sect" (for lack of a better name), sometimes appearing in militant program music linked to the civil rights movement and other social upheavals of the Sixties and Seventies, generated a new version of the jazz mystique and rituals which stressed African roots and pointedly abandoned the old hip attitudes in favor of a serious artistic demeanor. It also developed its own myths, critics, and fringe devotees who spread its evolving doctrines. The boppers, to say nothing of the declining number of early jazz holdouts, were puzzled and appalled by these strange new experiments.

The intersectarian fight which the "new thing" elicited was even smaller than the bop feud a generation earlier, although it raised similar issues. Again authoritarian voices warned against wild new noises that seemed devoid of organization and meaning. Trumpeter Roy Eldridge, a style setter in the late Thirties and Forties, declared of Ornette Coleman: "I listened to him all kinds of ways. . . . I even played with him. I think he's jiving, baby. He's putting everybody on. They start with a nice lead-off figure, but then they go off into outer space. They disregard the chords and they play odd numbers of bars. I can't follow them." Some veterans were more vehement, refusing to play with, or even listen to, the newcomers. In Los Angeles, star bop tenorman Dexter Gordon, arriving late for a job with his band, found young Ornette Coleman sitting in and sent him packing in the middle of a number. And in 1962 the bartender-manager of the Coronet bar, a hotbed of hard-bop sentiment in the Bedford-Stuyvesant area of Brooklyn, summarily fired Cecil Taylor's band after the first set on opening night. Unintimidated, the group remounted the stand after the break but was forced to leave by outraged habitués, one of them brandishing a switchblade. Yet, as before, the opposition of entrenched forces had little effect in the long run and served mainly to close the ranks of the schismatics. In the course of time, however, these rebels became increasingly established and by the Eighties were taking their place in the overall jazz denomination. And this denomination was more and more accepted by the evolving musical establishment, which, in its continuing spirit of accommodation and inclusiveness, had long since begun to make room for the sounds of the advancing twentieth century.

These, then, were the three jazz sects. They did not necessarily grow in similar ways; each had its distinctive character and pace of development. Yet they shared broad similarities with Troeltsch's "sect-type." Some of these are implicit in the above summary, and later I will discuss others in detail. But for now, I will spell them out in general terms.

Jazz movements suggest a blend of what Bryan Wilson calls gnostic and introversionist sects—gnostic in that they are inspired by positive, intuitive knowledge of the supernatural, and introversionist in that they withdraw socially and psychologically from unsympathetic, outside worlds in order to nurture and practice their beliefs. Animated by the messages of prophetic musicians and aided by distinctive myths and rituals of performance, initiation, language, dress, and humor, they rebel against the prevailing musical system, aggressively distancing themselves from its banalities, corruption, formalities, and supporters. Organization is simple, especially at first, with esteem and role resting on merit constantly reviewed by watchful peers.

Sectarian structure also depends on race. The ecstasy and fellowship of the music sometimes dissolve ethnic barriers, but both Jim Crow and "Crow Jim" (anti-white feelings among blacks) can be as strong in the jazz community as elsewhere in American society. Until recently blacks and whites did not customarily perform together, especially on records or broadcasts. And dance halls, theaters, and musicians' unions were generally segregated in a familiar pattern of pollution behavior, made all the more vehement by the unfathomable nature of the music. I do not mean to underemphasize this segregation in the following pages, but my main concern is with correspondences in the behavior of black and white followers who, despite obvious ethnic differences, demonstrated similar kinds of sect-like behavior. Thus, black and white jazz subgroups can be seen as related parts of a given jazz movement, much as black and white congregations and conferences of Methodists are related parts of an overall denomination (i.e., a mature sect).

In addition, organization depends on sex. Although not untouched by women's liberation, jazz fellowships remain heavily masculine in character and tone, particularly at their core. Women function in secondary roles as pianists, singers, dancers, den mothers, homemakers, breadwinners, and sex objects, but seldom are first-line musicians. The mystique and working conditions discourage domestic ties and reward the men's macho attitudes. Many performers feel a need for aggressive self-confidence on the bandstand, in the street, and in clubs in the midst of gangsters, vice, heavy drinking, and drugs. Even in the best of times, jobs are scarce for men, and far scarcer for women who compete in the face of ridicule or ostracism. One measure of the masculine tone of the jazz world is its fraternal argot, which is full of macho terms. And for many devotees the music itself is by definition masculine. As one pianist asserted in 1973, "Jazz is a male language. It's a matter of speaking that language and women just can't do it."

The sexual division of labor and prestige in music is ancient in most systems upheld by powerful taboos. In some African cultures women are still not allowed to play, hear, or even look at certain magically endowed instruments except in special, ritual circumstances. And until recently women were seldom seen in symphony orchestras. Yet extremes of male dominance did not come immediately to jazz. Like other ecstatic movements, jazz brotherhoods initially permitted women to play prominent ritual roles, relegating them to lesser functions only as the fellowship matured. In the early days, women stars such as Bessie Smith and Billie Holiday shone as brightly as male performers. But this is no longer the case. Many women now believe they must play twice as well to attract half the attention of their male counterparts receive. Contemporary guitarist Sonny Sharrock, whose wife, Lynda, a singer, has failed to break through the sexual barrier, told critic Valerie Wilmer, "If a woman is going to invade the holy territory of the artist, she's in a lot of trouble. . . . I know that people refuse to give Lynda any recognition at all." Wilmer herself, one of the few female jazz writers, observed that even when a woman performer is noticed, she is measured on masculine terms: "'You play like a man' was always the ultimate compliment a female musician could receive, fractionally better than the other painful cliché—'you sound good for a woman.'" Not a few jazzmen, as we'll see, feel that women's extreme susceptibility to the emotional power of the music makes them unpredictable front-line performers and potentially dangerous distractions both on and off the bandstand, a view shared by many in the classical-music world.

Not all jazzmen think this way, of course. Given their broad range of beliefs and practices, there is seldom unanimity on such questions and no one person or group can be called representative. Nevertheless, usually there is a consensus rooted in a pattern of priority and influence flowing from the core outward. Elite musicians and critics set the style and pace, dramatize ideals, and to some extent serve as role models. Their music and words are commanding and familiar while the evidence of more peripheral communicants remains relatively scanty. . . .

Jazz movements develop, I believe, along lines laid out by Max Weber and his followers. Weber demonstrated, among other things, that religious innovations come in "breakthroughs" inspired by prophets who generate feelings of ecstasy. At first the message attracts only a small group of apostles, but as it spreads the original circle expands into a congregation which, though simple at first, becomes increasingly complex. Eventually it begets priests and other functionaries who rationalize the prophecy and related values, clarifying, specifying, and systematizing the myths and rituals to meet contemporary demands, and writing them down in gospels, which has the effect of closing the canon and making them more accessible and palatable to a growing following. Thus, the prophecy, however watered-down, eventually becomes comfortably incorporated into the larger culture. . . .

Jazz sects start out in the cultic ferment of prophetic figures, like Bix Beiderbecke, Charlie Parker, and Ornette Coleman, men with messages and auras powerful enough to break through accepted customs and beliefs. Such charismatics change not only musical tastes but the outlooks and life-styles of listeners who fall under their spell. Before long the prophet acquires a small, elite following, mostly musicians, but gradually, as his message spreads in personal appearances, by word of mouth, and through recordings, he attracts a highly personalized and unstructured following composed of aesthetically adventurous individuals whose taste is volatile but who remain zealous while in the fold. Cultists demand stylistic purity of their idols and shun listeners who accept tainted music or musicians. For the most part, however, they readily tolerate other belief systems—including those of other art forms (including modern classical music) or religious (Christianity, Judaism, Islam, as well as more exotic faiths)—so long as they do not threaten the jazz life. Moreover, jazz cults, untroubled by most kinds of deviance or odd behavior, condone or even encourage them so long as they do not interfere with the music or its devotions. The cult asks only that believers revere the proper music, idols, and objects, and in some instances follow tacitly approved practices of dress, vocabulary, and association.

If it survives long enough, the jazz cult, like its religious counterparts, tends to merge with similar groups, becoming part of a more formal, increasingly structured body, a sect. Admirers of, say, Bix Beiderbecke extend their fascinations to Louis Armstrong and Duke Ellington, or the other way around. And, as the movement grows, its membership expands and differentiates. Elitists find discerning newcomers in their midst, gifted young musicians and critics whose hearts are in the music first and last. Newcomers also include less committed enthusiasts, fellow travelers, including musicians, writers, record collectors, hipsters, and others absorbed in the music but maintaining important links to the outside world. From these ranks come believers, some accredited by the establishment, who perform priest-like functions, rationalizing and certifying sectarian rituals and myths in broadly acceptable ways: critics, who explain and evaluate the new sounds; historians, who put the plots, characters, and settings of the music's past into meaningful order and perspective; and curators, including collectors and discographers, who preserve sacred objects and verify the details of the emerging canon. As the rationalization evolves, jazzmen with classical training come forward to blend the music with comfortably familiar forms of classical and popular music. Their dilutions attract large numbers of casual communicants—occasional record buyers, concert and club patrons, and recreational dancers—whose essentially conventional tastes are still adventurous enough to be intrigued by the now temperate sounds. The fringe followers acclaim the most celebrated diluters (mostly white), ignoring superior artists (mostly black), whose undiluted music has more power. Thus Paul Whiteman, a classical violinist bitten by the jazz bug during World War I, "refined" the new sounds into confections which made him the "King of Jazz" during the Twenties; in the next decade clarinetist Benny Goodman, at home with both Mozart and jazz, streamlined jazz of the Twenties so adroitly that he became wealthy and famous as the "King of Swing"; during the Fifties, pianist Dave Brubeck, who had sat at the knee of modernist composer Darius Milhaud, mixed jazz with classical and popular music in ways that put him high on the record charts and on the cover of *Time* magazine; and in the Seventies Miles Davis, a pioneer in the departures of the Fifties, led a "fusion" of jazz and rock music that brought him celebrity and fortune. The original prophets or their finest disciples are not displaced by such events, particularly in the opinion of elitists, but they rarely receive the popular rewards accorded celebrated diluters.

The population of listeners has a fluid membership. Elitist, fellow travelers, and marginal or casual fans—these are far from hard and fast categories. Many a casual listener, first attracted to the music through accessible dilutions, draws closer to the core after discovering purer sounds. And there are departures as well as arrivals. At the cult stage some devotees drop out when the novelty wears off and friends move on to other kicks. Then, too, as the fellowship moves in a churchly direction, it leaves behind early believers who object to compromises and reassert original purities, as in the Dixieland Revival of the Forties or the "hard-bop regression" in the succeeding decade.

At the other end of the fellowship Young Turks, chafing under restrictive sectarian clichés and rituals, seek out new prophets whose radical messages break through settled modes, thereby creating new cults and antagonizing unbending loyalists. Thus, in the early Forties, restless young jazzmen were mesmerized by the experiments of Charlie Parker and Dizzy Gillespie, much to the horror of aging idols, like Louis Armstrong, who had changed the face of jazz a generation earlier. And in the early Sixties adventurous young players and listeners, dissatisfied with tired bop formulas, discovered fresh enchantment in Ornette Coleman and John Coltrane, dismaying elder statesmen like Dizzy Gillespie and Dexter Gordon.

As sects mature in settled and formal ways, they join sympathetic groups evolving along churchly lines and grow increasingly open and tolerant. By now most of the original sectarian zeal has dissipated, along with much of the old inclusiveness. Time wears sharp edges smooth. Intractable positions and rigorous definitions soften, old antagonisms fade into a spirit of acceptance, even cooperation, a fixed establishment broadens to accommodate and include.

Today churchly movement abounds in the jazz world as old sectarian enmities cool and fade. The initial thrust of post–free jazz is not nearly so radical as that of its predecessors. Many avant-gardists now believe that free-jazz iconoclasm of the Sixties was too sweeping, particularly in its abandonment of traditional harmonic sequences. Reedman David Murray, who has returned to a big-band format with instrumental sections, tightly written arrangements, and repeated harmonic patterns, argues that it is time for jazz to return to ignored traditions. And Julliard-trained trumpeter Wynton Marsalis, seeking to reinstate some of the old harmonic rules, maintains that "Without the obstacles improvisation is nothing." The distinction between jazz and classical music has been blurring for years and is now impossible to make in much avant-garde work. And many musicians who in an earlier era would have identified themselves exclusively with jazz now draw on numerous native and national traditions and find the term "jazz" too restrictive. Ornette Coleman, unhappy with the category of "jazzman," recently said, "I've always classified myself as a composer who also performs music." Members of both classical and jazz camps now comfortably perform together and increasingly share similar skills and backgrounds. In 1984 Marsalis, who has played with Art Blakey's

Jazz Messengers and also at the Mostly Mozart Festival, won Grammy awards for recorded solo performances in both jazz and classical categories. Seminal jazzmen, including former radicals Richard Davis, Archie Shepp, and Max Roach, are finding places on university and conservatory faculties. And the music has established beachheads at the Smithsonian and at the National Endowment of the Arts, which awarded $1.3 million of its $13 million music budget for 1983–84 to jazz projects. As all this indicates, structural development now centers less on church-sect opposition or intersectarian battles than on amalgamation and synthesis in a churchly framework.

In sum, until recently jazz movements resembled sects, gnostically focused on spiritual knowledge accessible only to insiders and introversionist in their desire to withdraw socially and psychologically from an unsympathetic outside world. Jazz sects were multiethnic, male-oriented, liminal groups that began as loose, zealous cults, inspired by charismatic musical prophets, and gradually evolved in a churchly direction as their music, myths, and rituals become increasingly rationalized and moderated in ways that attracted a growing conventional following.

Prophets

The innovative jazzmen who inspired jazz sects were prophetic performers whose role harked back to the shaman, a figure traceable to Paleolithic times and still functioning in hunting and food-gathering cultures. A visionary and healer linked to the wizard and the medicine man, the shaman is marked by his capacity to evoke ecstasy and is the medium through which the gods speak to man.

A classic account of shamanic performance appears in Waldemar Bogaras's description of a séance among the Chuckchee of Siberia. Bogaras tells of the shaman occupying a special "master's place" near the back wall of a dark, crowded room after the evening meal; smoking strong tobacco, gyrating rhythmically while beating a drum, he employs ventriloquism and sleight of hand, singing repetitious, sometimes wordless songs especially identified with him or as part of a repertoire recognized and reacted to by his audience in words and gestures. As the spirit enters his body, the shaman moves and chatters ever more violently until the climactic moment when he communes with the supernatural before returning to his body for final incantations. Other shamen use different musical instruments and not uncommonly drugs, spiced water, or aromatic plants which help generate the magic "heat" indicative of ecstasy. "Getting hot," evidenced by emotional excitement, perspiration, or some other sign, is seen as an indication of superhuman power to produce ecstasy or trance.

Much of this behavior occurs in the performance of jazzmen. One thinks of a possessed Buddy Bolden transfixing the patrons of

Longshoreman's Hall in New Orleans; a perspiring Louis Armstrong, eyes shut and horn tilted up at a forty-five degree angle, galvanizing the faithful at the Sunset Café on Chicago's South Side; Charlie Parker hugging his saxophone to his stomach and fixing the rapt audience with a sightless stare while "blowing snakes" in the Yacht Club on Fifty-second Street; an intense John Coltrane mesmerizing the crowd at the Five Spot in lower Manhattan with one of his riveting, marathon solos. One of the best examples is King Oliver in 1923 at Lincoln Gardens in Chicago. An imposing figure who dominated the altar-like bandstand, he started performances by directing a stream of King Bee tobacco juice into the cuspidor, which he then beat with his foot to set the rhythm, and proceeded to blow the powerful, poignant sounds he was famous for. In the course of the evening he augmented his magic with a variety of tricks, such as making his cornet sound like a human or animal voice. Visiting musicians, gathered around the bandstand, were fascinated, and behind them entranced dancers performed Dionysian gyrations under a large revolving crystal ball that scattered specks of light around the dark, closely packed hall. After forty-odd minutes of "High Society" or "Dippermouth Blues," he might peer down at the acolytes ranged before him and say with a wink, "Hotter than a forty-five." Then he would drink deeply from the bucket of strongly sugared water he kept on the bandstand. . . .

But if the jazz prophet's magnetism was strongest onstage, his charisma often spread elsewhere. With or without his instrument he could electrify the atmosphere. Pianist Fats Waller needed only to enter a room to cause smiles. "His face would light up with such an expression that it was transmitted to everybody in the room," wrote clarinetist Mezz Mezzrow. "He was so magnetic with such a robust personality that you could never be sad in his presence." Duke Ellington radiated glamour. "There was some sort of magic to him you wouldn't understand," declared drummer Sonny Greer. "In my whole life, I've never seen another like him. When he walks into a room, the whole place lights up." Sometimes the charisma was even more enigmatic as in the haunting attraction of the introverted, saintly John Coltrane. But whatever the prophet's personality, the magic was an extension of his ecstatic music. . . .

Thus the afflicted jazz giant was cast in the role of psychotic genius, consumed prematurely by his fidelity to the ideals of the jazz world and posthumously reborn in myth to symbolize them. While he was still alive, however, his charisma helped obscure his personality. Even if he was a familiar figure, he remained curiously unknown, psychologically distant. Duke Ellington, for instance, though constantly in the spotlight, was almost inscrutable even to musicians who toured with him day after day. He cleaned them out at poker on payday, worked closely with them musically, yet remained essentially enigmatic and aloof. . . .

Successful religious prophets view themselves not as the deity, but as its agent, and jazz luminaries are no exception. As drummer Billy Higgins put it, "Music doesn't come from you, it comes through you." ...

Like the Weberian prophet, the jazz genius was a powerful agent for change, with charismatic power to defy the status quo and sweep whole groups into new paths. Ralph Ellison recalled how in 1929 Lester Young, tall and intense, newly arrived in Oklahoma City, "left absolutely no reed player and few young players of any instrument unstirred by the wild excitingly original flights of his imagination." ...

The prophet articulated for the inarticulate. He said dramatically and convincingly what his admirers felt most deeply but could not say themselves, things bottled up inside struggling to get out. Gerald McKeever, a would-be musician, recalled being devastated by the sounds of John Coltrane. "I was sitting there, digging ... screaming. ... I *felt* so much of what he was saying, I had so much I wanted to say to the whole world ... and *I didn't know how to get it out!* He was *my God!*" ...

Once the prophet's revelation had reached the audience, his image further elaborated and reinforced the message. ... A New Orleans veteran told how Jelly Roll Morton would sit at the keyboard all night and added, "We used to ask him, when do you sleep—he fool [*sic*] at the piano so much." Followers were in awe of such single-mindedness, and aspiring musicians sought to emulate it along with the prophet's sounds and technique. They also copied his walk, talk, and clothing. ...

The prophetic artist was a messenger from beyond who demonstrated the mystique, inspired the following, embodied the sectarian values, and provided a rallying symbol. In liminal jazz groups, lacking conventional guidelines and governing hierarchies, he provided followers noted for their individualism and idiosyncrasies with definitions, justifications, and discipline.

Note

1. Editor's Note: The author is referring to the church, sect, denomination typology developed by Ernst Troeltsch.

Hardcore

An Ethnographic Study of an Evolving Music Subculture

Kerry Hendricks

This qualitative study of a musical subculture used participant observation and in-depth interviews collected at eighteen concerts or shows of varying size. The collected data were analyzed using Glaser and Strauss's comparative method, and Donnelly's characteristics of a subculture were used to analyze identity formation of "hardcore" members.

Hardcore first emerged during the uncertainty of the Reagan administration as an underground movement resisting mainstream normalcy. Hardcore bands like Black Flag and Minor Threat used independent record labels, and included political statements in their lyrics. A splinter straight-edge subgroup developed that took a stance against drug use, smoking, drinking, and promiscuous sexual activity. Since the 1980s, the music of this subculture has evolved from aggressive punk to incorporate elements of metal, rap, and techno. It adopted its own fashion and "hardcore dancing," which has become a quintessential part of any "show"—the term used by participants in reference to hardcore concerts. The dancing is a somewhat violent form of physical contact between audience members triggered by musical cues of the "breakdown": it is an active role for the music as well as for the audience. Christian themes emerged in some hardcore music, prompting bands to distinguish themselves as either hardcore or "Christian hardcore."

While discussion of contemporary hardcore is not found in the literature, there is one source that provides considerable insight. Moore (2007) looks at the way punk music broke away from corporate intervention in popular culture. He shows how the "do-it-yourself ethic" of individualism challenged the mainstream rock scene, leading to the development of the hardcore subculture. This historical background provides a context for the emergence of hardcore. He also provides insight on the role of women in the new music. The aggressive angst that characterized the emergence of hardcore reinforced masculinity, pushing women into punk rather than hardcore. Moore also examines the way the group separated from mainstream music culture. Moore's analysis underscores the fact that hardcore was, and still is, an outlet for those who refuse to follow the conventional rock music norms. Not only is this rebellion still present, but it has evolved further due to legitimization of hardcore/metal record labels and bands.

Appearance or style of hardcore participants is also important. As noted by Hebdige (2004 [1979]), youth subcultures in the postwar UK, such as the mods and rockers, skinheads, and punks, adopted their own unique style. This style expressed their challenge of the cultural hegemony. Interestingly, one of the subcultures that developed was punk, which further evolved into hardcore. This idea of a group detaching itself from the "normalization" of society coincides with the separation of punk and hardcore from mainstream rock.

Haenfler's (2006) study of straight-edge—a subgroup within hardcore—goes a step further. Straight-edge members are dedicated to the prohibition of drugs, drinking, smoking, and promiscuous sexual activities. The trends in style and appearance of sXe (abbreviation for *straight-edge*) were adopted by the hardcore subculture, including (1) old school—typically punk hair styles of Mohawks or shaved heads, jeans, band T-shirts, spiked belts and wristbands, and bandanas; (2) youth crew (associated with both punk and hardcore)—clean-cut image, running shoes, hoodies, and cargo shorts; (3) metalcore (adopted by both metal and hardcore)—basketball jerseys with band names, cargo shorts, running shoes, gauges (a type of earring used to stretch the earlobes), and flat-billed hats.

Continuing with straight-edge, Mullaney (2006) gives personal accounts of being introduced to the subculture and discuss gender inequalities. Although straight-edge is seen as an open environment in hardcore music, gender inequalities still exist, making the open lifestyle a myth. Despite the fact that many of the sXe men and women interviewed by Mullaney downplayed the significance of gender, hardcore dancing at shows is dominated by men mainly because women fear injury or harm.

Regarding other hardcore, Purchla (2008) looks at hardcore "crews" and the social setting in which they thrive. A *crew* is simply a group of friends who regularly attend hardcore shows together, and while they have some characteristics of gangs, there is a distinction. He concludes that crews do, in fact, exercise social control within the hardcore subculture. They serve as authorities, intensifying male dominance in the subculture by creating norms of conduct for audience members that must be upheld to avoid confrontation.

While research on socialization, gender roles, subgroups, and historical background exists, there is little on the current developments of the hardcore subculture—for example, the new musical elements being used, the appearance/style of participants, and the way individuals establish their identities within the subculture. There is also little or no information about hardcore dancing.

This chapter addresses the question, What is "hardcore" and how did the current subcultures develop? It will look at the aspects of the subculture, such as the rapid expansion of artist labels and bands, the social settings, and the rules and norms of hardcore *shows* and hardcore dancing, as well as examine the differences between subgroups like straight-edge and Christianity.

The framework I will use to discuss subculture and identity formation was developed by Donnelly (1981) and Donnelly and Young (1988). Donnelly contends that subcultures have eight recognizable characteristics: (1) They are an identifiable group within or across cultures. (2) They are composed of both individuals and small groups. (3) They engage in specific types of behaviors and have recognizable norms and values. (4) They are distinctive in nature. (5) They represent different stages of membership. (6) The beliefs and behaviors that brought them together have scope and potential. (7) They are maintained by members of the subculture so long as individual needs are met. (8) They are maintained by face-to-face interaction and networking between members.

Donnelly and Young (1988) have a four-stage model of the way in which an actor's membership within a group or subculture affects the identity within that group. Presocialization is the first stage—information is gathered prior to one's involvement within a group. Selection and recruitment are the second stage—membership within a subculture. Socialization is third—an ongoing adoption of the rules and norms of the group. Acceptance or ostracism is the fourth stage—one's identity is either confirmed or not. Thus an individual learns through socialization and interaction the values and norms needed to construct an identity—from a novice to an experienced member—and that identity is confirmed by other members within the group. Donnelly and Young looked at identity constructions and confirmation in sport subcultures of rugby and rock climbing, but the model can be applied to other subcultures, such as hardcore. I will incorporate Erving Goffman's (1959) impression management, the process whereby an individual regulates and controls information in social interaction, to look at construction and reconstruction of identity within the subculture as it is confirmed and reconfirmed by members within the group. Impression management through the use of display tools such as appearance and behaviors is an important part of the hardcore subculture.

The Hardcore Subculture

Crowd Behavior

A crucial component of a subculture is members engaging in similar types of behavior. In hardcore, that occurs as people gather for a show. It is important for individuals attending hardcore shows to be knowledgeable of the unwritten rules and norms in order to avoid the hazards of a large number of audience members such as injury in the "pit" that inevitably develop in the crowd, and to maximize the viewing pleasure of the show.

> Anytime you have a full crowd that hasn't already made room for the pit, the pit will make room for itself. This meant that when the moshers and hardcore dancers pushed the rest of the crowd to the outside, it created a domino effect that sent somewhat of a "wave" through the entire crowd. [Excerpt from field notes—Macomb, IL, 2009]

Both verbal and nonverbal cues are used by performers and audience members. The actions in this setting are acceptable only within context, and would otherwise be deviant.

> Having no personal space to myself, the close proximity of the crowd created an intense amount of heat and humidity. As the crowd started to build up with the anticipation of a breakdown, Haste the Day's frontman addressed the crowd with "Dallas, Texas, show me what you got!" which led to the explosion of movement in response to the ensuing breakdown. [Excerpt from field notes—Dallas, TX, 2010]

Venues for the shows vary in size and shape but are typically small, darkened areas with the only light coming from the stage itself, drawing attention to the stage. The shows are extremely loud—the sound systems fill the room with music—and they're often humid because of the large number of people in a small space: there is risk of dehydration and hearing damage. This serves to maximize the musical experience rather than make audience members comfortable. The intensity of the music provokes excitement in the crowd and establishes behaviors of a subculture (Waksman 2001).

Because of the confined space, personal boundaries are crossed; physical contact is common. The main objective for some audience members is to be involved in the music close to the stage. This is not unique to hardcore but exhibits hardcore values. Thus audience members may be pushed, pressed against, and even stepped on by others. This situation becomes more severe when a pit emerges within the crowd—usually in the very center. This aggressive behavior would be considered deviant elsewhere, but here it is part of the hardcore crowd experience. Personal space is only restored by leaving the show, which ends with the headlining band's set (performance).

In the context of the show, the band and audience play off of one another using both verbal and nonverbal cues. The emergence of the pit is a result of the band's introducing a "breakdown" to the crowd by means of a verbal command (example: "I wanna see this place open up!") or nonverbal cue (specific musical note and tempo change) that is generally a widely accepted norm among audience members, regardless of the popularity of the band. However, some variables that can influence the facilitation of these behaviors are the number of people present at a show and the overall quality of the band itself.

> I began to notice that the frontman to Inhale/Exhale was getting frustrated. It was disappointing to see that even though the bands were really well established, the crowd was relatively weak. The energy just wasn't there, no matter how great the bands played. [Excerpt from field notes—Tyler, TX, 2010]

Forming the pit involves aggressive physical movements of hardcore dancing or moshing. Different rhythms are used to invoke different types of movement, such as (1) the slower-paced breakdown, which is responded to by the audience's hardcore dancing or moshing; (2) the two-step rhythm, which is responded to with the two-step dance rhythm; and (3) the increased speed in a song that builds up to a breakdown, which can lead to jogging as participants circle around the pit. The intensity of the crowd increases the intensity of the band's performance and is an indicator of how well the band is performing. These behaviors cease and the pit disperses at the end of the cued breakdown.

This synergistic effect among the audience is characterized as "synchronization and convergence" (Ginneken 2003). Individuals who come to these shows experience a sense of deindividuation as a fusion takes place within the group, and then leave as individuals once the particular show is over. Hardcore subculture is defined by the type of music and the behavior during a show; the movement is facilitated by the collective, and like-mindedness is displayed through appearance (clothing style, etc.). The compact space of the venues intensifies stress or arousal (Ginneken 2003).

Musical Elements

A crucial aspect of the hardcore subculture is the music. As with any genre of music, there are definitive musical elements that set it apart from other music and subgenres.

The hardcore music style is distinguished as a faster and more aggressive form of punk (Haenfler 2006). Hardcore also incorporates (in some cases) the use of synthesizers and double-bass kick drums to add to the overall rhythm progression of the music. A typical hardcore band would have two vocalists—a singer and a screamer—two guitarists (lead and rhythm), a bass player, a keyboardist or synthesizer player, and a drummer. Hardcore includes the rhythmic two-step beat created by a specific type of drum beat on the second and fourth beats in a rhythm, and the metal-influenced breakdown. Both of these musical elements are distinctive of hardcore music to drive the response to these types of elements, the hardcore dancing behavior.

> Breakdowns? . . . best way I can describe it is a rhythmic pattern in a song that's just . . . it's fun for people to dance to. Normally you have lower-tuned guitars for that, like D or A . . . maybe C for some of the newer bands. [Daniel, 20]

The musical elements of the breakdown follow a structure that almost every band adheres to: (1) If vocals are present during the breakdown, a single repeated statement is introduced to maintain the intensity; (2) the drummer will either emphasize the beat with a four-quarter-note symbol crash on top of double-bass kick drum, or will play half-notes on the symbol crash to give the music a slower feel; (3) guitarists use dissonant chords in rhythmic rifts (low-tuned in "drop-A") that create a heavier feel to the music.

> The slow breakdowns, like I said the chuggy breakdowns where you're barring-the-one [demonstrates on invisible guitar], it's gonna have like a minor sound to it along with a major to where it's catchy and dark, and evil, and heavy. [Blake, 21]

The song "Take the Crown" by the band Her Demise My Rise starts with the typical opening rhythms of a hardcore song but transitions into a breakdown early on in the song (0:33), maintaining the slow and steady rhythm supplemented with the repeated statement by the vocalist. Immediately following the breakdown, the song transitions again into a rhythm more closely related to the earlier versions of hardcore, which contains more punk undertones (1:13). The next transition changes the song rhythm into a two-step beat, in which the emphasis is on the second and fourth beats (1:45). Finally, the song closes with another breakdown (2:26) before ending (2:59).

By incorporating musical elements from other genres while still retaining the hardcore musical framework, subgenres have emerged. These include deathcore (characterized by speed and heaviness, with the incorporation of excessive breakdowns and death-metal riffs), melodic hardcore (with emphasis on more technical guitar riffs and melodic vocals), Christian hardcore and metalcore (inclusion of Christian values into song lyrics), and grindcore (includes both death metal and industrial music influences), as well as the emergence of subgenres not yet defined. All subgenres, however, are recognized as hardcore.

> Every year something new is coming out. . . . I mean, you've heard that new Her Demise My Rise; they've got the heaviest breakdowns ever and they've got the best two-step beats ever, but they mix it with like rap and that auto-tuned singing . . . it's like building blocks that just keep building and building on one another. [Blake, 21]

Thus hardcore music is constantly evolving and expanding to include a wider range of musical styles while still maintaining boundaries from other genres.

Identity Construction

Hardcore is not only being a supporter of the music but also exhibiting a subcultural identity. Hardcore identity is the expression of an individual's group affiliation—namely, participation in the hardcore subculture. An individual learns values and norms that lead to identity construction as a novice, and through impression management tactics and confirmation of that identity develops into an experienced member.

Hardcore identities vary according to the degree to which an individual embraces the characteristics of the subculture. Some individuals accept the subculture as the dominant factor in their lives, whereas others participate in the subcultural activities but do not accept it as their dominant identity. Clothing and hairstyles are characteristic of the hardcore subculture, as is engaging with the music, such as attending shows and engaging in "hardcore dancing" or moshing within the pit. Individuals who perform these roles fulfill the social expectations of the subculture and appear to have a personal identity associated with the subculture. But in addition to these impression management tactics, there are established rules that, when violated, are an indicator that someone is not hardcore.

Hardcore members regard appearance as a major factor of how "hardcore" someone is. Goffman (1959) used the theater image to understand social interaction; appearance is a "prop" that creates a convincing image to others and assists us in playing our roles. For hardcore, recent clothing styles include V-neck or band T-shirts, skinny or cut-off jeans, and TOMS or Vans shoes, worn by both guys and girls (also referred to as "scene kids"). "Old-school" clothing styles for guys include basketball jerseys, flat-billed hats, shorts, and Vans shoes. Along with clothing styles are unique hairstyles that can range from short to long hair for both men and women. Finally, gauges through the ears, piercings through the nose, and large and intricate tattoos can complete the appearance of being hardcore, but are optional. Any deviation from the specified style is an indicator of an individual who is not a member of the subculture.

> You listen to the CD, you wear the shirt, you pick up a pair of skinny jeans and they're hooked . . . you know, I've seen people like that. It's a transformation. . . . It's crazy . . . especially seeing guys go from wearing baggy jeans to skinny jeans on a whim like that. [Blake, 21]

However, appearance alone does not determine one's identity as a hardcore member.

> I mean, the dress thing . . . it only goes so far, you know, I mean . . . it is a good identifier if you're hardcore scene or not, but . . . there's some people out there that just dress like that and go to shows but they don't care about any of it. [Blake, 21]

An individual must also demonstrate how "hardcore" he or she is at a show. Such behavior gives them a hardcore identity in the subculture and confirms the identity of other participants as well. Display of movements and knowledge of the music is crucial—in conjunction with appearance—to the formation of identity. If an individual can discuss current bands with others, display an interest in the music by hardcore dancing or moshing, and have appropriate appearance, other members will confirm his or her membership.

> If you've got somebody in the back with their arms crossed, you know, looking at everyone with like a "what the hell?" look on their face, then it's pretty easy to tell they don't belong, but if you're getting out there, shooting the shit with people, having a good time, moving, and you dress the part, then you're in. [Daniel, 20]

Donnelly and Young's (1988) four-stage model of identity construction can be applied to identity construction within the hardcore subculture. During the first stage, *presocialization*, the individual gathers any and all information from any number of sources regarding the subculture before any participation in the subculture is made. An example of this would be for an individual to hear or listen to the hardcore music from an outside source, inquire about the clothing style associated with hardcore, or to be introduced by a family member or friend. As of today, hardcore is present in popular culture through means of magazines (*Alternative Press, HM Magazine*), social networking tools (Facebook, Myspace), and an Internet radio station (Hopecore.com).

Once the initial contact is made, the stage will continue until direct contact is made to the subculture by means of attending a show or by being received as a member.

> I like a lot of different kinds of music, but . . . as far as actually getting introduced and getting into it, it was because of my boyfriend . . . but I was first introduced to basically like . . . a slower version of it, and then getting closer to like . . . intense hardcore. [Ellen, 19]

The second stage, *selection and recruitment,* is a flexible stage characterized as membership within the subculture by means of actually selecting and seeking out membership, or by being recruited by another member. This process is important not only to the individual seeking membership but also to the subculture, as it needs new members to progress. In the hardcore subculture, an individual who has either taken interest in the music or has been motivated by peers to participate takes the step of attending a hardcore show and then decides whether to continue to take interest in the subculture.

> I've been to two shows so far. . . . I wouldn't say that I'm completely dedicated to it, but . . . I enjoy it. . . . I would say that I'm not a newbie anymore, because I know more about it, but I wouldn't say that I'm fully dedicated to it. . . . I wanna know more about it, learn about different bands and semi-dress the part. [Ellen, 19]

The third stage, *socialization,* refers to the active, ongoing stage where a member becomes familiar with the characteristics of the subculture. This happens through interaction when members share information. Through this communication and interaction, the norms and values of the hardcore subculture become established. Members then internalize the rules and norms of the subculture to help construct their identity within the subculture. Within hardcore, members learn the rules and norms of behavior for a show as well as for other times, and then "dress the part" and/or participate in crowd behavior.

> [Hardcore dancing] is more of a . . . it's an expression for them and to show the band that they're having a good time. My parents went to a show one time, just because they knew one of the kids that were playing. They saw some kids that were hardcore dancing and, you know . . . when we got home they were laughing about it and trying to imitate it and . . . making fun . . . making comments like "that's the dumbest thing," etc. and it's really not. It's your way of showing that "I really enjoyed this music and I'm really pumped." [Jordan, 18]

The fourth and final stage, *acceptance* (or *ostracism*), is essentially confirmation (or denial) of identity construction by the established members of the subculture; the individual's new identity is accepted (or the individual is rejected and possibly banished). Within hardcore, if the identity construction is unacceptable, it doesn't lead to banishment but rather a resocialization by the individual.

> When I first started going to shows . . . I'm not gonna say I felt out of place, because people are surprisingly accepting at shows . . . but I feel like the more shows I went to I could feel this routine starting to form: waiting in line, meeting people, knowing where to go . . . especially in the crowd if you don't wanna get hit. [Blake, 21]

The Donnelly and Young model determines the extent of an individual's involvement and membership within the hardcore subculture based on the stage of identity construction. Someone who has basic knowledge of hardcore, for instance, who has attended shows but is not fully committed to membership in the subculture, would be in the second stage of *selection and recruitment*, while an established member who has formed his identity within hardcore and has been supported by other members would be in the fourth stage of *acceptance*.

Conclusion

Since it separated from the punk music subculture, hardcore has incorporated new musical elements and developed a characteristic rhythmic "breakdown" and "two-step" beat. It has established itself as a unique musical subculture with its own set of rules and norms—for appearance and behavior—which have changed over the years. Donnelly and Young's study of subcultures and Donnelly's subcultural components have been used to identify the unique characteristics: specific types of crowd behavior, definitive musical elements, and the identity construction process within hardcore. While this study does not trace an informant's progress through the socialization model, it points to future research possibilities, which should include a closer look at religious groups established within the hardcore music subculture, as well as bands outside of the United States that have adopted the hardcore music style and have incorporated it into their own nationality.

16

Not Fade Away
Ritual Solidarity and Persistence in the Jamband Community
Pamela M. Hunt

The author discusses the sociological concept of ritual with regard to
the jamband music subculture. This social environment is an ephemeral
community. Specifically, it is not a community characterized by geographic
location, yet it allows for rituals that lead to collective effervescence
and social solidarity. In addition, the author proposes that there are four
processes by which this portable community persists: (1) the pilgrimage to
concerts and festivals, (2) rituals that members practice both in the parking
lot and in the concert experience, (3) the symbiotic relationship between
bands and the fans, and (4) the continual interaction among subculture
members.

Durkheim (1995 [1912]) first investigated the mechanisms by which
societies create and maintain unity. In his seminal text *The Elementary
Forms of Religious Life,* Durkheim focused on how rituals are a powerful source of social harmony. He theorized that religious rituals produce
an energized and focused type of interaction that, in turn, produces a
high level of social solidarity. Since Durkheim, several researchers have
found that other types of groups also use ritual to create and maintain
what he referred to as collective effervescence—a heightened sense of
group membership and the assignment of sacred value to items of significance in the group (Aguirre 1984, Grazian 2007, Jasper 1998, Kidder
2006). At the heart of this concept is the notion that items that reinforce
the moral order of the group are construed positively, and conversely,
those that violate the moral order of the group are considered negative.

This concept truly comes to life in the jamband music subculture.
This subculture grew from the Grateful Dead scene in the mid-1990s.
Bands like Phish, Widespread Panic, Moe, and the String Cheese

Incident have inspired a similar fan following to that of the Dead-heads. This colorful, lively, traveling music scene is similar to other music scenes in that there are several levels of involvement. At its core, this scene's music fans follow a band for weeks at a time. Once at a concert venue, fans share a temporary yet recurring community where many encourage a commitment to one another and to the Earth. Even as a portable, ephemeral community, this subculture is an exquisite portrayal of Durkheim's basic concepts that include the predictions of ritual solidarity.

What Is a Jamband?

Think of the term jamband as an umbrella term describing a band from any genre of music that has two particular characteristics: (1) playing improvisational jamming live music without a predetermined set list, and (2) allowing fans to freely tape and trade live music at each concert (Budnick 2003). This latter criterion is unique to this scene. And, as a result of the generosity of the bands, there are extensive live jamband music archives that are absolutely free to each fan to share and trade.

Using this definition, the jamband music scene has encompassed three generations of bands. In an interview with Dean Budnick, editor of *Relix Magazine* and the online live music magazine jambands.com, Barry Smolin names the Allman Brothers Band and the Grateful Dead as examples of first-generation bands, originating in the late 1960s to mid-1970s; Widespread Panic and Phish as second-generation bands, beginning in the mid-1980s; and Moe and String Cheese Incident as third-generation bands, starting in the early to mid-1990s (Budnick 1999).

The jamband subculture began as a result of fans leaving the Grate-ful Dead scene, with fans feeling more at home at smaller shows and festivals. However, within a matter of a few years, that small jamband scene became a very large scene, with some festivals boasting atten-dance in the tens of thousands. The jamband touring scene has, in fact, developed into a festival scene. In Budnick's words, "The summer of 2003 affirmed the import (and the perceived import) of festivals to the jamband community" (2003:253). In the past, jambands often played two- or three-day shows at the same venue, and for a while allowed camping, giving shows a type of festival feel. Now, many of the mem-bers attend several jamband-focused festivals each year in addition to touring with their favorite jamband from show to show.

The Subculture

The values of the jamband subculture include at the most general level individual freedom, cooperation, reciprocity, and the creation of a sustainable living environment. Simultaneously, members are also extremely cooperative and generous with one another. That is, although members embrace diversity, they are not necessarily tolerant with all behaviors, especially those that could harm another individual or invade another's freedoms. It is indeed a delicate balance trying to be tolerant of any and all people and behaviors and enforcing (without written rules) that people cooperate with and watch out for one another.

Being historically and culturally connected to the countercultural movement of the 1960s, jamband subculture members also value an alternative, anticapitalistic economic system. For example, it is quite commonplace in the jamband community to practice bartering and trading rather than selling for profit. A specific example is the practice of trading, but never selling, music to one another. It has been suggested that this value was perhaps transferred by the bands' allowance of members to freely trade and tape live music in return for members' continued dedication to the live music scene. The reciprocal nature of this relationship cultivates a culture of nurturing, sharing, and caring.

Many members claim that these prosocial values and behaviors such as bartering, trading, and living in community allow them to lead more meaningful lives. In fact, there are crews who travel and live in community for purposes of watching out for other members (Shenk and Silberman 1994). These teams ride in buses together, and most often live communally when not on tour. They help injured or intoxicated fans at shows by giving simple care and attention. Members also strive to protect the environment by promoting and using sustainable products like hemp and developing effective recycling and reusing habits. Additionally, members tend to buy others' handmade goods or only buy from the jamband community (rather than from corporate American retailers) to keep the scene alive and the people thriving.

The Jamband Scene and Solidarity

Recall that collective effervescence is a heightened feeling of group membership and the assignment of sacred value to artifacts in the culture. In the jamband scene this is referred to as the vibe. Specifically, there is a heightened sense of "emotional energy" among individuals in the parking lot vending community and within the concert setting (Collins 2004). The vibe generally refers to the level of decency and generosity experienced by members in interaction with one another as well as with venue security. If the vibe is "off," members will tell you so and inform you that bad experiences are a direct result. Additionally, after the concert begins, the x-factor refers to the "uncontrollable and unpredictable wild 'Good Thing' that comes into play when the music is at its best" (Shenk and Silberman 1994:333). This, according to some members, is the way in which they believe they can predict the next song. This believed symbiotic relationship between some members and the music is another example of a feeling of collective effervescence within this scene.

Consistent with this, there are symbols that become "sacred objects," as Durkheim would call them. Most objects, behaviors, and styles within this culture that support the moral order of the group are positively evaluated. In fact, members refer to these entities as *kynd*.[1] There is a kynd way to dance and a kynd way to behave. There is even a kynd way to dress. Dreadlocks, hemp clothing, and handblown glass are kynd ways to express oneself with fashion. But, arguably the most important kynd objects within this culture are the music and marijuana. The best homegrown marijuana in the scene is dubbed "kynd bud" or "kynd or heady nuggets."

How the Subculture Persists

Individuals with a high level of identification with this subculture often journey to these festivals and events several times each year. Once there, they congregate with each other in a fully functional community. Here, they hope to see acquaintances from earlier shows and also make new friends. Talk in the community generally consists of the ideals of working together, sharing rides, trading music, traveling, and musical experiences. Folks here often refer to one another as "brother" and "sister." They discuss the music and its deep meaning to them spiritually and emotionally. Inside the concert event, strangers become dancing partners, and no one is afraid of hugging or flashing a smile toward random individuals. After the event, they may travel to another concert or head away to rest, but one thing is for certain: they keep in touch with one another. This happens on a number of levels, including discussing the scene on an online message board.

The persistence of the subculture results from four social mechanisms: pilgrimage, ritual, relationships, and social networks. We'll look at each of these in turn.

Pilgrimage

A pilgrim is an individual who makes a journey to a specific location, and a pilgrimage is a voyage to that location with like-minded others who all value the shared experience of travel. Historically, pilgrims have made spiritual journeys (Bauman 1995, Dubisch 1995, Morinis 1984), and it has been argued that journeys to experience music and community are indeed spiritual (Baiano-Berman 2002, Sylvan 2002, Sutton 2000). Jamband subculture members make a pilgrimage each time they follow a band; this pilgrimage is a ritual to reaffirm subcultural values and ideals. Similarly, Turner and Turner (1978) observe that many Christian pilgrimages historically were (and continue to be) associated with festivals, noted to be the main attraction for the pilgrims. The festival scene of the jamband subculture is also a main attraction for jamband pilgrims.

After arriving at a show or festival, travelers share with one another the joys and the hardships of living on the road. The pilgrimage and shared experiences of travel forge strong bonds between members of the subculture. Specifically, some members make personal sacrifices in order to attend out-of-town concerts, and they have these sacrifices in common with one another. The journey sometimes generates feelings of personal and relational transformation for many. They truly become a community, with social support networks for one another (Pearson 1987:422).

Rituals

One of the most important rituals of this subculture is vending. In the main row of the parking lot, dubbed "Shakedown Street," independent vendors sell artwork, jewelry, food, and clothing. This title is from a Grateful Dead song about a certain street being the heart of a town with lots going on; "you just gotta poke around" to find it (Hunter 1990). This parking lot vending scene is one where people exchange their ideas and their goods in an open, friendly, and negotiable market.

Vendors in the community come from all over the United States, and many have been traveling for years. Vendors vary in style and merchandise, from those selling beer and water to those who travel the circuit to sell their artistic creations. By watching and networking, new vendors learn what and how to sell (Sheptoski 2000). Some vendors plan strategies for selling. For example, they might create a "rap" to grab people's attention. A woman selling sunglasses yells out, "Get some sunnies for your hunnies!" A man selling beer from a cooler stands on top of it as he shouts, "Get your icy cold beer right here!" "One for three, two for five!"

Taping live concerts is another ritual that some members engage in. "Tapers," as they are so aptly called, bring in recording equipment and are allowed special seating near the official soundboard with a taper's ticket (Whitman 2005). Taping, like vending, is an integral part of this scene. In fact, bands are labeled as "jam" when they allow free taping.

Finally, entering the concert, listening to the music, dancing, and smoking marijuana ceremoniously are the most joyous rituals enacted by members at each and every show. Within the venue, individuals often find their own niche. For instance, there are those who hoop around with LED hula hoops at the outer edge of the crowd. Also, there are folks who spin to the music (aptly called *spinners*). There are even those who join together around yellow balloons who call themselves

Wharfrats. This group is dedicated to remaining sober during the concert event. They help each other in this endeavor.

Relationships

As noted earlier, there exists a trusting relationship between subculture members and the bands. One of the defining characteristics of a jamband is permitting fans to tape the live performance within the concert venue (Budnick 2003). Recall that fans can tape, trade, and listen to the concert experience and relive those exciting live moments until the next concert, motivating them to attend future concerts. This provides a strong sense of trust and bonding between audience and band members.

Relationships among members are characterized by sharing. In addition to trading music, members share many things, including rides to the next show and concert tickets. For example, it is common to see individuals walking around the venue parking lot holding up one finger. This means that the individual needs a ticket to the evening's concert. Fellow members typically sell tickets to one another at no higher than face value. However, within this subculture, there is an amazing act of generosity known as "a miracle." Many times the person holding up that one finger either needs or would like a miracle, which is a free ticket to the show. Further, members engage in a bartering system with absolutely no hesitation. It is quite common in the scene for members to bring "extras," things that people need but have forgotten, and share these extras with each other. This generosity and thoughtfulness creates a family-like atmosphere.

Meeting new people is vital to the continuation of the jamband scene. Each time this community meets, new associations and new acquaintances are created. It is interesting to note that as the scene is recreated for each show, it consists of a different set of members. It is very important to socialize new members into the scene by teaching them the values and rules.

Interaction among Members

Just as relationships are crucial to the continuation of this scene, continued communication, outside the temporary parking lot community, is also important. Members are in continual interaction with one another, even when away from the concert or tour experience. When away from the traveling circuit, many members stay in touch via the Internet. This is not a new phenomenon. As early as 1985, Deadheads were logging onto online conferences and bulletin boards and using online services such as set lists and information about mail order tickets. Further, over 70,000 fans subscribe to a Dead Head Internet newsgroup (Shenk and

Silberman 1994). They also used the Internet to share media files, a common practice that was originally accepted by the Grateful Dead.

Today, the jamband community also stays connected via the Internet. Several bands and festivals have their own message boards and online forums. Jambands.com was created as an online magazine to keep members in touch with the scene when not touring. The site contains show reviews, forums, links, and news about the jamband scene. Jambase.com was created by one of the cofounders of jambands.com. At this one-stop site, members can keep a calendar of their favorite bands' upcoming performances, share information with one another, and search a database for upcoming shows. As a testament to the explosion of the festival scene, each year jambase.com provides a festival guide organized by region of the United States. The Homegrown Music Network, formed by Lee Crumpton in 1995, is an online source to find live shows, download samples, and listen to an online radio show. Here, tapers can learn how to tape, trade, and download live shows online.

An Ever-Changing Musical Landscape

In 2002, the very first Bonnaroo Music and Arts Festival (which began as a jamband festival), with minimal advertising, sold out in a matter of days. Dean Budnick (2003) attributes this to the fact that fans yearn for music and the community. At that time, there was little interest from the mainstream public in attending the festival. Since that time, however, mainstream acts such as Tom Petty, The Police, and Radiohead have been invited to the festival, bringing in what Budnick calls "the fringe element, who carry little interest in the long-term vitality of the scene, but rather appear solely to prey on concert goers" as well as bringing in curious mainstream-act followers (2003:253). This is fairly unique to Bonnaroo, as other large festivals in the United States have kept the music within the realm of jam and have not invited mainstream acts.

The jamband festival scene is likely to persist for many years to come. It bears resemblance to the folk and blues gatherings of the 1960s, which not only sustained a musical alternative to popular and rock music but also provided a venue for political and religious transformations and public expressions of ideology. Jamband subculture members also express themselves politically and free themselves to new experiences each time they convene in community. Their recurring scene provides many individuals the opportunity to become independent entrepreneurs in an alternative economic system. It also allows for new, as well as sustained, relationships. These relationships are enriched and their unity revived by the rituals enacted each time they gather. Thus, although their community is ephemeral and portable, members are able to create and maintain solidarity using the very basic sociological concepts Durkheim wrote about so many years ago.

Note

1. Other words in this subculture are often purposively misspelled, such as *Phriends,* which describes people who are helpful and friendly. The term is a play on the spelling of the jamband Phish (Shenk and Silberman 1994).

17

Taqwacore

An Introduction to Muslim American Punk Rock

Sarah S. Hosman

Taqwacore is a music subculture in the United States that can most basically be described as Muslim American punk rock. The word *taqwacore* is a hybrid that combines the Islamic term *taqwa,* which means "the fear or love of God," and *core,* short for *hardcore,* a term usually used to define a style of music characterized by an intense devotion to the subculture or community. As the word *taqwacore* indicates, the taqwacore subculture or community is a hybrid music subculture that in itself encompasses identities or aspects that are seemingly disparate: Islam and punk rock. This study, based on interview data, argues that taqwacore serves as a community-based form of resistance and identity formation, specifically through the development of a punk rock subculture.

Punk rock traditionally embraces a do-it-yourself ethic, an anti-authoritative attitude, and a disengagement from mainstream society and embracing of a marginalized identity (Davies 2005, Moore 2007, Traber 2001). Punk rock followers often elicit shock from others via their style and attitude, and their music often incorporates provocative discourses (e.g., death, violence, sex; Lang 1985). As a direct negation of the hippie movement of the 1960s and 1970s and the stadium rock movement of the 1970s, punk rock blurred the boundaries between performer and audience but also existed as a subculture that challenged norms and society openly, loudly, and sometimes violently (Davies 2005, McNeil and McCain 1997).

In contrast, Islam is a religion based on selflessness, devotion, and responsibility. Islam focuses on piety, cleanliness, and order—seemingly in direct opposition to punk rock's embracing of disorder, shocking styles, and "dirtiness" (Esposito 2005). The term *Islam* means "submission to God's will." Despite the perceived disjuncture between Islam and punk rock in the United States, taqwacore serves as a space for alternative identity production and a means of simultaneous rejection and embracing of these identities or cultures.

Emergence of Taqwacore

The conceptualization and emergence of taqwacore are unique. Part of this characterization of taqwacore as Muslim American punk rock is deeply rooted in its conceptual emergence. In 2004, Michael Muhammad Knight published a novel entitled *The Taqwacores*, which tells the fictional story of a young Muslim man who moves into a punk house in New York. The main character is surrounded by a variety of people, including a straight-edge Sunni, a Shi'a skinhead, a burqa-wearing riot grrrl, an Indonesian skater punk, and a queer Muslim punk. Despite the uniqueness of each character, all the people in the house question Islam, what it means to be a Muslim in the United States, and the reason Muslim punk rock exists in the United States. In Knight's novel, the Muslim punk house in New York serves as the backdrop for all of the characters to not only question Islam and the United States but also develop their own sense of or relationship with Islam. The novel culminates as one of the main characters brings taqwacore bands from California to New York for a house show. Ultimately, the novel provided a source of inspiration and community that led to the emergence of taqwacore in the United States because people identified with the struggles and characters in it.

Shortly after Knight published his novel, a real-life taqwacore subculture began to emerge as people across the United States and North America read Knight's novel and subsequently formed taqwacore bands. During the summer of 2007, the Taqwa Tour traveled across the United States playing shows, including the bands Al-Thawra, Diacritical, the Kominas, Secret Trial Five, and Vote Hezbollah. In 2009, various taqwacore bands went on tour across the United States and Europe, and they began to join forces with other artists in the United Kingdom, such as Riz MC and Citizen Vex, who also identified as taqwacore.

Further, director Eyad Zahra produced a movie version of the novel, also entitled *The Taqwacores*, that was released in 2009 and premiered at the 2010 Sundance Film Festival. Omar Majeed filmed a documentary about the real-life taqwacore subculture, released in 2009 and featured at film festivals around the world.

The Bands: A Description

Despite taqwacore's being characterized as Muslim American punk rock, the bands and artists who comprise taqwacore encompass a variety of genres and artistic styles. Al-Thawra is a self-described "doom-crust punk" (personal correspondence) or metal band from Chicago. Al-Thawra translates to "The Revolution," and the band's lyrics tend to be politically motivated, socially aware, and critical. Based in Washington, D.C., the taqwacore band Diacritical is now called Sarmust. On its Facebook page, Sarmust describes itself as "a mixture between alt-rock, post-hardcore, dance, funk, classical, and folk music from South Asia and Sufi musical traditions like Qawwali. In an attempt to create a new sound that is rooted in angst and spirituality but ultimately about activism. [sic]"

The Kominas, a taqwacore band from Boston, tends to encompass a more "traditional" punk rock sound and look. The band's lyrics are satirical and shocking, and its first album, *Wild Nights in Guantanamo Bay,* includes songs such as "Sharia Law in the USA," "Suicide Bomb the Gap," "Rumi was a Homo," "WalQaeda Superstore," and "Blow Shit Up." Because of their more "traditional" or classical punk rock musical style, attitude, and style of dress, the Kominas have received the most media attention of all the taqwacore bands. Another band associated with taqwacore is Secret Trial Five, an all-female band from Vancouver, Canada. The band's name references a group of Canadian Muslims held in Canada on suspected terrorism charges. Though Secret Trial Five participated in the 2007 Taqwa Tour and other taqwacore shows, it has since denounced its involvement with taqwacore music. This may reflect the increasing media attention given to taqwacore bands as a spectacle, rather than in-depth analyses of their music and actions.[1] Vote Hezbollah is a taqwacore band from San Antonio, Texas, that took its name directly from one of the bands in the novel *The Taqwacores.* Vote Hezbollah specifically turned the poem that appears on one of the introductory pages of the novel, entitled "Muhammad was a Punk Rocker," into a song.

There are also two musicians in the United Kingdom who identify with taqwacore: Riz MC, a hip-hop artist and actor who has written songs such as "Post-9/11 Blues"; and Citizen Vex, who produces music that he describes as "experimenting with industrial, punk, and Eastern influences to create music that's aggressive in sound and challenging in content" (personal correspondence).

People Involved

The people involved with taqwacore, as band members, artists, and supporters, represent a diverse community of people.[2] Those I am most familiar with and whose stories and experiences this analysis is based on do, however, share some specific characteristics. Many of the people whom I met who are involved with taqwacore are US-born children of immigrants. Many, but not all, come from Muslim backgrounds. Many, but not all, have Arab, Middle Eastern, or South Asian backgrounds as well. While the ethnicities and religious beliefs of those involved with taqwacore certainly exist upon a spectrum, a consistency among those I met was a feeling of being characterized as "the Other," within both US culture and their religious and/or ethnic culture. This feeling of being the Other within two cultures or communities is not only an important motivating factor for individuals' involvement with taqwacore but also explains its emergence as a subculture in the United States.

As scholars (Abdo 2005, Baker 2003, Byng 2008) have noted, Arabs and Muslims, specifically, in the West and particularly in the United States, have often been framed as the Other within these respective societies—as not quite existing within the social, political, religious, or cultural boundaries of the society. For many Muslim Americans, Arab Americans, Middle Eastern Americans, and South Asian Americans, 9/11 and the events that occurred and policies that were implemented immediately after served as another important reminder that they are outside the constructed boundaries of acceptability in the United States (Baker 2003, Byng 2008). Often, Muslims (or anyone perceived to be Muslim or Arab) were characterized and framed as terrorists, suicide bombers, or extremists (Abdo 2005, Baker 2003, Byng 2008). A definitive conflation of Islam with terrorism occurred after 9/11 that placed many Muslims and Arabs in the United States in the position of not just explaining their religion or culture but also defending their beliefs (Abdo 2005, Baker 2003, Byng 2008). In addition, those involved with taqwacore felt alienated within the Islamic community or their ethnic community. By not ascribing to the customs, rules, and so on of this religion or culture, they, too, felt as outsiders from a community to which they were supposed to belong.

This sense of a "dual frustration" toward two communities and the persistent desire to be a part of both communities actually defines taqwacore and makes it possible. As frustrated Muslim, Arab, Middle Eastern, and South Asian youth in the United States who felt isolated from both the United States society-at-large and their traditional religious or cultural communities, those who are involved with taqwacore developed a means of expressing this dual frustration, a means of questioning both communities, and a means of embracing or existing within both. As subcultural theory has previously indicated, this cultural "strain" (Merton 1938) experienced by immigrants and children of immigrants is not a new phenomenon; however, how taqwacore resolves this "conflict" or "struggle" is unique.[3] A clear example of this dual frustration can be illustrated in two anecdotes from those involved with taqwacore. The 2007 Taqwa Tour culminated at the annual Islamic Society of North America's (ISNA) annual conference. The bands on tour signed up to play at the ISNA "Open-Mike Night."

The first band to perform was Secret Trial Five, and shortly after they began to play, conference organizers called the police to have their performance shut down, primarily because there were women singing on stage. The other taqwacore bands, as well as Michael Muhammad Knight, responded by chanting "Pigs are haram in Islam!" playing on the reference to police as "pigs" and the fact that pork is forbidden, or "haram," according to Islam. This experience illustrates a certain alienation from and rejection of the mainstream, even progressive, Islam in the United States. Further, many people in the taqwacore subculture relayed stories of personal discrimination they experienced just days after 9/11, including one classmate asking an individual that I interviewed, "What did *your* people do?" These two examples illustrate how those involved with taqwacore have experienced a "two-front sort of struggle"[4] against both Islam and the United States, facing rejection and discrimination from both sides. Taqwacore, then, exists as a critique and response to both.

What Taqwacore Does

Faced with this frustration toward the United States, Islam, and their ethnic communities, these individuals not only formed a taqwacore community or subculture but also embraced the concept of taqwacore and its fluid nature. Finding a familiar voice, a familiar struggle, and a familiar need for a community among each other, the individuals involved with taqwacore drew strongly from Knight's novel in creating a community or a subculture in which to express these struggles, confront this dual frustration, and achieve solidarity—a sense that they were not the only ones dealing with these struggles.

As mentioned before, one immediate question that comes to mind when examining taqwacore as Muslim American punk rock is, How have these individuals combined Islam and punk rock, particularly within the United States context? Upon deeper analysis,[5] however, it becomes clear that the punk rock identity and the Muslim (or Arab, Middle Eastern, South Asian) identity are not the "conflicting" identities for the people involved with taqwacore. Rather, taqwacore exists as a means to navigate, question, criticize, and integrate this dual frustration for the individuals involved through the explicit creation of and membership in a music subculture. Important for those involved with taqwacore is not just the ability and openness to question Islam and the United States, but also the ability to be able to question, criticize, and challenge, as well as embrace and make sense of, these two aspects of "who they are."[6] As such, taqwacore has been a means of making sense of these identities and truly finding both an Islamic and US identity of their own.

The Fluidity of Taqwacore

Crucial to individuals' involvement with taqwacore is its fluidity. Despite the mainstream media's focus on taqwacore as Muslim punk rock, and particularly as a punk rock subculture comprised of Muslim Americans, taqwacore, as a personal identity concept and subcultural concept, exists as a much more fluid or indefinable concept. For those involved with taqwacore, it exists not just as "Muslim punk rock" but rather as a concept that represents the fluidity of their identities, the questioning and criticizing of all aspects of their identities, and a means of defining Islam and the United States on their own terms and in ways that makes sense for them. Those involved with taqwacore separate themselves from seemingly similar religiously based music subcultures (e.g., Christian punk rock, Christian hardcore, and punk rock in Malaysia/Indonesia) in that taqwacore does not espouse or promote religious beliefs or values but rather encourages critical social and political thinking about religion. Therefore, taqwacore exists as a minority subculture within the United States, not as an ethnic or religious subculture. As a result, members are marginalized by Americans and respective religious groups. Those involved with taqwacore are aware of their minority status and also of how both the US and Muslim communities view them.

Many of the individuals involved with taqwacore hesitate to describe it as "Muslim punk rock," instead using phrases such as "a community of like-minded individuals," "punk Muslims," "a community of friends," "a safe space," or just "friends."[7] These descriptions emphasize that, for those involved, the punk rock aspects of taqwacore are not the most prominent; rather, the sense of community and openness associated with taqwacore are far more important in characterizing its meaning.

Taqwacore as Punk Rock

Although taqwacore members emphasize the fluidity of the taqwacore identity and argue that "Muslim punk rock" does not adequately or fully encompass what taqwacore is, I would argue that taqwacore is in fact punk rock—in what it does and its place in society. As clearly defined Others in both US society and Muslim society, those involved with taqwacore not only exist within but embrace their outsider status. Further, as traditional analyses of punk rock have noted (Hebdige 2004 [1979]), punk rock historically has not just embraced this outsider status but also engaged in processes of rejection, reappropriation, and eliciting shock. Punk rock, here, is conceptualized not just as a musical style, aesthetics, or class-based rebellion (Hebdige 2004 [1979]), but as a more overarching attitude, behavior, and purpose. Whereas historical punk rock subcultures rejected mainstream norms and values and expressed this via their songs, behavior, musical style, and dress, taqwacore simultaneously rejects both US mainstream culture and mainstream Islam and embraces both. Further, whereas traditional punk rock reappropriated symbols, signs, and artifacts (e.g., the safety pin, swastika, or Doc Martins), taqwacore has, in ways, reappropriated punk rock and infused punk rock with new and shocking meanings. Echoing punk rock subcultures of the 1970s, taqwacore bands have created shocking lyrics (e. g., songs about suicide bombs and Guantanamo Bay) as well as taken the traditional punk rock image and infused it with Muslim/Arab imagery. By creating its own punk rock subculture, taqwacore has reappropriated "white people's music"[8] and claimed a subculture or community of its own. By reappropriating punk rock in a shocking and new way, taqwacore has developed a meaningful community of resistance.

Crucial in taqwacore's ability to reappropriate punk rock is the recent commercialization of punk rock and the images, styles, and popularity of punk rock since the 1970s. No longer shocking, traditional images and styles of punk rock are mass-produced and marketed to youth. In light of this commercialization of punk rock, taqwacore has created a new punk rock subculture in the traditional sense. To acknowledge that punk rock can and must go beyond style and aesthetics is to allow and encourage taqwacore as a punk rock subculture despite its fluid nature and rejection of strict labels. Similar to what Feixa (2006) found in local punk scenes in Mexico and Spain, taqwacore represents a link between a global culture and local forms of social resistance.

Further, taqwacore elicits shock from audiences and the media in ways similar to early or traditional punk rock. Due precisely to the mass commercialization of punk rock, the styles and attitudes of punk no longer elicit the kind or depth of shock as they did during punk rock's initial emergence in the 1970s. Taqwacore has, however, managed to successfully bring this shock value back into a music subculture. In addition to the song titles and themes listed previously, taqwacore bands' album titles and images, behavior at shows, and general attitude have elicited shock from mainstream US society and Muslims both in the US and abroad. In the United States, in a post-9/11 context, joking about suicide bombs and Guantanamo Bay, criticizing capitalistic ventures in the Middle East and in the United States, and making light of 9/11 are not just shocking but unacceptable to some people. As illustrated when taqwacore bands played at the ISNA conference, in many ways, what taqwacore is doing and when and where its members are doing it, makes it a very punk rock subculture.

Much of the shocking behavior, lyrics, and images of taqwacore is purposeful and intentional, and meant to be satirical and offensive.

However, members of taqwacore have experienced discrimination based on factors outside of their control. In many ways, those involved with taqwacore are shocking not because they sport Mohawks or wear offensive T-shirts but because they are Muslims or Arabs in the United States. Concert promoters and bar owners have canceled taqwacore shows once they found out that taqwacore has a Muslim or Arab component. It seems that being Muslim and playing loud music in the United States in itself is shocking behavior.

Conclusion

Taqwacore has been generally described as Muslim American punk rock, and while taqwacore is a punk rock subculture, it also goes beyond this simplistic definition. As a means of creating a safe space in which to explore various aspects of one's identity, taqwacore has allowed those involved to question, criticize, and embrace seemingly conflicting aspects of their identities. Existing within a socially constructed conflict between Islam and the United States, those involved with taqwacore have created and used a punk rock subculture as a means of resolving this conflict. Rather than punk rock and Islam clashing or requiring mediation, this historically grounded and socially constructed conflict between the United States and Islam has been the underlying motivation and influence for taqwacore's emergence. Taqwacore illustrates that, for those involved, membership in a punk rock subculture has served as a mediator and means of resolving and questioning an identity conflict.

Taqwacore also exists as a hybrid subculture and as such allows those involved to criticize, question, and resolve these various aspects of their identities and lives. It is specifically through the creation of a punk rock subculture that taqwacore has allowed and encouraged this. While the label "Muslim American punk rock" does not fully encompass what taqwacore is, taqwacore is definitively a punk rock subculture in various ways. Hebdige (2004 [1979]) described the emerging punk subculture in the 1970s as a hybrid of dissimilar ideas, and in many ways, taqwacore is similar to this tradition. However, taqwacore exists at a deeper level than a class-based rebellion or hybrid of two music styles, as Hebdige (2004 [1979]) found, as a hybrid of identities, ideas, and cultures. As mentioned throughout this chapter, taqwacore exists as an identity-building concept, a community of people facing similar struggles and questions, and as a safe space. Taqwacore, in embracing the DIY ethic, anti-authoritarian attitude, and eliciting shock, is specifically a punk rock subculture that is meaningful for those involved and represents a new type of music subculture in the United States. Importantly, taqwacore goes beyond a process of individual identity formation, as those involved with taqwacore hope to inform people outside the subculture of their own struggles and the possibilities taqwacore encompasses.

As Lee Childers—one of the founders of early punk rock—said, "To me, that's what rock & roll should always come down to—the unallowed" (quoted in McNeil and McCain 1997). Certainly taqwacore encompasses that which is "unallowed" in the United States, and as such, functions for those involved as a form of resistance and identity formation, specifically through the development of a punk rock subculture.

Notes

1. The focus on taqwacore as purely "Muslim punk rock" and as a spectacle was reaffirmed both in interviews with individuals involved with taqwacore and in a media analysis of popular media publications, both conducted by the author (Hosman 2009).

2. The analysis presented here is based on participant observations at taqwacore shows, as well as a series of interviews that the author conducted with various individuals involved with taqwacore, including three taqwacore band members, the director of *The Taqwacores* movie, and a self-identified taqwacore supporter/subcultural member (Hosman 2009).

3. This conflict or struggle is characterized as a socially constructed conflict between the United States and Islam/Arab/Middle Eastern/South Asian identities, that culminated in 9/11, but not conceptualized as an actual conflict between the various cultures/communities (e.g., "clashes of civilization"; Huntington 1993).

4. Direct quotation from an interview (Hosman 2009).

5. Based upon interviews and participant observations utilized in completing this research.

6. This is a phrase used commonly throughout the interviews conducted in reference to these two cultural aspects of individuals' lives.

7. Quotes directly taken from the individuals I interviewed who are involved with taqwacore.

8. Interviewee specifically said, "I always thought punk was white people's music and now I feel this [taqwacore] can be mine" (Hosman 2009).

Part V
Music as Social Change and Commentary

Street procession in LaBoca, Argentina, 2007. Photo by Sara Towe Horsfall.

18

Hitler, the Holocaust, and Heavy Metal Music:
Holocaust Memory and Representation in the Heavy Metal Subculture, 1980–Present[1]

Mark A. Mengerink

For historians, Holocaust memory involves more than the way that Jewish survivors remembered their experience decades after the event. It also involves the way survivors, scholars, artists, commentators, and the general public reconstruct the event. Holocaust memory is constructed in the same way that Berger and Luckmann (1966) have theorized that "reality" is socially constructed. It both reflects contemporary society and attempts to represent the events themselves. In essence, scholarly inquiry into the construction of Holocaust memory is an examination of cultural history and sociology of knowledge. The intense study of Holocaust memory from the 1990s to the present has overlooked the way extreme metal music lyrics represent Hitler, the Nazi Party, and the Holocaust. The author examines the representations constructed by extreme metal bands through archival analysis of their lyrics, revealing the ways the bands engage with these themes. More research is needed to determine whether or how the depictions in extreme metal lyrics influence contemporary society's understanding of the tragic events.

Whether presented authentically or inauthentically, in accordance with the historical facts or in contradiction to them, with empathy and understanding or as monumental kitsch, the Holocaust has become a ruling symbol in our culture. I am not sure whether this is good or bad, but it seems to be fact.[2]

This quote from the noted scholar Yehuda Bauer reflects the uneasiness with the growing number of ways the Holocaust is represented and Holocaust memory is created. As Holocaust survivors disappear, the social memory of the events becomes ever more important and more controversial. When all the survivors are gone, what memory of the murder of Jews and others by the Nazi regime will be passed on to future generations?

Pop culture contributes to this enterprise, and though it has not received enough attention from scholars, music helps construct and transmit memory of the period. Academics generally focus on classical music or music created during the Holocaust (Arnold 1992; Gilbert 2005a, 2005b; Wlodarski 2005). Extreme metal bands have been singing about the Nazi period for at least two decades, but no one to date has examined their role in this process. Historians have generally ignored or disparaged extreme metal music despite its growing presence in pop culture (Arnett 1996; Ballard and Coates 1995; Hansen and Hansen 1990; Mulder et al. 2007; North and Hargreaves 2006; Stack, Gundlach, and Reeves 1994).

Discussion must first focus on the lyrics—what is said about Hitler, the Nazi Party, and the Holocaust. This chapter introduces subgenres of extreme heavy metal and examines how bands portray the Holocaust, Nazis, and Hitler in their lyrics. It further suggests possible ways the topic of extreme metal music and Holocaust memory and representation can be approached. It does not address the issue of how fans and the general public receive these representations. Influence of the bands on Holocaust memory must await further study.

Definitions

Extreme heavy metal is a collection of musical subgenres distinguished from other forms of heavy metal by a certain kind of radicalism (Kahn-Harris 2007). Superlatives define extreme metal music. It is the fastest (or slowest, depending on subgenre), the loudest, the sickest, the harshest, and the most aggressive music. All extreme metal subgenres diverge radically from the more traditional metal music of the 1970s and 1980s. The most popular types of extreme metal are thrash metal, death metal, grindcore, and black metal.[3]

Thrash metal developed as a "fundamentalist" reaction against a perceived decadence found in more mainstream metal and reflects the influence of hardcore punk and the NWOBHM (New Wave of British Heavy Metal) of the early 1980s (Kahn-Harris 2007). Thrash metal bands moved to purify metal of commercialism. They play at a very fast tempo while generally singing about serious political and social issues, allowing the bands to avoid the perceived superficiality found in more commercial metal music. The most successful and representative bands of the genre were the "Big Four": Metallica, Megadeth, Slayer, and Anthrax.

Death metal and grindcore, even more "extreme" subgenres of extreme metal, share characteristics, namely, growled or screamed lyrics focused on violence, war, death, and mutilation. Generally, these lyrics seem indecipherable to the extreme metal neophyte. What separates death metal from grindcore is the influence of 1980s punk rock on grindcore and grindcore's use of extremely fast drumming, known as "blast beats," which are not typically utilized in death metal.[4] (Kahn-Harris 2007, McIver 2005). Among the bands attributed for death metal's development are Autopsy, Death, Morbid Angel, Deicide, Obituary, and Cannibal Corpse. Founders of grindcore include Napalm Death and Carcass (UK bands) and Repulsion and Terrorizer (US bands) (McIver 2005).

Extreme heavy metal also includes black metal. Original black metal bands from the 1980s, like Venom and Slayer, were essentially thrash bands that sang about Satan for shock purposes and to drive up album sales. However, some early black metal groups, like Bathory and Mercyful Fate, and many bands from the 1990s and 2000s "embraced Satanism wholeheartedly" and have made it a central feature of their lyrics and lifestyle (Kahn-Harris 2007). A new strand of black metal has now embraced nationalistic, Social Darwinist, and Romantic elements, with a hint of fascism thrown in, illustrating the black metal scene's desire to push the envelope into ever-more-extreme areas. The mid-1990s saw the eruption of controversy over the involvement of black metal scene musicians and fans in church burnings, graveyard desecrations, and homicides, mainly in Scandinavia (McIver 2005, Moynihan and Søderlind 2003).

Clearly extreme metal possesses a "transgressive" nature. Members of the extreme metal scene do not recognize boundaries established by society outside of the scene. They instead construct their own boundaries and rules to regulate activities within the scene and the relationship between the scene and the outside world. This transgressive aspect appears in the lyrics.

Holocaust Representation: Analysis of Lyrics

The heated debate over Holocaust memory and representation generally splits scholars into two camps. Exceptionalists believe the unprecedented nature of the crimes limits the possibility of true representations of them and that any attempt at representing the Holocaust devolves into vulgarization. Exceptionalists resent the appropriation of Jewish suffering by those advocating national interests, universalist ethics, or personal identity. Constructivists, in comparison, stress the subjective nature of the event and point out that individuals and societies perceive the Holocaust in relation to what they already know. Memories of the event are constructed and admitted into a society's historical consciousness as appropriations. As a result, different communities construct different meanings of the Holocaust based on their own motives and needs at that time (Mintz 2001).

Hitler and the Nazis

Because extreme metal bands sing about the darker side of humanity, it seems logical they would sing about one of the most destructive episodes in human history—an event that most clearly illustrates the baseness of humanity: the Nazi period and the Holocaust. The surprising aspect of this research is how bands address these issues. Some bands apparently use the music and lyrics to offend as many people as possible. This reflects a basic characteristic of extreme metal—the desire to give the "middle finger" to authority and convention. However, some artists address these issues in a tasteful and sophisticated, albeit controversial, way. Reflecting the diversity in the extreme metal scene, there is diversity in the way bands address these topics in their lyrics. An uncensored analysis of extreme metal lyrics with Nazi and Holocaust themes is crucial to understanding the creation of Holocaust memory and representation. However, the reader is warned that some of the lyrics may be offensive.[5] Further, preconceived notions about extreme metal music should not be allowed to cloud our analysis.

The songs roughly fall into categories based on their commentary on the notorious German dictator. The smallest group professes admiration for Hitler. A second group showers Hitler and his ideology with scorn. The largest group uses Hitler as a warning about the concentration of governmental power into the hands of one person.

Analysis uncovered only one song that seemed to profess admiration for the German dictator. Dismember's "Hate Campaign" (2000) juxtaposed Hitler with God, Allah, Krishna, and Satan. A strong antireligious streak runs through the song. According to the song, "lies and self-deceit" characterize all religions. Hitler receives praise for his antireligious stance. The song ends, "I met Krishna the clown / He showed me the celibacy [sic] but I fucked him anyway / I heard Satan today / Told me to burn churches in a broad way / Spoke to Hitler today / He gave me two options / Become a god my way or their martyr and slave."

The song has an undertone of sympathy for Hitler. The juxtaposition of Hitler with deities is interesting despite the ridicule the deities receive in the opening verses of the song. Dismember mocks the Christian God for his inability to address the current state of the world. Allah and Islam receive derision for the perceived link between religion and violence. While not a song about Hitler per se, it invokes Hitler to portray a political message. Hitler has risen above religion and these deities because he allegedly refused to be a martyr or slave to religious tradition. The lyrics paint Hitler's ability to resist the sway of religion as admirable, even heroic.

A few songs criticize or demonize Hitler and his ideology. Flotsam and Jetsam, a thrash metal act from Arizona, sees Hitler as "a demon with a man's face." "Sacred Reich," a song from a thrash metal band with the same name, calls Hitler a "madman" and explains how he threatened world peace, "killing millions of Russians and Jews." Only killing Hitler would "stop this Nazi disease."

Apprehension about government power seems a common lyrical theme among extreme metal bands. Most songs conjure Hitler and use him as a warning about abuse of governmental power. He serves as the standard against which we should judge all leaders. The concentration of political power in Hitler's hands illustrates the dangers of government power run amok. Songs about Hitler encourage vigilance in the face of government intrusion into individual lives. In this sense, a libertarian streak seems to run through the extreme metal scene. Seeing any government power as a slippery slope toward a Hitlerite dictatorship is a common theme in such songs. However, a strong liberal streak also emerges as well, especially when songs examine Nazi ideology's emphasis on racial inequality. A majority of the bands whose lyrics examine Hitler's worldview reject it for its racist foundation.

Despite the warnings of these songs, it appears that Hitler's ideology lives on—or more accurately, Hitler's ideology as these bands understand it. As exceptionalists of Holocaust memory have feared, creators of representations and memory of the Holocaust not only appropriate the Nazi period for their own political and ideological agenda but also try to engage it on terms recognizable to them. Government corruption and abuse of power remain popular lyrical themes for extreme metal bands. As they engage with Hitler, Nazi ideology, and the Holocaust, they do so in a way comfortable to them. That bands use the Nazis and Hitler as an example of current government action and tend to transmit Nazism in distorted form becomes obvious very quickly.

As is common in broader society, a fundamental misunderstanding of exactly what characterized Nazi ideology permeates extreme metal lyrics. The most common mistake is equating fascism/Nazism with communism. In line with contemporary political discourse, there is a deliberate distortion of the memory of Hitler and the Holocaust as a political weapon. Politicians and pundits routinely use the dirty "H-" and "N-" words ("Hitler" and "Nazi") to discredit a policy or political opponent. Distortions of Holocaust memory regularly appear in mainstream media.[6] Critics have labeled both George W. Bush and

Barack Obama as fascists, despite the very obvious differences in their political ideologies. It is not surprising that extreme metal bands lack clarity in their characterizations of fascism and Hitler as well.

While songs warn about possible future Hitlers, singers allude to contemporary Hitlers in control of current economic and political systems. A nebulous web of plutocrats, including those with Stalinist and communist tendencies, are at times likened to Hitler and Nazism. For example, "Destroy the Opposition," a song recorded in 2000 by the Maryland-based death metal band Dying Fetus, reviles the power of money, the exploitation of the weak, and conspicuous consumption, calling on people to resist such trends. "Without hesitation I will kick the TV in. / Sick of all these fuckers with their Prozac grins. / Always selling shit that no one wants or needs. / Choking up the planet with their get rich schemes. / A mediated world, what a sick reality / Wake the fuck up, smell the shit, then you will see. / What's good for them isn't good for everyone. / The future starts now, for a past yet to come. / Just ask them one question, / and they'll tell you fifteen lies. / They're Judas, Hitler, Stalin, and Brutus / all combined."

The song does not examine the real substantive differences between Hitler and Stalin, who seem indistinguishable. Reminiscent of the totalitarian paradigm developed in the immediate post–World War II period by Friedrich and Brzezinski (1956), this idea appears numerous times in extreme metal lyrics addressing Hitler and the Nazis. Both dictators perpetrated heinous crimes against the people, so bands conflate the two. Current plutocrats continue this treatment. More interestingly, the song includes two people known for their betrayal. So not only are the plutocrats controlling the world today in a brutal and dictatorial fashion, but they also are betraying society.

The Holocaust

When the analysis turns to how bands address the Holocaust, two trends immediately emerge. First, when extreme metal lyrics mention "holocaust," the majority of them do not apply the term to the murder of European Jews and other victims of the Nazi regime from 1939 to 1945. Second, these discussions of "holocaust" always involve ulterior motives. Bands that do refer to the murder of Jews and other targeted groups in their lyrics do so to forward their own political or social agenda, not to examine the systematic murder of an entire population.[7]

A majority of bands use the term *holocaust* to warn of some future catastrophic event resulting in the death of either the entire human race or a large portion of it. This future holocaust is not necessarily the death of the Jewish people in part or in total. For these bands, the murder of Europe's Jews is generally not even on the radar. However, other than a few exceptions, to say the murder of Jews does not concern these bands may go a bit too far. Persecution of social outsiders seems a behavior many extreme metal bands abhor, especially if perpetrated by a central government. Still, the/a holocaust is some future event that will occur concomitantly with the end of the world, not the past murder of Jews and other victims.

This holocaust will result from several factors, including nuclear war; a worldwide pandemic; natural disaster, including man-made environmental damage; or some final struggle between the forces of good and evil, in which evil (oftentimes explicitly identified as Satan) prevails. Different subgenres have their preferred "holocaust." Thrash metal bands typically sing about nuclear and environmental destruction, while black metal bands see the coming holocaust as the final victory of Satan.

With the heated rhetoric of the Cold War during the 1980s, fears of nuclear Armageddon seemed prevalent, and nuclear destruction remained a common theme among extreme metal bands. For example, in 1986 thrash metal band Nuclear Assault recorded "After the Holocaust," describing a grim postapocalyptic scene, complete with mutants, a crumbling civilization, and mass suicides.

Testament, a San Francisco Bay Area thrash metal band, sings of an "environmental holocaust" caused by the man-made destruction of the ozone layer in its 1989 classic, "Greenhouse Effect." The song's chorus runs, "And they don't even care / If they seal the planet's fate / Crimes they perpetrate / Wasting precious land / It's time to take a stand / Our only hope, to breathe again / To stop the madness closing in / What will we do, when all is lost? / Environmental holocaust." These lyrics reflect the growing concern about man's impact on the environment that emerged more broadly in the West at the same time.

Black metal bands tend to use "holocaust" to refer to some final glorious satanic slaughter of humanity and the Christian God: a victory of evil over good. Typically such lyrics appear in the first person. The narrator of Centurian's "Heading for Holocaust" (2001) revels "in the stench of decay" as "the death of god / and the end of the world" arrive. In the song "Under the Holocaust" (1996) by Enthroned, a black metal band from Belgium, the narrator "declare[s] an endless war" in the name of Satan. As Satan and his forces prevail in the war, "The whole universe, will then recognize / the supreme power of Satan, who will retake / his throne for eternity and will reign forever."

Other bands appropriate the Holocaust to support their positions on important social and political issues like abortion or animal rights. Abortion proves one of the most controversial issues in the United States today, and Count Raven tackles it in typical extreme metal style—by equating it to the deliberate, state-directed murder of Jews and other victim groups. Presented from the perspective of an aborted fetus, called "the avenger of the past," the 1993 song excoriates supporters of abortion rights, stating supporters "Made cosmetics of my placenta / Threw away and burned my remains / You use a fine word: abortion / It's children's holocaust to me."

Animal rights advocates within the scene have also appropriated the Holocaust to advance their cause. The best example comes from a band called Hades. Their song "In the Mean Time" opens, "Playing Hitler with defenseless pets / As far as I'm concerned there's no excuse / I wouldn't be surprised if you were taking bets / On just how much the poor creatures can take of your / Abuse!"

Hades proposes a genocidal alternative to animal research: "Why don't you get it straight before it's too late! / Relieve those crowded jails, redefine the word 'bail' / Take those sentenced to life put them under your knife! / There's no better answer! / Kill one bird with one stone, the other leave alone / Stop destroying animals, this choice is logical / Use humans for your tests, the results will prove best!"

Whether Hades takes the proposed solution seriously remains uncertain. While irony is rich throughout "In the Mean Time," we cannot determine whether the band also uses sarcasm. The extreme metal scene does have a strong tendency to avoid over-seriousness and to address issues sarcastically. Keith Kahn-Harris describes this tongue-in-cheek attitude in the UK extreme metal scene by declaring, "humour and irony have always had a very important place within [the UK] scene" (Kahn-Harris 2007).

Scene members acknowledge and sometimes even celebrate the more comic aspects of the subculture. They also generally celebrate lack of taste and decorum. More research should determine if "In the Mean Time" falls into this category. According to Kahn-Harris (2007), "extreme metal has, from the beginning, contained camp and comic elements." In most cases, bands use humor, satire, and a comic element to transgress what society outside the scene finds acceptable. Most times, those outside the scene find no humor where scene members do. The perfect example is a band called Anal Cunt.

Anal Cunt (A.C.) explores Hitler, the Nazis, and genocide from a unique perspective. The band's song "Body by Auschwitz" states, "You fat slob, you flunked Jenny Craig / You flunked Weight Watchers, you're 500 pounds / You hoard calories like Dig hoards cash / Here's the 'Final Solution' for your fat / Body by Auschwitz / Body by Auschwitz." Another song boldly proclaims, "I sent concentration camp footage to America's Funniest Home Videos" and then laments that the footage did not win the $10,000 prize.

A.C.'s 1999 song "Hitler Was a Sensitive Man" attempts to find the "good" side of Hitler by proclaiming, "He went to art school when he was younger / He wanted to be a painter / Hitler was a vegetarian / He was also a nonsmoker / Hitler was a sensitive man [4x]" The song, besides incorrectly stating Hitler went to art school, also diminishes his murderous Jewish policy by calling it a concern "about overpopulation."

The offensive offensive continues with A.C.'s 2000 track "I Went Back in Time and Voted for Hitler." In the song, Mr. Peabody, the fictional dog whose "Way-Back Machine" appeared on *The Rocky and Bullwinkle Show*, gets sold to a Chinese restaurant, and the narrator proudly declares, "I punched every girl I saw in the face / On the way to the booth to vote for Hitler." A.C. has achieved the trifecta with this song by offending those who abhor Hitler's ideology, by perpetuating a negative stereotype of Chinese culinary culture, and by mocking violence against women.

"Hogging Up the Holocaust" (2000) criticizes Jews because "other people got fucked with too / But all you care about is you / Faggots, Gypsies, others, too / But you just want people to care about you," while "Ha Ha Holocaust" (2001) finds humor in systematic murder. The opening verse declares, "I got tired of writing rape songs / Then I remembered the Holocaust / I couldn't write because it was so funny / I'm glad lots of people died. / Ha ha Holocaust [3x] / I'm glad lots of people died."

We must keep in mind that even among a scene that embraces transgressing normal societal boundaries, A.C. is not typical. No other bands sing of Hitler and the Holocaust in terms similar to A.C. While many extreme metal bands may have a distorted understanding of Hitler and Nazism (conflating Hitler with Stalin and Nazism with communism, for example) or have used the suffering of Jews for their own political purposes, very little evidence suggests that extreme metal subscribes to fascist ideology. In fact, "members with the most overtly fascist and racist views have been pushed to the furthest margins of the extreme metal scene" (Kahn-Harris 2007). A strong antigovernment message appears in many songs, but overall, it appears extreme metal bands reject Hitler and his ideology.

Conclusion

Extreme metal's engagement with the Holocaust fits the constructivist model. As musicians wrote songs addressing the Nazi period, they did so only gradually, and then on their own terms. In terms of Holocaust memory, scholars like Alan Mintz probably would celebrate the involvement of extreme metal bands in the process because their participation will keep the discourse and debate alive, despite the offensive nature of many of the lyrics. Mintz celebrates the multiplicity of views about Holocaust memory and representation. He writes,

Let there be many visions, and let them converse with one another and present attractive and persuasive arguments for their positions. But let no group, not even survivors, claim that only they guard the sanctity of Holocaust memory and only their motives are free from taint. For if the purity of Holocaust memory is cordoned off and protected—which I believe is impossible to begin with—and if it is not admixed with other values and aspirations, then it will wither to the point of becoming little more than a museum artifact. (Mintz 2001)

Mintz brings us full circle to Yehuda Bauer's observation that opened this chapter. Whether we like it or not, extreme metal music has established itself in the Holocaust memory and representation business. What is the effect of these representations on the listeners of metal music? And how does their Holocaust memory contribute to our societal understanding of the event? These are important questions to be further investigated. We now have the responsibility of taking it seriously.

Notes

1. I would like to thank graduate student Bruce Hodge of the Lamar University History Department for providing research assistance. I also extend a warm thanks to my colleagues Drs. Rebecca Boone, Jimmy L. Bryan Jr., and Yasuko Sato for their insightful comments on a previous draft. The editors of this anthology also have helped me tremendously in clarifying my argument. My thanks and appreciation extend to them as well.

2. Yehuda Bauer, quoted in Cole (1999).

3. This research excluded neo-Nazi extreme metal, a completely separate subgenre of extreme metal. Also called National Socialist metal, white power metal, skinhead metal, or NS metal (among others), neo-Nazi metal appears on the extreme fringe of an already extreme fringe of the music scene. In fact, only more recent black metal bands have flirted with similar ideas, while at the same time shunning NS metal as too extreme. For a somewhat brief and outdated summary of neo-Nazi metal, see the Anti-Defamation League's introduction to the scene (n.d.).

4. To the trained ear of extreme metal fans, the lyrics are not unintelligible. Those typically unfamiliar with the music describe the lyrics as unintelligible. Hansen and Hansen (1991) describe the process of schematic processing of metal music lyrics involving cognitive load. Essentially novices to extreme metal music cannot understand the lyrics because the cognitive load is too high. Cognitive load can be reduced through several means, including repeated listening to extreme metal music and having copies of written lyrics while listening. Most compact discs and cassette tapes come with the lyrics printed in the liner notes.

5. The online lyrics archive Dark Lyrics (2001–2011) proved crucial in conducting this research. Beginning in the summer of 2008 and continuing sporadically until April 2011, the website's search engine was used to search

for three terms: "Hitler," "Nazi," and "Holocaust." The "Hitler" search returned 92 hits, the "Nazi" search 101 hits, and the "Holocaust" search 628 hits. Certain methodological problems may result. Searching for specific terms could result in not detecting songs that address these issues allegorically. Some songs use two or more of these terms, resulting in overlapping hits on the term searches. Also, the website's creators update the site with new lyrics they receive from fans quite regularly. As a result, songs that discuss these topics posted after April 2011 will not be part of this study. Because fans submit lyrics they have deciphered, potential problems of accuracy result. When possible, accuracy of the posted lyrics was checked by comparing them to the lyrics printed in the CD or cassette tape liner notes and a second website called Encyclopaedia Metallum (2002–2011).

6. Dana Milbank, op-ed columnist for the *Washington Post*, has examined the distortion of the history of Hitler and the Nazis for political (and financial) gain in his recent book (2010), especially chapter 8, "Glenn Beck's Love Affair with Hitler." I have yet to find a similar extensive study of the exploitation of the Holocaust for political purposes by liberals in the current American political context. This does not mean liberals refrain from this behavior. Senator Sherrod Brown, a Democrat representing Ohio, received harsh criticism for playing "the Hitler card" in the debate over union workers' rights. Jack Torry (2011) provides an example.

7. The application of the term *holocaust* to the murder of Jews and other victim groups by the Nazi regime remains controversial, despite its acceptance by many scholars since at least the 1960s. "Critics consider the original Greek meaning of *holocaust*—a sacrifice totally consumed by fire—as singularly inappropriate terminology for mass murder without any sacrificial meaning and having nothing necessarily to do with fire." See "Historiography," in Laqueur and Baumel (2001). Kamens (2011) also examined the use of "holocaust."

19

Painful Listening
The Musical Noise and Cultural Transcendence
of Southern Italian Tarantism
Lee Robert Blackstone

The ancient music of the tarantism ritual, a ceremony to treat a supposed "spider bite," is a particular cultural formation of the southern Salento region of Italy. The music known as the *pizzica tarantata* allowed southern Italians to express, and endure, their conditions of hardship and alienation. In this selection, music is a healing medium against social alienation. It constituted painful listening that today has been superseded by cultural activism and commercialism, moving the once stigmatic music toward social acceptability. This example allows us to examine how tradition and local culture are shaped by history, and how they may be transformed and reclaimed again for political and cultural resistance. The chapter consists of the following: first, a discussion of music and its relevance to society; second, a discussion of the concept of "noise" and how it bridges concerns about music and deviance; and finally, a discussion of tarantism as found in the Salento.

After silence, that which comes nearest to expressing the inexpressible is music.

—*Aldous Huxley (1931)*

Since the time of Plato, the musical arts of the West have often been described as casting a spell over listeners. The art of music is a resource by which the harmony of the universe, society, and the individual may be achieved.

Pythagoras, a sixth-century BCE Greek philosopher, scientist, and musician, furnishes us with a resilient and influential view of musical order. According to legend, Pythagoras heard the sounds of a blacksmith's hammer beating iron out upon an anvil; the ringing tones sounded in harmonious combinations. Pythagoras replicated the effects of consonant sound via the use of an instrument known as the monochord, a device with one string stretched across its board. By moving the monochord's bridge, and by dividing the string into different lengths, Pythagoras discovered that the musical pitches obtained corresponded to mathematical ratios. Harmony could be scientifically expressed by numeric relationships, and sounds could now be arranged into what we recognize as the Western musical scales (James 1993, Levenson 1995). Crucially, Pythagoras's breakthrough insight went beyond humanly produced music to imply that "the idea that the plucking of a string or the sounding of a chime can give access to another plane of existence" (Cook 1998:32). This vibratory scheme bound the heavens to human existence on earth via sound. The Pythagorean principle of the "music of the spheres" proposed that the planets, as they traveled along their orbits, produced musical tones that could be deduced mathematically. The constant music of the universe "surrounded the listener from birth to death, with never a moment of true silence to act as its foil" (Levenson 1995:24). Access to the divine pattern in nature—and of people's own bodies in relation to the universe—could be sought via musical scales.

The Greek philosopher Plato's recording of Socratic dialogues in his *Republic* (c.380–340 BCE) established the Western linkage between music and the State. Plato believed that music should be subjected to control and censure, and he expressed ethical concern regarding how music might penetrate the minds of citizens. Order and law would allow the State to remain on guard against any alteration to musical form. Socrates states plainly in the *Republic*'s Book IV, 424 that *"any musical innovation is full of danger to the whole State, and ought to be prohibited"* (Vintage ed. 1991; emphasis added). In Plato's *Republic* and *Laws*, the point is argued that citizens should be steered away from dangerous, licentious rhythms so that "the whole community may come to voice always one and the same sentiment in song, story and speech." A harmonious society is invoked through musical control, which is one means of erecting moral boundaries to separate the socially threatening from political and civil ideals (Hamilton 2007).

St. Augustine (354–430 AD) Christianized the idea of a universe interwoven by sound. He believed that music, with its fleeting existence, was a perfect medium through which to perceive God's beauty and ordered plan for the cosmos (Richter 1967). Articulating connections between God, music, and man as representative of a harmonious, cosmic order became an interpretive project in the West for centuries. Pythagoras's work also birthed a magical system (linking the individual soul, nature, and all the heavens), which proved vital to Renaissance *magi*. Since the cosmos rang through with sound, such sounds vibrated in nature, and each person's soul and body were similarly attuned. Musical sounds could thus affect people's emotions and even be a resource through which to control others: perhaps people could be stirred to war, or to make love, or to fall asleep. Alternatively, music could be a medium of connection and reconnection; as a healing tool, music might bring body and soul to consort with Nature (Blackstone 2009, Godwin 1995, James 1993, Tomlinson 1993).

The Sociological Relevance of a Connected and Disconnected Universe

However, music—as a social construction—is also subject to control, and powerful social institutions may erect aesthetic (and sometimes physical) boundaries concerning which music in society is proper and legitimate listening, while other music may be deemed improper, deviant, or even threatening to society (Attali 1985, Becker 1974, Blackstone 2009, Hegarty 2007, Martin 1995, Meyer 1961). Music's attributed properties of harmony and unification are complicated by the conditions of modernity. The dominance of people over nature opens up the world not only to the exploitation of natural resources but also to the exploitation of other people under the modern capitalist system (Adorno 2002b [1938]; Marx and Engels 1988 [1845–1846]).

For millennia after Pythagoras, music in Europe was bound to social institutions where its use maintained hierarchical distinctions within religious ceremonies and the royal courts (Hamilton 2007, Mackerness 1964). But music could not remain untouched by the changes to the modern world, and it would be affected by the division of labor. Enlightenment rationality had its effect on music. Over the latter part of the eighteenth century and across the nineteenth century, the manufacturing and consumption of music was transformed forever: music became a commodity. Increasing consumer demand for new types of music—and for the instruments and accessories (such as sheet music) necessary to play it—spawned an autonomous music industry (Martin 1995).

The division of labor was also keenly felt in the hierarchical separation of the composer, the musician, and the listener into clearly defined roles. Composers sanctified their compositional art as "works," and concert halls became the new cathedrals for such musical pieces. Modern science and rationality bred skeptics of organized religion, and the concert hall was where individuals could gather and experience music, yearning for music to connect them with something "other": "music provided an alternative route to spiritual consolation" (Cook 1998:36).

However, the music business exposed listeners to music that conformed to a socially constructed "canon" of accepted musical works. Critiquing the popular music industry, Theodor Adorno argued that listeners were not challenged by the sounds that they heard. The repetitious nature of popular music song structure contributed to people's resigning themselves to the boring, repetitive nature of work in the capitalist marketplace: another version of control (Adorno 2002b [1938]). If people's ears were liberated by challenging sounds, ordinary folks might begin to think more critically and seek to change existing conditions. We must therefore account for noise if we are to understand music, particularly if one of music's main functions is to provide for listeners "*an affirmation that a society is possible*. Its order simulates the social order, and its dissonances express marginalities" (Attali 1985:29).

Hearing Noise

Every manifestation of life is accompanied by noise. Noise is thus familiar to our ear and has the power of immediately recalling life itself.
  —*Luigi Russolo (1913)*

The musicologist Nicholas Cook has argued that the notions that composers are more important than musicians, and that listeners are passive consumers of musical products, are hegemonic ideas that shape our own discourse and thought concerning music; "they are all human constructions, products of culture, and accordingly they vary from time to time and from place to place" (1998:17). Symbolic interactionists and social constructionists within sociology would likewise propose that the "naturalness" of performing and listening to music arises from processes of social interaction and collaboration between social actors. People respond to the stimuli in their physical and social environments, defining and redefining a palette of understanding (Berger and Luckmann 1966, Hewitt 1984, Martin 1995, Mead 1964). A search for meaning also occurs in the realm of music.

Comprehending music depends on a culture's musical norms. Listeners are socialized into hearing music in particular ways, so that the shared musical conventions garner the aura of "natural" perception. Unexpected sounds are labeled "unnatural" and stigmatized as "noise" or sonic deviance (Attali 1985, Becker 1974, Blackstone 2009, Hegarty 2007, Martin 1995, Meyer 1961). What is considered music therefore identifies membership in a social group that is its community of listeners (Martin 1995). Boundaries are constructed around tastes and aesthetic appreciation.

G. H. Mead, in his seminal symbolic interactionist work, stated that "it is the task . . . of the artist . . . to find the sort of expression that will arouse in others what is going on in himself . . . which will call out in others the attitude he himself has" (1964: 212). The idea of "calling out" emotion is applicable to music performance and composition. Howard Becker wrote that "only because artist and audience share knowledge of and experience with the conventions invoked does the art work produce an emotional effect" (1974:771). Jacques Attali's definition of music as "noise given form according to a code, that is theoretically knowable by the listener," is a similar argument (Attali 1985:25). The emotional content of the music is socially derived, because the emotions "called out" must correspond to the recognized, emotionally correct response within the society (Becker 1974, Martin 1995, Meyer 1961).

Noise, in contrast, is "something we are forced to react to." Paul Hegarty points out that—like music—"noise is cultural"—and so whether one judges a particular sound as noise depends on one's sociocultural context (Hegarty 2007:3). Noise signifies differences, threatens established systems, and jams information being presented to a listener. From the standpoint of those in power, noise is most often aligned with the marginalized, the alienated, and the politically oppressed within society. Even the most familiar song may turn deafening at high volume; even legitimate citizens of a State may be regarded as the "enemy within" if they practice an alternative lifestyle or question the powers-that-be (Blackstone 2005). Noise distorts familiar social terrain. To control noise and minimize its chaotic impact (i.e., to impose silence) becomes a significant political endeavor (Attali 1985).

The modern world produces noise. In the 1800s, cities exploded as people migrated from their towns and rural villages in search of a better life in the factory centers. Industrial noise was described as an aural threat to the natural world. The noise of the Industrial Revolution was thought to be damaging to "the overworked human mind" (Gordon 1992:197). No longer did the metal forge signify unified Pythagorean harmony; instead, noise heralded the dehumanizing division of labor.

Noise can also be utilized as a tool by the powerless. Noise, in the form of a deliberate disruption (i.e., sit-ins, protest songs, or living an alternative lifestyle), may be necessary to highlight social injustice. Within music, a transgression of accepted musical conventions may indicate new forms of music to come; what is perceived as noise can birth new social and artistic conventions (Attali 1985, Blackstone 2009). Or, as Adorno argued, challenging, avant-garde music that could be perceived as "noise" is essential to awaken people's minds (Adorno 2002b [1938]). Ironically, sounds dismissed as noise in one era may be accepted in another, establishing a new aesthetic (Attali 1985, Hegarty 2007).

In the case of southern Italy, we have an instance of a music/noise, the *pizzica tarantata*, which has been stigmatized and associated with the poor and the outcast, becoming not just fashionable but a state-ment of cultural and political presence. Such painful listening is being restored as a celebratory assertion of identity and a critique of modern, globalized capitalist society.

A Web of Rhythm

Let her dance 'cos she is a Tarantata
'Cos Taranta pinched her.
Where did the Tarantella pinch you?
Under the hem of the skirt.
    —*Traditional Salentinian folk song*
    (translation from Daniele Durante)

In the region of Apulia known as the Salento, the bite of a spider was thought to induce complex symptoms collectively referred to as taran-tism. Tarantismo—the name encompasses the entire phenomenon as process—survived from ancient times until the mid-twentieth century. The ritual of tarantism utilized a functional music for healing—a music that could initiate a trance state and that was not originally intended for reproduction on a concert stage.

The rough outline for southern Italian tarantism began with the bite, which predominantly occurred among poor rural peasant women. A *taranta*'s (spider's) bite could result in a continuum of effects, rang-ing from aggression to melancholia (Sigerist 1948). The remedy was to cure an individual (*tarantata*, female; *tarantato*, male) via a range of stimuli, "the symbolism of music, dance and colors" (De Martino 2005 [1961]:xxi). Once family, friends, or coworkers noticed that a person was acting out-of-sorts, a diagnosis of tarantism set in motion the hiring of musicians for the restorative ritual. Musicians had first to hunt for a *taranta*'s unique song, which was a clue to the infectious personality of the spider; arriving at the appropriate tune would be signaled by a response from the *tarantata*. What followed was a frenzied dance, which could continue for hours or even weeks, during which the *tarantata* maintained a conversation with her *taranta*. Dancing the spider's poison out would resolve the crisis, a denouement that came through equal parts exhaustion and negotiation with one's *taranta*. Grace would then be expressed to Saint Paul at his chapel in Gala-tina. The rhythmic music of *pizzica tarantata*, bounded by the ritual of *tarantismo*, made for a powerful folk production. The emphasis on musical skill was directed toward healing the tarantulated person, and possibly instructing concerned family and community members in the norms of the ritual (Blackstone 2009).

The genesis of the *pizzica tarantata* may extend into the world of the ancient Greeks, and in fact a cult of Dionysus was once centered in Apulia (De Martino 2005 [1961]:187; Lewis 1989:81, 91; Sigerist 1948:103). The repetitive crashing of tambourines was reported to strongly affect the *maenads*, women devoted to Dionysus, who worshiped the god in the throes of ecstatic dancing (Ehrenreich 2006:30–41). Such behavior may presage that of the *tarantati*, who similarly engaged in trance-dancing induced by the percussive tambourines.

Southern Noise

When the cultural anthropologist Ernesto De Martino and his research team descended on the Salento in 1959, their observation of a performed rite for a woman referred to as "Maria of Nardò" left De Martino and his compatriots feeling as though they had been "brutally hurled onto another planet" (De Martino 2005 [1961]:38). De Martino, in his landmark book *The Land of Remorse* (2005 [1961]), explained tarantism as a culturally specific practice that enabled some residents of Apulia to cope with the difficulties of their everyday lives. Further, the weird sense of mythic timelessness that surrounded the complex ritual highlighted what in the modern era has been referred to as the "Southern Question": the construction of differences between the north and the south of Italy.

Compared to the more industrialized and cosmopolitan north, the Salento has long been stigmatized as a backwards land, where one can find "at varying levels of consciousness—the space of the primitive, of superstition, the irrational, magic, desiccation, and death" (Crapanzano 2005:vii). Further, the history of Italy has been disjointed; the land had not only been divided up into many different city-states but also other countries such as France and Spain had controlled portions of the peninsula. The unification of Italy over the period of the Risorgimento (1848–1870) was thought necessary to create a single state, but contentious questions remained over differing dialects, regional cultures, and economic stratification. The people of the south remained mostly subjugated to wealthy landowners and to banks located in the north of Italy.

According to David Horn (2003), both Italian cultural anthropology and early Italian criminology following the Risorgimento highlighted the sense that southern Italians were less attuned to modernity. Unflattering portraits of southern Italians as premodern evolutionary throwbacks were popularized through the work of Cesare Lombroso (1835–1909). Lombroso's project used a musical metaphor to assess "deviant" individuals through bodily, physical features. "At times, Lombroso referred to anomalies as notes in a musical chord: the isolated anomaly had to be taken together with other physical and moral notes for the criminal type to take shape" (Horn 2003:16). In Lombroso's scheme, the south harbored dissonant criminal and barbaric beliefs within the newly modern nation-state of Italy. The south of Italy was, therefore, the embodiment of social noise.

"Civilizing" the South

In his 1930 essay "The Southern Question," the Italian Marxist theorist Antonio Gramsci addressed the north/south divide. Gramsci notes that the Socialists had also exacerbated antisouthern rhetoric, with people from the south routinely being portrayed as crude and biologically inferior beings. The peasants of the south were being exploited as part of one vast agrarian complex that served the interests of northern capitalists. In an effort to counter the racist logic levied against the south, Gramsci argued that northern proletarians needed to align themselves with the southern peasants in order to dislodge the influence of the capitalist north (Gramsci 2005 [1930], Verdicchio 2005).

De Martino addressed the abiding power of the "Southern Question" in *The Land of Remorse* (2005 [1961]) in myriad ways. In addition to dichotomies such as wealth/poverty, civilized/uncivilized, and city/country that characterize the Southern Question, De Martino also discusses the religious differences between the Catholic Church and indigenous pagan belief structures: another sociocultural battleground that remained contested in the south, and which also contributed to the "deeply discrediting" condition of the *tarantati*, the spider-bitten. The Italian Catholic Church co-opted indigenous folk beliefs into itself or otherwise eradicated them. The 1545 Council of Trent condemned dancing and other ecstatic activity; to engage in dance, therefore, was to court dissent. Seeking to bring tarantism in line with church orthodoxy, religious leaders settled upon utilizing Saint Paul as a figurehead for the afflicted *tarantati*. The people of the Salento were familiar with Paul's recovery from a poisonous viper bite in the *Acts of the Apostles* (28:1–6). According to folk music researcher and oral historian Luigi Chiriatti, the Catholic Church depicted *tarantismo* as sinful, gradually making the people of the Salento feel uncomfortable toward tarantism: "The people that were called *tarantati* . . . were ashamed of this dance, of this feeling, and people who were aware of the *tarantati* watched them as if they were something to hide."

Coping with Social Ills

Contributing to the stigmatization of tarantism in the modern world were social variables of sex and class. In the Salento, by the late 1950s "the vast majority of the populace continued to be day laborers— illiterate, poorly nourished, and without most forms of social assistance" (Del Giudice 2002). Italian newspaper *La Repubblica* reported in 2007 that nearly two-thirds of Italy's seven million poor remain rooted in the south. The Salento has historically also been a strict, patriarchal region. Many women were illiterate and unloved; a gendered division of labor, poverty, and patriarchy made for an oppressive life. Laura Fraser (2010:56) noted that in the south, "the local landowner had the right to sleep with a bride first on her wedding night." Small wonder, then, that the bite of the taranta held such erotic power, and tarantismo's capacity to channel melancholy and depression accrued symbolic power.

Importantly, De Martino described tarantism as a way of coping with what he refers to as the "crisis of presence." The ritual channeled alienation on the outskirts of society, and it aided in the recovery of a sense of purpose in one's lived history. Whereas women and the indigent were marginalized in Italian society, tarantism unveiled their suffering and demanded a social response. *Tarantismo* redirected peoples' frustrated inner worlds, which were assailed by destitution, church doctrine, and rigid social norms, and made of these sociopsychological complexes a public performance—an ecstatic protest—in music and dance.

Music may become an aural, political aesthetic. Because people often associate with others who understand the same musical norms, communities of listeners may be created (Martin 1995). The music one enjoys can become a source of empowerment, or what Grossberg (1997) describes as an "affective alliance." Norman Denzin wrote that not only do people fantasize and seek meaning through cultural objects, but also "these experiences become political when the actions and emotions they express connect to the political economies of everyday life in ways which reinforce class, race, and gender stereotypes" (Denzin 1992:135). Cultural expression can thus erect a boundary that valorizes a group's lived experience, setting that group apart from the wider society that judges their activities. Despite the shame attached to the ritual by outsiders, for southern Italians the magico-religious mystery of *tarantismo* spoke to their immediate conditions.

As tarantism settled into a stable cultural formation with its particular procedures, people who had been "bitten by spiders" became privileged pariahs in their social relationships. Stigma, defined by Erving Goffman (1963:3), is "an attribute that is deeply discrediting" that profoundly changes interpersonal interactions. Though *tarantati* might appeal in their crises to their spiders, rarely were actual bites found on afflicted persons; hence, attention focused on enacting symptoms through the public tarantism ritual. Further, the loss of income from leaving work, and the cost of maintaining musicians for the rite, was a burden for indigent families. As a form of stigma, *tarantismo* simultaneously delineated the "bitten" person as different, while also providing a structure wherein an individual could transcend her condition. Whether a person was unwanted, unloved, or suffered from a perceived helplessness in the face of grinding poverty, the *pizzica tarantata* functioned as "an outsider music for outsider individuals" (Blackstone 2009:192).

Musical Heritage

Historically, tarantism entered a long period of decline, gradually becoming regarded as an atavistic, shameful form of disease; empirical, rational science had abandoned tarantism's supernatural origins, cutting it off from its cultural lifeblood (Tomlinson 1993). No longer associated with Dionysian ecstasy, the ritual's purpose had become arcane by the mid-twentieth century. What lingered was a music that intimated unbearable sufferings. For the Salentinian community of listeners, the sound of the pizzica tarantata was akin to an aural wound, a passport to histories of exploitation and unhappiness.

Yet clearly, the efficacy of any ritual order depends on the shared understandings of the participants and possible observers; they are tightly bounded events (Lewis 1989), with an underlying logic that may belie apparent chaos (Ehrenreich 2006, Rouget 1985). So, despite the monetary expense and social cost, Apulians granted the *tarantati* the space and time to work through their crises:

> Music and dance are precisely the principal means of socializing or institutionalizing this hysteria, by providing it with stereotyped forms of trance forms. In tarantism, the tarantella (music and dance) does not have the function of curing the tarantulee of her hysteria, but on the contrary, provides her with a means of behaving like a hysteric in public, in accordance with a model recognized by all, thereby freeing her from inner misfortune. (Rouget 1985:164)

The 2004 documentary *Un Ritmo per L'Anima* (A Rhythm for Your Soul) explores the tarantism phenomenon, often echoing Rouget's insight above. In the film, the ancient ritual is compared with modern therapeutic methods such as psychoanalysis and transcendental meditation. Consistently stressed in *Un Ritmo per L'Anima* is the release of energy through tarantism: "a way," states therapist Antonio Fassina, "of resetting your mind." The goal of using music to heal is to restore harmony to the afflicted patient. Tullio Seppilli, president of the Italian Medical Anthropology Society, argues that a connection exists between contemporary therapies and Plato's epistemology: "If we look at modern scientific medicine, they talk not of harmony but of re-stabilizing or balancing different bodily functions, but it is still harmony they are talking about. . . . Everything works as a system" (Capani 2004). However, for *tarantismo* to bear healthy fruit, the afflicted individual had to be immersed into the ritual's choreography.

For any energies to be realigned, the *tarantata* had to be plugged into a "musical circuit," surrounded by the musicians and by the community. Salentinian society legitimated the ritual; the people provided *tarantismo* with power, which the *taranta* victim then found within herself. Much like the Pythagorean doctrine, music here becomes the thread linking people to society, and to ultimate harmony.

The Return of Noise

Agave: Now, now I see: Dionysus has destroyed us all.
Cadmus: You outraged him. You denied that he was truly god.
    —*Euripides,* The Bacchae

Jacques Attali wrote in *Noise* (1985) that noise is returning to society; it is never fully suppressed. Music serves the Dionysian impulse, the need to dance within a like-minded community (Blackstone 2009, Gaillot 1998). Perhaps it is not surprising that tarantism should return to Salentinian consciousness after its centuries-long decline. As Luigi A. Santoro, professor of theater at the University of Lecce in southern Italy, has stated, "These phenomena never really disappear—they get pushed into the shade, out of the way; underground, if you like, but as phenomena they remain" (Capani 2004).

The rebirth of *pizzica tarantata* was, however, fraught with difficulty, and musicians who performed the music suffered being discredited through association with the aural noise of the *pizzica*. Luigi Chiriatti described the transfer of stigma as being due to "broken memory"; the music conjured up the pains of poverty that families endured. As a result, the music was rarely performed. When musicians attempted to revive the music in the 1970s, they were met by protests in the painful form of a hail of thrown stones: a clear indication of how close to the surface sorrow lay in the Salentinian mindset (Chiriatti 1998:52).

Flaminia Vulcano, the manager of the band Nidi D'Arac, a group that derives its inspiration from the tarantism ritual, highlighted in an interview with me the different feelings that the "broken memory" aroused between city and country denizens:

> People who lived in the city [felt] high class, compared to people who were living in villages. . . . [But] the people that lived in the cities came from these people. . . . So, they kind of wanted to forget this rural part. This is why the people were ashamed of their roots.

However, Alessandro Coppola, the lead singer of Nidi D'Arac, argued that his return to the *pizzica* grew out of a "need," particular to his generation, to find his roots. Time had allowed for a reassessment of the *pizzica*, and time had forced a wedge between modernization and what had been "lost" in southern Italy. Tarantism was now poised to be rediscovered, not as an embarrassing relic of tradition but as a crucible for affirmative cultural and political identity-work.

The re-proposal of *pizzica tarantata* within the south of Italy partly resulted from an influx of immigrants into the Salento. Immigration has been an ongoing concern of the far right in Italy, for groups such as Lega Nord per L'Indipendenza della Padania, and even Silvio Berlusconi's center-right Forza Italia. The Lega Nord, in particular, argued for the north's racial superiority over the south (Verdicchio 2005); and, with increased immigration occurring in the south from Albania and African countries, the already-denigrated south was perceived as contributing excessively to the immigration "problem." As for the people of southern Italy, the arrival of a wave of immigration after the fall of the Berlin Wall in 1989 resulted in regional soul-searching. The new immigrants did not abandon their traditions or cultural beliefs, leaving many southern Italians to wonder what defined their own culture (Chiriatti, personal interview, 2006).

The answer was to be found in *pizzica*, and in the specific cultural formation of the tarantism ritual. With young people moving toward identifying themselves with southern Italian life, *tarantismo* no longer appeared stigmatic; in fact, it was a basis of "self-assertion" (Chiriatti 2006) that tied people to their land. One could argue that the power within oneself that tarantism allowed one to seek, the grace bestowed either by the spider or Saint Paul, was once more released to establish the worth of the community. As a result, a new cultural activist movement emerged in the Salento: *neotarantism*. Many bands formed to perform *pizzica* music, either traditionally (such as Alla Bua and Zoè) or combined with modern electronics and dance rhythms (such as Nidi D'Arac and Mascarimiri). The audiences for the *pizzica* are referred to as the *nuovi tarantati*, the "new tarantati," who dance and identify themselves with this music. Where classic tarantism offered a means for an individual to be reintegrated back into his or her family and society, neotarantism creates an opportunity for people to integrate themselves into a renewed culture.

A New-Old Music

The political dimension to the sounds and performance of the contemporary pizzica movement lies in its alterity. Alessandro Coppola describes the music itself as "exotic"; it is not music that one would readily hear on the radio or find performed on the television. Neotarantismo set itself against not only the hegemony of Prime Minister Silvio Berlusconi, who long represented the north's concerns in Italian politics, but also Berlusconi's domination of the mainstream Italian media. The rise of neotarantismo, with its emblematic pizzica music steeped in the historical subjugation of southern Italian women, under Berlusconi's reign was particularly apt given the prime minister's frequent derogatory comments about Italian women, and the numerous sex scandals that occurred during his administration.

The cultural movement also exalts what the Salentine accordionist Claudio Prima refers to as the "slow time" of the Apulia region, as compared to both the urban bustle of the north and the racing pace of globalization (Prima, personal interview, 2006). In the process of building a powerful local movement that affirms the Salento's values and difference, the *nuovi tarantati* are likewise addressing the "Southern Question" and biting back against its pernicious influence. To expose other people to the culture of the south means to infect them with its value. Ironically, the power of *pizzica tarantata* has not been lost on politicians. Each summer, towns in southern Italy have their *feste*, street festivals that may coincide with saints important to that locale. Music is prominently featured at the *feste*, and politicians of both the right and the left have sponsored some of the most popular *pizzica* bands to perform for their constituents. While musicians such as Coppola and Prima agree that such exposure is good, they are also wary of appearing to support a particular politician's agenda. However, the essential aspect of modern *pizzica* is that it exalts community and the power of the people; as an outsider music, it has long served as a subtle critique against authority. For politicians to court a music that has the danger of noise within it is to take a risk at undermining themselves. The mayor of Melpignano, a small town that hosts the famous *La Notte della Taranta* music festival (which has attracted upwards of 50,000 people), has acknowledged that

> What we want to show by means of "The Night of the Tarantula" is that our traditions aren't some kind of ornament which we keep in the best room in the house. . . . [It] has to be something dynamic, it has to be a product that in some way will enable you to build a project for the future of our area It is rather extraordinary that such old music has slipped through the clutches of time; it gets the generations together, and it makes them dance. When those bodies begin to dance, to the notes of that music, we are carrying out a remarkable political office. (in Pisanelli 2005)

The power of tarantism to bring people together, to knit them together in a shared choreography, remains undiminished.

Conclusion

On a much larger scale, tarantism today is a vastly changed ritual, one based on performance and marketing the Salento in a positive light. The *pizzica tarantata* is a vehicle against alienation: no longer is the music performed solely for a stricken victim, but the music is experienced in groups in concert settings that foster ecstasy and joy. However, the commercialization of tarantism takes genuine emotional release and cuts a route to spirituality through the market.

In this light, the idea of tarantism is as important under modern conditions as it was in its premodern context. No matter how stigmatized the tarantism tradition became, the emphasis on a harmonious union between music and dance still serves to bring together individuals and their world, combating the crippling "crisis of presence" described by De Martino. The *neotarantismo* revival therefore serves a reconnective function that delivers on sociology's promise to face a fragmented, modern world. The music of *pizzica tarantata* reminds us that "society is possible" (Attali 1985:29). The question now is how far neotarantism may be exported, and how much it may utilize the modernity that has caused so much pain for the south, without vanishing into the noise of itself.

20

An International Comparison of the Politics of Straight-Edge
William Tsitsos

The author examines the political message of straight-edge music in Europe and the United States. In the latter, the music reflects the individualistic, liberal ideology with an emphasis on personal morality that has been common since the 1960s. In contrast, in European countries with strong welfare states, the medium is a means of challenging capitalist oppression.

Straight-edge is a musical (and life-) style centered on rejecting drugs, alcohol, and (in some cases) meat-eating. The term comes from a song entitled "Straight Edge," by the early-1980s Washington, D.C., hardcore punk band Minor Threat. Although Minor Threat broke up in 1984, straight-edge did not end. To the contrary, it has become an international subculture. In this chapter I will compare straight-edge in the United States with European straight-edge, focusing on influential bands from the 1980s and 1990s. Like bands in the larger punk subculture from which straight-edge emerged, straight-edge bands voiced dissatisfaction with society's mainstream. The specific sources of this dissatisfaction differed, however, for straight-edge bands in the United States in comparison to their European counterparts. US straight-edge bands emphasized issues of personal morality and individual choice (particularly abstinence from drugs and alcohol) as central to the subculture. In contrast, in Europe a leftist, Marxian brand of straight-edge emerged in many of the most influential bands of that period.

I contend that straight-edge in the United States reflects the emergence of hyper-individualistic, neoliberal ideology in the nation since the 1960s. Specifically, I am referring to the increased focus on personal morality, rather than structural conditions, as the root of social problems, which was a defining characteristic of the post-1960s United States (Luhr 2009:9). I argue that this preoccupation with individual values and morals in the United States helped shape the US version of straight-edge into one that was similarly preoccupied with individualistic morality. By contrast, straight-edge in Europe took shape in an environment without the US aversion to structural explanations (and remedies) for social problems. The most influential European straight-edge bands from the 1980s and 1990s, as indentified in the literature on European straight-edge, came from nations with strong welfare states, such as the Netherlands and Sweden. For these bands, straight-edge was a means to clear the mind in preparation for challenging the oppressive structures of capitalism.

Literature Review

Wood's 1999 article provided an overview of the processes of development and schism in the US straight-edge scene's history. As described below, the straight-edge message has taken various forms as it evolved, with some straight-edgers speaking out against meat-eating, caffeine, and even abortion, in addition to alcohol and drugs. The book *All Ages: Reflections on Straight Edge* (1997), by Beth Lahickey, compiled interviews with musicians and fans, primarily from the New York straight-edge scene of the late 1980s, but also with Ian MacKaye, the vocalist for Minor Threat. In *Burning Fight: The Nineties Hardcore Revolution in Ethics, Politics, Spirit, and Sound* (2009), Brian Peterson interviewed prominent figures, including many straight-edgers, from the 1990s hardcore scene. Meanwhile, Gabriel Kuhn's *Sober Living for the Revolution: Hardcore Punk, Straight Edge, and Radical Politics* (2010) collected interviews with individuals associated with the straight-edge scene in Europe and elsewhere. The interviews published in these books provide the main material that I analyze here.

When not relying upon these interview data, I base my analyses on primary source accounts written by those who were present and central actors in the events that they describe, such as *Dance of Days: Two Decades of Punk in the Nation's Capital* (Andersen and Jenkins 2001). Another resource for information on straight-edge in Europe is Marc Hanou and Jean-Paul Frijns's (2009) book, *The Past The Present 1982–2007: A History of 25 Years of European Straight Edge,* which combines interviews with analysis. Overall, I am attempting to understand straight-edge by studying the words of those individuals who have played central roles as performers and organizers in the straight-edge scene over the years. This is different from works (Williams 2003, Williams and Copes 2005, Wilson and Atkinson 2005) that focus on straight-edge fans.

Since 2006, there have been two book-length scholarly analyses of straight-edge, by Wood (2006) and Haenfler (2006). In their work, Haenfler and Wood treated straight-edge as a subculture. Haenfler, for example, cited Bennett's (2001) definition of a subculture as "a social subgroup distinguished from mainstream culture/dominant society by its own norms, values, rules, and, especially in youth subcultures, its own music and style" (Haenfler 2007:33). For Haenfler, "subcultures are made up of youth dissatisfied with the mainstream adult world who seek to carve out their own niche" (2007:33). But what is the source of this dissatisfaction? In this chapter, I argue that the answer to this question varies when comparing straight-edge bands in the United States with their European counterparts through the 1980s and 1990s. While there were exceptions to this pattern, on the whole the most influential US straight-edge bands were more likely to cite others' moral choices as the main source of their dissatisfaction, while the most influential bands from Europe more often spoke out against structural conditions at the societal level.

While Haenfler emphasized the antimainstream component of straight-edge, Wood, citing the work of David Matza (1964, 1969), pointed out how subcultural identity is not formed in a vacuum but rather is influenced by mainstream society. As Wood stated, "it is not simply a coincidence that an antidrug culture should emerge in the United States at a time when prominent politicians, celebrities, and other cultural agents were vehemently declaring a 'war on drugs' in American society" (Wood 2006:17). This point, that subcultures are in fact products of the larger society in which they emerge, is central to my analysis of the distinct evolutionary paths of straight-edge in the United States and Europe.

Straight-Edge in the United States

In songs like "Straight Edge," Minor Threat showed little interest in larger sociopolitical issues, focusing more on the personal choice of sobriety. Andersen and Jenkins quoted Minor Threat's vocalist, Ian MacKaye, in an early-1980s interview discussing his "inward-looking ethic: 'If you want to keep an eye on what's going on, that's cool, but you are not as capable of changing politics as you are capable of changing yourself. If you're able to change yourself, that's for the better. When you get that out of the way, then maybe other things will shape up'" (Andersen and Jenkins 2001:80). In *All Ages*, MacKaye reiterated this, stating, "It's not my fucking business to be telling people what to do with their own lives" (Lahickey 1997:100–101). Overall, Minor Threat embodied the total focus on individual moral choices that characterized straight-edge at its beginning.

In the late-1980s, the second wave of straight-edge took shape around New York City, although many of the "New York City" straight-edge bands were actually from suburban Connecticut and New Jersey. As Lahickey wrote in the introduction to her book, *All Ages*, "I view this particular era to be the second wave of straight edge. DYS [Department of Youth Services, a Boston straight-edge band], SSD [Society System Decontrol, also from Boston], and Minor Threat, whether deliberately or not, provided the initial inspiration of the straight edge scene on the East coast. These bands were influences of Youth of Today, Bold, Judge, and so on" (Lahickey 1997:xx). The last group of bands mentioned by Lahickey spearheaded a revival of straight-edge in a city whose punk scene was long known for excessive drug use (Lahickey 1997:25).

Youth of Today introduced vegetarianism into the straight-edge code of ethics (Wood 1999a:139). To the degree that the band helped increase fans' awareness of cruelty to animals in "a selfish, hardened society" (Youth of Today 1988), it was celebrated for its combination of "the hardcore, the energy, the straight edge and the politics" (Hanou and Frijns 2009:30). However, the politics of Youth of Today focused on individual moral choices, particularly vegetarianism, involved in being straight-edge. As such, this version of straight-edge was fundamentally similar to that of the first wave. Perhaps the best example of this individualistic focus was the emergence in the late 1980s of the archetypal straight-edge song in which the lyrics are directed at a (former) friend who is "perceived not to be 'living up' to the straight-edge philosophy and lifestyle" (Wood 1999a:140). Songs from the late 1980s that exemplify this include Youth of Today's "Stabbed in the Back," Bold's "Talk Is Cheap," and "New York Crew," by Judge (Wood 1999a:140). The emergence of the "stabbed in the back" archetype stemmed from its pure focus on the individualistic morality that was at the core of straight-edge from the start.

The early 1990s, meanwhile, brought the third wave of straight-edge. The most visible part of the third wave was the militant, vegan straight-edge movement, which focused on animal rights in addition to the antidrug, anti-alcohol straight-edge message. In the song "Ecocide" (1992) the band Earth Crisis decried the ways "corporations with their dollar sign focus ravage the Amazon like a plague of locusts, plumes of black smoke ascend into the sky, a forest of beautiful creatures senselessly dies." In the band's most well-known song, "Firestorm," Earth Crisis openly called for street warfare against drug dealers. In calling for various types of social action, Earth Crisis seemed to have broadened the focus of straight-edge beyond just personal intoxication.

One of the most controversial aspects of the third wave of straight-edge was the pro-life, anti-abortion message conveyed by some bands.

In the 1992 song "Stand By," Earth Crisis sang, "For the fetus, for the cat, for the cow, for the rat, for innocent victims we will attack." In the liner notes for the *All Out War* EP (1992), the band explained the use of the term *fetus*. They wrote, "Respect for innocent life must encompass all those who are unable to defend themselves. Be it animals or unborn children, all must be given the same right to live free from enslavement, torture, and pain." Much like Youth of Today placed cruelty to animals on the straight-edge radar, bands like Earth Crisis extended this to awareness of cruelty to the unborn. Although bands such as Earth Crisis displayed greater willingness to address larger-scale social issues than did Minor Threat, they approached these issues with a focus on individual morality rather than upon larger, structural social conditions. When these bands did discuss larger issues, it was in the context of diatribes against enemies, such as corporations or drug dealers, who chose to engage in immoral actions. There is not as much hostility directed toward the social systems that structured those choices.

The most extreme variation of the third wave of straight-edge was arguably the "hardline" movement, which influenced bands like Earth Crisis. Hardline was started in Southern California as a record label by Sean Muttaqi, the singer of the band Vegan Reich, which existed from 1987 to 1992. Peterson described hardline as "a militant move-ment in the hardcore scene that combined revolutionary politics, Old Testament style spirituality, and veganism" (Peterson 2009:85), along with opposition to abortion and homosexuality (Peterson 2009:96). According to Muttaqi, his "initial goal was to spread a militant animal liberation message, as well as radical political messages" (Peterson 2009:483). However, as with bands like Earth Crisis, the radical and revolutionary politics of hardline seemed mainly to focus on attacking the most visibly corrupt actors, rather than the structural causes behind them. For example, the 1995 Vegan Reich song "Stop Talking—Start Revenging!" called for attacks against laboratories conducting experi-ments on animals.

Hardline clearly had a broader, more political focus than early straight-edge. However, this political focus still interpreted problems as rooted in individual moral failings. Vegan Reich, with songs like "I, the Jury," "No One Is Innocent," and "Letter to Judas," demonstrated this moral emphasis most clearly. In fact, Sean Muttaqi explained the demise of hardline as a consequence of its excessive emphasis on individual morality, stating that "hardline lost any aspect of militancy and was all-consumed with minute details or inward shit. It was like how inwardly introspective can you get about where something was grown and whether a chocolate bar had an ounce of caffeine in it? It got absurd to the point where they weren't getting anything done" (Peterson 2009:489). Although Muttaqi described these "inwardly introspective" debates as contrary to the radical goals of hardline, they were, in fact, consistent with hardline's fixation on individual morality as the root of larger problems. In this sense, hardline was a quintessential product of the neoliberal United States, a society that it did not hesitate to criticize.

Straight-Edge in Europe

The US straight-edge bands discussed above do not, of course, capture the wide variety of straight-edge bands that existed in the US during the 1980s and 1990s. However, they are among the most well-known and influential bands of the time period. Similarly, European straight-edge of that time assumed a variety of styles, both musically and ideologically. However, among the most influential bands identified in the literature on European straight-edge music are bands whose political orientation was virtually nonexistent in US straight-edge. These bands—Lärm, Manliftingbanner (which included members of Lärm), and Refused—viewed straight-edge as part of a larger Marxian critique of capitalism. It is significant that the early-1980s Dutch band Lärm, Europe's first straight-edge band (Hanou and Frijns 2009:12), formed in the European nation known for having relatively liberal laws regarding drugs and alcohol. Hanou and Frijns described Lärm as "a political band that witnessed the destructive power of drugs amongst their friends. Their song 'It's up to you' sends a strong straight edge message but it was actually nothing less than a call for political action" (Hanou and Frijns 2009:12). In 2007, to celebrate Lärm's twenty-fifth anniversary reunion show, Way Back When Records re-released the band's two seven-inch records from the 1980s, including new liner notes. In the liner notes, the band presented "Straight Edge as a stepping out of main stream culture. A decision not to take part in a shitty cultural pass time [sic] that is cast down by heartless corporate monsters. An opiate for the horrendous conditions of the capitalist system." With the use of the term opiate, the Marxian orientation of the band becomes clear. Third-wave straight-edge bands from the United States, like Earth Crisis and Vegan Reich, did not hesitate to criticize corporations either. However, for those bands, this more often took the form of criticisms of corporations for their evil (i.e., immoral) actions, rather than criticisms of the larger social structure of capitalism.

Members of Lärm played in the band Manliftingbanner in the early 1990s. Manliftingbanner, like Lärm, placed political issues at the lyrical forefront. Michiel from Manliftingbanner described this as a reaction to the larger society's belief "in hollow phrases like 'the end of history,' proclaiming that capitalism had defeated socialism, and that (neo-) liberalism was the path to success. We decided to change gears and put politics before straight edge. Not that we were getting rid of it, politics just became in the first place and straight edge in the second place" (Hanou and Frijns 2009:39). But what did it mean to place "politics before straight edge?" Paul from Manliftingbanner (and Lärm) conveyed his sense of what this meant by stating that "to us it seemed self-explanatory that, after you've taken the blindfold of intoxication off, your interests would venture towards examining the oppressive conditions of capitalism, the fucked-up gender dynamics, consumerism, class, race" (Kuhn 2010:51). For bands like Manliftingbanner and Refused, straight-edge was a means to achieving the end of a challenge to capitalism. As Michiel from Manliftingbanner stated, "The lifestyle alone doesn't lead to any sort of change" (Kuhn 2010:48) in the larger social system. In contrast, in the United States, the straight-edge lifestyle, and the moral purity that it symbolized, often became an end itself.

Manliftingbanner was a strong influence on the band Refused, who "became the flagship of a remarkably strong vegan straight edge movement that engulfed Sweden throughout the 1990s" (Kuhn 2010:53). Dennis Lyxzén, the vocalist of Refused, cited the band's biggest inspirations as "bands that talked about politics, about communism/socialism *and* straight edge, and they interlinked the two" (Kuhn 2010:55). The popularity of Refused was not limited to Europe, as they were signed to Chicago's Victory Records, perhaps the best-known label for third-wave straight-edge music. Besides Refused, Victory also released records by Earth Crisis. Like Manliftingbanner, Refused prioritized politics over straight-edge. In the words of Lyxzén, the members of the band "were into politics and kinda [*sic*] used straight edge as a base for our political ideas" (Kuhn 2010:55).

In the mid-1990s, Refused toured the United States with the band Snapcase, an American band also signed to Victory Records. Dennis Lyxzén's description of the band's experiences on tour with Snapcase reveals the apolitical nature of the American straight-edge scene. According to Lyxzén, the members of Snapcase were "really cool people. But they were not into politics, they were not radical people, they were like, you know, 'yeah, we are sort of straight edge kids, vegetarian guys . . .' and that was it. I mean, we got into fights with them during the tour 'cause they thought we talked way too much about politics and got upset that we were so radical" (Kuhn 2010:55–56). This apolitical attitude was not limited to bands. Lyxzén went on to state that "when we played in the States, we constantly had to defend ourselves 'cause we talked about equality and feminism and gay rights. People were just like, 'What's your problem?'"

Ultimately, many of the members of Manliftingbanner and Refused who viewed straight-edge as a prerequisite for bringing down capitalism tended to drift away from the straight-edge scene and from labeling themselves as straight-edge, even if they themselves continued to abstain from drugs and alcohol (Kuhn 2010:51–62). This, too, can be attributed to their prioritizing of politics. As Michiel from Manliftingbanner stated, "Moralism and materialism just don't mix" (Kuhn 2010:47). This distinction between moralism and materialism corresponds almost perfectly with the distinction between US and European straight-edge discussed in this chapter. On one hand are the moralists, bands like Minor Threat, Youth of Today, and Vegan Reich, whose dissatisfaction with the mainstream was rooted in objection to immoral behavior. On the other hand are the materialists, bands like Manliftingbanner and Refused, whose dissatisfaction was with the larger socioeconomic structures of capitalism. For the materialists, the challenge to capitalism was ultimately more important than the pursuit of moral purity. Indeed, when asked by Kuhn to explain his statement regarding moralism and materialism, Michiel asserted that "it's utterly impossible to lead a pure life, whatever that may be, while living under capitalism" (Kuhn 2010:48).

Conclusion

The late-twentieth-century context in which straight-edge emerged was defined by a number of ideological and intellectual trends. In the ideological realm, the growing influence of neoliberalism shaped political and economic policy in the United States, as described by scholars such as Luhr (2009), Harvey (2007), and Hardt and Negri (2000). I have argued that the most influential bands in US straight-edge reinforced neoliberal ideology. This ideology emphasizes the importance of individual characteristics in explaining life outcomes, at the expense of attention to structural conditions. In the late twentieth century, the atrophy of any potential for structural criticism drove dissatisfied Americans, including straight-edgers, to rely on calls for greater personal morality. Unsurprisingly, the most influential bands in American straight-edge reflected this preoccupation with moralism. Even when they criticized corporations, such criticisms were directed at corporate actors for their immoral actions, not at the larger capitalist system. The calls for social change by various straight-edge bands in the United States tended to focus on the revolutionary potential of individual morality. In this sense, the growth of straight-edge in the United States mirrored the rise of the "personal-is-political" viewpoint.

By contrast, straight-edge music in Europe took shape in an environment without an aversion to structural explanations (and remedies) for social problems. For some of the most influential European straight-edge bands from the 1980s and 1990s, straight-edge was a means to clear the mind in preparation for challenging the oppressive structures of capitalism. The limits of applying a moralistic code of ethics to a materialist cause led some of the members of these European bands to cease using straight-edge as a personal identity marker as they grew older, because they perceived an incompatibility of moralism and materialism.

More generally, the tension between moralism and materialism is at the core of social science itself. On one hand, moralists (sometimes called "idealists") believe that society can be understood by examining the characteristics of individuals, including their morals and values. On the other hand, materialists attempt to understand society by examining the economic conditions and social systems in which people live. In this sense, the study of the contrasts between straight-edge in the United States and in Europe is an examination of the way that two different worldviews manifest themselves in one international subculture.

21

Sing Out!
Collective Singing Rituals of Folk Protest Music in US Social Movements
Jeneve R. Brooks

This chapter examines the communal feeling and solidarity building that happens in folk protest music. The rituals of sing-alongs have played an important role in social movement activism, especially in the nineteenth and twentieth centuries. Folk protest musicians and activists see it as an important part of their social change work, providing much-needed emotional cohesion and strength.

So being in touch with the idea as a group we can affirm that we have a community experience not just at a football game or in church. But in a vernacular sense, in a people sense, in yearning for something in life that we all have in common. That is the nature of folk music. It allows you to be in touch with authentic moments of common sensibility. And when you have that in your lexicon, you have the tools of a protest song.
—Interview with Peter Yarrow
of the 1960s folk group Peter, Paul, and Mary

As Peter Yarrow's comment illustrates, there is a communal experience of solidarity building in folk protest music that is similar to the experience of religious rituals or major popular cultural events. Three different areas need to be explored when examining the role of music rituals in American social movements. First is the way that traditional group sing-alongs, with their strong emphasis on emotion, coincide with sociological ideas of ritual. Second is an examination of the use of collective singing rituals in social movements. Here, four progressive movements of the nineteenth and twentieth centuries are used—

(1) the abolition movement (Eyerman and Jamison 1998; Horsfall 2013, Chapter 5, this volume; Southern 1997; Wright 2006); (2) the early labor movement (Fowke and Glaser 1973; Horsfall 2013, Chapter 2, this volume; Roscigno, Danaher, and Summers-Effler 2002); (3) the civil rights movement (Eyerman and Jamison 1998, Reagon 1975); and (4) the anti–Vietnam War movement (Lynskey 2011).The third area to be explored is the way that musicians and activists themselves explain the importance of singing to their social change work. Drawing on interviews and focus groups, I found it provides a link to historical social activism and gives them needed emotional cohesion and strength to participate in social movements

Defining Ritual: The Folk Protest Music Tradition and the Role of Emotion

Numerous studies by sociologists and others show that rituals are not just routinized practices taking place in formal settings (e.g., a Catholic high mass) but also refer to the everyday actions in all areas of life that over time become repeated or customary. According to Smith (2007:1), "Ritual involves conventionalized and stylized human actions. These are often organized with reference to overarching cultural codes, have a communicative intent, and generate powerful emotional responses among participants."

Smith's definition provides a starting point for discussing the rituals of group sing-alongs in the folk protest music tradition. Folk protest music, following in the genre of folk music more generally, refers to melodies of the common people that are easy to learn and sing, that are passed to different generations through oral transmission, that are conventionally sung a capella or accompanied by simple instrumentation such as the guitar, and that have a political or social message.[1] Folk protest songs of previous social movements are often rediscovered by younger activists and recycled, although the words are slightly altered to reflect the concerns of the current social movement. Within the United States, collective singing of folk protest music has served the tradition of activism throughout many generations. It creates cultural codes of group singing that span more than 150 years. Folk protest music traditions "are inherited ways of interpreting reality and giving meaning to experience; they are constitutive of collective memory and thus provide the underlying logical structure upon which all social activity is constructed" (Eyerman and Jamison 1998:20).

Emotion also plays an important role in the collective singing of protest music. This music has the ability to construct and reflect the emotions of individual activists within a larger collective: "The construction of meaning through music and song . . . exemplifies how collective structures of feeling are actually made and reorganized, in part, through song. . . . Songs and music give us access to both feelings and thoughts that are shared by larger collectivities and that make better claim, perhaps, for cultural representativity" (Eyerman and Jamison 1998:161). This notion of music as an emotional ritual and as a hotline to the collective consciousness is also discussed by Horsfall (Chapter 6, this volume), who argues that a successful ritual of collective music makes us feel that we are emotionally resonating not only with others in our immediate group but also with the larger culture, giving us a certain type of energy.

Connecting to the larger culture is a key aspect of music's emotional power. The famous neuroscientist Levitin explains that many studies show not only that music is related to areas of the brain involved in emotional reactions (e.g., thalamus, hippocampus, amygdala, prefrontal cortex, midbrain, etc.) but also that emotional reactions to different musical pitches are culturally determined:

> Certain sequences of pitches evoke calm, others excitement. The brain basis for this is primarily based on learning, just as we learn that a rising intonation indicates a question. All of us have the innate capacity to learn the linguistic and musical distinctions of whatever culture we are born into, and experience with the music of that culture shapes our neural pathways so that we ultimately internalize a set of rules common to that musical tradition. (Levitin 2006:26)

Various tempos are used purposefully by composers and singers to express and elicit different emotional states. The legendary folk protest singer Pete Seeger explains how the tempo of the famous protest song "We Shall Overcome" changed in the group sing-alongs over time:

> "We Shall Overcome" was originally a fast gospel song. [Sings and claps], "I overcome; I overcome." And in the late nineteenth century, they turned it into a union song, "We Will Overcome." And in 1946, there were 300 tobacco workers on strike in Charleston, South Carolina, and one of them liked to sing this song very slow. Around the picket line, they might have been warming themselves around the little fire. And they say, "Oh here comes Lucille!" Her name was Lucille Simmons. "And now we'll hear that song sung slower than we've heard it ever sung." [Sings] (Brooks 2010:62)

Perhaps Miss Lucille deliberately led "We Shall Overcome" in a slower tempo to reinforce the somber feeling of the tobacco workers' determined struggle for equality, or perhaps it was to recreate a connection to Negro spirituals from the nineteenth century abolition movement. Whatever her original intent, it will soon become clear that emotion played a key role in the collective singing rituals of folk protest music.

Collective Singing Rituals in Four US Social Movements

I now turn to the collective singing rituals of the four aforementioned American social movements.

The Abolition Movement

Cultural researchers emphasize the significance of collective singing rituals of Negro spirituals in galvanizing the US abolition movement in the eighteenth and nineteenth centuries. Negro spirituals, sung collectively among the slaves working the fields, were often encoded with double meanings that highlighted the injustice of slavery while drawing on the hopeful Christian metaphors of God's leading the Israelites out of bondage in Egypt (Horsfall, Chapter 2, this volume; Southern 1997; Wright 2006). According to the famous abolitionist Frederick Douglass, "Canaan," "heaven," and "run to Jesus" "simply meant a speedy pilgrimage toward a free state, and deliverance from all the evils and dangers of slavery" (Southern 1997:87). Wright states, "Enslaved African Americans turned to song, in the tradition of their West African ancestors, to tell their histories, record experiences, articulate aspirations for justice, vent anger, and protest the institution of slavery" (2006:414). In this way, the Negro spirituals—or "sorrow songs," as W. E. B. Du Bois termed them—helped develop a shared black consciousness among African Americans living in slavery and instilled hope for a better, more just world.

> Through all the sorrow of the Sorrow Songs there breathes a hope—a faith in the ultimate justice of things. The minor cadences of despair change often to triumph and calm confidence. Sometimes it is faith in life, sometimes a faith in death, sometimes assurance of boundless justice in some fair world beyond. (Du Bois 1997 [1903])

The Early Labor Movement

Historical treatment of the early-twentieth-century US labor movement highlights the presence of collective singing among labor activists. The Industrial Workers of the World (IWW, or the Wobblies) were particularly well known for collective singing. Troubadour activists like Joe Hill often wrote parodies of labor relations to the melodies of well-known Christian hymns. With the publishing of *The Little Red Songbook* in 1909, the IWW intended to teach an array of movement songs to a broad audience, given that the IWW was the only American union that accepted women, immigrants, and African Americans into its ranks at that time. *The Little Red Songbook* proved to be extremely popular, with 10,000 copies of its first edition sold in only a month.

And it has continued to be published more than thirty times since then, with the most recent printing in 2010. Others have examined ritualistic group singing in the southern textile strikes of 1929–1934. Analyzing archival data on former mill-worker musicians and interviews and correspondence with surviving musicians, one group of researchers found that "music that was disseminated appears to have been influential both prior to and during actual protest events. The use of pre-existing melodies . . . seems to have been important, as was the ritual and community-centered character of performances" (Roscigno, Danaher, and Summers-Effler 2002:154). Thus the use of music in the labor movement is well documented (Brazier 1968; Fowke and Glaser 1973; Horsfall, Chapter 2, this volume; Renshaw 1999; Roscigno, Danaher, and Summers-Effler 2002).

The Civil Rights Movement

Collective singing, born out of the African American rituals of the Negro spiritual and church gospel music, helped to strengthen the resolve and commitment of activists during the civil rights movement. Group sing-alongs served as an inspiration for activists engaged in high-risk protest activities (i.e., facing police dogs, clubs, fire hoses, and sneering counter protestors) or after the protests to lift their spirits as they were held in lonely jail cells. Collective singing also acted as a bridge to coalesce the wide range of groups that were involved in the civil rights movement (e.g., varying class and status groups, black and white supporters, and blacks from different regions). Finally, group sing-along songs led to shared performance of simple melodies with easily repeatable choruses. Not dogmatic or overly ideological, the songs were hence inclusive and reflective of universal themes of brotherhood and integration (Eyerman and Jamison 1998).

The Anti–Vietnam War Movement

The movement against the Vietnam War also utilized simple melodies and universalistic themes. John Lennon's "Give Peace a Chance" was written specifically as a group sing-along song for protests. With its broad, general appeal and easy-to-sing melody, it became a favorite. Pete Seeger led a spontaneous sing-along of the song with a half a million protestors at the October 15, 1969, Moratorium to End the War in Vietnam in Washington, D.C. Lennon was gratified:

> I was pleased when the movement in America took up "Give Peace a Chance" because I had written it with that in mind really. I hoped that instead of singing "We Shall Overcome" from 1800 or something that they would have something contemporary. I felt an obligation to

write a song that people would sing in the pub or on a demonstration. (Lynskey 2011:137)

During my interview and focus groups, I was surprised by how many musicians and activists connected with the folk protest music of prior social movements. It made them feel as if they were a part of a larger legacy of activism. They also noted that the tradition of collective singing provided them with much-needed emotional cohesion and strength. However, Lennon's criticisms are well-taken; even given the rich history of the folk protest music, one would hope that there would still be an infusion of new songs to enliven the rituals of collective singing instead of solely relying on the historical repertoire. I will take up this issue later.

Reflections on Collective Singing Rituals by Musicians and Activists

From a larger study of thirty-six interviews, I selected twenty-eight to examine here—focusing on musicians and activists.[2] Some respondents acknowledged the folk protest music tradition as an ever-evolving progression that interwove new lyrics for the purposes of the new generation's collective singing rituals. The protest music legend Pete Seeger explained that the definition of a folk protest song was constantly changing due to this iterative process.

> It all depends on your definition of protest. For many people, protestant hymns are protest! And gospel songs. . . . During the civil rights movement, they just put slightly new words to old gospel songs and they had a whole lot of new songs. There used to be an old spiritual in the nineteenth century, [sings] "Got my hand on the gospel plow, wouldn't take nothing for my journey now. Keep your hand on the plow, hold on."

And during the civil rights movement it was, "Keep your eyes on the prize, hold on. Hold on." You still sing the same chorus (Pete Seeger, interview).

In the same way, folksinger Peter Siegel related how he often relied on some of the standard songs in the folk protest music repertoire when asked to lead sing-alongs at rallies. He added that he updated the protest songs with new verses to make them relevant.

> I feel like there's this whole pool of songs that has been around for forty or fifty years—that are all perfectly effective. So whenever I am asked to play a rally—it's like—that's what I play. . . . So that's one of the reasons

why I haven't written a song about George Bush. . . . I'll write and add verses. And when I'm in concert—I'll sing a verse about George Bush. And it gets a laugh and it's funny. (Peter Siegel, interview)

Peter Yarrow, of Peter, Paul, and Mary fame, questioned the whole conceptualization of "protest music" as he sought to explain the linkages between the songs of different American social movements and generations of activists—particularly labor movement songs that were then reused by the civil rights movement. He stated,

> I think proprietary to asking a question about the relationship of a person to music of conscience, music of commitment, music of political/social change, music of protest, you have to say: "What are the sensibilities that make up the capacity of a person to embrace and then be a purveyor of this kind of music?" And I maintain that it's a whole language unto itself related to folk music. . . . I sang "We Shall Overcome" long before I sang it in the civil rights movement there. I was singing it in 1954–1955. I learned "If I Had a Hammer" at that concert in 1955, long before we marched and sang with Dr. Martin Luther King Jr. in 1963. (Peter Yarrow, interview)

The activists I interviewed made some of the most poignant statements about the ways the collective singing rituals of folk protest songs made them feel a part of a rich legacy of activism. One example:

> I think that's a really powerful thing and maybe why we keep singing them—some of the same ones [songs] over and over again because they helped us articulate what we wanted or believed or who we hoped to be in some way or something like that. And then you sang them—because those were the words that we had. And so I feel like it has been a powerful tool—probably not for converting people—but certainly for instructing or making/growing a movement in some way. (Amanda, focus group participant)

Correspondingly, other activists noted how songs that are associated with one social movement were actually the musical legacy of older social movements. When asked what anti–Vietnam War songs came immediately to mind, many responded with civil rights' anthems: "I feel like some of the ones we're mentioning are not actually anti-war songs. They come out of the civil rights [movement] (Jim, focus group participant).

Besides appreciating how the collective singing rituals of folk protest music connected them to a rich, historical legacy of social change activism, some respondents also noted how the emotional power of collective singing had a motivational effect. They explained how the songs at times reflected what they wanted to feel in any given moment of their activist action. For instance:

> When you're protesting, you're marching, and you're singing, it takes on a totally different context than when you're in a classroom and you're talking about things. . . . It has an urgency that is hard to replicate on a recording, on an mp3 that you'd hum a tune on. (Dan, focus group participant)

Another respondent noted how collective singing in other social movements such as the anti-apartheid movement created the emotional cohesion and strength needed to make social change possible:

> Because it is really something amazing . . . singing together, vocalizing together . . . this expression of emotion. It anesthetizes—it does counter fear . . . you just watch . . . those movies from South Africa—and people are just singing but . . . moving their bodies together and harmonizing. And you watch that and you're like, "They could do anything." . . . and they did it. They were sort of propelled by that collective engagement. (Frida, focus group participant)

When Peter Yarrow was asked about protest music's emotional power, he concentrated on music's ability to affect people deeply and revitalize hopes and dreams for a better life. He stated,

> It's music that creates community around hoping, dreaming, mobilizing to do something. It affects people dramatically and deeply. It makes them remember what they truly care about. It focuses them on real issues rather than on power, money, and fame.

Finally, Michael Lydon, artist and one of the founding editors of *Rolling Stone* magazine, argued that the folk protest music tradition offered both an emotional release and inspiration for people to be more musical:

> Those songs were being taken up, and they were inspiring hundreds and thousands of people like me to take up music ourselves. Well, I can do that. I can just bang my guitar and I can do something. . . . A lot of the simple folk songs are the first songs you play—so you are starting to learn music by playing "Down by the Riverside" or "We Shall Not Be Moved.". . . People say, "Oh well, how much did it matter? All the hippies grew up and they turn into bankers or something like that." It's

not true; it really affected people. And gave them a touchstone—so that it counted. (Michael Lydon, interview)

Conclusion

This chapter explored the importance of group sing-alongs to US social movements and examined the way that the collective singing tradition of folk protest music is an emotion-laden and solidarity building ritual. It also looked at the use of collective singing rituals in four American social movements and considered comments of activists and musicians that their collective singing experience was a way to elicit or reflect certain emotional states and to connect historically with the rich history of progressive social movement activism of the past.

Obviously, American social movements are not the only ones to use the collective singing rituals of folk protest music. Internationally, it was used successfully in the South African struggle against apartheid (noted above) and in the Nueva Canción movement against growing trends in imperialism, fascism, and economic inequality in Spain, Portugal, and Latin America. And it must be remembered that not all movements that emphasize group singing are progressive. There is significant historical documentation that the Nazi Party used singing to spread fascist propaganda, and currently many studies have examined the use of music by white power movements. It should also be remembered that not all activists want to sing collectively and may even find the ritual trite. One activist told me that she usually tried to avoid the singing part of most demonstrations. She found that most of the standard protest sing-alongs had been done too much and "lost their juice" (Sarah, focus group participant).

Her criticism of the group sing-along harkens back to John Lennon's concern that civil rights songs such as "We Shall Overcome" and "This Little Light of Mine" would be overused. This propelled him to write a sing-along for his generation. Yet, the question remains: Could a song be written today for a collective singing ritual that would impact the Net Generation in the same way that "Give Peace a Chance" impacted Baby Boomers? Given the waning appeal of the folk music genre, in general, and the current means of accessing music through individualized means such as iPods, the future of the group sing-along seems precarious. Journalist David Bauden noted that Occupy Wall Street's lack of anthem is partly reflective of how the "new generation experiences music: through personalized iPod playlists streaming through headphones instead of communal sing-alongs" (Bauder 2011). At the risk of sounding like the child of the 1960s that I am—someone who remembers how vibrant progressive change efforts can be when accompanied by the unity and sheer power of group singing—I hope this is not the case. I hope there will be a song that carries on the SING OUT! tradition for the next generation, and generations to come.

Notes

1. "Folk music" is a misnomer. Please see Chapter 2, which explains why folk music is difficult to define.

2. For a full description of the methodology used in the larger study, please consult http://musicandartsinaction.net/index.php/maia/article/viewArticle/ antiwarsongs (Brooks 2010). Of the twenty-eight respondents, seventeen were from two focus groups with activists, and eleven were from interviews with folk protest musicians; the total sample included fifteen men and thirteen women; and all respondents self-identified as "white" except for two college-age Palestinian youth—one male and one female.

Part VI
Commodification of Music

A youth band playing at Dreamworld, a nonalcoholic nightclub for young people in Arlington, Texas, 2000.

22

The Industrialization of Popular Music—Part II
Simon Frith

The modern music industry was basically in place by 1945. There has since been a steady professionalization of every facet of music making. Independent producers continue to play an important role in the ebb and flow of the music industry.

The Making of the Rock Industry

By 1945 the basic structure of the modern music industry was in place. Pop music [short for "popular music"] meant pop records, commodities, [and] a technological and commercial process under the control of a small number of larger companies. Such control depended on the ownership of the means of record production and distribution and was organized around the marketing of stars and star performances (just as the music publishing business had been organized around the manufacture and distribution of songs). Live music making was still important but its organization and profits were increasingly dependent on the exigencies of record making. The most important way of publicizing pop now—the way most people heard most music—was on the radio, and records were made with radio formats and radio audiences in mind.

The resulting shifts in the distribution of musical power and wealth didn't occur without a struggle. The declining significance of New York publishing houses and big city session musicians, the growing

Originally published in James Lull, ed., Popular Music and Communication, *2nd ed. (Thousand Oaks, CA: Sage, 1992), pp. 49–74. Condensed from the original. Reprinted with permission.*

importance of radio programmers and record company A & R [artists and repertoire] people, were marked by strikes, recording bans, disputes over broadcasting rights and studio fees, and, outside the United States, such disputes were inflected with the issue of "Americanization" (and anti-Americanism). The United States's influence on international popular music, beginning with the worldwide showing of Hollywood talkies, was accelerated by the US entry into World War II—members of the service became the most effective exporters. By the end of the war the pop music people heard on radio and records across Europe— and even in parts of Southeast Asia—was either directly or indirectly (cover versions, copied styles) American. Hollywood's 1930s success in defining internationally what "popular cinema" meant was reinforced in the 1940s and 1950s by the American record industry's success in defining the worldwide sound of "popular music."

Outside the United States the ending of the war and wartime austerity and restraint meant a new boom for the record industry (in Britain, for example, Decca's turnover increased eightfold between 1946 and 1956). In the United States, postwar euphoria was short lived. By the end of the 1940s, television seemed to carry the same threat to the pop industry as radio had twenty years earlier. The industry's resistance to this threat and its subsequent unprecedented profits were due to technological and social changes that, eventually, turned the record industry into the rock business.

The technological developments that began with CBS's experiments with microgroove recording in the late 1940s and culminated with digital recording and the compact disc in the 1980s, had two objects: to improve recorded sound quality and to make record storage and preservation easier. . . . By the end of the 1960s, records, not concerts, defined the "best" sound. Nowadays both classical and popular musicians have to make sure that their live performances meet the sound standards of their records. The acoustic design of concert halls has changed accordingly, and rock groups take sound checks, sound mixers, elaborate amplification systems, and these days the use of taped material to enhance their "live" performances for granted. The increasing "purity" of recorded sound—no extraneous or accidental noises—is the mark of its artificiality. Prewar records were always heard as a more or less crackly mediation between listeners and actual musical events; their musical qualities often depended on listeners' own imaginations. To modern listeners these old discs (and particularly classical 78s) are "unlistenable"—we're used to treating albums as musical events in themselves.

. . . The late 1940s "battle of the speeds" between CBS's 33-1/3 LPs and RCA's 45 rpm records was resolved with a simple market division—LPs were for classical music collectors, 45s for pop, which continued to be organized in three minute segments, as music of convenience and of the moment (a definition reinforced by the continuing significance of jukeboxes for pop sales).

Record companies' assumptions about "true" reproduction and pop-triviality were, in the end, undermined by the invention that made hi-fi records feasible—magnetic tape. . . .

Hence arose the problem of home taping that, in the 1950s, was certainly not foreseen. Tape recording, initially developed by German scientists for broadcasting purposes in the war, was initially picked up not by the music biz but by radio stations (as a relatively cheap way of rerecording talk and jingles) and film studios (as an aid to making soundtracks), but record companies quickly realized tape's flexibility and cheapness too, and by 1950 tape recording had replaced disc recording entirely. This was the technological change that allowed new, independent producers into the market—the cost of recording fell dramatically even if the problems of large-scale manufacture and distribution remained. Mid-1950s United States indie labels such as Sun were as dependent on falling studio costs as late-1970s punk labels in Britain, the latter benefiting from scientific breakthroughs and falling prices in electronic recording.

But tape's importance wasn't just in terms of costs. Tape was an intermediary in the recording process. The performance was recorded on tape, the tape was used to make the master disc. And it was what could be done during this intermediary stage, to the tape itself, that transformed pop music making. Producers no longer had to take performances in their entirety. They could cut and splice, edit the best bits of performances together, cut out the mistakes, make records of ideal, not real, events. And on tape sounds could be added artificially. Instruments could be recorded separately; a singer could be taped, sing over the tape, and be taped again. Such techniques gave producers a new flexibility that enabled them to make records of performances, like a double tracked vocal, that were impossible live (though musicians and equipment manufacturers were soon looking for ways to get the same effects on stage). By the mid-1960s the development of multi-track recording enabled sounds to be stored separately on the same tape and altered in relationship to each other at the final mixing stage, rather than through the continuous process of sound addition. Producers could now work on the tape itself to "record" a performance that was actually put together from numerous, quite separate events, happening at different times and, increasingly, in different studios. The musical judgments, choices, and skills of producers and engineers became as significant as those of the musicians and, indeed, the distinction between engineers and musicians has become meaningless. Studio-made music need no longer bear any relationship to anything that can be performed live; records use sounds, the effects of tape tricks and electronic equipment, that no one has ever heard before as music (Frith 1983). And the digital storage of sound has made its manipulation even easier. Computers can be used to isolate, extract, and distort any element from a digital recording (a drum sound, a bass note). Such "sampling" is now a norm of record production, though the legal implications in terms of authorship and "theft" remain unresolved. . . .

The rise of rock depended too on a broader social change—the appearance of youth as the pop music market. . . . Teenagers were the one age group that still wanted to be out of the house and they began to take over public leisure spaces, to display a distinct teen culture in their own codes of dress and noise. These new leisure consumers were not, at first, catered to by the major leisure companies, and American teenagers had to find their style where they could—in black music, in certain Hollywood images. The resulting demands for records and clothes were first met by small, independent companies, looking for opportunities not already covered by the majors. Their success (and need for further advertisement outlets and promotion) opened the new market to media like radio and cinema desperately in need of it. The Elvis Presley story is typical. His commercial potential was first realized by his local independent label, Sun, but once his potential was realized (and his television appearances proved to the doubter that he could, indeed, be a national youth star) then he was quickly used as a way of selling records, cinema seats, magazines, merchandise, and advertising time on radio (which was adapting easily to Top 40 and rock and roll formats). From the industry perspective rock and roll was a means to an end. As music it was taken to be silly, gimmicky, and with a short shelf life; but as a way to control teenage spending, it couldn't be beaten. . . .

The record industry's post-Presley focus on youth had spectacular results. In 1955 US record sales increased 30 percent (from their postwar low point) to $277 million; in 1956 they reached $377 million; in 1957 $460 million; and in 1959 a peak of $605 million. . . .

In the United States this market was first tapped not by local independent producers (though significant independent servicing companies were involved—FM radio stations, *Rolling Stone,* new promoters like Bill Graham) but by British acts, and the immediate result of this was the direct entry of the US majors, CBS, RCA, and Warner's, into the British pop scene. They set up offices in London in pursuit of British musicians, not fans. The Beatles and Rolling Stones, Dave Clark, Herman's Hermits, and the rest of the British invasion groups were almost all signed to EMI or Decca, which made them vast profits, but by the end of the 1960s British rock groups such as Led Zeppelin, who made even vaster profits, were on American labels. By the end of the 1970s Decca itself had been taken over by the German-Dutch company, Polygram, and EMI had been reabsorbed by Thorn, the electrical goods manufacturer it had sold off fifty years earlier.

Rock, even more dramatically than rock and roll, reached sales levels previously thought impossible. In 1967 the American record industry passed the billion-dollar annual sales mark for the first time. By 1973 annual sales had reached $2 billion, record companies were taking two million sales of single rock LPs for granted, and classical music's market share, 25 percent in the 1950s, had dropped to 5 percent. By 1978 the industry had reached sales of more than $4 billion. This was the industry I described in my book, *Sound Effects*: "music had become the most popular form of entertainment—the sales of records and tapes easily outgrossed the returns on movies or sport" (Frith 1981, pp. 4–5). . . .

Throughout the 1970s, on the other hand, 80 percent of records released failed to cover their costs and so there developed a sharp distinction between "hit" groups, for whom the first sign of success meant a sudden surge of record company investment designed to realize the sales potential to the full, and "miss" groups, the majority, whose records were released without fanfare, vanished without a trace. . . . Record flops are made, then, with little additional costs for the companies, and just often enough a hit is released that covers all these costs anyway. . . .

[The rock business] involved, first of all, the steady professionalization of every facet of music making. Hucksters, amateurs, and gamblers were replaced by responsible team players—musicians, managers, promoters, pluggers, agents, and so on, who were paid not to take risks but to provide a fixed skill. The industry began to be dominated by lawyers and accountants, and by the mid-1970s there was very little tension between musicians and the business. Rock performers were more likely to complain about companies not exploiting them properly than to object to being "commercialized."

Second, "independent" producers and label owners were part of this system. They became, in effect, talent scouts and market researchers for the major companies, while being driven, for survival, into dependent manufacturing and distribution deals. They were the main victims of the ever-increasing financial demands made by each professional in the system, made by the artists and producers and engineers and promotion crews. The costs of success were inflationary and it made sense to let the majors bear them. . . .

The rock business faced a crisis at the end of the 1970s not because of punk or the cycle of business competition but because of "outside" technological and social change parallel to those that gave birth to rock and roll in the first place. On the one hand, the demographic structure of Western countries was shifting (the number of teenagers fell, the number of people over twenty-five increased) while mass youth unemployment meant young people had less money to spend on leisure goods anyway. On the other hand, the spread of home taping, computer games, and video recording gave recorded music new sorts of competition for people's time and interest. In Britain, for instance, 1984 market research suggested that 97 percent of teenagers had access to tape recorders and that 85 percent used them to record music. By the same year 35 percent of households had videocassette recorders and 20 percent home computers, equipment that no one had in 1976. . . .

This is the context for the end of the rock boom. Between 1973 and 1978 world record sales expanded from $4.75 to $7 billion, but in 1978–1979 there was a 20 percent drop in record sales in Britain, [and] an 11 percent fall off in the United States. The growth rate of the rock business (which had reached 25 percent per year in 1976) was down to 5–6 percent, and record companies had to stop assuming ever-increasing sales, an expanding number of platinum discs. . . .

The industry also benefited from consumer shift from vinyl to compact discs, which have a much higher profit margin (especially as the bulk of CD sales so far have come from back catalog). The number of actual titles released remains much lower than it was in the mid-1970s.

The Politics of Technology

Most explanations of change in the music industry are derived from general theories of corporate strategy and market control. . . .

I'm dubious about this model. . . . As Heikki Hellman puts it:

> The pattern is rather that the smaller companies offer a test market for the competition between the larger companies, through which these companies can outline their music production. The smaller companies have gained a permanent and important although subordinate position in the music industry. The cycles have changed into symbiosis. (Hellman 1983, p. 355)

This is not to say that there are no longer contradictions and struggles in the music business, but that they can't be reduced to a simple lineup of goodies and baddies (independent companies, bold musicians, and adventurous fans versus the multinationals, designer groups, and easy listeners). If there's one thing to be learned from twentieth-century pop history it is that technological inventions have unexpected consequences. The "industrialization of music" has changed what we do when we play or listen to music, and it has changed our sense of what "music" is, both in itself and as an aspect of our lives and leisure, but these changes aren't just the result of producer decisions and control. They also reflect musicians' and consumers' responses.

Music "machines" have not, in short, been as dehumanizing as mass media critics from both left and right perspectives have suggested. For a start, it was technological developments that made our present understanding of musical "authenticity" possible. Recording devices enabled previously unreproducible aspects of performance—improvisation, spontaneity—to be reproduced exactly, and so enable Afro-American music to replace European art and folk musics at the heart of Western popular culture. . . . Recording gave a public means of communication to otherwise socially inarticulate people, and its continuing technical refinement, particularly since the development of the electrical microphone, has extended the possibilities of expression in all pop genres. Out of such developments came the star system—the marketing of individual performers as spuriously "knowable" friends and idols—but out of these same developments also came new means of self-definition, musical identities that could (as in "minority" cultures and subcultures) challenge the common sense of bourgeois ideology (Frith 1986).

Technological change has also been the basic source of resistance to the corporate control of popular music. Examine the history of inventions in the recording industry and you will find that those that catch on are the ones that lead, at least in the short term, to the decentralization of music making and listening—video tapes caught on, for example, video discs did not. The music industry uses new instruments and devices to do old things more efficiently or cheaply; it is musicians and consumers who discover their real possibilities. The mechanization of popular music has not, then, been a simple story of capitalist takeover. Think, for example, of how Jamaican dub culture and New York hip-hop took over the technology of recording to undermine the status of the record as a finished product; scratching and mixing "found" sounds together, challenging the whole idea of copyright.

But the most significant example of new technological habits challenging old record company ways is home taping. Cassette recorders have given fans a new means of control over their sounds; they can compile LPs and radio shows for themselves, use a Walkman to carry their soundscapes around with them. And, for the industry, this is the source of all its troubles. Behind the recurring (and increasingly successful) campaigns for levies to be imposed on blank tapes is the suggestion that people are using them to acquire music illicitly, without paying for it, without even giving the musicians involved their just reward. Every blank tape sold is a record not sold. This is another example of the multinationals' inability to control the use of their own inventions (the effects of home taping were not anticipated) and their failure to grasp the point that to throw another electronic toy into the leisure market is to disrupt all consumer habits. The suggestion that blank tapes are simply replacing records is, therefore, misleading. What home taping signifies, rather, is the changing place of music in leisure generally. Records are being replaced not by tapes as such but by other leisure activities: music is being used differently and in different, more flexible forms.

Multinational profits are, meanwhile, being defended against new technology in the language of individual creativity. Home taping, scratch mixing, and the various forms of piracy have disrupted the equation of artists' "ownership" of their creative work and companies' ownership of the resulting commodities—the latter is being defended by reference to the former. Copyright has become the legal and ideological weapon with which to attack "illegal" copying, and the battle is being fought in the name of justice for the artist.

Conclusion

. . . Record executives no longer wake up in the night worried they were the ones who turned down the next Michael Jackson. They've got a worse nightmare now: They sign up the next MJ and then make no money out of him! For every record they sell, 1,000 are copied onto tape by fans at home and 100,000 are produced illicitly in Singapore and Taiwan! His video clips are stolen from satellite services, and the world is awash with unauthorized posters and tee-shirts!

Even by 1982 the piracy figures were daunting—66 percent of the Asian record and tape market, 30 percent in Africa and in the Middle East, 21 percent in South America, 11 percent in Canada and the United States. . . .

What we have seen is, effectively, the "death of black vinyl." As John Qualen (1985) points out, the "crisis" in the music industry in the last decade has been marked by three important shifts in the organization of profit making. First, recording and publishing companies are now integrated, and an increasing proportion of record company profits come from the exploitation of publishing copyrights. Second, the majors now derive a regular source of income from licensing material from their back catalogs to independent TV and specialist music packagers. Third, record companies have begun to treat radio and TV use of records and videos not as advertisements for which they provide new material cheaply, but as entertainment services that should pay competitive prices for the recordings they use. . . .

The move from record sales to rights exploitation as the basic source of music income has two implications. First, as Bill Graham (1986) suggests, it puts rock in corporate America. Already the biggest stars, like Michael Jackson and Bruce Springsteen, are being offered their biggest pay checks by companies keen to use their names in advertisements, and get their biggest concert returns not from ticket sales but from the tie-in merchandise. Companies are lining up to sponsor rock tours and TV shows. . . . One interesting aspect of the new global leisure market is that it is not dominated by American-based corporations. CBS is now part of the Japanese SONY empire (as a hardware manufacturer looks to its software interests in classic fashion); RCA has been absorbed by the Bertlesmann Group (BMG), a German-based company whose central interests are publishing and distributing books and magazines. As the other two "majors" (Thorn-EMI and Polygram) are also based in Europe, WEA is the only American major label left, though the MCA-Geffen conglomerate is rather more a major these days than an independent.

Second, as the majors' interest in individual record buyers falls and the promotional drive shifts from radio to TV and video, new opportunities will arise for the independents. . . .

And this reference to the "sound of the streets" brings me back to my starting point—music as human activity. The industrialization of music hasn't stopped people from using it to express private joys or public griefs; it has given us new means to do so, new ways of having an impact, new ideas of what music can be. Street music is certainly an industrial noise now, but it's a human noise too, so it is perhaps fitting to conclude that the most exciting and political music of the early 1990s should be the hip-hop sounds of young urban black bands like Public Enemy, groups that are heavily dependent on both the latent technology and street credibility. The struggle for fun continues!

23

Authenticity and Independence in Rap Music and Other Genre Communities

Jennifer C. Lena

For fans and practitioners of commercial rap music, authenticity is one of the most important values we hold. We tend to associate it with independence, as if one necessarily implied the other. Some of us feel strongly that "real" or authentic rappers must create their music free from (corporate) control. Conversely, we feel that inauthentic rappers have allowed the dictates of the marketplace to influence the music they make. I will argue these values are not unique to rap music, and are found in other musical communities, including New Orleans jazz and country. I examine the features of a music community that permit definitions of authenticity and independence to take hold. My examination of three features—the size of a genre community, its market and industry structure, and the race and class of performers—reveals that authenticity is not a stable attribute of people, places, or things. Instead, it is redefined as fans and artists face shifting social conditions.

Authenticity in Music Communities

Which style of country music do you think is more authentic? Performers like Roy Acuff and Hank Williams use exaggerated Southern accents, lyrical themes of personal and family problems, "country" musical instruments (e.g., banjo, fiddle, and steel pedal guitar), yodeling, and other distinctive vocalizations. These performers present themselves—in their music and in their public persona—as sincere, original, and as having a deep commitment to the life and lifestyle of a country artist. In contrast, performers like John Denver and Taylor

Swift employ complex lyrical themes associated with middle-class morality and behavior, their orchestration is drawn from other genres (e.g., acoustic guitar, piano), and they de-emphasize any Southern accent they might have. These performers often work within other musical styles, including pop music.

For most of us, Williams wins in a landslide, both because the musical elements he employs are more "traditional" and because he is seen to be more sincere—writing the music he loves, not what record label executives ask him to produce for the charts. But this perception obscures the truth: both styles of country—what one sociologist dubbed the "hardcore" and "soft shell" (Peterson 1997)—are products created for the marketplace by teams of music workers (producers, arrangers, music executives, agents) trying to sell tickets and records (Ryan and Peterson 1982). The teams "share beliefs about what they think people will listen to on the radio and what they will buy in stores" and combine these beliefs with elements that "infuse [them] with the legitimacy already established for that form" (Hughes 2000:200, 190). This is no less true of seemingly more authentic, or hardcore, artists. So ultimately, neither group has anticommercial objectives. Nor is one style of artist necessarily more "sincere" about their dedication to musical craftsmanship.

In contrast to an essentialist view, sociologists define authenticity as a *description* of a person, thing, or place that matches a set of expectations about what people, things, or places should be. We know that different groups are unlikely to agree on the symbols (practices, etc.) that denote or connote authenticity. For example, feminists may define a "real woman" as one who is independent, self-supporting, and pro-choice, while fundamentalist Christians may say a "real woman" is financially dependent, home-bound, and outside of the political matrix (and so her opinion on reproductive technologies is irrelevant or nonexistent). Rather than adjudicating between these two definitions, a sociologist would examine the relationship between each group's definition and its history, values, and economy, for example. This "network of commodified signs, social relations, and meanings, a world of human experience and subjectivity" is what creates definitions of, and disputes over, authenticity (Grazian 2003:17).

Sociological studies of authenticity in music help us to predict how and when authenticity disputes will erupt, and also how the disputing groups will define authenticity (Peterson 1997, Grazian 2003, Lena 2006). Music communities must acquire the *capacity* to make authenticity claims; they do not occur arbitrarily within the life course of a musical style. When musical communities are young and small—when they are avant-garde genres (Lena 2012)—there is little consensus about stylistic conventions, so musicians and fans don't police deviations from them. There's no sense in making distinctions based on claims of sincerity or fidelity to a tradition when there is no tradition to reference. Disputes over authenticity emerge much later, after the community has matured into a scene-based genre, in which multiple groups share performance spots, audience and band members, and advice on how to perform the new musical style (Lena 2012).

The size of the genre community is only one resource needed before a musical style can play host to authenticity claims. Perhaps the most important resource is the availability of recording contracts with the so-called major labels. Columbia, Warner Brothers, BMG, and other major labels offer artists big production and promotion budgets to work with, and they are especially good at the global distribution of entertainment products, but they lack the management expertise required to discover and incubate innovative music. In contrast, independent labels like the famed Sun Records excel at finding and developing innovative talent (like Johnny Cash and Elvis), but their small size and meager resources force them to sell artist contracts when the majors come knocking. Arthur Levy, a former Columbia Records executive, summarizes, "It sounds funny, but independent, small labels just can't afford to have hits" (Eliot 1989:230–231). Consequently, the music industry was characterized for many years by a simple distinction between organizational size and musical style: small, independent labels made innovative music while large, major labels made popular music that was less innovative (Peterson and Berger 1975). As a result of this historical association between size and innovation, musical artists under contract with independent record labels are still regarded as having more creative freedom, while major labels are seen as stifling artistic creativity. Major label management is seen as an impediment to innovation, and, by extension, to authenticity. This association between independence and authenticity, and major label contracts and inauthenticity, is a mechanism that promotes the emergence of authenticity disputes.

The conflation of authenticity and independence is so strong that every popular music community has experienced conflict when major firms move in to take over production of the music. In contrast, music communities that are only produced for local constituencies rarely, if ever, host debates over the authenticity of fans or performers. That is, mass production by major labels is a necessary and sufficient condition for authenticity debates in music. To demonstrate this relationship, I now turn to the history of rap music production, and the effect of major label oligopolistic production on musical content and authenticity.

Rap Music, Authenticity, and "Independence"

The music industry was characterized for many years by a simple distinction between organizational size and musical quality: small, independent labels were viewed as making innovative music while large, major labels produced popular music that was seen as being much less

creative (Peterson and Berger 1975). The relationships between organizational size and perceptions of musical innovation and authenticity
were transformed in the 1970s when major label management discovered a new way to organize production.[1] The changes were inspired
by a report on the state of the industry commissioned by Clive Davis
at Columbia Records (Charnas 2010:12). The report recommended
a change in management strategy; in particular, that Columbia stop
buying artist contracts and buy entire independent labels instead,
including their management teams. The newly acquired labels would
become semi-autonomous divisions of Columbia (or "label groups");
the executive staff would not interfere in the creative process but only
retain budgetary control (Dowd 2004:1417). Columbia instituted this
"open system of production," and the other major labels followed suit
(Lopes 1992; Dowd 2000, 2004; Dowd and Blyler 2002; Charnas
2010: 12). This change in management strategy allowed major firms
to harness their strengths—big production budgets and wide distribution networks—while taking advantage of the ability of independent
labels to find and develop talent.

   Such was the state of the industry when rap music was first recorded,
in 1979.[2] At the time, "black music divisions" at major labels were
pumping out funk, disco, and R&B, but they were hesitant to record
rap. However, by the late 1980s, they finally added formerly independent rap labels to their label groups and quickly established a foothold
in the market. As Figure 1 demonstrates, by 1987, independent labels
owned only 60 percent of rap songs charting on the weekly Top 100
R&B charts, and the following year, major labels seized oligopolistic
control of the rap music market (Lena 2003).[3]

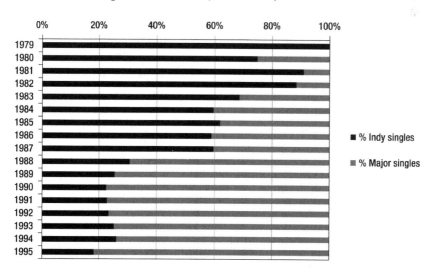

*Figure 1: Comparative percentage ownership of rap market by label type,
1979–1995.*
Source: Lena (2003).

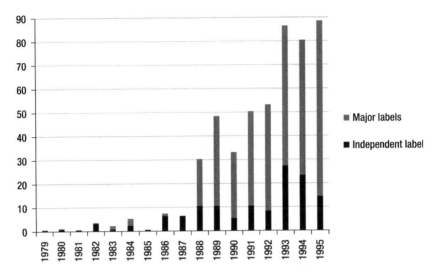

Figure 2: Count of "rough" rap songs by label type, 1979–1995. Source: Lena (2006).

For the purposes of this chapter, the most interesting aspect of this buyout of independent rap labels was that the artists retained their authentic image after joining the major label rosters (within label groups). For the first time, a musical genre played host to artists who were both major label artists and authentic performers. How was this possible? How was authenticity generated by major label artists? Looking more closely at the rap music produced in this period reveals how this was accomplished.

Rap songs and videos, particularly after the late 1980s, frequently depicted their protagonists and performers as angry, violent, unintelligent, criminally minded, and hyper-sexualized. In these years, rap protagonists were often "gangstas," engaged in various forms of illegal activity. After all, "the more rappers were packaged as violent black criminals, the bigger the white audiences became" (Samuels 2005:24).

The dominance of violent and sexually explicit music within popular rap is unquestionably a consequence of major label control. As is shown in Figure 2, the majority ownership of such "rough" material is clearly in the hands of the major labels.[4] Between 1988 and 1995, major labels charted up to five-and-one-half more songs with these vulgar lyrics than all their independent competitors combined (Lena 2006).

Such "rough" music was extremely popular, and it increasingly featured a hustler as a protagonist who represented an emergent set of values: a love of money *and* the 'hood. This combination of values resolved the potential conflict between major label ownership and authenticity. By using a hustler protagonist, major label artists (particularly, formerly independent ones) were able to blend "street" credibility—authenticity—with commercial success. In interviews and song lyrics, on websites, and in promotional materials, rappers emphasized that it was possible to "keep it real" while also "gettin' paid." For example, in 1990, rapper Bosco Money described the goal of his group Downtown Science in these terms: "Our crusade is to fuse street credibility with a song that's accessible to the mainstream" (quoted in Light 2004:138). Here, "credibility" is synonymous with authenticity, and mainstream "accessibility" is a reference to financial success. Groups like Downtown Science sought to "maintain connections to the 'hood and to 'keep it real' thematically, rapping about situations, scenes and sites that comprise the lived experience of the 'hood"; the continued emphasis on the 'hood was "an attempt to mitigate the negative accusations that they have sold out in the event of commercial or crossover success" (Forman 2005:207). After all, "A dichotomy was firmly in place—rappers knew that they could cross over to the pop charts with minimal effort, which made many feel an obligation to be more graphic, and attempt to prove their commitment to rap's street heritage" (Light 2004:142). The hustler protagonist accomplished this aim. The emergence and popularity of the hustler at a key moment in the industry—when major labels established control over the production of music—was no accident.

This history of rap music reveals the conflation of authenticity and independence in mass-marketed music communities and that authenticity and industrial production do not necessarily exist in an antagonistic relationship. We can see that a redefinition of rap authenticity was a means of accommodating the shifting sands of industrial production. As major firms owned more and more rap music, artists adjusted their sound and image—primarily by adopting a hustler protagonist—to infuse it with legitimacy and authenticity.

On the Importance of Race to Authenticity

My argument has focused on the link between community structure and belief in order to illustrate when and why debates over authenticity erupt. I now turn to a final, important facet of how authenticity debates are structured within music community: the race and class of performers. It is often assumed that to play bluegrass, a musician must be working-class, white, and hail from the Appalachian Mountains (Rosenberg 1985), while salsa musicians must be Latin American (Urquía 2004), and punk musicians must be young (Laing 1985). Well-meaning fans of the blues arrive in Chicago clubs expecting to find the music being played by "uneducated American black men afflicted with blindness or some other disability, playing in ramshackle joints that are dimly lit, unbearably smoky, and smelling as funky as their music sounds" (Grazian 2003:13). While music communities need to acquire the capacity to make authenticity claims, performers also often need to have particular attributes in order to be seen as authentic purveyors of a tradition.

In music communities dominated (or perceived to be dominated) by black performers, critics and fans often find it difficult to ennoble the music without invoking essentializing narratives of racial consciousness or musical talent. Thus, the authenticity of performers in styles like jazz, blues, rap, and gospel is usually a function of how well they express or demonstrate attributes associated with blackness. The skill of black musicians—rappers included—has often been described as if it were an instinctual, even genetic, gift. For example, nonwhite New Orleans jazzmen like Buddy Bolden were described as being "fresh off the plantation" when they "gained possession" of European instruments, and although "they really didn't have anyone to teach them or, especially to *tell them the official limits of their horns,*" they "just blew them their own way." The tonalities of the instruments combined with "their African rhythms," and "they just played like they felt and sang" (Buerkle and Baker 1973:14; emphasis in original). Jazzmen and other black musicians were seen as having an innate sensitivity to rhythm, engaging in wild and irresponsible expressions of identity, masculinity, force, and power, and living close to nature, particularly as expressed in irrepressible, wanton sexuality (Lena and Peterson 2008, Lena 2012). Black American musicians are often described as instinctual bearers of African rhythms, as if this were a genetic trait.

Turning toward more contemporary styles, it is the "specter of mainstream dilution, the threat to every emergent form of cultural production in American society, particularly the fecund musical tradition that comes from black America," that haunts rappers contracted with major labels (Dyson 2005:64). Self-actualized, "authentic" "street" artists—"real black men"—must not allow major labels to control their fate. In this way, authenticity and independence become twinned within the discourse of rap and inexorably linked with race. In rap, the hustler is prized for traits *imagined* to be a function of instinct, experience, and genetics. These traits are not a function of training, diligence, or intelligence. In their association with blackness (and especially poor urban blacks), the values of "rough" rap tend to reinforce, not undermine, pernicious racist sentiments.

In hardcore country music, a style dominated by white performers, authenticity debates often surround the class attributes of performers. Fans typically expect that hardcore country artists are accessible to fans, unpretentious in their demeanor, appreciate rural life and physical labor, and have an accompanying distrust or dislike of "city folks" and white-collar labor (Peterson 1997:6–9). "Authentic" country artists are white men who maintain relatively conservative views of women's roles in public and private life, as well as "traditional" family values of faith and tradition, rural life, Christianity, alcohol, death, humor, and nostalgia (Mann 2008). The music valorizes a return to "'simplicity,' moral clarity, social stability and cohesion, small-scale community and a 'slow pace,' honesty, loyalty, tradition—all of which are usually framed as in decline" (Mann 2008:87). Almost every scholar of country music notes the association of these values with whiteness (Peterson 1997, Fox 2004, Mann 2008).

When hardcore country artists fabricate their image as authentic performers, they adopt the "pose of rustics resigned to the march of time" (Mann 2008:87) and act like "exiles in their own homeland, painfully holding on to closeness in a world that has already deserted them" (Stewart 1988:235). It is this last point that bears repeating: the rustic pose is an *adopted* one (Lena 2012). The image of country music as local, intimate, folk, and anticommercial is compelling for fans but is at odds with the reality that country music has always been mass produced and commercial (Peterson 1997). The same can be said of rap and gospel performers, who adopt the pose of the hustler, and the god-fearing supplicant, both of which are marked by a particular notion of what black men and women should and can be. Music is a reflection of our societal norms, just as much as it reflects the characteristics of a specific community of fans and artists.

Conclusion

This chapter illustrates that a full understanding of musical myths—the ideological commitments that animate membership in the community—can only be achieved when we examine the social structures in which they take shape. In particular, mass production by major labels is a necessary and sufficient condition for authenticity debates in music. However, the shape or content of claims to authenticity are not unchangeable and are influenced by larger cultural norms governing race and class.

Notes

1. Negus (2005:629) identifies a second factor that contributed to the increase of major label contracts with black artists over the 1970s, and that was pressure put on the labels by civil rights workers and particularly the NAACP. Pressure was also applied by the Fairplay Committee, a group of DJs and radio workers who fought racial underrepresentation, harassment, and payola.

2. On October 13, 1979, "Rapper's Delight" by the Sugar Hill Gang became the first rap single to enter the *Billboard* R&B singles chart—it would later peak at number four. Sugarhill Records, the independent label on which the single was recorded, was the leading producer of rap music in the Top 100

charts from 1979 to 1983. Independent labels like Sugarhill owned 84 percent of the charting rap singles over these four years (Lena 2003).

3. These data include all rap singles that appeared in the weekly *Top 100 R&B Billboard Magazine* charts between January 1, 1979, and December 31, 1995. A detailed description of the data collection, cleaning, and analysis can be found in Lena 2003.

4. Using the same data as in Figure 1, and employing a taxonomy of four characteristics, rap songs were sorted into subgenre categories. The taxonomy was influenced by Krims (2000) and first published in Lena (2006). The four characteristics are flow, musical style, rhythmic style, and semantic content. Thirteen subgenres were inductively produced from iterative coding of the songs and matched with various expert texts on the genre. These subgenres were then combined into "rough" (and not-rough) groups based on the single characteristic of semantic content.

24

"A Piece of Art Is Not a Loaf of Bread"

Indie Rock's Challenge to Commodification

Jeffrey Nathanial Parker

In terms of the evolution of music consumption, there are bellwether events that help us understand the direction of change. This chapter examines three bellwether events involving three well-known bands: (1) Pearl Jam's protracted 1994–1998 battle with Ticketmaster; (2) Wilco's attempt to release *Yankee Hotel Foxtrot* in 2001 against the wishes of Reprise Records; and (3) Radiohead's circumvention of the label system in its digital release of *In Rainbows* in 2007 on a pay-what-you-want model.

On December 19, 2008, the *Wall Street Journal* reported that the Recording Industry Association of America (RIAA) would end individual lawsuits of illegal file-sharers outside of cases of particularly egregious offenders (McBride and Smith 2008)—a distinct policy change for an organization that had spent over a decade litigating against those involved in illegal file sharing, often suing its consumers. On February 5, 2009, a *New York Times* blog reported that Bruce Springsteen was upset about the prospect of a merger between concert ticket-seller Ticketmaster Entertainment and Live Nation, a live events company, which "would place the dominant players in all sides of the live concert business under one corporate umbrella: the sale of tickets, the representation of artists and the control of concert halls." Springsteen's ire was raised when fans had trouble getting tickets to one of his shows from Ticketmaster and "were redirected to TicketsNow.com, a ticket resale site, where tickets were offered for considerably more than face value." The blog post quotes Springsteen from his website as saying "the one thing that would make the current ticket situation even worse for the fan than it is now would be Ticketmaster and Live Nation coming up with a single system, thereby returning us to a near monopoly situation in music ticketing" (*New York Times* DealBook Blog 2009).

These events are points along the way in an evolution of music consumption, an evolution that draws on the diversification of mass mediation as well as a shift in the conception of the rock audience. While this evolution is comprised of myriad tiny changes that ultimately result in paradigm shifts, certain bellwether events can be pointed to that help us understand the direction of music consumption in America in the past few decades and its potential direction in decades to come. Three events centering on three different "independent" bands exemplify these changes: Pearl Jam's protracted battle with Ticketmaster, from 1994 to 1998; Wilco's attempt to release *Yankee Hotel Foxtrot* in 2001 against the wishes of Reprise Records; and Radiohead's circumvention of the label system in the digital release of *In Rainbows* in 2007 on a pay-what-you-want model.

Background

In 1994, Pearl Jam was thought by some to be "the biggest rock band in the world" (Strauss 1998), having "sold six million copies each of its first two albums, 'Ten' (1991) and 'Vs.' (1993)" just in the United States (Pareles 1994). Ticketmaster was a ticket-selling corporation that had exclusive "contracts with halls and arenas representing 63.2 percent of the country's 9.9 million seats" at the time, according to Pollstar, an industry publication (Ramirez 1994). The organization "maintained marketplace supremacy by locking venues and promoters into exclusive contracts and, in return, sharing millions of dollars' worth of ticket service fees" (Boehlert 1996:22). Pearl Jam attempted to tour in the summer of 1994 with tickets under $20, which would have required that Ticketmaster lower its service charges. The band claimed Ticketmaster refused to lower service charges sufficiently. Pearl Jam tried to organize its tour without Ticketmaster (Goodman 1994:21) but ended up canceling it (Herbert 1994). Pearl Jam filed a memorandum to the US Justice Department accusing Ticketmaster of operating a monopoly and "using that influence to keep promoters from booking the band" (Strauss 1994). Members of the band testified in Congress on the matter (Reuters 1994). Pearl Jam spent the next few years attempting to circumvent Ticketmaster while touring—and mostly failed in its attempt. (*New York Times* 1994; Strauss 1995a, 1995b; Pareles 1996). In 1995 the Justice Department announced that it was closing the investigation into Ticketmaster's anticompetitive practices (Blumenthal 1995), and by 1998 the band was back playing Ticketmaster venues (Strauss 1998:21).

In 2001, Wilco was not as popular as Pearl Jam was in 1994, putting up modest sales figures on its first three records (Pareles 2002).

Wilco had helped "to popularize one of the most conservative rock 'n' roll movements of the last few decades," alternative country, a genre that updated old country and roots music with an indie rock sensibility (Sanneh 2004). However, "the band, and [singer Jeff] Tweedy in particular, grew restless with the music and wanted to push some of the conventions of the rock song (Shorto 2004)," which they did on their fourth record, *Yankee Hotel Foxtrot*. Wilco's record company, Reprise Records—a subsidiary of AOL Time Warner—refused to release "as is" *Yankee Hotel Foxtrot*, "apparently for its lack of commercial-radio potential" (Kot 2001:38) and because it "veered too far from the rootsy rock that Wilco was known for" (Pareles 2002). Instead of changing what "one executive reportedly called a 'career-ending' album" (Kot 2002:42), the band "bought back the record from Reprise and [found itself] in the enviable position of fielding more than thirty offers from other labels" (Kot 2001:38). Wilco finally released the album, after streaming it for free, on Nonesuch Records (also a subsidiary of AOL Time Warner), and "where the band's previous album, 'Summerteeth,' sold 20,000 in its first week according to SoundScan, 'Yankee' sold 57,000 copies in its first week and went on to sell more than 500,000" (Carr 2005).

Our third bellwether example, Radiohead, was an established critical and commercial force with a reputation for challenging prevailing notions of what a rock band ought to do when it released *In Rainbows* in October 2007 (Robbins 1993; Drozdowski 1995:88; Kemp 1997:118). The band, which had been signed to EMI, was out of contract with a label when it finished *In Rainbows* (Pareles 2007b). On October 1, guitarist Jonny Greenwood posted a brief message on the band's website: "Hello everyone. Well, the new album is finished, and it's coming out in 10 days; We've called it *In Rainbows*. Love from us all. Jonny (*Dead Air Space*)." In addition to releasing the album with such a short turnaround from the announcement, the band also allowed consumers to choose what price they wished to pay for it (Levy 2007). A physical version of the CD was released on January 1, 2008, as a venture with independent labels TBD and XL (Pareles 2007b). The physical album moved 122,000 copies in the United States in its first week and debuted at number one (Leeds 2008). The physical disc went on to sell 636,000 copies in the United States (*Rolling Stone* 2008b). In addition, 100,000 copies of a deluxe version of the album, which sold for $81, were sold, with a total of more than three million copies of the album in all forms. Notably, Radiohead "claim[ed] to have made more money on the digital release of *In Rainbows* than they made for their total take on 2003's *Hail to the Thief,* which has sold 1 million copies in the US" (*Rolling Stone* 2008a).

These three events represent a shift away from typical challenges to appropriation and commodification posed by artists, insofar as the events are built around economics, not aesthetics. Rock rebellion has traditionally just led to bigger sales for those supposedly being rebelled against. Affect a rebel stance today, and see it on a T-shirt tomorrow.[1] Indie[2] rock is different, because it appears less dangerous aesthetically and politically than previous iterations of the genre—it is not as confrontational in challenging social mores within the context of the music itself. One real way indie bands *are* dangerous, though, is the way in which they have subverted major systems of distribution. Economic necessity has caused bands to take steps to ensure not only that their audiences hear their music but that they survive as artists. It is these steps taken out of economic necessity, not ones taken out of aesthetic desire, that represent real problems for the record industry. That said, my research also focuses on the limitations of this new form of rebellion.

I argue that these particular challenges from indie bands to hegemonic regimes offered the potential for a legitimate challenge to a system of authority in a way previous aesthetic rebellions and anti-authority attitudes had not. Looking at these three examples, I explore the ways some indie bands have subverted outside efforts to market to and monetize tastes, the ways the larger music industry has handled alternative economies created by these indie bands, and the ways key players have used new media in this dramaturgy of art and commerce. Ultimately, I explore why one set of challenges (Wilco and Radiohead's redefinition of the way recorded music could be distributed and heard) gained some measure of success, while the other (Pearl Jam's attempt to wrest live music from the hands of multinational conglomerates) looks in retrospect like a fool's errand.

Methods

I did a content analysis of two archived databases to identify how the press represented these three situations: the *New York Times* (as my non-music-centric source) and *Rolling Stone* (as my music-centric source). I combed my way through each of the hundreds of articles, highlighting passages and taking notes. As I read, I identified themes I saw emerging. By the end of my reading, I had picked out three: band motivation behind the challenge to authority, understanding of the power of the artists relative to the industry they were challenging, and type of systems the artists were challenging. After coding my notes, I examined these events in terms of the analytical categories.

Analysis

In the first section of my analysis, I evaluate the motivations attributed to each band for making a stand. In the second section, I investigate the amount of power each band was perceived to have during their confrontations with the music industrial complex. Most crucially, in the third section, I explore the types of challenge each band made, specifically what segment of the music industry each band sought to circumvent.

Attributed Motivations

Pearl Jam's challenge to Ticketmaster was portrayed as an altruistic crusade on behalf of its fans: "We remember what it's like to not have a lot of money," said man of the people Stone Gossard, testifying before Congress" *(Rolling Stone* 1994:60). Singer Eddie Vedder was explicit about his altruistic intentions, as he long "claimed that his goal was to be a different kind of rock star. He would resist the temptations of power, wealth, and ego" (Boehlert, Colapinto, and Hendrickson 1996:52). It was not just Pearl Jam making these claims—other music industry figures classified Pearl Jam's motivations as pure, with the manager of another band saying, "I'm not sure it helped Pearl Jam . . . but it definitely helped consumers" (Boehlert 1995:81).

Wilco's challenge to Reprise was also portrayed as a stance based on idealism. In this instance, though, it was not a concern for fans that was seen as a primary motivation, but a concern for the integrity of the band's music. Wilco's refusal to work within the system is seen as a refusal based on an instinct to protect its art. Singer Jeff Tweedy has spoken openly about the issue in starkly idealistic terms. "We realized we just weren't interested in making records like the ones they're trying to sell," he said in a 2002 article (Kot 2002). Later that same year, he said, "We never made any money off records. . . . But I never wanted to be in a band where the only reason we're together is to sell a record" (Scaggs 2002). As with Pearl Jam, Wilco's stance was not one of just an artist perpetuating a notion of idealism. In an article titled "The Ever-Expanding Legend of Wilco," Kelefa Sanneh said, "slowly, improbably, unwillingly, Wilco has become one of those bands that stands for something" (Sanneh 2004).

To an extent, however, Radiohead's challenge was conceived of in idealistic terms. The ideals were a bit different—mostly offering audiences control and tearing down an industry the band saw as corrupt and/or impotent. Band members spoke some about their audience—singer Thom Yorke said, "We just wanted to get the album to people who'd been waiting patiently for four years" (Binelli 2008)—but most of their more idealistic quotes have more to do with destroying the record industry as it existed. "I like the people at our record company, but the time is at hand when you have to ask why anyone needs one," Yorke said. "And, yes, it probably would give us some perverse pleasure to say 'F_you' to this decaying business model" (Tyrangiel 2007). The band sometimes backed off the idea that *In Rainbows* was some grand gesture against the industry, though. Greenwood claimed the band released the record the way it did "partly just to get it out quickly, so everyone would hear it at the same time, and partly because it was an experiment that felt worth trying" (Hiatt and Knopper 2007).

There is another reason attributed to Radiohead, though, that maybe band members did not talk about explicitly but that others did: self-interest. Jeff Leeds said, "Initially, they viewed it as a way to let fans preview Radiohead's music without the guidance—or filter—of radio programmers, music critics, or other conventional tastemakers" (Leeds 2007). Mark Binelli claimed that "the download idea was partly a response to the fact that every Radiohead album since *Kid A*, in 2000, had leaked in some form online" (Binelli 2008). These assertions, if true, display a recognition on Radiohead's part of the power of the Internet—both to help a band (by delivering material directly to an audience without interference from gatekeepers) and to potentially harm a band (by providing an arena in which an album can leak before a band is ready for it to be heard).

Perceived Power

If understanding the presumptive motivations behind each act of resistance might tell us why the bands did what they did, understanding the amount of power each band was assumed to have vis-à-vis the industry they were challenging might tell us something about the status of those industries during the time period. Pearl Jam, "the intense Seattle-based band that has become the top rock act in the country," was pitted against Ticketmaster, "the colossus of American ticket brokers, a tough, aggressive computerized service that sells more than $1 billion in sports and entertainment tickets annually" (Herbert 1994). Most coverage made sure to emphasize who had the power in the struggle, and it was not Pearl Jam. "Although it is the most popular American rock band of the 1990s, Pearl Jam finds struggles everywhere," Pareles (1995) said. *Rolling Stone* referred to Vedder's "unwinnable war with Ticketmaster" (Boehlert, Colapinto, and Hendrickson 1996:52). Pareles wrote a piece for the *New York Times* called "Pearl Jam Gives Voice to Sisyphus" (1994)—Sisyphus being the Greek mythological figure whose punishment in death was to push a boulder up a hill for all eternity, only to have it perpetually roll back down as soon as he neared the top. Sisyphus was not the literary figure who showed up time after time in coverage of Pearl Jam, though. A constant allusion used when discussing Pearl Jam's challenge to Ticketmaster is that of David and Goliath. "David and Goliath redux?" *Rolling Stone* asked (1994:60). "Pearl Jam just can't take this fight on," a band spokesman said. "It's very hard for them to be the David against a very powerful Goliath" (Wiederhorn 1995:20). Eric Boehlert acknowledged that

Pearl Jam was a big band by saying "a showdown of Goliath vs. Goliath was set" (Boehlert 1995:81). Vedder himself did not refer to Goliath specifically, but he did lament from the stage in Chicago, "I hate to think it's the wave of the future—corporate giants that can't be toppled" (Weisel 1995:30).

Wilco's story was portrayed in a similar way, with a key difference. *Rolling Stone* highlighted Wilco by saying, "The story should have been a simple one: The band fought the suits, and the suits won" (2002:96). But the suits did not win, of course, and this is the twist that makes the coverage of Wilco's story different from the coverage of Pearl Jam's. Wilco's story became one of a record industry that was not competent enough to recognize quality. So, power relations in the story of Wilco are complicated, insofar as the music industry that the band challenged is understood to possess more institutional power, while the band is understood to possess power rooted in music and ability to relate to its audience. The fact that AOL Time Warner paid for the album twice—once to make it while the band was signed to Reprise, and once to sign the band to Nonesuch after it was let go with a completed record—gets mentioned a lot. "That's the coup, that's like the coup of all time for us, to basically get one of the biggest entertainment corporations in the world to release us from a contract essentially scot-free with a record that they had already paid for, and then sell it back to them for three times the money," Tony Margherita, Wilco's manager, said (Jones 2002).

Radiohead's was not portrayed as an underdog story. EMI was in financial trouble before the release of the album (*Rolling Stone* 2007:21). The recorded music industry in general was suffering, and had been since 2000, with drops in sales leading to "massive layoffs at the major labels" (Knopper 2008). Because of the rise of new forms of media, one writer declared in 2008 that "the labels are less necessary than ever" (Serpick 2008). In 2008, EMI had to make massive layoffs, underlining the point that the recording industry was in trouble (*New York Times* 2008).

Nature of the Challenge

If Radiohead—and to a lesser extent, Wilco—were understood to be better positioned in their challenges than Pearl Jam, at least part of the reason is the type of challenge each band made. The most crucial distinction to be made among the three cases is that between recorded music and live music. Their challenges are remarkably similar up to this point, insofar as all three bands challenged the way music is distributed to fans/consumers. Whereas Pearl Jam contested the way live music was controlled and how the rights to capitalize on it were distributed, Wilco and Radiohead were concerned with the way recorded music was distributed and monetized. Both these concerns have to do with distribution of music, but it is important to recognize that the two distribution modes are distinct and offer differing obstacles to any effort to fundamentally change them.

This distinction is important to make because the nature of the live show is fundamentally different from the nature of the piece of recorded music, and the difference between the two is integral to understanding why Wilco and Radiohead succeeded where Pearl Jam did not. The ways recorded music can be distributed have multiplied in recent years, whereas the ways live music can be distributed have remained relatively static. While the two systems of distribution are different, they are related, and understanding their interconnections can offer some insight into the shifting ways artists (and corporations) understand the monetization of music.

To understand the actions of Wilco and Radiohead, one must understand the nature of rock and roll at the turn of the twentieth century, and indeed the nature of all culture. Essentially, mass culture as it existed earlier in the century has ceased to exist. Michael Kammen (1999) argues that sometime after the middle of the twentieth century, "the more familiar markets for popular culture became fragmented so that almost no one with something to sell, except for the major television networks, tried to target everyone with a singular product" (Kammen 1999:179). The breakdown of this consolidation and the increasing fracture of culture bring up new challenges for conceiving of the rock and roll audience. The balkanization of culture is far more prevalent than it ever was, and the Internet is the best example of it. Whereas old media like newspaper, radio, and television were one-way and allowed entertainment industry types and advertisers with enough power to shape the discourse, the Internet is a multi-channel network that allows users not only to receive information from a wider variety of sources but to input information into that same wide variety of sources. No longer can youth culture be thought of as a dominant singular force that is easy to market to.

The record label has traditionally functioned as a way to expand an artist's potential audience. In exchange, the artist gives the record label a cut of the profits from the record—a rather large one, as "artists only get pennies on the dollar" (Porter 2007). What happens when (1) cultural fracture means potential audiences for even the biggest bands are smaller than they were in the past, and (2) emergent technologies like the Internet allow artists to reach more people than they ever could in the past directly?

Eventually the size of the potential audience and the size of the group an artist can reach without the help of a label get close enough for a record label to not make much sense financially for an artist. The former president of Reprise Records, Howie Klein, sums it up: "Maybe without [major labels] I'm going to sell 25 percent less records," he said, "but they're taking 40 percent more money that I wouldn't have to spend—so it's not worth it" (Nelson 2003). This is even more feasible when one considers that recording costs have dropped dramatically—"10 percent of what it would have cost 10 years ago," Wilco's manager estimated in a 2003 article (Nelson 2003)—meaning the upfront costs that labels traditionally provide are less necessary. Wilco and Radiohead certainly benefited in publicity from years at Reprise and EMI, but there is some thought that the Internet can do what labels did in the past in this regard (Pareles 2007a).

While Wilco and Radiohead had the technology to circumvent the traditional distribution mechanism for recorded music in America (the major label), no equivalently powerful technology exists for live music.[3] The CD (or the MP3) is infinitely reproducible (and in today's environment, infinitely reproducible outside the traditional channels of the major record company). The concert is different, though. The concert is the holdover from the days of yore, and it cannot be reproduced in totality. As such, those who control the consumption of live music have a much easier time retaining that control.

The inflexibility of the market for concerts as opposed to that for recorded music is born out by the numbers. In 2007, *Rolling Stone* reported that "album sales are down 36 percent since their peak in 2000, the year Napster took off," while also reporting that "the concert business boomed in 2007" as "revenues surged eight percent, to $3.9 billion" (Knopper 2008). This reality is reflected in the attitudes of artists themselves. Giving material away for free, despite the RIAA's protestations, is one way of monetizing music, as artists tend to make more money from live performance and merchandise than music sales, and many artists actually believe file-sharing can be helpful (Mason 2008:156). This is the interconnection of these two distribution systems: recorded music almost acts as publicity for live music, where the most secure money is made. Labels seem to have figured this out, too, as Pearl Jam manager Kelly Curtis believes that labels "will push harder for young acts to sign '360-degree' deals—in which the labels get a chunk of touring, merchandise, and other income" (Hiatt and Knopper 2007).

Summary and Conclusion

In order to understand economic rebellion in rock and roll, it is not enough to know that an artist has challenged a system of distribution—one must know what type of system of distribution the artist has challenged. Pearl Jam challenged the distribution of the live concert experience, while Wilco and Radiohead challenged the distribution of recorded music. This distinction makes a difference, as the live concert experience cannot be infinitely replicated and easily distributed locally the way recorded music can. More to the point, recorded music has begun to be viewed as a sort of marketing tool for the more financially lucrative live music show, so there has come to be more investment in distributing music as widely as possible, even at the risk of not monetizing it. Changes in the systems of distribution between 1994 and 2007 have transformed the way musicians (and their fans) can challenge the music industrial complex.

"A piece of art is not a loaf of bread," Wilco's Tweedy said, explaining,

> When someone steals a loaf of bread from the store, that's it. The loaf of bread is gone. When someone downloads a piece of music, it's just data until the listener puts that music back together with their own ears, their mind, their subjective experience. How they perceive your work changes your work. Treating your audience like thieves is absurd. Anyone who chooses to listen to our music becomes a collaborator. (Jardin 2004)

This quote speaks to a reality about recorded music right now. A piece of art really is not a loaf of bread, because a loaf of bread cannot be replicated infinitely at no real cost. More to the point, niche markets that limit the consumption of certain types of bread to certain audiences have not developed so far as I know, threatening the very existence of larger bakeries as they currently operate. Bakeries can presumably still monetize their bread (and concert promoters can still monetize the live experience) to an extent record companies cannot monetize their music, and that will not change until bread (and live experience) is infinitely replicable.

This is the unifying issue that ties the three case studies together: monetization. Pearl Jam, Wilco, and Radiohead all effected economic rebellions, not aesthetic ones, and all three bands brought attention to the problem of who gets paid off rock and roll. Of course, their stories were told differently, but ultimately, how the stories ended can be largely attributed to the *types* of challenges each band made.

Bands are in a much better position to take control of the means of production in regard to recorded music than live music at the moment. It is worth noting that this success regarding the distribution of recorded music has bearing on what kind of music a band can potentially make. The success of the economic rebellions over recorded music is important because they represent efforts to remove music from the music industrial complex's commodification machine, thereby allowing more aesthetic freedom.

The evasion of corporations like Ticketmaster might be possible if bands book smaller venues not controlled by the corporation (like clubs and amphitheatres). In recent years the indie rock band Bright Eyes has put on reasonably successful tours playing independent venues while conscientiously avoiding venues controlled by Live Nation (a spinoff of Clear Channel), something Pearl Jam of course had trouble with when trying to avoid Ticketmaster (Ryzik 2007). The fact remains, though, that Ticketmaster controls the market for large-scale concerts to an extent that major labels just do not control the market for recorded music anymore.

Ultimately, an understanding of this new economic rebellion is important because it flies in the face of a general understanding that rock and roll revolt can be easily co-opted, and that rock and roll rebellion is primarily aesthetic. The fact that the bands used as my case studies could be classified as "indie" (in designation or action) also calls for a serious reconsideration of the subculture(s) as politically significant. Moreover, this research points to many of the issues that face a failing record industry right now. A big issue here, the one the RIAA is perhaps beginning to face, is that the major record label is in danger, if it does not change its model, of becoming the appendix of the musical body politic: a vestigial organ that served a purpose at some point in evolutionary history that is no longer necessary. The Internet is the first mass medium to reflect the way people actually absorb art—as a community of people communicating with each other, rather than a captive audience being broadcast to—and this shift in relational dynamics diminishes the relevancy of the recorded music industry as it has historically operated.

Notes

1. Sometimes quite literally: when Nirvana first made the cover of *Rolling Stone* (RS 628), lead singer/guitarist Kurt Cobain appeared wearing a shirt that read "Corporate Magazines Still Suck." A quick Google search reveals you can now buy T-shirts emblazoned with the phrase.

2. The term is heavily contested, but for my purposes, *indie* will mean underground rock music made after 1979 that is characterized largely by independent labels, strong local community formation, lo-fi recording, and alternative forms of distribution.

3. Recordings of live concerts made available on CD or, more recently, digital video on DVDs and on websites like YouTube, do bring something of a live event into a reproducible context, but ultimately these artifacts are shadows of the actual event. See Fonarow's (2006) description of the ritualistic nature of the indie concert and Durkheim's (1995 [1912]) discussion of the way rituals can funnel public affect for further discussion.

25

Operating Outside of the Music Industry
Strategies of Production in a Scene-Based Music Genre
Diana Miller

In the absence of a corporate music industry, how do musicians and other producers create and distribute music? What opportunities and constraints does this organizational form provide? This chapter outlines two strategies that individuals in a local music scene use to produce and distribute music: cooperative rather than competitive networking, and promotion geared toward existing audiences rather than new fans. Both strategies are creative responses to the lack of opportunity in this scene to earn a living at music; both strategies also reduce the likelihood that this local scene will develop into a profit-oriented music industry.

Music, like most art, is fundamentally a collective activity (Becker 2008 [1982]). Although we may romanticize the imagined lone creative genius, artists and other creative producers rely heavily on "support personnel" to perform tasks that are not considered "art," although they are necessary for artistic production. Painters rely on craftspeople to supply materials like canvases and paints, and gallery owners to display and sell their work; dance companies rely on publicists to gain media exposure for their productions and sell tickets. Howard Becker (2008 [1982]) uses the concept of "art world" to describe these networks of artists and support personnel, and the practices through which they produce and distribute art.

Viewed through this lens, the extensive cooperation required to produce music becomes obvious. Although popular musicians (usually) write and play their own music, sound engineers record and produce their albums, publicists and promoters arrange their concerts and sell tickets, and media representatives like journalists and video jockeys expose their music to audiences. Even with modern social media that allow musicians to distribute their work online, bands and musicians have difficulty reaching a wide audience without these support personnel (Leonard 2007, Martin 2006b). Musicians and support personnel can liaise in many different ways: for example, through informal amateur experimentation (Lee 2009), freelance project-based work in independent music scenes (Leonard 2007), or large-scale standing organizations like corporate record labels (Negus 1999). The sociologist's task is to pinpoint how art world participants relate to each other, and how it matters.

I use Becker's (2008 [1982]) "art worlds" as a theoretical framework to (1) describe the "conventions" or patterns of cooperation in the underground heavy metal music community in Toronto, Canada; and (2) explain how these conventions shape the resulting music and the future opportunities available to musicians. This community is what Lena and Peterson (2008) call a "scene-based" genre, where music production happens through informal personal relationships, and musicians and support personnel make little, if any, money through music. This differs from an "industry-based genre" (Lena and Peterson 2008), where music production is mediated through large-scale for-profit organizations like corporate record labels. Though the music played in this scene resembles that of industry-based heavy metal bands, the two kinds of bands operate under vastly different conditions of production.

In this chapter, I ask, In a scene-based music community, how do musicians and other producers create and distribute heavy metal music? What opportunities and constraints does this organizational form provide? My answers draw on participant-observation at thirty concerts and eighteen interviews with individuals in the Toronto heavy metal scene, including musicians, fans, and support personnel like show promoters and independent label owners. My ethnographic description highlights two strategies of production and distribution: a focus on cooperative rather than competitive networking, and insider-oriented promotion strategies that target existing fans rather than mass audiences.

Features of the Scene

Participants in the Toronto heavy metal scene develop stable networks and practices for creating music, but they do so without corporate or industry-based support. Bands often play together for years, performing in bars and other small venues locally and in nearby cities. They frequently write and produce full-length albums, with some putting out multiple records, and make small amounts of money from selling these CDs and performing live. Most bands are not signed to record labels, or are signed to little-known, metal-focused independent labels rather than major corporate ones. Most musicians distribute some of their music for free through websites with user-generated content (e.g., YouTube, MySpace, Facebook). Their music is rarely sold digitally online (e.g., on iTunes) and is almost never found in national chain music stores. Musicians frequently achieve recognition within the local metal community, but not outside of this scene. The bulk of musicians' media exposure occurs through media created by and for the metal community (e.g., blogs and discussion boards focused on the Toronto metal scene), as opposed to national or mainstream press.

In a corporate, industry-based music genre, most fans may never meet artists in person; yet, in the Toronto metal community fans and musicians often know each other, and committed fans frequently take on support roles like organizing shows or writing CD and concert reviews. While professional, industry-based bands socialize backstage before and after performing, most local concerts have no backstage area and musicians socialize with the audience before and after performing. Support personnel in this scene typically work informally as part-time freelancers, rather than working for record labels or other formal businesses; most recording, show organizing, and review writing is done by scene members in their spare time, rather than promotion companies or music magazines with a core full-time staff. These freelance support personnel typically have full-time jobs outside the metal scene.

These features make the Toronto metal community a quintessential "scene-based genre" (Lena and Peterson 2008). A scene-based genre is a community of music production centered on personal networks, and usually based in a specific city or neighborhood. Scene-based musicians and support personnel do not support themselves from music; music production is self-funded rather than profit-making. Media coverage in a scene is local and community-based, as opposed to national or mainstream. The Toronto metal community meets all these criteria.

Aspiring artists similar to the ones in the Toronto metal scene, and all scene-based genres (i.e., unsigned, achieving mostly local recognition, distributing free music via social media), are certainly found within music industries, particularly early in their careers; however, in a music scene, *all* participants including support personnel operate on this freelance and often self-funded basis. An aspiring musician in an industry-based scene might hope to eventually affiliate with a major corporate record label or talent agency and earn a living; in a scene-based genre like the Toronto metal community, these organizations do not exist.

While some scene-based genres eventually develop into larger-scale music industries, some genres stay scenes[1] (Lena and Peterson 2008). Without longitudinal data, we cannot know whether the Toronto metal scene is developing into an industry; however, the available evidence suggests that it is not. Although classic heavy metal was briefly popular with audiences in North America and the UK through the late 1970s and 1980s, today those same audiences widely report disliking it (Hall 2007, Bryson 1996). The underground Toronto scene is also centered on subgenres like black metal and death metal, which never developed into industries (Lena and Peterson 2008). Finally, as I will show, conventional production and distribution strategies in the Toronto metal scene are creative solutions to the lack of corporate support and profit-making opportunities but also reproduce these conditions; these strategies are unlikely to attract the attention of mass audiences or corporate music industries.

Heavy Metal and Expectations of Success

Participants in all local scene-based music genres confront a similar challenge: how to produce music with no guarantee of financial support or profit. However, participants' responses to this challenge may vary. Musicians in some scenes may actively work to increase profit-making opportunities, like early scene-based jazz musicians who affiliated with record labels and classical musicians to develop a jazz industry (Phillips and Owens 2004). Alternatively, scene-based musicians may find methods of creating and distributing music that do not require the music to be profitable. Participants in the Toronto metal scene adopt the latter strategy. They largely believe that heavy metal is unmarketable to mass audiences. Musicians in this scene clearly want to reach audiences, and explicitly state as much, but they do not expect to earn a living from music. This attitude shapes the two strategies of production outlined in this chapter: cooperative networking, and an orientation toward existing audiences rather than new fans.

We can better understand Toronto metal musicians' attitudes toward financial success by distinguishing between ideals and realistic expectations, as Paul, a twenty-three-year-old white metal musician, does here:

> The dream would be touring around the world playing music and stuff like that, but that's a long shot. And even, the majority of metal bands that do that don't make a living at it. You have to have some sort of part-time job, which is why I've been keeping this one around, because if we did start touring more, I could always just go back and work there afterwards.

Although Paul might "dream" of supporting himself by playing music, he does not expect this. Because he expects to always work outside the music scene, he deliberately looks for a job with a flexible schedule that will not interfere with his music. Taylor, a twenty-four-year-old female metal fan and former fanzine editor, similarly explains,

> For people who want careers in music, I find they get very torn. You can't make a successful living off metal. It's just not an option. So either you bridge the gap and, you know, mix in some elements of popular music with your metal or you have two bands, one that makes money and one that doesn't. Take your pick. But metal is either a hobby or a failed career.

Here, Taylor echoes the widely shared sentiment that metal—at least, the kind of metal played in the local scene—is simply not profitable. Matthew, a twenty-six-year-old white male musician, does exactly what Taylor describes. He plays the bass in three bands—two metal bands that he does for enjoyment, and one Top 40 cover band that earns money playing in bars. As he says of the cover band, "it's not that I don't like it but it wouldn't be my first choice for music to listen to." In conversations at shows, I also heard many cautionary tales of metal bands who broke up after touring or recording a CD because they exhausted their savings and had to go back to work.

Becoming famous and touring the world playing metal might be many musicians' dream; however, they do not treat it as a realistic possibility that they should act toward. Of course, not every industry-based band becomes famous, either; however, in industry-based genres making a living in the music business might be possible. Although they did not use these terms, participants in this metal community did not expect the scene to become an industry-based genre that would give them this chance to earn a living. Interestingly, participants in the Toronto metal scene treat this lack of earning potential as an advantage rather than a limitation, explicitly justifying their music through a rhetoric of anticommercialism. Fans and musicians spoke disparagingly about pop music, which they described as "manufactured," "a big lie," "just pandering to whatever the label tells them to do," and "like someone who's really well dressed and really, really fucking stupid." As Paul explains,

> [nu metal] is . . . the sort of new popular metal. Because that sort of stuff appeals to the wide masses and of course it needs some, some like real metalheads into it. But it's just the fly-by-nighter people . . . it doesn't seem like it's played for the sake of playing music. It seems more played for like commercial success and games and things like that. You see these songs on WWE Raw and all this stuff and, you know, it's all over MuchMusic.

Paul takes the commercial success of heavy metal—particularly its ties with corporate entities like WWE and MuchMusic—as evidence of its aesthetic failure. Echoing what others have found (Halnon 2006, Weinstein 2000), Toronto metal fans and musicians defined commercial pop music as lacking artistic integrity, and defined themselves and their music in explicit contrast to it; unlike successful pop musicians, they see themselves as devoted to art for art's sake.

Strategies of Production in a Scene-Based Genre

In this section I show that the ways that people in the Toronto metal scene produce and distribute music are creative responses to their belief in heavy metal's unprofitability. Musicians and support personnel typically mobilize resources and people through cooperating rather than competing with each other, and through use of distribution strategies that target existing fans rather than new fans or mass audiences. As I will argue, these strategies of production and distribution actively reduce the likelihood that the Toronto underground metal scene will develop into an industry.

Problems of Mobilization: Resource Scarcity and Cooperation

Musicians operating in scenes rather than industries must obviously forego the resources those industries might offer, which makes resource mobilization challenging. One conventional solution is for scene-based musicians to perform tasks that industry-based musicians would have support staff carry out. Industry-based rock musicians (usually) write and play their own music, but support personnel put that music onto a CD, book and promote concerts, and produce merchandise. Record labels also fund many of these expenses for professional musicians (Negus 1999). In contrast, when scene-based heavy metal musicians wish to tour, design merchandise, or produce a CD, they do much of the support work themselves.

For many musicians, this involves acquiring technical skills; for example, some musicians learn the technical skills of recording instead of hiring a pricey professional sound engineer. Jake, a heavy metal musician, obtained a college education in music engineering and originally hoped to work at a studio. Although he did not find a studio job, he owns professional-quality sound equipment and maintains a personal studio in his basement, which he used to record his band's CD. Similarly, rather than depending on promoters to book concerts and invite his band to play, Ethan taught himself business and marketing principles and now organizes shows.

Once this expertise is acquired, it is often shared. Jake records other bands' CDs on a freelance basis, and Ethan promotes and finances shows for other bands as frequently as his own. As is customary for support personnel in this scene, Jake and Ethan are frequently paid for doing this work for other bands; however, they (and other support personnel) explained that they do not charge what they "should," or what they consider "market rates." Musicians arguably have incentives to view other bands in the scene as competitors and therefore keep this technical expertise to themselves—or at least charge higher prices for their labor. In fact, some aspiring professional musicians form "defensive exclusionary networks" to survive in competitive industry-based genres (Hracs 2010). In an industry-based genre, this makes sense; when it is possible to "make it," but not all bands do, bands have incentives to compete with each other for audiences, media coverage, and industry attention. Yet, cooperation is more conventional in the Toronto underground metal scene than competition. Bands often develop stable friendships, play together repeatedly, promote each other's shows, encourage audiences to buy each other's CDs, and trade favors such as loaning equipment, connecting each other to promoters, and doing work for each other for free or relatively low rates.

Musicians also manage financial scarcity by treating money earned from music as a way to finance further musical activity, rather than as a source of income.[2] Virtually all musicians and support personnel in the Toronto metal scene maintain jobs or other income sources outside the scene. Musicians typically spend more money purchasing equipment than they ever earn back; in contrast, support personnel might legitimately expect to earn some money from music, although not all do. Take the example of promoters: "promoting," or organizing, a show involves booking a venue, arranging bands to play, advertising the show, charging admission, and paying the bands out of ticket sales. In theory, a good promoter should earn a small profit for each show, but the consensus in the Toronto scene was that promoters more often lose money than make money. Christian, a white, mid-twenties bassist in a local band, stopped promoting shows because he was "tired of losing money at it." He found that relatively unknown bands wanted more money to play than Christian estimated he would make in ticket sales, or that many people who said they would attend a show never showed up. Although he still books shows occasionally as a favor for his friends' bands, he no longer considers it a job. Heath, a heavy metal fan in his early twenties, quit his job to start a promotion company but became similarly frustrated and stopped promoting shows after a few months.

In short, few participants in the Toronto metal scene earn reliable income from music, and so rely on their own expertise and that of friends to accomplish the routine tasks of music production. Most income from musical activities goes toward covering expenses; the goal is not to make a profit, but to break even. It is unsurprising to find musicians struggling to break even (Menger 1999), even in industry-based genres. However, note that in this scene-based music genre it is not just artists who must manage financial uncertainty; support personnel like promoters do as well.

Problems of Distribution: Targeted vs. Mass Audiences

The conventional distribution system in the Toronto metal scene is noteworthy because it is largely oriented toward audiences that already listen to heavy metal, rather than mass-market audiences or potential new fans. Musicians state that they want to reach more listeners and express a vague desire to "get the music out there," as Ethan put it. As performance implies a desire for an audience, this is unsurprising. However, in practice musicians' distribution strategies primarily reach people who already listen to heavy metal.

Musicians and promoters typically advertise concerts on websites created by and for members of the Toronto metal scene. New fans and mass-market audiences are largely unaware of these websites and are thus unlikely to hear about shows posted there. Metal musicians and promoters normally do not list their shows in mainstream concert listings, which in Toronto are typically found in weekly general-interest music magazines (i.e., magazines that focus on all music rather than a specific genre). The use of metal-focused rather than non-genre-specific media reduces the likelihood that a fan of related music genres (e.g., hard rock) might hear about a metal show. Show promoters also use word-of-mouth and social media like Facebook to advertise shows; promoters commonly invite all their Facebook friends to a show (after building up a friends list of heavy metal fans) or invite all the people who have "liked" a band's Facebook page. CDs are primarily sold at shows but may also be available online through bands' websites or through independent metal-focused distributors' websites—not major outlets like amazon.com, but distributors emerging from and focusing on the metal community. Musicians may make samples of their music available on websites with user-generated content, such as Facebook, MySpace, and YouTube.

These methods of distribution primarily reach fans with prior knowledge of these bands or websites, or who are already connected to the bands using social media. Industry-based bands obviously use websites like Facebook and YouTube as well; however, industry-based metal bands do this as one of many distribution strategies, while for scene-based musicians these websites may be the primary or only method for musicians to publicize their music. Furthermore, whereas industry-based bands might send out press releases or use a print advertising campaign to publicize upcoming shows, shows in the Toronto metal scene are usually only posted on websites created by and for scene members.

These strategies make vastly different assumptions than strategies of distribution in corporate music industries. In professional music industries, many musicians and publicists use distribution strategies that target as many people as possible, such as radio airplay, televised music videos, billboard ads, press releases that generate coverage in national and worldwide media outlets, and even television commercials. These strategies assume that many people who hear the music will like it and might purchase a CD or attend a concert; the central problem is ensuring that as many people as possible hear the music, or hear about an upcoming concert. In contrast, scene-based heavy metal musicians assume that most mass audiences will not like their music so the central problem is reaching *the right people.*

Paul explained that heavy metal is "music for musicians"; he describes it as so technically complex and difficult to appreciate that most listeners are other metal musicians, or dedicated fans who have learned to appreciate it. This sentiment was widely shared among fans and musicians in the Toronto metal scene. Because they assume that most audiences will not like heavy metal, musicians and support personnel use media centered on the local metal scene rather than mainstream press. When I asked musicians if they ever used more mass-oriented distribution strategies—for example, sending demo CDs to radio stations, potential agents, non-genre-specific music magazines, corporate record labels, or iTunes representatives—most reported that they did not. Some musicians had never used these strategies; others had tried them and found them less successful than niche marketing strategies. Despite the high potential payoff, most musicians believed that marketing strategies geared toward corporate music industries had a low chance of success; in contrast, inviting active members of the heavy metal scene to a self-promoted concert via Facebook would certainly draw an audience. Put another way, these distribution strategies are unlikely to lead to financial success, but they can and do help musicians gain recognition and esteem from a community of like-minded peers.

Participants in the heavy metal scene do sometimes use more mass-oriented strategies, even if they are rare. Grace, a freelance publicist, sends demo CDs to radio stations—she is the only person I encountered who used this strategy. However, she still looks for relatively targeted audiences. She says,

> I won't send [a demo CD] to a radio station that does all, like, country. I, I do a lot of research before I send it out to make sure that there are shows that have metal. . . . I'm not going to send it to CHFI [a major Toronto radio station]. . . like, if they don't have a metal show I'm not going to send it, because the bands paid so much money to have PR done and I want to make sure that I'm gonna get reviews.

This quote shows that Grace shares most musicians' assumption that heavy metal is not marketable to mass audiences—or, at least, she expects radio hosts to share this assumption. She does not expect that a Top 40 or rock DJ might hear a heavy metal song and view it as appropriate for his or her audience; in fact, she expects that a radio host might avoid an album specifically because it is a metal album. Consequently, Grace looks for DJs and radio stations that explicitly self-identify with the heavy metal genre, which typically means that she will not send CDs to major radio stations. Rather, she sends CDs to smaller, less popular niche radio stations—for example, the Governor's Ball, which is actually not a radio station but a radio-style online podcast based in the Toronto metal scene. Interestingly, although most heavy metal musicians assume that their music is unmarketable to mass audiences, they do not seriously consider altering their music to appeal to mass tastes.

Discussion and Conclusion

The conventional strategies of production and distribution in the Toronto metal scene limit producers' opportunities for commercial success but also provide opportunities for potentially unmarketable creative experimentation. A lack of affiliation with corporate music industries means that musicians often do support work themselves; however, they are also freed from accountability to industry demands, particularly the pressure to write marketable music. Industry-based genres actively attempt to predict what audiences will buy, and then produce that kind of music, leading to frequently repetitive content (Hirsch 1972, Negus 1999). In contrast, people in the Toronto metal scene routinely break music industry conventions, such as song length. A song length of approximately three to five minutes originally became conventional because that was what early records could play, and this has remained conventional because it is now what audiences expect to hear and therefore what music industries expect musicians to produce (Peterson 1997). While some heavy metal bands play three-to-five-minute songs, others play songs that are shorter than one minute or longer than twenty-five minutes. Reaching a smaller audience means a smaller market for CDs and concert tickets; however, these audiences tend to be highly committed metal fans who appreciate creative experimentation. Music producers tend to be more concerned with peer recognition and community esteem rather than financial profits.

The strategies of production found here may not hold true for other scene-based music communities. Industry-based music genres develop different strategies of production and distribution (Martin 2006b; Negus 1999), and we should expect different scene-based music genres to do so as well. In particular, because some scenes have developed into industries (Lena and Peterson 2008), we should expect that some music scenes use methods of production and distribution that encourage, or are at least more amenable to, corporate organizations and profit-making as a main goal. Differences among strategies of production in scene-based music genres may therefore help to explain which music communities will transition into music industries, and which will not. Future research should compare the conventional processes of music production described here to those found in a scene that is transitioning to an industry-based genre, or that has made the tradition already.

Notes

1. Lena and Peterson (2008) cite Chicago jazz, folk rock, alternative country, and punk rock as examples of scenes that developed into industries, and doo-wop, death metal, garage, and jungle as examples of scene-based genres that remained scenes.

2. Of course, bands' earnings rarely cover their expenses, particularly when they tour and need accommodations. I attended more than one concert where bands offered free T-shirts and CDs to fans that could offer them a place to sleep that night.

26

Why Pay for Music?
How College Students Rationalize Illegal Downloading
Jason S. Ulsperger, Kristen Ulsperger, and Stan H. Hodges

The authors conducted a study of 800 college students from four universities in the United States. The majority routinely downloaded music from the Internet and other sources, knowing it was illegal. They were interested to understand why these students, who otherwise were law-abiding persons, chose to do this. Neutralization theory, a classic sociological perspective in the study of crime, was used to study the rationalization techniques used to justify their illegal behavior. These techniques include the denial of responsibility, condemnation of condemners, denial of the victim, denial of injury, and appealing to higher loyalties.

The use of peer-to-peer networks to exchange music files gained popularity in the late 1990s. Napster, one of the most notorious networking programs at that time, let users exchange compressed audio files known as MP3s. Soon after its inception, thousands of users were sharing copyrighted songs through the Internet. It was a great way for people to obtain desired music without paying for what many consumers perceived to be an overpriced commodity. The Recording Industry Association of America (RIAA) hurriedly sued Napster and won, but other programs quickly replaced it. Fighting program designers was a dead end, so in 2003, the RIAA announced it was going to start suing individual file sharers—a policy that continues (Moore and McMullan 2004, Bhattacharjee et al. 2006).

In defense of the recording industry, illegal downloading has big financial effects. In 2000, consumers in the United States bought over

785 million albums. In 2006 they purchased just over 588 million. By 2010 only 326 million albums sold, down nearly 13 percent from the previous year. Digital sales from outlets such as iTunes and sales of ringtones for cellular telephones are balancing out some of the losses. However, the music industry still appears to be struggling, and the largest block of music pirates—college students—continues to download illegally more than ever before (Graham 2004, Christman 2011, Perpetua 2011).

Neutralization Theory

In sociology, a popular theoretical framework for analyzing illegal behavior is neutralization theory (Sykes and Matza 1957). Neutralization theory focuses on how criminals justify their illegal behavior with specific rationalization techniques. This includes the denial of responsibility, condemnation of condemners, denial of the victim, denial of injury, and appealing to higher loyalties.

Denial of responsibility involves people shifting the blame for criminal behavior to someone or something else. The *condemning of condemners* implies people in the system judging criminals are hypocrites. Whether it is police, lawyers, or judges, those pointing the finger do things far worse. *Denial of the victim* implies the person harmed by criminal actions deserved it. *Denial of injury* means the perpetrator thinks he or she did no harm to anyone. With *appealing to higher loyalties,* the criminal will claim unyielding allegiance to another person or group. The criminal will then argue that his or her actions took place because of, or for, that allegiance. In turn, loyalty to others is more important than social rules (Sykes and Matza 1957).

Findings

Thirteen percent of respondents in this study claimed they do not engage in illegal music downloading. The following section analyzes the ways the remaining 87 percent neutralize the illegality of their actions.

Denial of Responsibility

With this research, denial of responsibility included any illegal downloading justification that shifts blame to technology, time constraints, economic disadvantage, or access issues. This represents the highest frequency of neutralization techniques in this study: 278 (36 percent) of the respondents claimed their illegal downloading is not their fault (see Table 1).

With blaming technology, the mere presence of the Internet is enough to condone illegal downloading. One student noted, "Anything on the

Table 1. Justifications for Illegal Internet Downloading of Music*

Technique of Neutralization	Frequency	Percentage
Download Illegally		
Denial of Responsibility	278	36
Condemnation of the Condemners	142	18
Denial of the Victim	113	15
Denial of Injury	91	12
Appeal to Higher Loyalties	49	6
Do Not Download Illegally	105	13
Total	778	100

*Note: Twenty-two responses were not included due to either nonresponse or ambiguity in response.

Internet is fair game. . . . If it is such a problem, why don't they get rid of the sites that supply the music?" Other respondents negated their responsibility due to the ability to rip and burn off music. However, other arguments dealt with time constraints and economic disadvantage. On one survey, a student indicated her life is hectic and illegal downloading is "a convenient way to get the [songs] you need." Another respondent noted, "I couldn't listen to music if I couldn't download it. I don't have the time or energy to go to the mall." In terms of economic disadvantage one respondent claimed, "I'm a college student. Like I can afford to buy CDs." With the theme of access, another respondent stated, "I download the songs I can't buy at the store because I am underage."

Condemnation of the Condemners

Condemning the condemners involved statements relating to everyone downloading and governmental apathy. Here, 142 (18 percent) respondents indicated those who are after them, such as the government or RIAA, are no different from them. One student noted, "Everyone does it. I can't think of someone who wouldn't want to." Others stated, "It is done so much it is not a big deal" and that it is just a way to "work the system" that consistently "works you." With governmental themes, one student commented, "I feel [illegal downloading] is acceptable because as a middle-class American I am already paying enough [to other people] because of taxes." Another argued, "[It] is stealing, but . . . [The government] should go after people committing worse crimes." Students also indicated the government could do more to take greed out of the recording industry. One respondent said the "government should make the RIAA decrease prices." With hypocrisy, the basic component of neutralization involves the idea that the industry has been stealing from consumers with high prices. One student argued, downloading copyrighted songs is only "illegal so [record companies] can hold a monopoly and charge outrageous prices for something that will be [worthless] in a year."

Denial of the Victim

Denial of the victim included aggressive, nonsympathetic statements toward victim greed, overpriced CDs, and general comments toward persistent exploitation of consumers by the recording industry. Here, 113 (15 percent) respondents believed victims deserve it. With greed, multiple statements related to the music industry and its ravenous desire for profit.

One student stated, "I think the music industry is wrong. [They] already make enough money from radio, publicity, and concerts." Another respondent agreed with this feeling. He elaborated to the point of describing the luxury office furniture he believes greedy executives surely have. He pointed out, "The music industry doesn't need money. They all sit in leather chairs with massagers built in them while [I] scrounge around. I'm left looking for pennies to get something to eat." With excessive pricing, multiple respondents provided thoughts similar to one student who argued, "If [companies] would make CDs cheaper I would buy them." Some responses took on a more aggressive tone. One student denied artists as victims because of their music industry ties when he stated, "I do rip off [music] artists, but I do not mind because they are all little corporate bitches these days."

Denial of Injury

Denial of injury included themes such as a lack of moral harm, music not being a tangible product, previewing music for later purchase, and informal artist promotion. It also included comparisons to earlier forms of music sharing and passive statements about victims having a high level of economic prosperity. As shown in Table 1, ninety-one (12 percent) students in this study claimed their actions cause no harm.

With morals, one student noted that illegal downloading "doesn't violate any morals" and that it "doesn't directly affect anyone." Another student claimed his music piracy is a legitimate behavior because he was not "physically hurting anyone." Many respondents argued no one is hurt, but few followed the argument that illegal downloading is actually moral. However, some did indicate that as long as it is limited, it is suitable. One respondent argued, "If you don't do it in excess then it is not so bad." With this category, some respondents implied they actually provide a service to music artists in two ways when they illegally download. First, they create a preview outlet for themselves. Second, they create a preview outlet for others by serving as informal, small-scale promoters. One student stated, "Many people who [illegally] download a song, like it enough that they go buy the whole CD anyway." Echoing that idea, another student indicated, "If it is a band I like, I will go buy their music."

Creating promotion outlets for others involves not only listening to illegally downloaded music on your own but also sharing it with other people who might enjoy it and end up being a fan. One student explained, "A lot of bands get started by people [obtaining their music without paying for it]. You don't hear them complaining until they get to be famous . . . like Metallica—poor Metallica." Someone else made a similar point when he argued, "Most of the bands I listen to now, I heard their music from [illegal] downloading. . . . Downloading is a good thing for fans and bands." Interestingly, several respondents argued that illegal downloading is nothing new. One stated that "in the 'old days' [people] just recorded songs they liked off of the radio." Another noted, "For years people borrowed music from their friends. . . . It's not like I am stealing. It's like borrowing from a friend's collection." Even if it is more like stealing and less like borrowing, students believe artists experience such a high level of economic prosperity that they can take the monetary loss. Another student stated, "The only thing I know is [downloading music] off the Internet is okay because the [artists] get money from other sources like tours."

Appeal to Higher Loyalties

In this project, appealing to higher loyalties included justifications based on relationships, free trade, God, the higher power of music, environmental concerns, and basic ideas of freedom. Here, forty-nine (6 percent) of the respondents said they download illegally because of an allegiance they have to someone or something else.

With relationships, responses indicated college students sometimes download for family members and friends who do not have Internet access or the know-how to do it. Many implied that family knew they were doing it but thought it was a legitimate behavior. One respondent stated, "My parents know [I download illegally] and they don't care." Free-trade rationalizations concerned arguments with idealistic perspectives of an Internet void of capitalistic motives. As one student said, "I believe that the Internet was designed to be a database for the free trade of information. Bans on downloading are wrong. They defeat the true purpose of the Internet." Interestingly, a related argument brings in references to God and the supernatural forces of music. One student argued, "[Music] is an art form just as paintings are. God gave us our mind to be able to express ourselves. . . . So, why charge for music when it is an expression of someone's mind and enables them to get their point across to people." Along similar lines, another respondent indicated that downloading illegally is wrong, but that it is less important than music existing in new formats for people to "listen to and enjoy." One respondent even argued, "With today's horrific consumerism, illegal downloading is to be expected as part of the [student] counter culture."

With environmentalism, a student contended that her illegal downloading of music is "beneficial for us because it reduces waste from CD packages." In terms of basic freedoms, one student argued that laws making the downloading of copyrighted material illegal are "a ploy by the recording industry and artists." He stated that the industry's covert goal is to "impede upon the freedoms of information enjoyed by everyday Americans."

Conclusion

Substantial amounts of college students who download illegally neutralize their activity by denying responsibility. Moreover, a sizable number say hypocrites are the ones condemning their actions. Fewer deny injury and victimization. Though some respondents indicated victimization does happen, many contend the music industry and artists can handle it or deserve it. In this study, the lowest frequency of neutralization among college students who download music illegally involved appealing to higher loyalties. Though this represented the smallest category, respondents did reveal some interesting rationalizations on music as a free form of expression versus its continuing to be a commodity. In terms of its capitalist viability as a consumer good, it is obvious that the future of the recording industry seems uncertain. However, one thing seems sure—illegal downloading and the fight to stop it will probably continue for years, and justifications for illegal downloading probably will as well.

References

Books and Journal Articles

Abbott, A., and A. Hrycak. 1990. "Measuring Resemblance in Sequence Data: An Optimal Matching Analysis of Musician Careers." *American Journal of Sociology* 96:144–185.

Abdo, G. 2005. "Islam in America: Separate but Unequal." *Washington Quarterly* 28:7–17.

Adorno, T. W. 2002a [1938]. "On the Social Situation of Music." In *Essays on Music*, ed. R. Leppert, 391–436. Berkeley: University of California Press.

———. 2002b [1938]. "On the Fetish-Character in Music and the Regression of Listening." In *Essays on Music*, ed. R. Leppert, 288–317. Berkeley: University of California Press.

———. 1976. *Introduction to the Sociology of Music*. New York: Seabury Press.

———. 1973. *Philosophy of Modern Music*. New York: Seabury Press.

Aguirre, B. E. 1984. "The Conventionalization of Collective Behavior in Cuba." *American Journal of Sociology* 90:541–566.

Ahlkvist, J. A., and R. Faulkner. 2002. "Will This Record Work for Us? Managing Music Formats in Commercial Radio." *Qualitative Sociology* 25:189–215.

Allen, W. F., C. P. Ware, and L. M. Garrison. 1995 [1867]. *Slave Songs of the United States*. New York: Dover.

Allmendinger, J., and R. J. Hackman. 1996. "Organizations in Changing Environments: The Case of East German Symphony Orchestras." *Administrative Science Quarterly* 41:337–369.

———. 1995. "The More the Better? A Four-Nation Study of the Inclusion of Women in Symphony Orchestras." *Social Forces* 74:423–460.

Andersen, M., and M. Jenkins. 2001. *Dance of Days: Two Decades of Punk in the Nation's Capital*. New York: Soft Skull.

Anderson, C. A., N. L. Carnagey, and J. Eubanks. 2003. "Exposure to Violent Media: The Effects of Songs with Violent Lyrics on Aggressive Thoughts and Feelings." *Journal of Personality and Social Psychology* 84:960–971.

Arnett, J. J. 1996. *Metalheads: Heavy Metal Music and Adolescent Alienation*. Boulder, CO: Westview.

Arnold, B. 1992. "Art Music and the Holocaust." *Holocaust and Genocide Studies* 6:335–349.

Asai, S. 2008. "Firm Organization and Marketing Strategy in the Japanese Music Industry." *Popular Music* 27:473–485.

Aschaffenburg, K., and I. Maas. 1997. "Cultural and Educational Careers: The Dynamics of Social Reproduction." *American Sociological Review* 62:573–587.

Attali, J. 1985. *Noise*. Minneapolis: University of Minnesota Press.

Baiano-Berman, D. J. 2002. *Deadheads as a Moral Community*. PhD dissertation, Department of Sociology, Northeastern University, Boston, MA.

Baker, H. A. 1984. *Blues, Ideology, and Afro-American Literature: A Vernacular Theory*. Chicago: University of Chicago Press.

Baker, R. W. 2003. "Screening Islam: Terrorism, American Jihad, and the New Islamists." *Arab Studies Quarterly* 25:33–56.

Ballard, M. E., and S. Coates. 1995. "The Immediate Effect of Homicidal, Suicidal, and Non-Violent Heavy Metal and Rap Songs on the Moods of College Students." *Youth and Society* 27:148–168.

Baraka, A., and L. Jones. 1967. *Black Music*. New York: Morrow.

Bauman, Z. 1995. *Life in Fragments: Essays in Postmodern Morality*. Hoboken, NJ: Wiley-Blackwell.

Bayton, M. 1998. *Frock Rock: Women Performing Popular Music*. Oxford: Oxford University Press.

———. 1990 [1988]. "How Women Become Musicians." In *On Record: Rock, Pop, and the Written Word*, ed. S. Firth and A. Goodwin, 238–257. London: Routledge.

Becker, H. S. 1982. *Art Worlds*. Berkeley: University of California Press.

———. 1974. "Art as Collective Action." *American Sociological Review* 39 (December):767–776.

———. 1973 [1963]. *Outsiders: Studies in the Sociology of Deviance*. New York: Free Press.

Becker, J., and A. Becker. 1981. "A Musical Icon: Power and Meaning in Javanese Gamelan Music." In *The Sign in Music and Literature*, ed. W. Steiner, 203–215. Austin: University of Texas Press.

Beer, D. 2008. "Making Friends with Jarvis Cocker: Music Culture in the Context of Web 2.0." *Cultural Sociology* 2:222–241.

Benjamin, W. 1969. "The Work of Art in the Age of Mechanical Reproduction." In *Illuminations*, trans. Harry Zohn, 217–251. New York: Schocken.

Bennett, A. 2006. "Punk's Not Dead: The Continuing Significance of Punk Rock for an Older Generation of Fans." *Sociology* 40:219–235.

———. 2004. "Consolidating the Music Scenes Perspective." *Poetics* 32:223–234.

———. 2001. *Cultures of Popular Music*. Buckingham, UK, and Philadelphia: Open University Press.

Bennett, H. S. 1980. *On Becoming a Rock Musician*. Amherst: University of Massachusetts Press.

Benzecry, C. E. 2009. "Becoming a Fan: On the Seductions of Opera." *Qualitative Sociology* 32:131–151.

———. 2006. "Curtain Rising, Baton Falling: The Politics of Musical Conducting in Contemporary Argentina." *Theory and Society* 33:445–479.

Berg, B. L. 1995. *Qualitative Research Methods for the Social Sciences*, 2nd ed. Needham Heights, MA: Allyn and Bacon.

Berger, K. 2007. *Bach's Cycle, Mozart's Arrow: An Essay on the Origins of Musical Modernity*. Berkeley: University of California Press.

Berger, P., and T. Luckmann. 1966. *The Social Construction of Reality: A Treatise on the Sociology of Knowledge*. New York: Anchor.

Berliner, P. F. 1994. *Thinking in Jazz: The Infinite Art of Improvisation*. Chicago: University of Chicago Press.

Bevers, T. 2005. "Cultural Education and the Canon: A Comparative Analysis of the Content of Secondary School Exams for Music and Art in England, France, Germany, and the Netherlands, 1990–2004." *Poetics* 33:388–416.

Bhattacharjee, S., R. D. Gopal, K. Lertwachara, and J. R. Marsden. 2006. "Impact of Legal Threats on Online Music Sharing Activity: An Analysis of Music Industry Legal Actions." *Journal of Law and Economics* 49:91–114.

Bielby, D. D., and W. T. Bielby. 1996. "Women and Men in Film: Gender Inequality among Writers in a Culture Industry." *Gender and Society* 10:248–270.

Bielby, W. T., and D. D. Bielby. 1999. "Organizational Mediation of Project-Based Labor Markets: Talent Agencies and the Careers of Screenwriters." *American Sociological Review* 64:64–85.

Binder, A. 1993. "Constructing Racial Rhetoric: Media Depictions of Harm in Heavy Metal and Rap Music." *American Sociological Review* 58:753–767.

Binning, K., M. Unzueta, Y. Huo, and L. Molina. 2009. "The Interpretation of Multiracial Status and Its Relation to Social Engagement and Psychological Well-Being." *Journal of Social Issues* 65:35–49.

Blackstone, L. R. 2009. "'The Spider Is Alive': Reassessing Becker's Theory of Artistic Conventions through Southern Italian Music." *Symbolic Interaction* 32(3):184–206.

———. 2005. "A New Kind of English: Cultural Variance, Citizenship, and DIY Politics amongst the Exodus Collective in England." *Social Forces* 84(2):801–818.

Blumer, H. 1969. *Symbolic Interactionism*. Englewood Cliffs, NJ: Prentice Hall.

Bohlman, P. V. 1999. "Ontologies of Music." In *Rethinking Music*, ed. N. Cook and M. Everist, 17–34. Chicago: University of Chicago Press.

Bonilla-Silva, E. 1997. "Rethinking Racism: Toward a Structural Interpretation." *American Sociological Review* 62:465–480.

Bourdieu, P. 1984. *Distinction: A Sociological Critique of the Judgment of Taste*. Cambridge: Cambridge University Press.

Brake, M. 1985. *Comparative Youth Culture: The Sociology of Youth Culture and Youth Subcultures in America, Britain, and Canada*. New York: Routledge.

Brazier, R. 1968. "The Story of the I.W.W.'s 'Little Red Song Book.'" *Labor History* 9(1):91–105.

Brodkin, K. 1998. *How Jews Became White Folks*. New Brunswick, NJ: Rutgers University Press.

Brooks, J. 2010. "Peace, Salaam, Shalom: Functions of Collective Singing in US Peace Movements." *Music and Arts in Action* 2(2):56–71.

Bryson, B. 1996. "Anything but Heavy Metal: Symbolic Exclusions and Musical Dislikes." *American Sociological Review* 61(5):884–899.

Budnick, D. 2003. *Jambands: The Complete Guide to the Players, Music, and Scene*. San Francisco: Backbeat Books.

Buerkle, J., and D. Baker. 1973. *Bourbon Street Black: The New Orleans Black Jazzman*. New York: Oxford University Press.

Bull, M. 2007. *Sound Moves: iPod Culture and Urban Experience*. London: Routledge.

Burleigh, H. T. 1984. *The Spirituals of Harry T. Burleigh: High Voice*. Indianapolis: Belwin-Mills.

Burnett, R. 1996. *The Global Jukebox: The International Music Industry*. London: Routledge.

Byng, M. D. 2008. "Complex Inequalities: The Case of Muslim Americans after 9/11." *American Behavioral Scientist* 51:659–674.

Cantwell, R. 1997. *When We Were Good: The Folk Revival*. Cambridge, MA: Harvard University Press.

Cerulo, K. A. 1995. *Identity Designs: The Sight and Sounds of a Nation*. New Brunswick, NJ: Rutgers University Press.

Chandler, M. 2003. "Soloing." *Studies in Symbolic Interaction* 26:293–294.

Charnas, D. 2010. *The Big Payback: The History of the Business of Hip-Hop.* New York: New American Library.

Chasteen, A. L., and T. Shriver. 1998. "Rap and Resistance: A Social Movement Analysis of the Wu-Tang Clan." *Challenge: A Journal of Research on African American Men* 9:1–24.

Chaves, M. 2004. *Congregations in America.* Cambridge, MA: Harvard University Press.

Cheng, S., and K. Lively. 2009. "Multiracial Self-Identification and Adolescent Outcomes: A Social Psychological Approach to the Marginal Man Theory." *Social Forces* 88:61–98.

Christe, I. 2004. *Sound of the Beast: The Complete Headbanging History of Heavy Metal.* New York: HarperCollins.

Christian, M. 2000. *Multiracial Identity: An International Perspective.* London: MacMillan.

Clark, D. 2001 [1994]. *Rise and Fall of Popular Music.* Norfolk, England: Viking.

Clarke, E. F. 2005. *Ways of Listening: An Ecological Approach to the Perception of Musical Meaning.* New York: Oxford University Press.

Clawson, M. A. 1999. "When Women Play the Bass: Instrument Specialization and Gender Interpretation in Alternative Rock Music." *Gender and Society* 13:193–210.

Cohen, A. K. 1955. *Delinquent Boys: The Culture of the Gang.* New York: Free Press.

Cohen, S. 1995. "Sounding Out the City: Music and the Sensuous Production of Place." *Transactions of the Institute of British Geographers* 20(4):434–446.

Cole, T. 1999. *Selling the Holocaust: From Auschwitz to Schindler—How History Is Bought, Packaged, and Sold.* New York: Routledge.

Coleman, J. 1988. "Social Capital in the Creation of Human Capital." *American Journal of Sociology Supplement* 94:S95–S120.

Collins, R. 2004. *Interaction Ritual Chains.* Princeton, NJ: Princeton University Press.

Cook, N. 1998. *Music: A Very Short Introduction.* New York: Oxford University Press.

Cooke, D. 1959. *The Language of Music.* London: Oxford University Press.

Cooley, C. 1902. *Human Nature and the Social Order.* New York: Scribner.

Cornell, S., and D. Hartmann. 2006. *Ethnicity and Race: Making Identities in a Changing World.* Thousand Oaks, CA: Pine Forge.

Cottrell, S. 2004. *Professional Music-Making in London: Ethnography and Experience.* London: Ashgate.

Coulangeon, P. H., and Y. Lemel. 2007. "Is 'Distinction' Really Outdated? Questioning the Meaning of the Omnivorization of Musical Taste in Contemporary France." *Poetics* 35:93–111.

Coulangeon, P., H. Ravet, and I. Roharik. 2005. "Gender Differentiated Effect of Time in Performing Arts Professions: Musicians, Actors, and Dancers in Contemporary France." *Poetics* 33:369–387.

Crapanzano, V. 2005. "Forward." In *The Land of Remorse*, by Ernesto De Martino, vii–xiv. London: Free Association Books.

Cross, B. 1993. *It's Not about the Salary: Rap, Race, and Resistance in Los Angeles.* New York: Verso.

Cross, I. 1997. "Pitch Schemata." In *Perception and Cognition of Music*, ed. I. Delige and J. Sloboda, 353–386. East Sussex, UK: Psychology Press.

Crossley, N. 2008. "The Man Whose Web Expanded: Network Dynamics in Manchester's Post/Punk Music Scene, 1976–1980." *Poetics* 73:24–49.

Cruz, J. 1999. *Culture on the Margins: The Black Spiritual and the Rise of American Cultural Interpretation.* Princeton, NJ: Princeton University Press.

Curran, G. M. 1996. "From 'Swinging Hard' to 'Rocking Out': Classification of Style and the Creation of Identity in the World of Drumming." *Symbolic Interaction* 19:37–60.

Cutting, J. 2000. *Analyzing the Language of Discourse Communities.* New York: Elsevier.

Davies, M. 2005. "Do It Yourself: Punk Rock and the Disalienation of International Relations." In *Resounding International Relations: On Music, Culture, and Politics,* ed. M. I. Franklin, 113–140. New York: Palgrave MacMillan.

Davis, F. J. 1991. *Who Is Black? One Nation's Definition.* University Park: Pennsylvania State University Press.

De Martino, E. 2005 [1961]. *The Land of Remorse.* Trans. D. L. Zinn. London: Free Association Books.

Dempsey, N. P. 2008. "Hook-Ups and Train Wrecks: Contextual Parameters and the Coordination of Jazz Interaction." *Symbolic Interaction* 31(1):57–75.

Denisoff, R. S. 1972. *Sing a Song of Social Significance.* Bowling Green, KY: University Popular Press.

DeNora, T. 2003. *After Adorno: Rethinking Music Sociology.* Cambridge: Cambridge University Press.

———. 2002. "Music into Action: Performing Gender on the Viennese Concert Sage, 1790–1810." *Poetics* 30:19–33.

———. 2000. *Music in Everyday Life.* New York and London: Cambridge University Press.

———. 1991. "Musical Patronage and Social Change in Beethoven's Vienna." *American Journal of Sociology* 97:310–346.

———. 1986. "How Is Musical Meaning Possible? Music as a Place and Space for 'Work.'" *Sociological Theory* 4:84–94.

Denzin, N. K. 1992. *Symbolic Interactionism and Cultural Studies.* Cambridge: Blackwell.

DeVeaux, S. K. 1997. *The Birth of Bebop: A Social and Musical History.* Berkeley: University of California Press.

DiMaggio, P. J. 2006. "Nonprofit Organizations and the Intersectoral Division of Labor in the Arts." In *The Nonprofit Sector: A Research Handbook,* ed. W. W. Powell and R. Steinberg, 432–461. New Haven, CT: Yale University Press.

———. 1992. "Cultural Boundaries and Structural Change: The Extension of the High Culture Model to Theater, Opera, and the Dance, 1900–1940." In *Cultivating Differences: Symbolic Boundaries and the Making of Inequality,* ed. M. Lamont and M. Fournier, 21–57. Chicago: University of Chicago Press.

———. 1991. "Social Structure, Institutions, and Cultural Goods: The Case of the United States." In *Social Theory for a Changing Society,* ed. P. Bourdieu and J. S. Coleman, 133–155. Boulder, CO: Westview.

———. 1987. "Classification in Art." *American Sociological Review* 52:440–455.

———. 1982. "Cultural Entrepreneurship in Nineteenth-Century Boston." *Media, Culture, and Society* 4:33–55, 303–322.

Dollar, N. 1988. *The Development of a Strong Musical Taste Culture: The Deadheads.* Master's thesis, Arizona State University.

Donnelly, P. 1981. "Toward a Definition of Sport Subcultures." In *Sport and the Sociocultural Process,* 565–588. Dubuque, IA: Wm. C. Brown.

Donnelly, P., and K. Young. 1988. "The Construction and Confirmation of Identity in Sports Subculture." *Sociology of Sports Journal* 5:223–240.

Douglass, F. 1993 [1845]. *Narrative of the Life of Frederick Douglass, an American Slave*. Boston: Bedford.

Dowd, T. J. 2007. "Sociology of Music." In *21st Century Sociology: A Reference Handbook*, ed. C. D. Bryant and D. L. Peck, (2):249–260, 440, 505–512. Thousand Oaks, CA: Sage.

———. 2004. "Concentration and Diversity Revisited: Production Logics and the US Mainstream Recording Market, 1940–1990." *Social Forces* 82(4):1411–1855.

———. 2003. "Structural Power and the Construction of Markets: The Case of Rhythm and Blues." *Comparative Social Research* 21:147–201.

———. 2000. "Musical Diversity and the US Mainstream Recording Market, 1955 to 1990." *Rassegna di Italiana di Sociologia* 41(2):223–263.

Dowd, T. J., and M. Blyler. 2002. "Charting Race: The Success of Black Performers in the Mainstream Recording Market, 1940 to 1990." *Poetics* 30:87–110.

Dowd, T. J., K. Liddle, and M. Blyler. 2005. "Charting Gender: The Success of Female Acts in the US Mainstream Recording Market, 1940 to 1990." *Research in the Sociology of Organizations* 23:81–123.

Dowd, T. J., K. Liddle, K. Lupo, and A. Borden. 2002. "Organizing the Musical Canon: The Repertoires of Major US Symphony Orchestras, 1842 to 1969." *Poetics* 30:35–61.

Dubisch, J. 1995. *In a Different Place: Pilgrimage, Politics, and Gender at a Greek Island Shrine*. Princeton, NJ: Princeton University Press.

Du Bois, W. E. B. 1997 [1903]. *The Souls of Black Folk*. Boston: Beacon.

———. 1969. "Of the Sorrow Songs." In *The Souls of Black Folk*, 264–277. New York: Signet Classic.

Duffins, R. W. 2007. *How Equal Temperament Ruined Harmony: And Why You Should Care*. New York: Norton.

Dumais, S. A. 2002. "Cultural Capital, Gender, and School Success: The Role of Habitus." *Sociology of Education* 75:44–68.

Durkheim, E. 1995 [1912]. *The Elementary Forms of Religious Life*. New York: Free Press.

Dyson, M. E. 2005. "The Culture of Hip-Hop." In *That's the Joint! The Hip-Hop Studies Reader*, ed. M. Forman and M. A. Neal, 61–68. New York: Routledge.

Early, G. 1998. "Pulp and Circumstance: The Story of Jazz in High Places." In *The Jazz Cadence of American Culture*, ed. R. O'Meally, 393–430. New York: Columbia University Press.

Ehrenreich, B. 2006. *Dancing in the Streets*. New York: Metropolitan.

Eliot, M. 1989. *Rockonomics: The Money behind the Music*. New York: Watts.

Epstein, J., and D. Pratto. 1990. "Heavy Metal Rock Music, Juvenile Delinquency, and Satanic Identification." *Popular Music and Society* 14(4):67–76.

Epstein, J. S., D. J. Pratto, and J. K. Skipper. 1990. "Teenagers, Behavioral Problems, and Preferences for Heavy Metal and Rap Music: A Case Study of a Southern Middle School." *Deviant Behavior* 11:381–394.

Engels, F., and K. Marx. 1988 [1845–46]. *The German Ideology*. New York: International Publishers.

———. 1964 [1848]. *The Communist Manifesto*. New York: Monthly Review Press.

Esposito, J. L. 2005. *Islam: The Straight Path*, 3rd ed. New York: Oxford University Press.

Eyerman, R., and A. Jamison. 1998. *Music and Social Movements: Mobilizing Tradition in the Twentieth Century*. New York: Cambridge University Press.

Fabbri, F. 1989. "The System of Canzone in Italy Today." In *World Music, Politics, and Social Change*, ed. S. Frith, 122–142. Manchester, UK: Manchester University Press.

———. 1982. "A Theory of Musical Genres: Two Applications." In *Popular Music Perspectives*, ed. P. Tagg and D. Horn, 52–81. Exeter, UK: International Association of the Study of Popular Music.

Faulkner, R. R. 1971. *Hollywood Studio Musicians: Their Work and Careers in the Recording Industry*. Chicago: Aldine-Atherton.

Feixa, C. 2006. "Tribas Urbanas and Chavos Banda: Being a Punk in Catalonia and Mexico." In *Global Youth? Hybrid Identities, Plural Worlds*, ed. P. Nilan and C. Feixa, 149–166. New York: Routledge.

Feld, S. 1984. "Sound Structure and Social Structure." *Ethnomusicology* 28:383–409.

Fine, G. A. 2003. "Crafting Authenticity: The Validation of Identity in Self-Taught Art." *Theory and Society* 32(2):153–180.

———. 1979. "Small Group and Culture Creation." *American Sociological Review* 44:733–745.

Fonarow, W. 2006. *Empire of Dirt: The Aesthetics and Rituals of British Indie Music*. Middletown, CT: Wesleyan University Press.

Forman, M. 2005. "'Represent': Race, Space, and Place in Rap Music." In *That's the Joint! The Hip-Hop Studies Reader*, ed. M. Forman and M. Anthony Neal, 201–222. New York: Routledge.

Fowke, E., and J. Glaser. 1973. *Songs of Work and Protest*. Mineola, NY: Dover.

Fox, A. A. 2004. "White Trash Alchemies of the Abject Sublime: Country as Bad Music." In *Bad Music: The Music We Love to Hate*, ed. C. J. Washburne and M. Derno, 39–61. New York: Routledge.

Fraser, L. 2010. "Dance of the Spider Women." *Afar* 2(3):50–57 (July/August).

Friedrich, C. J., and Z. Brzezinski. 1956. *Totalitarian Dictatorship and Autocracy*. Cambridge, MA: Harvard University Press.

Frith, S. 1996. *Performing Rights: On the Value of Popular Music*. Cambridge, MA: Harvard University Press.

———. 1986. "Art vs. Technology." *Media, Culture, and Society* 8:263–279.

———. 1983. "Popular Music, 1950–1980." In *Making Music: The Guide to Writing, Performing, and Recording*, ed. G. Martin. London: Robert Hale.

———. 1981. *Sound Effects*. New York: Pantheon.

Gaillot, M. 1998. *Multiple Meaning Techno*. Paris: Dis Voir.

Gaisberg, F. W. 1946. *Music on Record*. London: Robert Hale.

Garcia-Alvarez, E., T. Katz-Gerro, and J. Lopez-Sintas. 2007. "Deconstructing Cultural Omnivorousness, 1982–2002: Heterology in Americans' Musical Preferences." *Social Forces* 86:755–764.

Gardner, R. O. 2004. "The Portable Community: Mobility and Modernization in Bluegrass Festival Life." *Symbolic Interaction* 27:155–178.

Gelatt, R. 1977. The *Fabulous Phonograph, 1877–1977*. London: Cassell.

Gennari, J. 2006. *Blowin' Hot and Cold: Jazz and Its Critics*. Chicago: University of Chicago Press.

Genovese, E. 1974. *Roll Jordan Roll: The World the Slaves Made*. New York: Pantheon.

George, N. 1988. *The Death of Rhythm and Blues*. New York: Pantheon.

Gibson, W. 2006. "Material Culture and Embodied Action: Sociological Notes on the Examination of Musical Instruments in Jazz Improvisation." *Sociological Review* 54:171–187.

Gilbert, S. 2005a. "Music as Historical Source: Social History and Musical Texts." *International Review of the Aesthetics and Sociology of Music* 36:117–134.

———. 2005b. *Music in the Holocaust: Confronting Life in the Nazi Ghettos and Camps*. Oxford: Oxford University Press.

Gilroy, P. 1993. *The Black Atlantic: Modernity and Double Consciousness*. Cambridge, MA: Harvard University Press.

Ginneken, J. 2003. *Collective Behavior and Public Opinion*. Mahwah, NJ: Lawrence Erlbaum.

Gioia, T. 1997. *The History of Jazz*. New York: Oxford University Press.

———. 1988. *The Imperfect Art: Reflections on Jazz and Modern Culture*. Oxford: Oxford University Press.

Giuffre, K. 1999. "Sandpiles of Opportunity." *Social Forces* 77(3):815–832.

Glaser, B., and A. Strauss. 1967. *The Discovery of Grounded Theory: Strategies for Qualitative Research*. New York: Aldine De Gruyter.

Glynn, M. A. 2000. "When Cymbals Become Symbols: Conflict over Organizational Identity within a Symphony Orchestra." *Organization Science* 11:285–298.

Glynn, M. A., and T. J. Dowd. 2008. "Charisma (Un)Bound: Emotive Leadership in *Martha Stewart Living* Magazine, 1990–2004." *Journal of Applied Behavioral Science* 44:71–93.

Glynn, M. A., and C. Marquis. 2004. "When Good Names Go Bad: Symbolic Illegitimacy in Organizations." *Research in the Sociology of Organizations* 22:147–170.

Godwin, J. 1995. *Harmonies of Heaven and Earth*. Rochester, VT: Inner Traditions International.

Goffman, E. 1974. *Frame Analysis: An Essay on the Organization of Experience*. Cambridge, MA: Harvard University Press.

———. 1967. *Interaction Ritual: Essays on Face-to-Face Behavior*. New York: Doubleday Anchor.

———. 1963. *Stigma*. New York: Touchstone.

———. 1959. *The Presentation of Self in Everyday Life*. Garden City, NY: Doubleday Anchor.

Gordon, M. 1992. "Songs from the Museum of the Future: Russian Sound Creation (1910–1930)." In *Wireless Imagination: Sound, Radio, and the Avant-Garde*, ed. D. Kahn and G. Whitehead, 197–243.Cambridge, MA: MIT Press.

Gramsci, A. 2005 [1930]. *The Southern Question*. Trans. P. Verdicchio. Toronto: Guernica.

Grazian, D. 2010. "Demystifying Authenticity in the Sociology of Culture." In *Handbook of Cultural Sociology*, ed. J. Hall, L. Grindstaff, and M. Lo, 191–200. New York: Routledge.

———. 2007. "The Girl Hunt: Urban Nightlife and the Performance of Masculinity as Collective Activity." *Symbolic Interaction* 30:221–243.

———. 2003. *Blue Chicago: The Search for Authenticity in Urban Blues Clubs*. Chicago: University of Chicago Press.

Greenway, J. 1953. *American Folk Songs of Protest*. Philadelphia: University of Pennsylvania Press.

Griswold, W. 1987. "The Fabrication of Meaning: Literary Interpretation in the United States, Great Britain, and the West Indies." *American Journal of Sociology* 92:1077–1117.

Gross, R. L. 1990. "Heavy Metal Music: A New Subculture in American Society." *Journal of Popular Culture* 24(1):119–130.

Grossberg, L. 1997. *Dancing in Spite of Myself.* Durham, NC: Duke University Press.

Gruenewald, D. A. 2003. "Foundations of Place: A Multidisciplinary Framework for Place Conscious Education." *American Educational Research Journal* 40(3):619–654.

Guan, J., and J. D. Knottnerus. 1999. "A Structural Ritualization Analysis of the Process of Acculturation and Marginalization of Chinese Americans." *Humboldt Journal of Social Relations* 25:43–95.

Guerra, C. 2001. "The Unofficial Primer on *Conjunto.*" In *Puro Conjunto: An Album in Words and Pictures,* ed. J. Tejada and A. Valdez, 3–9. Austin: University of Texas Press.

Haenfler, R. 2006. *Straight Edge: Clean-Living Youth, Hardcore Punk, and Social Change.* New Brunswick, NJ: Rutgers University Press.

———. 2004. "Rethinking Subcultural Resistance: Core Values of the Straight Edge Movement." *Journal of Contemporary Ethnology* 33:406–436.

Hall, A. 2007. "The Social Implications of Enjoyment of Different Types of Music, Movies, and Television Programming." *Western Journal of Communication* 71(4):259–271.

Hall, G. M. 2005. *Slavery and African Ethnicities in the Americas.* Chapel Hill: University of North Carolina Press.

Halnon, K. B. 2006. "Heavy Metal Carnival and Dis-alienation: The Politics of Grotesque Realism." *Symbolic Interaction* 29(1):33–48.

Hamilton, A. 2007. *Aesthetics and Music.* New York: Continuum.

Hamm, M. S. 1993. *American Skinheads: The Criminology and Control of Hate Crime.* Westport, CT: Praeger.

Hanou, M., and J. P. Frijns. 2009. *The Past The Present 1982–2007: A History of 25 Years of European Straight Edge.* Warsaw, Poland: Refuse Records.

Hansen, C. H., and R. D. Hansen. 1991. "Schematic Information Processing of Heavy Metal Lyrics." *Communication Research* 18:376–378.

———. 1990. "Rock Music Videos and Antisocial Behavior." *Basic and Applied Social Psychology* 11:357–369.

Hanslick, E. 1957 [1854]. *The Beautiful in Music.* New York: Liberal Arts Press.

Hardt, M., and A. Negri. 2000. *Empire.* Cambridge, MA: Harvard University Press.

Harris, D., and J. Sim. 2002. "Who Is Multiracial? Assessing the Complexity of Lived Race." *American Sociological Review* 67:614–627.

Harvey, D. 2007. *A Brief History of Neoliberalism.* New York: Oxford University Press.

Hebdige, D. 1987. *Cut 'n' Mix: Culture, Identity, and Caribbean Music.* London: Methuen.

———. 2004 [1979]. *Subculture: The Meaning of Style.* Spanish ed. New York: Methuen.

Hegarty, P. 2007. *Noise/Music.* New York: Continuum.

Hellman, H. 1983. "The New State of Competition in the Record Industry." *Sociologia* 20.

Hennion, A. 2001. "Music Lovers: Tastes as Performance." *Theory, Culture, and Society* 18:1–22.

Herrmann, D. 1998. *Helen Keller.* New York: Knopf.

Hesmondhalgh, D. 2007. "Aesthetics and Audiences: Talking about Good and Bad Music." *European Journal of Cultural Studies* 10:507–527.

———. 1998. "The British Dance Music Industry: A Case Study of Independent Cultural Production." *British Journal of Sociology* 49:234–252.

Hewitt, J. 1984. *Self and Society*. Boston: Allyn and Bacon.

Hilliard, C. 1998. *Intellectual Traditions of Pre-Colonial Africa*. Boston: McGraw-Hill.

Hirsch, P. M. 1972. "Processing Fads and Fashions: An Organizational-Set Analysis of Culture Industry Systems." *American Journal of Sociology* 77:639–659.

Hodson, R. 2007. *Interaction, Improvisation, and Interplay in Jazz*. New York: Routledge.

Horn, D. G. 2003. *The Criminal Body*. New York: Routledge.

Hosman, S. 2009. *Muslim Punk Rock in the United States: A Social History of the Taqwacores*. Master's thesis, University of North Carolina.

Hracs, B. J. 2010. *Working in the Creative Economy: The Spatial Dynamics of Employment Risk for Musicians in Toronto*. PhD dissertation, University of Toronto, Department of Geography.

Hughes, M. 2000. "Country Music as Impression Management: A Meditation on Fabricating Authenticity." *Poetics* 28(2–3):185–205.

Hunter, R. 1990. *A Box of Rain*. New York: Penguin.

Huxley, A. 1931. *Music at Night and Other Essays*. New York: Doubleday, Doran and Co.

Irwin, D. 1999. "The Straight Edge Subculture: Examining the Youths' Drug-Free Way." *Journal of Drug Issues* 29(2):365–380.

Irwin, J. 1977. *Scenes*. Beverly Hills, CA: Sage.

James, J. 1993. *The Music of the Spheres*. New York: Grove.

Janssen, S., G. Kuipers, and M. Verboord. 2008. "Cultural Globalization and Arts Journalism: The International Orientation of Arts and Cultural Coverage in Dutch, French, German, and US Newspapers, 1955 to 2005." *American Sociological Review* 73:719–740.

Jaquez, C. F. 2002. "Meeting la Cantante through Verse, Song, and Performance." In *Chicana Traditions: Continuity and Change*, ed. N. E. Cantu and O. N. Ramirez, 167–182. Chicago: University of Illinois Press.

Jasper, J. M. 1998. "The Emotions of Protest: Affective and Reactive Emotions in and around Social Movements." *Sociological Forum* 13:397–424.

Jenkins, C. J., and C. M. Eckert. 1986. "Channeling Black Insurgency: Elite Patronage and the Development of the Civil Rights Movement." *American Sociological Review* 51:812–830.

Jeppesen, L. B., and L. Frederiksen. 2006. "Why Do Users Contribute to Firm-Hosted User Communities? The Case of Computer-Controlled Musical Instruments." *Organization Science* 17:45–63.

Johnson, C., T. J. Dowd, and C. L. Ridgeway. 2006. "Legitimacy as a Social Process." *Annual Review of Sociology* 32:53–78.

Johnson, J. R. 1947. *Twentieth Century Music*. New York and London: G. P. Putnam's Sons.

———. 1937. *Rolling along in Song*. New York: Viking.

Johnson, V. 2007. "What Is Organizational Imprinting? Cultural Entrepreneurship in the Founding of the Paris Opera." *American Journal of Sociology* 113:97–127.

Kahn-Harris, K. 2007. *Extreme Metal: Music and Culture on the Edge*. Oxford: Berg.

Kammen, M. 1999. *American Culture, American Tastes: Social Change and the Twentieth Century*. New York: Knopf.

Kassabian, A. 1999. "Popular." In *Key Terms in Popular Music and Culture*, ed. B. Horner and T. Swiss, 113–123. Malden, MA: Blackwell.

Katz, M. 1998. "Making America More Musical through the Phonograph, 1900–1930." *American Music* 15:448–476.

Kennedy, R. 2003. *Nigger: The Strange Career of a Troublesome Word*. New York: Vintage.

Khanna, N. 2010. "If You're Half Black, You're Just Black: Reflected Appraisals and the Persistence of the One-Drop Rule." *Sociological Quarterly* 51:96–121.

Khanna, N., and C. Johnson. 2010. "Passing as Black: Racial Identity Work among Biracial Americans." *Social Psychology Quarterly* 73:380–397.

Khodyakov, D. M. 2007. "The Complexity of Trust-Control Relationships in Creative Organizations: Insights from a Qualitative Analysis of a Conductorless Orchestra." *Social Forces* 86:1–22.

Kidder, J. L. 2006. "Bike Messengers and the Really Real: Effervescence, Reflexivity, and Postmodern Identity." *Symbolic Interaction* 29:349–371.

Killian, C., and C. Johnson. 2006. "'I'm Not an Immigrant': Resistance, Redefinition, and the Role of Resources in Identity Work." *Social Psychology Quarterly* 69:60–80.

Klineberg, S. L. 2009. *Houston's Economic and Demographic Transformations: Findings from the Expanded 2009 Survey of Houston's Ethnic Communities*. April. Houston: Rice University Publications.

Knight, M. M. 2004. *The Taqwacores*. Brooklyn, NY: Autonomedia.

Knoke, D. 1990. *Political Networks: The Structural Perspective*. New York: Cambridge University Press.

Knottnerus, J. D. 2011. *Ritual as a Missing Link: Sociology, Structural Ritualization Theory, and Research*. Boulder: Paradigm.

———. 2010. "Collective Events, Rituals, and Emotions." In *Advances in Group Processes*, ed. S. R. Thye and E. J. Lawler, 27:39–61. Bingley, UK: Emerald Group.

———. 1997. "The Theory of Structural Ritualization." In *Advances in Group Processes*, ed. B. Markovsky, M. J. Lovaglia, and L. Troyer, 14:257–279. Greenwich, CT: JAI.

Knottnerus, J. D., and D. G. LoConto. 2003. "Strategic Ritualization and Ethnicity: A Typology and Analysis of Ritual Enactments in an Italian American Community." *Sociological Spectrum* 23:425–461.

Korgen, K. 1998. *From Black to Biracial: Transforming Racial Identity among Americans*. Westport, CT: Praeger.

Kotarba, J. A., B. Merrill, J. P. Williams, and P. Vannini. 2013. *Understanding Society through Popular Music*. New York: Routledge.

Kotarba, J. A., J. L. Fackler, and K. M. Nowotny. 2009. "An Ethnography of Emerging Latino Music Scenes." *Symbolic Interaction* 32(4):310–333.

Kotarba, J., and P. Vannini. 2009. *Understanding Society through Popular Music*. London: Routledge.

Kraszewski, J. 2010. "Multiracialism on *The Real World* and the Reconfiguration of Politics in MTV's Brand during the 2000s." *Popular Communication* 8:132–146.

Kremp, P. A. 2010. "Innovation and Selection: Symphony Orchestras and the Construction of the Musical Canon in the United States (1879–1959)." *Social Forces* 88(3):1051–1082.

Krims, A. 2000. *Rap Music and the Poetics of Identity*. New York: Cambridge University Press.

Kubrin, C. E. 2005. "Gangstas, Thugs, and Hustlas: Identity and the Code of the Street in Rap Music." *Social Problems* 52:360–378.

Kuhn, G., ed. 2010. *Sober Living for the Revolution: Hardcore Punk, Straight Edge, and Radical Politics.* Oakland, CA: PM Press.

Lahickey, B. 1997. *All Ages: Reflections on Straight Edge.* Huntington Beach, CA: Revelation Records Publishing.

Laing, D. 1985. *One-Chord Wonders: Power and Meaning in Punk Rock.* Milton Keynes, UK: Open University Press.

——. 1997 [1985]. "Listening to Punk." In *The Subcultures Reader,* ed. K. Gelder, 448–459. New York: Routledge.

Lamont, M., and V. Molnár. 2002. "The Study of Boundaries in the Social Sciences." *Annual Review of Sociology* 28:167–195.

Lang, D. 1985. "Listening to Punk." In K. Gelder (Ed.), *The Subcultures Reader* (2nd Edition.) New York: Routledge, pp. 448–459.

Laqueur, W., and J. T. Baumel. 2001. *Holocaust Encyclopedia.* New Haven, CT: Yale University Press.

Latour, B. 1987. *Science in Action: How to Follow Scientists and Engineers through Society.* Cambridge, MA: Harvard University Press.

Lawler, E. J. 2001. "An Affect Theory of Social Exchange." *American Journal of Sociology* 107:321–352.

——. 1998. "Network Structures and Emotion in Exchange Relations." *American Sociological Review* 63(6):871–894.

——. 1996. "Commitment in Exchange Relations: Test of a Theory of Relational Cohesion." *American Sociological Review* 61:89–108.

Lawler, E. J., S. R. Thye, and J. Yoon. 2000. "Emotion and Group Cohesion in Productive Exchange." *American Journal on Sociology* 106(3):616–657.

Lawler, E. J., and J. Yoon. 1993. "Power and the Emergence of Commitment Behavior in Negotiated Exchange." *American Sociological Review* 58(4):456–481.

Lee, J. 2009. "Open Mic: Professionalizing the Rap Career." *Ethnography* 10(4):475–495.

Leichtentritt, H. 1951. *Music Form.* Cambridge, MA: Harvard University Press.

Lena, J. C. 2012. *Banding Together: How Communities Create Genres in Popular Music.* Princeton, NJ: Princeton University Press.

——. 2006. "Social Context and Musical Content: Rap Music, 1979–1995." *Social Forces* 85(1):479–495.

——. 2004. "Sonic Networks: Economic, Stylistic, and Expressive Dimensions of Rap Music, 1979–1995." *Poetics* 32:297–310.

——. 2003. *From "Flash" to "Cash": Producing Rap Authenticity, 1979 to 1995.* PhD dissertation, Columbia University.

Lena, J. C., and R. A. Peterson. 2008. "Classification as Culture: Types and Trajectories of Music Genres." *American Sociological Review* 73(5):697–718.

Lenneberg, H. 2003. *On the Publishing and Dissemination of Music, 1500–1850.* Hillsdale, NY: Pendragon.

Leonard, M. 2007. *Gender in the Music Industry: Rock, Discourse, and Girl Power.* London: Ashgate.

Levenson, T. 1995. *Measure for Measure.* New York: Touchstone.

Leverette, T. 2009. "Speaking Up: Mixed Race Identity in Black Communities." *Journal of Black Studies* 39:434–445.

Levine, L. 1988. *Highbrow, Lowbrow: The Emergence of Cultural Hierarchy in America.* Cambridge, MA: Harvard University Press.

Levitin, D. 2006. *This Is Your Brain on Music: The Science of a Human Obsession.* New York: Dutton.

Lewis, I. M. 1989. *Ecstatic Religion.* New York: Routledge.

Leyshon, A., P. Webb, S. French, N. Thrift, and L. Crewe. 2005. "On the Reproduction of the Musical Economy after the Internet." *Media Culture and Society* 27:177–209.

Lhamon, W. T., Jr. 1998. *Raising Cain: Blackface Performance from Jim Crow to Hip Hop.* Cambridge, MA: Harvard University Press.

Light, A. 2004. "About a Salary or Reality?—Rap's Recurrent Conflict." In *That's the Joint! The Hip-Hop Studies Reader,* ed. M. Forman and M. A. Neal, 137–146. New York: Routledge.

Lomax, A. 1968. *Folk Song Style and Culture.* New Brunswick, NJ: Transaction.

———. 1962. "Song Structure and Social Structure." *Ethnology* 1:1–27.

Lopes P. 2002. *The Rise of a Jazz Art World.* Cambridge: Cambridge University Press.

———. 1992. "Innovation and Diversity in the Popular Music Industry, 1969 to 1990." *American Sociological Review* 57(1):56–71.

Lott, E. 1993. *Love and Theft: Blackface Minstrels and the American Working Class.* New York: Oxford University Press.

Luhr, E. 2009. *Witnessing Suburbia: Conservatives and Christian Youth Culture.* Berkeley: University of California Press.

Lynskey, D. 2011. *33 Revolutions per Minute.* New York: HarperCollins.

Mackerness, E. D. 1964. *A Social History of English Music.* London: Routledge and Kegan Paul.

MacLeod, B. A. 1993. *Club Date Musicians: Playing the New York Party Circuit.* Urbana: University of Illinois Press.

Maisonneuve, S. 2001. "Between History and Commodity: The Production of a Musical Patrimony through the Record in the 1920–1930s." *Poetics* 29:89–108.

Mann, G. 2008. "Why Does Country Music Sound White? Race and the Voice of Nostalgia." *Ethnic and Racial Studies* 31(1):73–100.

Margolick, D. 2001. *Strange Fruit: The Biography of a Song.* New York: The Ecco Press.

Marotto, M., J. Roos, and B. Victor. 2007. "Collective Virtuosity in Organizations: A Study of Peak Performance in an Orchestra." *Journal of Management Studies* 44:388–413.

Marshall, G. 1991. *The Spirit of '69: A Skinhead Bible.* Scotland: S. T. Publishing.

Martin, P. J. 2006a. *Music and the Sociological Gaze: Art Worlds and Cultural Production.* Manchester, UK: Manchester University Press.

———. 2006b. "Musicians' Worlds: Music-making as a Collaborative Activity." *Symbolic Interaction* 29(1):95–107.

———. 1995. *Sounds and Society: Themes in the Sociology of Music.* Manchester, UK: Manchester University Press.

Martineau, H. 1989 [1838]. *How to Observe Morals and Manners.* New Brunswick, NJ: Transaction.

Mason, M. 2008. *The Pirate's Dilemma: How Youth Culture Is Reinventing Capitalism.* New York: Free Press.

Matza, D. 1969. *Becoming Deviant.* Englewood Cliffs, NJ: Prentice Hall.

———. 1964. *Delinquency and Drift.* New York: John Wiley and Sons.

Mazlish, B. 1989. *A New Science.* New York: Oxford University Press.

McClary, S. 1991. *Feminine Endings: Music, Gender, and Sexuality.* Minneapolis: University of Minnesota Press.

McCormick, L. 2009. "Higher, Faster, Louder: Representations of the International Music Competition." *Cultural Sociology* 3:5–30.

McIver, J. 2005. *Extreme Metal II.* London: Omnibus Press.

McLeod, B. A. 1993. *Club Date Musicians: Playing the New York Party Circuit.* Urbana: University of Illinois Press.

McNeil, L., and G. McCain. 1997. *Please Kill Me: The Uncensored Oral History of Punk.* London: Abacus.

McNeil, W. H. 1995. *Keeping Together in Time: Dance and Drill in Human History.* Cambridge, MA: Harvard University Press.

Mead, G. H. 1964. *On Social Psychology.* Chicago: University of Chicago Press.

———. 1934. *Mind, Self, and Society.* Chicago: University of Chicago Press.

Mellers, W. 1950. *Music and Society.* New York: Roy.

Menger, P. M. 1999. "Artistic Labor Markets and Careers." *Annual Review of Sociology* 25:541–574.

Merton, R. K. 1938. "Social Structure and Anomie." *American Sociological Review* 3:672–682.

Meyer, L. 1961. *Emotion and Meaning in Music.* Chicago: University of Chicago Press.

Milbank, D. 2010. *Tears of a Clown: Glenn Beck and the Tea Bagging of America.* New York: Doubleday.

Mintz, A. 2001. *Popular Culture and the Shaping of Holocaust Memory in America.* Seattle: University of Washington Press.

Mitra, A., and J. D. Knottnerus. 2004. "Royal Women in Ancient India: The Ritualization of Inequality in a Patriarchal Social Order." *International Journal of Contemporary Sociology* 41:215–231.

Monson, I. 1996. *Saying Something: Jazz Improvisation and Interaction.* Chicago: University of Chicago Press.

Moore, R. 2007. "Friends Don't Let Friends Listen to Corporate Rock: Punk as a Field of Cultural Production." *Journal of Contemporary Ethnography* 36:438–474.

———. 2004. "Postmodernism and Punk Subculture: Cultures of Authenticity and Deconstruction." *Communication Review* 7:305–327.

Moore, R., and E. C. McMullan. 2004. "Perceptions of Peer-to-Peer File Sharing among University Students." *Journal of Criminal Justice and Popular Culture* 11:1–19.

Morinis, A. E. 1984. *Pilgrimage in the Hindu Tradition: A Case Study of West Bengal.* Delhi: Oxford University Press.

Moynihan, M., and D. Søderlind. 2003. *Lords of Chaos: The Bloody Rise of the Satanic Music Underground.* Port Townshend, WA: Feral House.

Mulder, J., T. ter Bogt, Q. Raaijmakers, and W. Vollebergh. 2007. "Music Taste Groups and Problem Behavior." *Journal of Youth and Adolescence* 36:313–324.

Murninghan, J. K., and D. E. Conlon. 1991. "The Dynamics of Intense Work Groups: A Study of British String Quartets." *Administrative Science Quarterly* 36:165–186.

Natella, A. A. 2008. *Latin American Popular Culture.* Jefferson, NC: McFarland.

Negus, K. 2005. "The Business of Rap: Between the Street and the Executive Suite." In *That's the Joint! The Hip-Hop Studies Reader*, ed. M. Forman and M. A. Neal, 607–625. New York: Routledge.

———. 1999. *Music Genres and Corporate Cultures.* London: Routledge.

Neil, L. 1987. "Sect." In *Jazz: Myth and Religion*, 19–34. Oxford: Oxford University Press.

Nicholson, S. 2005. *Is Jazz Dead? (Or Has It Moved to a New Address).* New York: Routledge.

North, A. C., and D. J. Hargreaves. 2006. "Problem Music and Self-Harming." *Suicide and Life Threatening Behavior* 36:582–590.

Ollivier, M. 2008. "Modes of Openness to Cultural Diversity: Humanist, Populist, Practical, and Indifferent." *Poetics* 36:120–147.

Omi, M., and H. Winant. 1994. *Racial Formation in the United States: From the 1960s to the 1990s.* 2nd ed. New York: Routledge.

Oware, M. 2009. "A 'Man's Woman'? Contradictory Messages in the Songs of Female Rappers, 1992–2000." *Journal of Black Studies* 39:786–802.

Pearson, A. 1987. "The Grateful Dead Phenomenon: An Ethnomethodological Approach." *Youth and Society* 18:418–432.

Peña, M. 1985. *The Texas-Mexican Conjunto: History of Working-Class Music.* Austin: University of Texas Press.

Perry, I. 2004. *Prophets of the Hood: Politics and Poetics in Hip Hop.* Durham, NC: Duke University Press.

Peterson, B. 2009. *Burning Fight: The Nineties Hardcore Revolution in Ethics, Politics, Spirit, and Sound.* Huntington Beach, CA: Revelation Records Publishing.

Peterson, R. A. 2005. "Problems in Comparative Research: The Example of Omnivorousness." *Poetics* 33:257–282.

———. 1997. *Creating Country Music: Fabricating Authenticity.* Chicago: University of Chicago Press.

———. 1994. "Cultural Studies through the Production Perspective: Progress and Prospects." In *The Sociology of Culture: Emerging Theoretical Perspectives,* ed. D. Crane, 163–189. Cambridge: Blackwell.

Peterson, R. A., and N. Anand. 2004. "The Production of Culture Perspective." *Annual Review of Sociology* 30:311–334.

Peterson, R. A., and D. Berger. 1975. "Cycles in Symbolic Production: The Case of Popular Music." *American Sociological Review* 40(2):158–173.

Phillips, D. J., and Y. K. Kim. 2009. "Why Pseudonyms? Deception as Identity Preservation among Jazz Record Companies." *Organization Science* 20:481–499.

Phillips, D. J., and D. A. Owens. 2004. "Incumbents, Innovation, and Competence: The Emergence of Recorded Jazz, 1920 to 1929." *Poetics* 32:281–295.

Pinckney, W., Jr. 1989. "Puerto Rican Jazz and the Incorporation of Folk Music: An Analysis of Musical Directions." *Latin American Music Review/Revista de Musica Latinoamericana* 10(2):236–266.

Pinheiro, D. L., and T. J. Dowd. 2009. "All That Jazz: The Success of Jazz Musicians in Three Metropolitan Areas." *Poetics* 37:490–506.

Plato. 1991. *The Republic.* New York: Vintage Classics.

Potter, R. 1995. *Spectacular Vernaculars: Hip-Hop and the Politics of Postmodernism.* Albany: State University of New York Press.

Prior, N. 2008. "Putting a Glitch in the Field: Bourdieu, Actor Network Theory, and Contemporary Music." *Cultural Sociology* 2:301–319.

Qualen, J. 1985. *The Music Industry.* London: Comedia.

Reagon, B. 1975. *Songs of the Civil Rights Movement, 1955–1965: A Study in Culture History.* Washington, DC: Smithsonian Institute.

Regev, M. 1998. "Who Does What with Music Videos in Israel?" *Poetics* 25:225–240.

Renshaw, P. 1999. *The Story of the IWW and the Syndicalism in the United States.* Chicago: Ivan R. Dee.

Reuter, E. 1969. *Race Mixture: Studies in Intermarriage and Miscegenation.* New York: Greenwood.

Richter, P. E., ed. 1967. *Perspectives in Aesthetics*. New York: Odyssey.

Ridgeway, J. 1990. *Blood in the Face: The Ku Klux Klan, Aryan Nations, Nazi Skinheads, and the Rise of a New White Culture*. New York: Thunder's Mouth.

Robbin, A. 2000. "Classifying Racial and Ethnic Group Data in the United States: The Politics of Negotiation and Accommodation." *Journal of Government Information* 27:129–156.

Robeson, P. 1958. "A Universal Body of Folk Music—A Technical Argument by the Author." In *From Here I Stand*, 124–125. New York: Othello.

Rockquemore, K. A., and D. Brunsma. 2002. *Beyond Black: Biracial Identity in America*. Thousand Oaks, CA: Sage.

Rockquemore, K. A., D. Brunsma, and D. J. Delgado. 2009. "Racing to Theory or Retheorizing Race? Understanding the Struggle to Build a Multiracial Identity Theory." *Journal of Social Issues* 65:13–34.

Rodriquez, J. 2006. "Color-Blind Ideology and the Cultural Appropriation of Hip-Hop." *Journal of Contemporary Ethnography* 35:645–668.

Roman-Velazquez, P. 1999. *The Making of Latin London: Salsa Music, Place, and Identity*. Aldershot, UK: Ashgate.

Root, M. 1992. "Within, Between, and Beyond Race." In *Racially Mixed People in America*, ed. M. Root, 3–11. Thousand Oaks, CA: Sage.

Roscigno, V. J., and W. F. Danaher. 2004. *The Voice of Southern Labor: Radio, Music, and Textile Strikes, 1929–1934*. Minneapolis: University of Minnesota Press.

Roscigno, V. J., W. F. Danaher, and E. Summers-Effler. 2002. "Music, Culture, and Social Movements: Song and Southern Textile Worker Mobilization." *International Journal of Sociology and Social Policy* 22:141–174.

Rose, T. 1994. *Black Noise: Rap Music and Black Culture in Contemporary America*. Middleton, CT: Wesleyan University Press.

Rosenberg, N. V. 1985. *Bluegrass: A History*. Urbana: University of Illinois Press.

Rosenblum, B. 1975. "Style as Social Process." *American Sociological Review* 43:422–438.

Rossmann, G. 2004. "Elites, Masses, and Media Blacklists: The Dixie Chicks Controversy." *Social Forces* 83:61–79.

Rouget, G. 1985. *Music and Trance*. Chicago: University of Chicago Press.

Roy, W. G. 2010. *Reds, Whites, and Blues: Social Movements, Folk Music, and Race in America*. Princeton, NJ: Princeton University Press.

———. 2004. "'Race Records' and 'Hillbilly Music': The Institutional Origins of Racial Categories in the American Commercial Recording Industry." *Poetics* 32:265–279.

———. 2002. "Aesthetic Identity, Race, and American Folk Music." *Qualitative Sociology* 25:459–469.

———. 2001. *Making Societies: The Historical Construction of Our World*. Thousand Oaks, CA: Pine Forge.

Roy, W. G., and T. J. Dowd. 2010. "What Is Sociological about Music?" *Annual Review of Sociology* 36:183–203.

Rublowsky, J. 1971. *Black Music in America*. New York: Basic.

Russolo, L. 2004 [1913]. "The Art of Noises: Futurist Manifesto." In *Audio Culture: Readings in Modern Music*, ed. C. Cox and D. Warner, 10–14. New York: Bloomsbury Academic.

Ryan, J. 1985. *The Production of Culture in the Music Industry: The ASCAP-BMI Controversy*. Lanham, MD: University Press of America.

Ryan, J., and R. A. Peterson. 1982. "The Product Image: The Fate of Creativity in Country Music Song Writing." *Sage Annual Reviews of Communication Research* 10:11–32.

Salagnik, M., and D. J. Watts. 2008. "Leading the Herd Astray: An Experimental Study of Self-fulfilling Prophecy in an Artificial Cultural Market." *Social Psychology Quarterly* 71:338–355.

Samuels, D. 2005. "The Rap on Rap: The 'Black Music' That Isn't Either." In *That's the Joint! The Hip-Hop Studies Reader*, ed. M. Forman and M. A. Neal, 147–153. New York: Routledge.

Sanjek, R., and D. Sanjek. 1991. *American Popular Music Business in the Twentieth Century*. New York: Oxford University Press.

Santoro, M. 2010. "Constructing an Artistic Field as a Political Project: Lessons from La Scala." *Poetics* 38(6):534–554.

———. 2004. "What Is "Cantautore"? Distinction and Authorship in (Italian) Popular Music." *Poetics* 30:11–32.

Sarabia, D., and T. Shriver. 2004. "Maintaining Collective Identity in a Hostile Environment: Confronting Negative Public Perception and Factional Divisions within the Skinhead Subculture." *Sociological Spectrum* 24:267–294.

Sardiello, R. 1998. "Identity and Status Stratification in Deadhead Subculture." In *Youth Culture: Identity in a Postmodern World*, ed. J. S. Epstein, 118–147. Malden, MA: Blackwell.

———. 1994. "Secular Rituals as Popular Culture: A Case for Grateful Dead Concerts and Deadhead Identity." In *Adolescents and Their Music: If It's Too Loud You're Too Old*, 115–140. New York: Garland.

Savage, M. 2006. "The Musical Field." *Cultural Trends* 15:159–174.

Sawyer, R. K. 2003. *Group Creativity: Music, Theatre, Collaboration*. Mahwah, NJ: Lawrence Erlbaum.

Scherer, F. M. 2001. "The Evolution of Free-Lance Music Composition, 1650–1900." *Journal of Cultural Economics* 25:307–319.

Schmutz, V. 2009. "Social and Symbolic Boundaries in Newspaper Coverage of Music, 1995–2005: Gender and Genre in the US, France, Germany and the Netherlands." *Poetics* 37:298–314.

Schutz, A. 1951. "Making Music Together: A Study in Social Relationships." *Social Research* 18:76–97.

Seeger, A. 2004. *Why Suyá Sing: A Musical Anthropology of an Amazonian People*. Urbana: University of Illinois Press.

Seeger, P. 1972. *The Incompleat Folksinger*. New York: Simon and Schuster.

Sewell, W. H., Jr. 1992. "A Theory of Structure: Duality, Agency, and Transformation." *American Journal of Sociology* 98:1–29.

Sheehy, D. 1999. "Popular Mexican Musical Traditions: The Mariachi of West Mexico and the *Conjunto* Jarocho of Veracruz." In *Music in Latin American Culture: Regional Traditions*, ed. J. M. Schechter, 34–79. New York: Shirmer.

Shenk, D., and S. Silberman 1994. *Skeleton Key: A Dictionary for Deadheads*. New York: Doubleday.

Shepherd, J., and P. Wicke. 1997. *Music and Cultural Theory*. Malden, MA: Polity.

Sheptoski, M. 2000. "Vending at Dead Shows: The Bizarre Bazaar." In *Deadhead Social Science: You Ain't Gonna Learn What You Don't Want to Know*, ed. R. G. Adams and R. Sardiello, 157–181. Walnut Creek, CA: Alta Mira.

Sherman, B., and J. Dominick. 1986. "Violence and Sex in Music Videos: TV and Rock 'n' Roll." *Journal of Communication* 36(1):73–93.

Sigerist, H. E. 1948. "The Story of Tarantism." In *Music and Medicine*, 96–116. New York: Henry Schuman.

Singer, S. I., M. Levine, and S. Jou. 1993. "Heavy Metal Music Preference, Delinquent Friends, Social Control, and Delinquency." *Journal of Research in Crime and Delinquency* 30:317–329.

Skinner, K. 2006. "Must Be Born Again": Resurrecting the Anthology of American Folk Music." *Popular Music* 25:57–75.

Small, C. 1998. *Musicking: The Meanings of Performing and Listening.* Hanover, CT: University Press of New England.

Southern, E. 1997. *The Music of Black Americans: A History.* New York: W. W. Norton.

Stack, S., J. Gundlach, and J. L. Reeves. 1994. "The Heavy Metal Subculture and Suicide." *Suicide and Life-Threatening Behavior* 24:15–23.

Steinberg, M. 2004. "When Politics Goes Pop: On the Intersection of Popular and Political Culture and the Case of Serbian Student Protests." *Social Movement Studies* 3:3–29.

Steward, G. A., Jr., T. E. Shriver, and A. L. Chasteen. 2002. "Participant Narratives and Collective Identity in a Metaphysical Movement." *Sociological Spectrum* 22:107–135.

Stewart, K. 1988. "Nostalgia—a Polemic." *Cultural Anthropology* 3(3):227–241.

Stolzoff, N. C. 2000. *Wake the Town and Tell the People: Dancehall Culture in Jamaica.* Durham, NC: Duke University Press.

Stonequist, E. 1937. *The Marginal Man: A Study in Personality and Culture Conflict.* New York: Charles Scribner's Sons.

Suall, I., and T. Halpern. 1993. *Young Nazi Killers and the Rising Skinhead Danger.* New York: Anti-Defamation League.

Sudnow, D. 1978. *Ways of the Hand: The Organization of Improvised Conduct.* Cambridge, MA: Harvard University Press.

Supicic, I. 1987. *Music in Society: A Guide to the Sociology of Music.* Stuyvesant, NY: Pendragon.

Sutton, S. C. 2000. "The Deadhead Community: Popular Religion in Contemporary American Culture." In *Deadhead Social Science: You Ain't Gonna Learn What You Don't Want to Know,* ed. R.G. Adams and R. Sardiello, 109–127. Walnut Creek, CA: Alta Mira.

Swidler, A. 1986. "Culture in Action: Symbols and Strategies." *American Sociological Review* 51(2):273–286.

Sykes, G., and D. Matza. 1957. "Techniques of Neutralization." *American Sociological Review* 22:664–670.

Sylvan, R. 2002. *Traces of the Spirit: The Religious Dimensions of Popular Music.* New York: New York University Press.

Taylor, V., and N. E. Whittier. 1992. "Collective Identity in Social Movement Communities: Lesbian Feminist Mobilization." In *Frontiers in Social Movement Theory,* ed. A. D. Morris and C. M. Mueller, 104–129. New Haven, CT: Yale University Press.

———. 1995. "Analytical Approaches to Social Movement Culture: The Culture of the Women's Movement." In *Social Movements and Culture,* ed. H. Johnston and B. Klandermans, 163–187. Minneapolis: University of Minnesota Press.

Thornton, S. 1996. *Club Cultures: Music, Media, and Subcultural Capital.* Hanover, CT: Wesleyan University Press.

Toll, R. C. 1982. *The Entertainment Machine.* Oxford: Oxford University Press.

Tomlinson, G. 1992. "Cultural Dialogics and Jazz." In *Disciplining Music: Musicology and Its Canons,* ed. K. Bergeron and P. V. Bnohlman, 64–94. Chicago: University of Chicago Press.

———. 1993. *Music in Renaissance Magic.* Chicago: University of Chicago Press.

Toop, D. 1992. *Rap Attack No. 2: African Rap to Global Hip-Hop.* London: Serpent's Tail.

Traber, D. S. 2001. "L.A.'s White Minority: Punk and the Contradictions of Self-Marginalization." *Cultural Critique* 48:30–64.

Trachtenberg, A. 1982. *The Incorporation of America: Culture and Society in the Gilded Age.* New York: Hill and Wang.

Tsitsos, W. 1999. "Rules of Rebellion: Slam-dancing, Moshing, and the American Alternative Scene." *Popular Music* 18(3):397–414.

Turino, T. 2008. *Music as Social Life: The Politics of Participation.* Chicago: University Chicago Press.

———. 2001. "The Music of Sub-Saharan Africa." In *Excursions in World Music,* ed. B. Nettl, C. Capwell, P. V. Bohlman, I. K. F. Wong, and T. Turino. Upper Saddle River, NJ: Prentice Hall.

Turner, B. S., and S. P. Wainwright. 2006. "Just Crumbling to Bits? An Exploration of the Body, Aging, Injury, and Career in Classical Ballet Dancers." *Sociology* 40:237–255.

Turner, V. 1995 [1969]. *The Ritual Process: Structure and Anti-Structure.* Piscataway, NJ: Aldine.

Turner, V., and A. Turner. 1978. *Image and Pilgrimage in Christian Culture.* New York: Columbia University Press.

Ulsperger, J. S., and J. D. Knottnerus. 2010. *Elder Care Catastrophe: Rituals of Abuse in Nursing Homes—And What You Can Do about It.* Boulder, CO: Paradigm.

———. 2006. "Enron: Organizational Rituals as Deviance." In *Readings in Deviant Behavior,* ed. A. Thio and T. C. Calhoun, 279–282. Boston: Allyn and Bacon.

Urquía, N. 2004. "Doin' It Right: Contested Authenticity in London's Salsa Scene." In *Music Scenes: Local, Translocal, and Virtual,* 279–282. Nashville, TN: Vanderbilt University Press.

Valdez, A., and J. A. Halley. 1996. "Gender in the Culture of Mexican American *Conjunto* Music." *Gender and Society* 10(2):148–167.

van Eijck, K. 2001. "Social Differentiation in Musical Taste Patterns." *Social Forces* 79:1163–1185.

van Venrooij, A. 2009. "The Aesthetic Discourse Space of Popular Music, 1985–86 and 2004–05." *Poetics* 37:295–398.

van Venrooij, A., and V. Schmutz. 2010. "The Evaluation of Popular Music in the United States, Germany, and the Netherlands: A Comparison of the Use of High Art and Popular Aesthetic Criteria." *Cultural Sociology* 4(3):395–421.

Vanderwood, P. 1981. *Disorder and Progress: Bandits, Police, and Mexican Development.* Lincoln: University of Nebraska Press.

Vannini, P., and J. P. Williams. 2009. "Authenticity in Culture, Self, and Society." In *Authenticity in Culture, Self, and Society,* ed. P. Vannini and J. P. Williams, 1–20. Burlington, VT: Ashgate.

Verdicchio, P. 2005. "Introduction." In *The Southern Question,* ed. A. Gramsci, 7–26. Toronto: Guernica.

Waksman, S. 2009. *This Ain't the Summer of Love: Conflict and Crossover in Heavy Metal and Punk.* Berkeley: University of California Press.

———. 2001. *Instruments of Desire: The Electric Guitar and the Shaping of Musical Experience.* Cambridge, MA: Harvard University Press.

Walser, R. 1993. *Running with the Devil: Power, Gender, and Madness in Heavy Metal Music.* Hanover, CT: Wesleyan University Press.

Warde, A., D. Wright, and M. Gayo-Cal. 2008. "The Omnivorous Orientation in the United Kingdom." *Poetics* 36:148–165.

Watkins, S. C. 2001. "A Nation of Millions: Hip Hop Culture and the Legacy of Black Nationalism." *Communication Review* 4:373–398.

Waxer, L. 2002. *Situating Salsa: Global Markets and Local Meanings in Latin Popular Music.* New York: Routledge.

Weber, M. 1958 [1905]. *The Protestant Ethic and the Spirit of Capitalism.* New York: Charles Scribner's Sons.

———. 1958. *The Rational and Social Foundations of Music.* Carbondale: Southern Illinois Press.

Weber, W. 2006. "Redefining the Status of Opera: London and Leipzig, 1800–1848." *Journal of Interdisciplinary History* 36:507–532.

———. 1984. "The Contemporaneity of Eighteenth-Century Musical Taste." *Musical Quarterly* 70:175–194.

Weinstein, D. 2000. *Heavy Metal: The Music and Its Culture.* London: Da Capo.

———. 1991. *Heavy Metal: A Cultural Sociology.* New York: Lexington.

Whitman, M. L. 2005. *"When We're Finished with It, Let Them Have It": Jamband Tape-Trading Culture.* Thesis, University of Chicago, Chicago, IL.

Widdicombe, S., and R. Wooffitt. 1995. *The Language of Youth Subcultures: Social Identity in Action.* New York: Simon and Schuster.

Wilder, A. 1972. *American Popular Song: The Great Innovators 1900–1950.* New York: Oxford.

Williams, J. P. 2003. "The Straightedge Subculture on the Internet: A Case Study of Style-Display Online." *Media International Australia Incorporating Culture and Policy* 107:61–74.

Williams, J. P., and H. Copes. 2005. "How Edge Are You? Constructing Authentic Identities and Subcultural Boundaries in a Straightedge Internet Forum." *Symbolic Interaction* 28(1):67–89.

Willis, P. 1977. *Learning to Labor: How Working-Class Kids Get Working-Class Jobs.* Farnborough, UK: Saxon House University Press.

Wilson, B., and M. Atkinson. 2005. "Rave and Straightedge, the Virtual and the Real: Exploring Online and Offline Experiences in Canadian Youth Subcultures." *Youth and Society* 36(3):276–311.

Witmark, I., and I. Goldberg. 1939. *From Ragtime to Swingtime: The Story of the House of Witmark.* New York: Lee Forman.

Wlodarski, A. 2005. *The Sounds of Memory: German Musical Representations of the Holocaust, 1945–1965.* PhD dissertation. University of Rochester, Rochester, NY.

Wood, R. T. 2006. *Straightedge: Complexity and Contradictions of a Subculture.* Syracuse, NY: Syracuse University Press.

———. 1999. "'Nailed to the X': A Lyrical History of the Straightedge Youth Subculture." *Journal of Youth Studies* 2:133–151.

———. 1999. "The Indigenous, Nonracist Origins of the American Skinhead Subculture." *Youth and Society* 31:131–151.

Woodard, V. 1955. *The Strange Career of Jim Crow.* New York: Oxford University Press.

Wright, J. 2006. "Songs of Remembrance." *Journal of African American History* 91(4):413–424.

Wright, R. 2000. "I'd Sell You Suicide: Pop Music and Moral Panic in the Age of Marilyn Manson." *Popular Music* 19(3):365–385.

Wu, Y., and J. D. Knottnerus. 2005. "Ritualized Daily Practices: A Study of Chinese

'Educated Youth.'" *Shehui* [Society] 6:167–185. [Chinese academic journal. English translation available upon request.]

Wuthnow, R. 2003. *All in Sync: How Music and Art Are Revitalizing American Religion.* Berkeley: University of California Press.

Young, K., and L. Craig. 1997. "Beyond White Pride: Identity, Meaning, and Contradiction in the Canadian Skinhead Subculture." *Canadian Review of Sociology and Anthropology* 34:175–206.

Zellner, W. W. 1995. *Countercultures: A Sociological Analysis.* New York: St. Martin's.

Zerubavel, E. 1991. *The Fine Line: Making Distinctions in Everyday Life.* New York: Free Press.

———. 1985. *The Seven Day Circle: The History and Meaning of the Week.* Chicago: University Chicago Press.

Media and Digital Sources

Addicted to Noise (an online music magazine featuring the writings of G. Marcus, D. Marsh, and other contemporary pop critics): http://www.addict.com/.

Aitken, L. 1970. "Skinhead Invasion." On *High Priest of Reggae* [CD]. London: Pressure Drop Records.

Amato, R. 2007. "Istat, in Italia 7 Milioni e Mezzo di Poveri i 2/3 Vivono al Sud, Sempre Peggio Gli Anziani." *La Repubblica.it.* October 4.

Anal Cunt. 2001. "Ha Ha Holocaust," from album *Defenders of the Hate.* http://www.darklyrics.com/lyrics/analcunt/defendersofthehate.html#2. Accessed 8/15/2008.

———. 2000a. "I Went Back in Time and Voted for Hitler," from album *Split with the Raunchous Brothers.* http://www.darklyrics.com/lyrics/analcunt/splitwiththeraunchousbrothers.html#2. Accessed 8/15/2008.

———. 2000b. "Hogging Up the Holocaust," from album *Split with the Raunchous Brothers.* Retrieved from http://www.darklyrics.com/lyrics/analcunt/splitwiththeraunchousbrothers.html#3. Accessed 8/15/2008.

———. 1999a. "Body by Auschwitz" and "I Sent Concentration Camp Footage to America's Funniest Home Videos," from album *It Just Gets Worse.* http://www.darklyrics.com/lyrics/analcunt/itjustgetsworse. Accessed 8/15/2008.

———. 1999b. "Hitler Was a Sensitive Man," from album *It Just Gets Worse.* http://www.darklyrics.com/lyrics/analcunt/itjustgetsworse. Accessed 8/15/2008.

Anti-Defamation League. (n.d.). "Neo-Nazi Hate Music: A Guide." http://www.adl.org/main_Extremism/hate_music_in_the_21st_century.htm. Accessed 8/16/2008.

Bauder, D. 2011. "New Generation of Music Central to Protest." Music Yahoo.com. November 14. http://music.yahoo.com/news/generation-music-central-protest-171334345.html. Accessed December 30, 2011.

Berlinkski, C. 2005. "Das Jackboot: German Heavy Metal Conquers Europe." *New York Times.* January 9:A32, A36.

Best, W. 2006. "Gospel According to … The Ever-Evolving Soundtrack of Black America." *Harvard Divinity Bulletin* 34(2) Spring.

Binelli, M. 2008. "The Future According to Radiohead." *Rolling Stone.* February 7:54–59.

Blumenthal, R. 1995. "US Ends Ticketmaster Investigation." *New York Times.* July 6.

Bodleian Library. University of Oxford. "The Ballads Project." http://www.bodley
.ox.ac.uk/ballads/project.htm Accessed 5/4/2011.

Boehlert, E. 1996. "Altered Stakes." *Rolling Stone.* March 21:22.

———. 1995. "Taking on Ticketmaster." *Rolling Stone.* December 28:81.

Boehlert, E., J. Colapinto, and M. Hendrickson. 1996. "Who Are You? Pearl Jam's
Eddie Vedder." *Rolling Stone.* November 28:51–54, 57, 146–148.

Boyer, H. C. 1999–2000. "The Negro Spiritual." *Jubilee Singers: Sacrifice and
Glory,* PBS. http://www.pbs.org/wgbh/amex/singers/filmmore/reference/inter-
view/boyer02.html. Accessed 10/2009.

Budnick, D. 1999. "The Music Never Stops for Barry Smolin." Jambands.com.
http://www.jambands.com. Accessed 5/15/2011.

Capani, G. 2004. *Un Ritmo Per L'Anima.* Director. Anima Mundi Video.

Caramanica, J. 2005. "Heavy Metal Gets an M.F.A." *New York Times.* September
18:A1, A28.

Carr, D. 2005. "Exploring the Right to Share, Mix, and Burn." *New York Times.*
April 9.

Center for American Music. 2010. "Stephen C. Foster Biography." University of
Pittsburg Library System. http://www.pitt.edu/~amerimus/FosterProfessional
career.html. Accessed 5/2/2011.

Centurian. 2001. "Heading for Holocaust." On *Liber Zar Zax* [CD]. Wimereux,
France: Listenable Records. http://www.darklyrics.com/lyrics/centurian/liber
zarzax.html#2. Accessed 8/15/2008.

Chiriatti, L. 1998. *Opillo pillo pà.* Edizioni Aramirè.

Christman, E. 2011. "US Album Sales Fall 12.8% in 2010, Digital Tracks Eke
Out 1% Gain." *Billboard.* http://www.billboard.com/news/u-s-album-sales
-fall-12-8-in-2010-digital-1004137859.story#/news/u-s-album-sales-fall-12-8
-in-2010-digital-1004137859.story.

Cockrell, D. "Black Faced Minstrelsy." PBS. http: www.pbs.org/wgbh/amex/foster/
sfeature/sf_minstrelsy_6.html. Accessed 7/30/2012.

Cohen, R. 2002. "Alan Lomax: Citizen Activist." Obit from ISAM Newsletter,
Fall, 32(1). http://depthome.brooklyn.cuny.edu/isam/cohen1.html. Accessed
7/30/2012.

Coldwell, C. 1998. "The Westminster Directory for Public Worship and the Lining of the Psalms." First Presbyterian Church of Rowlett. http://www.fpcr.org/
blue_banner_articles/lining.htm. Accessed 7/30/2012.

Count Raven. 1993. "Children's Holocaust." On *High on Infinity* [CD]. Germany:
Hellhound Records. Retrieved from http://www.darklyrics.com/lyrics/count
raven/highoninfinity.html#2. Accessed 8/16/2008.

"Dark Lyrics." 2001–2011. Dark Lyrics Metal Archive. http://www.darklyrics
.com. Accessed 8/15/2008.

Dekker, D. 2009 [1969]. *Unity: On This Is Desmond Dekker* [CD]. London:
Trojan Records.

Del Giudice, L. 2002. "Historical Introduction to Puglia and the Salento." Liner
notes. *Puglia: The Salento.* Rounder Records. 82161–1805–2.

Dismember. 2000. "Hate Campaign." On *Hate Campaign* [CD]. Donzdorf,
Germany: Nuclear Blast. Retrieved from http://www.darklyrics.com/lyrics/
dismember/hatecampaign.html#11. Accessed 8/16/2008.

Dove, I. 1975. "South Rocks Again at Music Academy." *New York Times.* February 2:47.

Drozdowski, T. 1995. "The Bends." *Rolling Stone.* May 18:88.

Durante, D. (n.d.). "Testi e spartiti a cura di Daniele Durante." Booklet included with CD set *Viva Ci Balla* by Canzoniere Grecanico Salentino. Anima Mundi.

Dying Fetus. 2000. "Destroy the Opposition." On *Destroy the Opposition* [CD]. Upper Darby, PA: Relapse Records. Retrieved from http://www.darklyrics.com/dyingfetus/destroytheopposition.html#2. Accessed 8/15/2008.

Earth Crisis. 1992. *All Out War* EP [audio cassette]. Conviction Records (address unknown).

Edwards, H. 1975. "There's Art in the Led Zep's Heavy-Metal Hullabaloo." *New York Times.* February 2:X20.

Encyclopaedia Metallum. 2002–2011. http://www.metal-archives.com. Accessed 8/15/2008.

Enthroned. 1996. "Under the Holocaust." On *Prophecies of Pagan Fire* [CD]. Nesles, Nord Pas-de-Calais, France: Evil Omen Records. http://www.darklyrics.com/lyrics/enthroned/propheciesofpaganfire.html#3. Accessed 8/16/2008.

Flotsam and Jetsam. 1986. "Der Führer." On *Doomsday for the Deceiver* [CD]. Agoura Hills, CA: Metal Blade Records. http://www.dakrlyrics.com/lyrics/flotsamandjetsam/doomsdayforthedeceiver.html#9. Accessed 8/15/2008.

Garner, F. H. 1955. "Musical Semantics." *New York Times,* May 15:X7.

Gonzales, S. 1991. "History of the Mariachi," Excerpts from *Mexico, The Meeting of Two Cultures.* New York: Higgins and Associates. http://www.mariachi.org/history.html. Accessed on October 2, 2009.

Goodman, F. 1994. "The Price Is Not Right." *Rolling Stone.* October 6:21–22.

Goodman, G., Jr. 1975. "Jazzmen in City Still Battle Old Myths." *New York Times.* September 1:6.

Graham, B. 1986. *Guardian.* May 30.

Graham, J. 2004. "Colleges Sing Discount Tunes." *USA Today.* December 13:7B.

Hades (USA). 1988. "In the Mean Time." On *If at First You Don't Succeed* [CD]. United States: Torrid Records. Retrieved from http://www.darlyrics.com/lyrics/hadesusa/ifatfirstyoudontsucceed.html#2. Accessed 8/15/2008.

Harding, R. E. 2005. "You Got a Right to the Tree of Life: African American Spirituals and Religions of the Diaspora." http://ctl.du.edu/spirituals/Religion/index.cfm. Accessed 10/9/2010.

Herbert, B. 1994. "In America: Ticket Trust Busters." *New York Times.* June 5.

Hiatt, B., and S. Knopper. 2007. "Inside Radiohead's Biz-Shaking Release." *Rolling Stone.* November 1:15–16.

Higginson, T. W. 1867. "Negro Spirituals." In *Atlantic Monthly.* Available online at http://xroads.virginia.edu/~hyper/twh/higg.html.

Holden, S. 1985. "Jazz: Chick Corea Leads Trio." *New York Times.* January 3:C18.

Huntington, S. 1993. "The Clash of Civilizations." *Foreign Affairs* 72:22–49.

I Am Trying to Break Your Heart. 2002. Dir. S. Jones. Perf. J. Tweedy, J. Bennett, L. Bach, G. Kotche, J. Stirratt. Plexifilm.

"In Rainbows." *Dead Air Space.* http://www.radiohead.com/deadairspace/index.php?a=292 . Accessed 3/15/2009.

Isbell, C. (the "Homeboy from Hell"), with links to his New Jack Hip-Hop Reviews: http://www.ai.mit.edu/~isbell/isbell.html.

J. M. K. "Oh God Our Help in Ages Past." *Christian Biography Resources.* http://www.wholesomewords.org/biography/bwatts3.html. Accessed 7/30/2012.

Jardin, X. 2004. "Music Is Not a Loaf of Bread." *Wired.* November 15. http://www.wired.com/culture/lifestyle/news/2004/11/65688?currentPage=all. Accessed 11/8/2011.

"Jazz at Lincoln Center." 2011. Available at http://www.jalc.orc. Accessed 12/7/2011.

Jones, C. C. 1842. *The Religious Instruction of the Negroes in the United States.* http://docsouth.unc.edu/church/jones/jones.html. Accessed 10/2010.

Jones, R. A. 1994. "The Scene: Identity Crisis; Skinheads Aren't All Alike, O. C. Teen-Agers Say in Defense of Their Subculture That Believes in Racial Harmony." *Los Angeles Times*, September 30:E1.

Jones, S. (Dir.) 2002. "I Am Trying to Break Your Heart." Perf. J. Tweedy, J. Bennett, L. Bach, G. Kotche, J. Stirratt. *Plexifilm.*

Kamens, T. 2011. "What's in a Name?" June 1. http://blogs.rj.org/reform/2010/04/what-in-a-name-1.html?utm_source=feedburner&utm_medium=feed&utm_campaign=Feed%3A+rjblog+%28RJ+Blog%29.

Kemp, M. 1997. "Deep Blue." *Rolling Stone.* July 10:117–118.

Kennedy, S. "What Alan Lomax Meant to Me and This World." http://www.alan-lomax.com/about_StetsonKennedy.html. Accessed 5/20/2011.

Knopper, S. 2008. "2007: From Bad to Worse." *Rolling Stone.* February 7:15–18.

Kot, G. 2002. "The Classic Album That Almost Wasn't." *Rolling Stone.* May 23:42.

———. 2001. "Wilco." *Rolling Stone.* October 11:38.

Kotarba, J. A. 1998. "The Commodification and Decommodification of Rock Music: Rock en Espanol and Rock Music in Poland." Paper presented at the Annual Meeting of the SSSI Couch-Stone Symposium, February 21, Houston, TX.

Lärm. 2007. *No One Can Be That Dumb* and *Nothing Is Hard in This World If You Dare to Scale the Heights* [vinyl records]. Warmond, Netherlands: Way Back When Records.

Leeds, J. 2008. "Radiohead Finds Sales, Even after Downloads." *New York Times.* January 10.

———. 2007. "In Radiohead Price Plan, Some See a Movement." *New York Times.* October 11.

Leonard, R. C. (n.d.). "Singing the Psalms: A Brief History of Psalmody." http://www.laudemont.org/index.html?MainFrame=http://www.laudemont.org/a-stp.htm. Accessed 5/1/2011.

Levy, J. 2007. "Just $9,250 a Song!" *Rolling Stone.* November: 83.

McBride, S., and E. Smith. 2008. "Music Industry to Abandon Mass Suits." *Wall Street Journal.* December 19.

Minor Threat. 1981. *In My Eyes* EP [vinyl record]. Washington, DC: Dischord Records.

Moore, N. (n.d.). "The Big Red Songbook: Over Sixty Years of Wobbly-lore." Interview and book review. http://www.eugeneiww.org/articles/archiegreen.htm. Accessed 5/2/2011.

Moore, R. 2003. "Friends Don't Let Friends Listen to Corporate Rock: The Independent Media of Punk Subculture." Paper presented at the Annual Meeting of the American Sociological Association, Atlanta Hilton Hotel, Atlanta, GA. http://www.allacademic.com/meta/p108081_index.html.

Mr. Symarip. 2006. "Skinheads Dem a Come." *The Skinheads Dem a Come* [CD]. Madrid, Spain: Liquidator Records.

Mullaney, J., and C. Kolb. 2006. "Having the Edge or Edged Out? Women's Experiences in the Straight Edge Hardcore Music Scene." Paper presented at the Annual Meeting of the American Sociological Association, Montreal, Quebec, Canada.

NegroSpirituals. "Dr. Watts." http://www.negrospirituals.com/song.htm. Accessed 10/20/2010.

Nelson, C. 2003. "MEDIA; One Music Label or Several? Pearl Jam Weighs Options." *New York Times*. 14 July.

Nelson-Burns, L. (n.d.). The Contemplator's Folk Music Site. http://www.contemplator.com. Accessed 5/2/2011.

———. (n.d.). "Contemplations from the Marianas Trench: Music and Deep Thought." http://www.contemplator.com. Accessed 5/4/2011.

NetHymnal. *Isaac Watts: 1674–1748*. http://www.cyberhymnal.org/bio/w/a/t/watts_i.htm. Accessed 10/11/2010.

New York Times. 2008. "EMI Reportedly Cutting 2,000 Jobs." January 14.

———. 1994. "Offering Pearl Jam Tickets in a Lottery." December 23.

———. 1985. "Kansas City Revives Jazz Landmark." May 2:A16.

———. 1955. "Parisian Jazz Fans Riot at Concert by Bechet." October 20:42.

———. 1945. "Jazz Maestro Prepares for Concert Debut." February 11:X5.

———. 1935a. "College Curbs Jazz." March 28:23.

———. 1935b. "Reich Bars Radio Jazz to Safeguard 'Culture.'" October 13:N3.

———. 1935c. "To Fight American Jazz." February 24:N8.

New York Times [DealBook Blog]. 2009. "Springsteen: This Merger Isn't Born to Run." February 5. http://dealbook.nytimes.com/2009/02/05/bruce-springsteen-this-merger-isnt-born-to-run/. Accessed 7/21/2012.

"*New York Times*: Media Kit." 2011. http://nytmarketing.whsites.net/mediakit/newspaper. Accessed 12/7/2011.

Newsweek. 2004. "The Norah Jones Effect." February 2:55–56.

Nuclear Assault. 1986. "After the Holocaust." On *Game Over* [CD]. United States: Combat Records. http://www.darklyrics.com/lyrics/nuclearassault/gameover.html#7. Accessed 8/15/2008.

Nzewi, M. 2006. "African Music Creativity and Performance: The Science of the Sound." *Voices: A World Forum for Music Therapy* 6(1). http://www.voices.no/mainissues/mi40006000199.html. Accessed 4/1/2006.

Palmer, R. 1980a. "In Pop, It Was Conservatives vs. the Progressives." *New York Times*. December 28:D19.

———. 1980b. "Pop: AC/DC and Def Leppard." *New York Times*. August 3:42.

———. 1980c. "Rock: Black Sabbath 4." *New York Times*, October 19:59.

Pareles, J. 2007a. "MUSIC; Radiohead, Big Enough to Act Like a Baby Band." *New York Times*. 11 October.

———. 2007b. "Radiohead's experiment with 'virtual busking.'" *New York Times*. 12 November.

———. 2002. "A Jilted Band Finds Love After All." *New York Times*. 21 April.

———. 2000. "Ozzy Osbourne, without the Birds and Bats." *New York Times*. July 26:E1, E3.

———. 1996. "Two Jams (Pearl and Traffic) for One Price." *New York Times*. September 30.

———. 1995. "Musical History of the Art Called Jazz." *New York Times*. September 1:D16.

———. 1994 "RECORDINGS VIEW; Pearl Jam Gives Voice to Sisyphus." *New York Times*. 4 December.

———. 1990. "Heavy Metal from an Era Before Poses." *New York Times*. September 30:59.

———. 1985a. "Jazz: At Town Hall Charlie Parker Tribute." *New York Times*. September 2:36.

———. 1985b. "Jazz Service Group Formed." *New York Times*. May 1:C25.

———. 1985c. "Music: Ellington's Sacred Concerts." *New York Times.* September 3:C13.

———. 1985d. "Should Rock Lyrics Be Sanitized?" *New York Times.* October 13:H1, H5.

PBS. "Minstrels." *American Experience: Stephen Foster and the Minstrels.* http://www.pbs.org/wgbh/amex/foster/sfeature/sf_minstrelsy_1.html. Accessed 6/15/2011.

Perpetua, M. 2011. "Jay-Z and Kanye Break iTunes Sales Record." *Rolling Stone.* http://www.rollingstone.com/music/news/jay-z-and-kanye-break-itunes-sales-record-20110817.

Piazza, T. 1995. "How Two Pianists Remade (and Upheld) a Tradition." *New York Times.* January 1:H29.

Pisanelli, P. 2005. *Il Sibilo Lungo Della Taranta.* Director. Big Sur.

Porter, E. 2007. "Radiohead's Genius? Making Music Downloading Pay." *New York Times.* November 27.

Powers, A. 2000. "A Kind of Boutique Metal Offers a Refined Approach to Head-banging." *New York Times.* July 18:E3.

Purchla, J. 2008. "Crews in the Hardcore Music Subculture." Paper presented at the Annual Meeting of the American Sociological Association, Boston, MA.

Ramirez, A. 1994. "Ticketmaster's Mr. Tough Guy." *New York Times.* November 6.

Ratliff, B. 2005. "New Orleans Musicians Ask if Their Scene Will Survive." *New York Times.* September 8:E1.

Red Hot Jazz Archive. http://www.redhotjazz.com. Accessed 7/30/2012.

Reuters. 1994. "Pearl Jam Musicians Testify on Ticketmaster's Prices." *New York Times.* 1 July.

Riding, A. 1985. "From Rod Stewart to Heavy Metal at Rock Festival near Rio de Janeiro." *New York Times.* January 21:C21.

Robbins, I. 1993. "Radiohead." *Rolling Stone.* 8 July: 95.

Rockwell, J. 1985. "Jazz: Threadgill's Classical Style." *New York Times.* September 13:45.

———. 1975. "Alice Cooper Blends Rock with Theatrics." *New York Times.* May 7:48.

Roddy, D. B. 2002. "Clashing in York—Street Fighting between Neo-Nazis, Anti-Racists Leads to 25 Arrests." *Pittsburgh Post-Gazette.* January 13:C–9.

Rolling Stone. 2008a. "In the News." November 13:24–25.

———. 2008b. "The Good, the Bad, and the Weird." December 25:36.

———. 2007. "In the News." August 23:21–22.

———. 2002. "Wilco." April 11: 96.

———. 1994. "July." December 29:60.

———. 1992. "Nirvana." April 16: cover.

Ruggles, L. 1997. "The Regular Singing Controversy: The Case against Lining Out." http://earlyamerica.com/review/fall97/sing.html. Accessed 5/20/2011.

Ryzik, M. 2007. "Bright Eyes in the Big City, Sporting a Prada Suit and a Hot Album." *New York Times.* May 24.

Sacred Reich. 1987. "Sacred Reich." On *Ignorance* [CD]. Agoura Hills, CA: Metal Blade Records. http://www.darklyrics.com/lyrics/sacredreich/ignorance.html#8. Accessed 8/16/2008.

Sanneh, K. 2005. "Heat, Good Cheer, Jagged Music, and Even Some Melody." *New York Times.* July 28:E5.

———. 2004. "The Ever-Expanding Legend of Wilco." *New York Times.* 20 June.

Scaggs, A. 2002. "Jeff Tweedy." *Rolling Stone.* December 12:78.

Schreck, C. 2004. "Skinhead vs. Skinhead in Anti-Racist Fight." WorldSources Online. Accessed 6/5/2011, NewsBank on-line database (Access World News).

Serpick, E. 2008. "NIN, Eagles, Pumpkins: Who Needs Labels?" *Rolling Stone.* April 17:11–12.

Shorto, R. 2004. "The Industry Standard." *New York Times Magazine.* 3 October.

Ska-P. 2001. "Mestizaje." *Planeta Eskoria.* [CD]. New York: RCA Records.

Smarsh, S. 2001. "What It Means to Be a Skinhead." *Kansan.* April 30:1–11.

Smith Creek Music. "What Is a Gospel Hymn (Song)?" http://www.smith creekmusic.com/Hymnology/American.Hymnody/Gospel.hymnody/Gospel .hymnody.html. Accessed 5/1/2001.

Smith, P. 2007. "Ritual." *Blackwell Encyclopedia of Sociology.* Ed. G. Ritzer. Blackwell Reference Online. Accessed 7/1/2011.

Soyka, D. 1985. "Censorship: What Next?" *New York Times.* December 8:NJ40.

Strauss, N. 2000. "Antiheros Made of Metal." *New York Times.* April 4:E1.

———. 1998. "Maui Wowie." *Rolling Stone.* April 2:20–22.

———. 1995. "Pearl Jam Cancels Its Troubled Tour." *New York Times.* June 27.

———. 1995. "The Pop Life." *New York Times.* April 6.

———. 1995a. "Being Smart about Music That Isn't." *New York Times.* May 16:C17.

———. 1995b. "Death and Madness Remain the Basics in Slayer's Repertory." *New York Times.* February 20:C14.

———. 1995c. "Raw Roots of What Became Today." *New York Times.* April 18:C16.

———. 1994. "In the News." *Rolling Stone.* July 14:35.

Testament. 1989. "Greenhouse Effect." On *Practice What You Preach* [CD]. New York: Atlantic Records. http://www.darklyrics.com/lyrics/testament/practice-whatyoupreach.html#6. Accessed 8/16/2008.

Torry, J. 2011. "Sen. Brown Compares Anti-Union Governors to Hitler, Stalin." *Dayton Daily News.* March 3. http://www.daytondailynews.com/blogs/content/ shared-gen/blogs/dayton/ohiopolitics/entries/2011/03/03/sen_brown_compares _antiunion_g.html.

Tyrangiel, J. 2007. "Radiohead Says: Pay What You Want." *Time.* October 1.

"Vaudeville! A Dazzling Display of Heterogeneous Splendour, Designed to Educate, Edify, Amaze, and Uplift." http://wroads.virginia.edu/~ma02/easton/vaudeville/ vaudevillemain.html. Accessed 5/2/2011.

Vegan, R. 1995. *Vanguard* 10-inch [vinyl record]. Laguna Beach, CA: Uprising Communications.

Watermulder, D., J. A. Hudlin, and E. Kaufman. (n.d.). "A Tradition of Spirituals." http://www.gwu.edu/~e73afram/dw-ah-ek.html#wade. Accessed 10/5/2008.

Watrous, P. 1995. "A Night of 100 Years of Onstage Experience." *New York Times.* May 6:16.

Weisel, A. 1995. "In the News." *Rolling Stone.* August 24:30.

Wernowsky, K. 2006. "A Clash of Ideas and More/Racial Views a Leading Reason for Skinheads Fighting Each Other." *Times Leader.* February 4:1A.

Wiederhorn, J. 1995. "The Road Less Traveled." *Rolling Stone.* August 10:19–20.

Wilson, J. S. 1975a. "Jazz Repertory Company Recalls Basie Sound." *New York Times.* January 19:46.

———. 1975b. "Mary Lou Takes Her Jazz Mass to Church." *New York Times.* February 9:120.

———. 1965. "Septet Attempts History of Jazz." *New York Times*. September 15: 42.

Wright, D. 1995. "Out of the Comfort Zone, On to New Adventures." *New York Times*. May 7:H42.

Youth of Today. 1988. "We're Not in This Alone" [vinyl record]. NY: Caroline Records.

Index

Musicology, 3, 37, 82, 191
Muslim, xxi, 15, 120, 166–174

Narcotics. *See* Drugs
Nationalism, 101, 117
Nationhood, 73
Native Americans, xx, 111
Network(ing), 22, 25, 90, 119, 133,
   150, 155, 161–162, 164, 233, 235,
   248, 252–255, 258, 263
Neo institutional theory, 14
Neoliberalism, 209
Norms, xxi, 14, 53, 68, 82, 89, 149–
   151, 154, 156–157, 166, 172, 191,
   193, 196, 204, 239
NWOBHM (New Wave of British
   Heavy Metal), 178
Noise(s), xv, 33, 45, 81, 88, 94, 99,
   140, 188, 191–192, 194–195, 198,
   200–201, 224, 226, 231
North America, 13, 15, 32, 42, 77,
   167, 169, 255
Nu metal, 63, 256

Objectification, 37, 71
Oi, 117
Oligopoly, 34
Opera, 39, 132

Pacific, 15
Parlor singing, xviii
Pentatonic, xix, 3–5, 7, 17, 54
Percussion, 64, 77
Perform: performance, xix–xx, 10,
   14–15, 22, 24, 26, 30, 35, 38–39,
   42, 52, 59, 67, 74, 76, 78, 80–81,
   83–89, 234–235, 237–132, 140,
   145–146, 152, 163–164, 170, 192,
   196, 199–200, 215, 223– 225,
   229, 234, 249, 259; performed/
   performing, xiv, xviii, xxii–xxiii,
   9–10, 14, 16–18, 20, 22, 25, 27,
   34–35, 37, 58, 65, 72–74, 82–84,
   87–88, 90, 97, 106–107, 125,
   132–133, 140, 143–144, 146, 152,
   154, 170, 191, 194, 198–201, 225,
   234, 252–254, 257; performer(s),
   xvii, xx, 8–11, 14, 22–23, 32–33,
   40, 45, 75, 81, 83, 87–88, 94, 99,
   119, 141–142, 145, 151, 166,

203, 227, 229, 232–234, 236–239;
   performing rights 9, 34
Persistence, 158, 161
Personal identity. *See* Identity
Phonograph, 31-33
Pianos, xviii–xix, 4–5, 11, 17, 19, 28,
   31, 33, 76, 84, 147, 233
Piercings, 44, 155
Pilgrimage, 158, 161–162
Pitch, xix, 37, 73, 84, 189, 213
Player(s), 25–26, 30, 33–34, 82–83,
   87, 128, 144, 147, 227, 241, 244
Poland, 4
Political, xxii, 14–15, 66–67, 93,
   118, 121, 123, 148, 164, 168–169,
   171, 178, 181, 183, 185, 187–189,
   192–193, 196, 199–200, 202, 204,
   206–209, 212, 217, 231, 233, 244,
   251
Political power. *See* Power
Polka, 71, 74
Polyphonic, 15
Polyrhythmic, 15
Popular: music, xiii, xvii–xviii, xxiv,
   6–7, 11, 16, 19–22, 29–30, 33, 35,
   42–43, 75, 93, 95, 99, 102, 126,
   138, 143, 191, 223–224, 229, 234–
   235, 256, 269–270, 272, 274–275,
   278–281, 283, 285, 296, 287–288;
   musician, 24, 252
Post hardcore. *See* Hardcore
Postmodern, xx, 93, 98, 102
Power(ful), xxi, 13, 35, 43, 63, 68,
   73, 102, 117, 119, 123, 138,
   141–143, 145–147, 158, 180–183,
   186, 190–193, 195–196, 198–200,
   207, 212–213, 217–220, 223, 238,
   244–249, 267
Prejudice, xxiv, 108, 110–111, 113,
   117
Product, xxiii, 23–24, 30, 33, 37, 42,
   90, 124–125, 128–129, 131–133,
   160, 191, 200, 204, 207, 229,
   233–234, 248, 266; production,
   xxiii, 14, 24, 29–30, 32, 34, 36, 38,
   40–42, 68, 82, 93, 167, 193, 223,
   226, 228, 234–239, 250 252–255,
   257–258, 261–262; reproduction,
   32, 102, 193, 225
Profane, 62, 82, 131

About the Editors

Sara Towe Horsfall has specialties in theory, social psychology, social problems, music, and religion. Her books include *Social Problems: An Advocate Group Approach* (Westview Press 2012), *A Neighborhood Portrait: Polytechnic Heights of Inner City Fort* (ed. Sunbelt Eakin 2002), *Chaos, Complexity and Sociology* (ed. with Ray Eve and Mary Lee, Sage Publications 1997), and *Identifying the Spiritual Experience* (Texas A&M University 1996). She received her Ph.D. from Texas A&M University in 1996 and worked as an Associate Professor at Texas Wesleyan University for fifteen years. She was president of the Southwestern Sociological Association in 2009–2020 and held other offices in the association prior to that. She is a member of the American Sociological Association, Society for the Study of Social Problems, Association for Sociology of Religion, Phi Kappa Phi, Alpha Kappa Delta, and the Institute of Noetic Sciences. Before focusing on a career in sociology, she worked as a journalist and foreign correspondent in England, Greece, and India. She also spent several years as a church choir director, music program director, and music teacher.

Jan-Martijn Meij is an assistant professor of sociology at Florida Gulf Coast University with a specialization in environmental sociology, social inequality, and social psychology. He obtained his Ph.D. at Oklahoma State University in 2009 and has a master's degree in International Strategy and Marketing from the Catholic University of Nijmegen (currently known as the Radboud University). In his dissertation, he explored diagnostic, prognostic, and motivational framing by the various discursive communities of the modern American environmental movement of environmental degradation aimed at individuals and their households. In other words: What do social movement organizations communicate to their members regarding the causal links between their individual and household consumer behaviors and environmental degradation? Other environmental-related research interests include world systems theory and the environment as well as the persistence of environmental justice concerns, especially as they pertain to Native Americans. Other non-environmental-related research activities include sociology of music. His book on social problems and solutions will be published by Cognella in 2013.

Meghan D. Probstfield received his M.A. in Applied Sociology (2001) from the University of Central Florida–Orlando, and his Ph.D. from Oklahoma State University (2006). He is currently associate professor of sociology in the Department of Social Sciences at Indian River State College in Fort Pierce, Florida, and actively involved in organizing the Center for Media and Journalism Studies. He is also coordinator of a community-based project involving a marginalized and lower income population. Areas of interest include social psychology, dying and death, and social theory. He has taught a variety of sociology courses, with a special emphasis on symbolic interaction, including Self, Society, and Everyday Life; Sociology of Body and Emotion; Clinical Sociology; Sociology of Death; Social Theory; Social Psychology; Gender and Sexuality; and Race/Ethnic Relations. His book contributions include a test bank and other contributions for Robert Kastenbaum's *Death, Society, and Human Experience, 10th edition* (Pearson Allyn & Bacon 2009) and the "W.I. Thomas" entry in *Dictionary of Modern American Philosophy* (Thommes Press 2005).